Dungeons & Dragons® 4th Edition FOR DUMMIES®

by Bill Slavicsek and Richard Baker

Foreword by Mike Mearls
Lead Game Developer for the DUNGEONS & DRAGONS game

WILEY
Wiley Publishing, Inc.

Dungeons & Dragons® 4th Edition For Dummies®

Published by
Wiley Publishing, Inc.
111 River Street
Hoboken, NJ 07030-5774

www.wiley.com

Copyright © 2008 by Wiley Publishing, Inc., Indianapolis, Indiana

Published by Wiley Publishing, Inc., Indianapolis, Indiana

Published simultaneously in Canada

For general information on our other products and services, please contact our Customer Care Department within the U.S. at 877-762-2974, outside the U.S. at 317-572-3993, or fax 317-572-4002.

For technical support, please visit www.wiley.com/techsupport.

Wiley also publishes its books in a variety of electronic formats. Some content that appears in print may not be available in electronic books.

Library of Congress Control Number:

ISBN: 978-0-470-29290-7

Manufactured in the United States of America

10 9 8 7 6 5 4 3 2

WILEY

About the Authors

Bill Slavicsek began playing the DUNGEONS & DRAGONS roleplaying game with his friends during his formative teenage years in New York City. This was in 1977, the same year that *Star Wars* and Terry Brooks's *The Sword of Shannara* debuted. This trilogy of epic fantasy combined with comic books and horror novels to forever influence Bill's outlook on life and entertainment. In 1986, Bill's hobby became his career when he joined the staff of West End Games. There, as an editor and game designer, Bill worked on a number of board games and roleplaying games, including *Ghostbusters*, *Paranoia*, *Star Wars: The Roleplaying Game*, and *Torg: Roleplaying the Possibility Wars*. Later, Bill went on to use his vast knowledge of the *Star Wars* films and associated extensions to write two editions of *A Guide to the Star Wars Universe* for Lucasfilm, Ltd. (published by Del Rey Books).

1n 1993, Bill joined the staff of TSR, Inc., then publishers of the DUNGEONS & DRAGONS game lines, as a game designer and editor. His design credits for the company include the *Alternity Science Fiction Game* (which he co-designed with Richard Baker), the *d20 Modern Roleplaying Game*, the *d20 Star Wars Roleplaying Game*, the *Star Wars Miniatures Game*, *Urban Arcana*, *Council of Wyrms*, and the EBERRON *Campaign Setting*.

Since 1997, Bill has been the R&D Director for Roleplaying Games, Book Publishing, and D&D Games for Wizards of the Coast, Inc., the company that now publishes all DUNGEONS & DRAGONS novels and game products. He oversaw the creation of the d20 Roleplaying Game System and the newest edition of the DUNGEONS & DRAGONS game. Bill leads a talented staff of game designers, developers, and editors who produce award-winning game products for DUNGEONS & DRAGONS and other d20 System game lines, including roleplaying game supplements and accessories, adventures and campaign books, and prepainted plastic miniatures. He lives with his wife Michele, their cat Pooh, and more comics, toys, and books than he knows what to do with — and that's okay by him.

Richard Baker is an award-winning game designer and a best-selling author. He's worked on the DUNGEONS & DRAGONS game lines since 1991. Rich traces his D&D experience back to 1979, when he began playing the DUNGEONS & DRAGONS game as a 7th-grader. He spent a significant amount of his high school and college years playing D&D at every opportunity, and after serving as a surface warfare officer in the United States Navy, Rich decided to take a shot at working on the game he grew up playing — and so he joined the staff of TSR, Inc. and became a game designer.

Rich's list of D&D design credits numbers over 60 game products, including the Origins Award–winning *Birthright Campaign Setting*, the *Alternity Science Fiction Roleplaying Game* (which he co-designed with Bill Slavicsek), and the

3rd Edition Dungeons & Dragons game. He has also served as creative director for the Alternity and Forgotten Realms game lines. As an author, Rich has published ten fantasy and science fiction novels, including *Swordmage*, the *Last Mythal* trilogy, and the New York Times bestseller *Condemnation*.

Rich is currently employed as a senior game designer at Wizards of the Coast, Inc. and works every day on new products for the Dungeons & Dragons game. He married his college sweetheart Kim in 1991; they have two daughters, Alex and Hannah. When he's not writing (a rare occurrence), Rich likes to hike in the Cascades, play wargames, and root for the Philadelphia Phillies — because somebody has to.

Dedication

Bill Slavicsek: To everyone who ever imagined an amazing adventure, I offer this key to D&D. When I first found the game, it helped focus and expand my imagination and creativity. And it was a lot of fun. Today, I still have fun playing the game, and my gaming group meets every Thursday evening to brave whatever new challenges I dream up for them. I hope you'll find the same outlet for imagination and fun as I've enjoyed for more than 30 years.

Richard Baker: To Kim, Alex, and Hannah for being patient with me through nigh-constant work in evenings and on weekends for many months now. I promise that I'm going to take my computer for a drive deep into the woods sometime soon and leave it there so it can't ever find its way home again.

Author's Acknowledgments

Bill Slavicsek: The newest edition of the Dungeons & Dragons game owes its existence to a lot of talented people. The work that Rich and I have done on this *For Dummies* book would not have been possible if not for the original effort of a formidable team of creatives and business people. Thank you to my creative team on the massive redesign project, which included Rob Heinsoo, Andy Collins, James Wyatt, Mike Mearls, Chris Perkins, Kim Mohan, Michele Carter, and Jeremy Crawford. Also thank you to the brand team, who help bring D&D products to market, which includes Liz Schuh, Scott Rouse, Kieren Chase, Sarah Girard, Linae Foster, and Martin Durham.

I have to also acknowledge the efforts of the rest of my game design staff. This amazing collection of designers, developers, and editors work every day to push the envelope and expand the horizons of our products, and as much as

I lead them, they influence the way I think about and approach game design and D&D. Every part of this *For Dummies* book owes at least a little to the ideas and work of Richard Baker, Greg Bilsland, Logan Bonner, Bart Carrol, Bruce Cordell, Peter Lee, Stephen Radney-MacFarland, Julia Martin, David Noonan, Peter Schaefer, Stephen Schubert, Chris Sims, Rodney Thompson, Rob Watkins, Jennifer Clarke Wilkes, Steve Winter, and Chris Youngs.

Finally, thanks to everyone at Wiley Publishing who worked with us on this book, including Amy Fandrei, Jean Nelson, and Virginia Sanders, and to everyone at Wizards of the Coast, Inc. who help us make great games and other great products on a regular basis.

Richard Baker: Many people of exceptional creativity have worked on the D&D game over the years. Without the work of game designers, editors, and artists such as Gary Gygax, Dave Arneson, Jim Ward, Kim Mohan, Zeb Cook, Jeff Grubb, Steve Winter, Bruce Nesmith, Tim Brown, Troy Denning, Roger Moore, Ed Greenwood, Mike Carr, Harold Johnson, Andrea Hayday, Jon Pickens, Lawrence Schick, Skip Williams, Dave Sutherland, Jeff Easley, Larry Elmore, and countless others, D&D would not have grown into the beloved hobby of millions of fans across the world. Countless other authors, artists, developers, and editors have contributed over the years; we're sorry that we can't thank them all.

A special acknowledgment is in order for Peter Atkinson, Ryan Dancey, and other folks who were instrumental in bringing the D&D game and many of its designers to Wizards of the Coast, Inc. Through their efforts, they reinvented and reinvigorated the game at a difficult and crucial time in its life cycle.

I'd like to add a special thank you to good friends and colleagues who have shared in my own D&D games over the years, including Ed Stark, John Rateliff, David Eckelberry, Shaun and Miranda Horner, David Wise, Thomas Reid, David Noonan, James Wyatt, Warren Wyman, Duane Maxwell, Andy Weedon, and Dale Donovan. I've had a lot of fun saving the world with you guys!

Publisher's Acknowledgments

We're proud of this book; please send us your comments through our online registration form located at `www.dummies.com/register/`.

Some of the people who helped bring this book to market include the following:

Acquisitions and Editorial

Project Editor: Jean Nelson

Acquisitions Editor: Amy Fandrei

Copy Editor: Virginia Sanders

Technical Editor: Christopher Perkins

Editorial Manager: Kevin Kirschner

Editorial Assistant: Amanda Foxworth

Sr. Editorial Assistant: Cherie Case

Cartoons: Rich Tennant (`www.the5thwave.com`)

Composition Services

Project Coordinator: Erin Smith

Layout and Graphics: Reuben W. Davis, Alissa D. Ellet, Joyce Haughey, Tobin Wilkerson, Christine Williams

Proofreader: Mary Lagu

Indexer: Potomac Indexing, LLC

Art Credits: William O'Connor, David Griffith, Wayne Reynolds, Lars Grand-West, Wayne England, Adam Gillespie, Thomas M. Baxa, Jim Nelson, Steve Prescott, Eva Widermann, Anne Stokes, Fred Hooper, James Zhang, Lee Moyer, Stephen Crowe

Publishing and Editorial for Technology Dummies

    Richard Swadley, Vice President and Executive Group Publisher

    Andy Cummings, Vice President and Publisher

  Mary Bednarek, Executive Acquisitions Director

    Mary C. Corder, Editorial Director

Publishing for Consumer Dummies

    Diane Graves Steele, Vice President and Publisher

    Joyce Pepple, Acquisitions Director

Composition Services

    Gerry Fahey, Vice President of Production Services

    Debbie Stailey, Director of Composition Services

Contents at a Glance

Foreward..xxiii

Introduction 1

Part 1: D&D Crash Course 7

Chapter 1: Preparing for Adventure...9

Chapter 2: Your First Character...21

Chapter 3: Starting Out as a Fighter...31

Chapter 4: Starting Out as a Rogue...41

Chapter 5: Starting Out as a Wizard..51

Chapter 6: Starting Out as a Cleric..61

Chapter 7: Playing the Game..71

Chapter 8: Practice Session 91

Chapter 9: Finding a D&D Game to Join 99

Part 11: Building a D&D Character 109

Chapter 10: Defining Your Character 111

Chapter 11: Choosing a Class 127

Chapter 12: Picking a Race 143

Chapter 13: Figuring Out Your Character's Ability Scores 151

Chapter 14: Choosing Powers 159

Chapter 15: Selecting Feats 185

Chapter 16: Picking Skills 199

Chapter 17: Choosing Armor, Weapons, and Gear 209

Chapter 18: Advancing Your Character 223

Part 111: Playing Your Best Game...........................229

Chapter 19: Handling Yourself in a Fight 231

Chapter 20: Making the Most of Magic 251

Chapter 21: Roleplaying and Working Together 275

Chapter 22: Character Building for Experts...291

Part IV: The Art of Dungeon Mastering 301

Chapter 23: Running the Game 303

Chapter 24: Building a Dungeon 323

Chapter 25: Keeping Your Players Happy 345

Part V: The Part of Tens 355

Chapter 26: The Ten Best Fighter Powers 357

Chapter 27: The Ten Best Rogue Powers 363

Chapter 28: The Ten Best Wizard Powers 369

Chapter 29: The Ten Best Cleric Powers 373

Chapter 30: The Ten Best Low-Level Monsters 377

Chapter 31: The Ten Best Mid-Level Monsters 383

Chapter 32: The Ten Best High-Level Monsters 389

Chapter 33: The Ten Best D&D Novels 393

Appendix A: Glossary 397

Index 411

Table of Contents

Foreward ....*xxiii*

Introduction 1

About This Book...1
Why You Need This Book..2
How to Use This Book 2
How This Book Is Organized..3
    Part I: D&D Crash Course 3
    Part II: Building a D&D Character....................................3
    Part III: Playing Your Best Game 4
    Part IV: The Art of Dungeon Mastering...............................4
    Part V: The Part of Tens..4
Icons Used in This Book..4
Where Do I Go From Here?...5

Part 1: D&D Crash Course.................................... 7

Chapter 1: Preparing for Adventure 9
What Is D&D? 10
Objectives of the D&D Game 12
    Storytelling..12
    Adventure goals..12
    Character victories 12
Looking at the Components of the Game....................................13
    Players and characters 13
    The Dungeon Master 14
    The adventure...14
    Supplies you need 15
One Game Rule to Rule Them All 17
Joining a D&D Game..19

Chapter 2: Your First Character 21
Defining Your Character 21
    Name 22
    Race..22
    Class 23
    Level and XP..24

Ability scores 24
Special abilities 25
Key statistics...25
Feats 26
Skills 26
Gear 26
Powers 27
Playing Your Character..27
Taking turns 27
Roleplaying..28
Your imagination is the limit 29
Character Roles...29
Choosing Your Character 30

Chapter 3: Starting Out as a Fighter **31**
Who Should Play a Fighter? 31
How to Play a Fighter 32
Fighter builds 32
The fighter's role 32
Selecting a Fighter...33
Regdar, 1st-Level Human Fighter 34
Tordek, 1st-Level Dwarf Fighter 36
Calia, 1st-Level Elf Fighter...38

Chapter 4: Starting Out as a Rogue **41**
Who Should Play a Rogue?...41
How to Play a Rogue 42
Rogue builds 42
The rogue's role 43
Selecting a Rogue 43
Jax, 1st-Level Human Rogue 44
Shadow, 1st-Level Human Rogue..46
Lidda, 1st-Level Halfling Rogue 48

Chapter 5: Starting Out as a Wizard **51**
Who Should Play a Wizard? 51
How to Play a Wizard..52
Wizard builds 52
The wizard's role 53
Selecting a Wizard...53
Beryn, 1st-Level Human Wizard 54
Dreggu, 1st-Level Dwarf Wizard 56
Telsa, 1st-Level Elf Wizard..58

Chapter 6: Starting Out as a Cleric .... .61

Who Should Play a Cleric? 61
How to Play a Cleric...62
    Cleric builds 62
    The cleric's role 63
Selecting a Cleric 63
Thomm, 1st-Level Human Cleric 64
Chenna, 1st-Level Halfling Cleric.................................66
Eberk, 1st-Level Dwarf Cleric.....................................68

Chapter 7: Playing the Game .... .71

Understanding the D&D Game 71
Rolling Dice 72
Exploring the Dungeon...73
    What can you do while exploring? 74
    Ability checks 75
Combat Basics 75
    Determining who goes first 76
    Taking your turn 76
Engaging in Combat 78
    Combat sequence..78
    Attacking with a weapon 79
    Other defenses 79
    Attacks and damage 80
    Critical hits..80
    Flanking...80
    Combat advantage 80
    Other actions in combat....................................81
Using Powers in Combat 81
    Types of powers used in combat 81
    Power attack types...83
Movement in Combat 84
    Move actions...84
    Forced movement..85
    Distance and movement 85
    Occupied squares...85
    Difficult terrain 86
    Obstacles..86
Spending and Gaining Action Points 86
Facing Skill Challenges 87
Hit Points, Healing, and Dying 87
    Healing in combat 88
    Healing the dying 88
Rest and Recovery 88
Conditions That Affect Combat.....................................88

Chapter 8: Practice Session **91**

    The Battle Grid and Markers 91
        Markers...92
        Moving on the battle grid...92
    A Practice Combat 93
        Placing characters on the battle grid and rolling initiative 93
        What to do on a turn..94
        The Dungeon Master...95
        Example of player versus monster combat 95
    Adding Story Elements 97

Chapter 9: Finding a D&D Game to Join **99**

    A Typical Game Session 99
    Finding Someone to Play With...100
        Joining someone else's game..101
        Organizing your own game..102
    Starting Off with a High-Level Character 103
    Regdar, 4th-Level Human Fighter 104
    Regdar, 8th-Level Human Fighter 106

Part II: Building a D&D Character *109*

Chapter 10: Defining Your Character **111**

    Your Character Sheet...111
    Filling Out the Character Sheet 112
        Names 112
        Class and level 113
        Level modifier 113
        Path and destiny..114
        Race and size 114
        Alignment, deity, and personality 115
        Character description..117
        Ability scores 117
        Hit points and healing surges 117
        Senses 118
        Initiative...119
        Defenses 119
        Speed...121
        Action points..121
        Basic attacks 121
        Skills 122
        Feats 123

Race and class features 123
Powers 124
Magic items 124
Other equipment 125

Chapter 11: Choosing a Class 127

Character Roles...128
The controller 128
The defender...129
The leader 129
The striker 130
Class Descriptions 130
The fighter is the best class 131
The rogue is the best class...134
The wizard is the best class...136
The cleric is the best class...139
Other classes 141

Chapter 12: Picking a Race 143

Humans..143
Ability adjustments 144
Special traits 144
Best class..145
Dwarves...145
Ability adjustments 146
Special traits 146
Best class..146
Elves...147
Ability adjustments 147
Special traits 147
Best class..148
Halflings..148
Ability adjustments 148
Special traits 149
Best class..150
More Races to Choose From..150

Chapter 13: Figuring Out Your Character's Ability Scores 151

How the Ability Scores Work 151
Generating Ability Scores...155
The standard array..155
The customizing scores method 156
Assigning Ability Scores by Class 157

Chapter 14: Choosing Powers 159

Navigating through Powers 160
Powers you don't choose 161
Learning new powers 162
Replacing powers 162
Choosing Fighter Powers 163
The Great Weapon Fighter 164
The Guardian Fighter 166
Choosing Rogue Powers 168
The Brawny Rogue 169
The Trickster Rogue 170
Choosing Wizard Powers 172
The War Wizard 173
The Control Wizard 175
Choosing Cleric Powers 177
The Battle Cleric 178
The Devoted Cleric 180

Chapter 15: Selecting Feats 185

What's a Feat? 186
The Basics of Acquiring Feats 187
Planning Your Feat Choices 187
Choosing fighter feats 188
Choosing rogue feats 190
Choosing wizard feats 193
Choosing cleric feats 195

Chapter 16: Picking Skills 199

All about Skills 199
Using skills 201
Choosing your character's skills 202
Quick Picks: Using Skill Packages 203
Fighter skill packages...204
Rogue skill package 204
Wizard skill package 205
Cleric skill package..207

Chapter 17: Choosing Armor, Weapons, and Gear 209

Going Shopping 210
Choosing the Right Weapon...212
Fighter weapons 213
Rogue weapons 214
Cleric weapons 214
Wizard weapons 215

Choosing Armor 215
    Shield or no shield?..216
    Light versus heavy 216
Everything Else Your Character Is Carrying................................218
    Useful gear...218
    Write it down and forget it 219
Improving Weapons and Armor 220
    Masterwork armors...220
    Magical arms and armor 221

Chapter 18: Advancing Your Character **223**
Gaining Experience Points 223
    Where do XP come from? 224
    For the Dungeon Master 224
Gaining Levels..225
    Ability score increases...226
    Level modifier 226
    New powers..226
    Feats 227
Advancing a Level 227

Part III: Playing Your Best Game **229**

Chapter 19: Handling Yourself in a Fight **231**
Choosing the Right Weapon for the Job.......................................231
    Killing 'em quickly: Attacking hit points...........................232
    Playing for time: Action-denial powers..............................232
    Beating 'em with footwork: Maneuver.................................233
    Winning with a smile: Negotiation.......................................233
    Bugging out: Knowing when to retreat 234
Managing Expendable Powers and Resources 235
    Fire away: Using encounter powers 235
    Hold on, there: Using daily powers......................................236
Putting It All Together: Developing Your Combat Strategy 237
    Step 1: Define the situation 237
    Step 2: Evaluate your foes 239
    Step 3: Choose the right tactic 239
    Step 4: Rethink your assumptions..241
Using Advanced Tactics 241
    Flanking..241
    Beating the initiative order 241
    Charging..242
    Avoiding opportunity attacks 243
    Concentrating on defense 244

Setting up opportunity attacks 245
Adapting Your Tactics to Your Foes 247
Beating ranged controllers 247
Handling numerous foes 248
Fighting monsters your character can't hurt 248

Chapter 20: Making the Most of Magic 251

Selecting Wizard Spells for the Adventure..............................252
Casting in Combat 254
Rituals: The Magic You Didn't Know You Had 255
Learning rituals 256
Using rituals 257
Powering Up with Magic Items 257
Types of magic items 259
Acquiring magic items 261
Defining the Magic Item Baseline 262
Fighter magic items 264
Rogue magic items 267
Cleric magic items 268
Wizard magic items 271

Chapter 21: Roleplaying and Working Together 275

Roleplaying with Style 275
Choosing your character's alignment 276
Building a persona 277
Creating mannerisms 278
Knowing when to stop 280
Working Together 280
Cooperating in a fight 281
Buffing your teammates 282
Saving downed characters 284
Minding Your Table Manners 285
Five do's 285
Five don'ts 287

Chapter 22: Character Building for Experts .291

Min-Maxing Your Character 291
Min-maxing strategies 293
Exploiting good interactions 293
Choosing a Paragon Path 294
Epic Destiny for the Win! 296
Multiclassing: Maxing Out Your Choices...................................297

Part IV: The Art of Dungeon Mastering........................301

Chapter 23: Running the Game 303

DMing: The Best Role in the Game...304
    Preparing an adventure 304
    Building the world...304
    Playing NPCs 305
    Running monsters 306
    Adjudicating results 307
    Keeping up with the characters 308
Choosing an Adventure to Run 308
Task-Oriented DMing 309
    The exploration task...312
    The conversation task...313
    The combat task..314
    The free time task...317
Getting the Most out of Your Monsters........................318
    Figuring out monster stats 318
    Deciding what the bad guys do 320
    Fighting smart, fighting dumb 321

Chapter 24: Building a Dungeon 323

Creating a D&D Adventure...323
    Parts of an adventure...324
    An adventure-builder checklist 327
Sample Dungeon: Hall of the Spider God 328
    Adventure premise..328
    Using the battle grid...329
    Using the character and monster markers 329
    Adventure key...329
    Starting the adventure 330
    Wrapping up the adventure 342

Chapter 25: Keeping Your Players Happy 345

Figuring Out Your Players 345
Narrating the Adventure 348
    Getting ready, getting organized.................................349
    Creating evocative scenes...349
    Using the cut-scene..350
Running a Fun Game 351
    Using props 351
    Table rules...352
    Game balance..353

Part V: The Part of Tens *355*

Chapter 26: The Ten Best Fighter Powers **357**

10. Anvil of Doom 358
9. Reaping Strike 358
8. Precise Strike 358
7. Serpent Dance Strike 359
6. Unbreakable 360
5. Sweeping Blow 360
4. Dizzying Blow 360
3. Come and Get It 361
2. Comeback Strike 361
1. Tide of Iron 362

Chapter 27: The Ten Best Rogue Powers **363**

10. Tornado Strike 363
9. Sly Flourish 364
8. Crimson Edge..364
7. Leaping Dodge 365
6. Cloud of Steel 365
5. Blinding Barrage 365
4. Bait and Switch 366
3. Tumble 367
2. Slaying Strike 367
1. Piercing Strike 367

Chapter 28: The Ten Best Wizard Powers **369**

10. Magic Missile 369
9. Dispel Magic 370
8. Ice Storm 370
7. Mirror Image 370
6. Sleep...371
5. Lightning Bolt 371
4. Fireball..371
3. Shield 372
2. Thunderlance 372
1. Cloud of Daggers 372

Chapter 29: The Ten Best Cleric Powers **373**

10. Cure Light Wounds...373
9. Lance of Faith 374
8. Flame Strike 374
7. Cure Serious Wounds...374
6. Awe Strike...374

5. Healing Strike..375
4. Daunting Light 375
3. Mantle of Glory..375
2. Mass Cure Light Wounds..375
1. Sacred Flame..376

Chapter 30: The Ten Best Low-Level Monsters 377

10. Stirge (Level 1 Lurker)..377
9. Hell Hound (Level 7 Brute) 378
8. Young White Dragon (Level 3 Solo Brute) 378
7. Deathjump Spider (Level 4 Skirmisher) 378
6. Werewolf (Level 8 Brute)..379
5. Ghoul (Level 5 Soldier)...379
4. Dire Rat (Level 1 Brute)..379
3. Ogre Skirmisher (Level 8 Skirmisher) 380
2. Blazing Skeleton (Level 5 Artillery) 380
1. Orc Raider (Level 3 Skirmisher)..................................380

Chapter 31: The Ten Best Mid-Level Monsters 383

10. Cyclops Impaler (Level 14 Artillery) 383
9. Flesh Golem (Level 12 Elite Brute)..............................383
8. Wailing Ghost (Level 12 Controller)............................384
7. Umber Hulk (Level 12 Elite Soldier).............................384
6. Beholder Eye of Flame (Level 13 Elite Artillery) 384
5. Mummy Lord (Level 13 Elite Controller) 385
4. Mind Flayer Mastermind (Level 18 Elite Controller) 385
3. Vrock Demon (Level 13 Skirmisher) 385
2. War Troll (Level 14 Soldier) 386
1. Adult Red Dragon (Level 15 Solo Soldier)....................387

Chapter 32: The Ten Best High-Level Monsters 389

10. Yuan-ti Anathema (Level 21 Elite Skirmisher)...............389
9. War Devil (Level 22 Brute) 389
8. Voidsoul Specter (Level 23 Lurker) 390
7. Elder Purple Worm (Level 24 Solo Soldier)....................390
6. Death Knight (Level 25 Elite Soldier)............................390
5. Pit Fiend (Level 26 Elite Soldier) 390
4. Storm Giant (Level 24 Elite Controller) 391
3. Ancient Blue Dragon (Level 28 Solo Artillery) 391
2. Tarrasque (Level 30 Solo Brute) 391
1. Orcus (Level 33 Solo Brute)..392

Chapter 33: The Ten Best D&D Novels 393
Dragonlance Chronicles 393
Dragonlance Legends 393
Icewind Dale Trilogy 394
R.A. Salvatore's War of the Spider Queen 394
A Practical Guide to Dragons 394
Storm Dragon...394
Swordmage...395
The Orc King...395
The Sword Never Sleeps..396

Appendix A: Glossary *397*

Index *411*

Foreword

You have to realize that, if you've never played DUNGEONS & DRAGONS before, I am incredibly jealous of you on two counts.

For one thing, you're about to experience a whole truckload of awesome firsts. Your first dungeon, your first critical hit, your first dragon slain, your first go at saving the world — all these await you. D&D is more than a game. It's an operating system for the imagination, a tool to craft and share dreams of epic battles, horrific villains, and noble heroes with your friends. If you've never played the game before, you are in for a wild ride.

For another, you have a pair of experts showing you the ropes. Between the two of them, Bill Slavicsek and Rich Baker have put more time into thinking, writing, and building D&D than any other pair of game designers you could name. Back in the day, learning D&D consisted primarily of getting the rules wrong, arguing over what was supposed to happen next, and making things up on the fly. If D&D is the imagination's operating system, then this book is your user's manual.

You might be intimidated by the size of this book or the sheer length of D&D's three core rulebooks: the *Player's Handbook,* the *Dungeon Master's Guide*, and the *Monster Manual*. Unlike many games, D&D isn't about memorizing the rules and following them to the letter. Having a good time, telling an exciting story, and hanging out with your friends is more important than getting everything right. D&D is a cooperative game where you and your friends work together. That applies equally to fighting a dragon and to learning the rules. So, if you have any worries about memorizing the entire game, set them aside. The rules are there to keep everything organized, make things fair for everyone, and help determine what happens next. They're guidelines, not inalterable, unquestionable laws.

As you set out on your career as a D&D player, allow me to offer my own little contribution to your growing understanding of the game. The nice thing about writing a foreword is that I get in a word before Bill and Rich. So, here's my bit of advice:

Thou shalt be a hero. If there is a dragon that needs slaying, a kingdom that needs liberating, or a demon that needs to be chased back to the Abyss, draw your sword, ready your spells, and leap to action. All of us are great in our dreams, and D&D is where our dreams come a little bit closer to life.

Have fun, may you roll many 20s, and may the orcs, trolls, and giants you face be plagued with rolling 1 after 1. (Don't worry! Just read ahead and soon that will make perfect sense.)

—Mike Mearls

Mike is Lead Game Developer for the DUNGEONS & DRAGONS game at Wizards of the Coast. In addition to all the work Mike has done on the 4th Edition of the game, he has co-authored a number of 4E adventures, including *Keep on the Shadowfell*, *Thunderspire Labyrinth*, and *Pyramid of Shadows*.

Introduction

*Y*ou crave action and adventure. You revel in the fantastic. You want to play DUNGEONS & DRAGONS. The DUNGEONS & DRAGONS game has been around for more than 30 years, and it stands as the pinnacle of fantasy-adventure games (also known as *roleplaying games*). The concepts and play patterns of D&D (as it is affectionately referred to) harken back to the games of make-believe that almost everyone played as a little kid. However, D&D provides form and structure, making game play more satisfying and robust for kids and adults alike.

This book makes the mysterious and often arcane world of fantasy roleplaying games — specifically the DUNGEONS & DRAGONS Roleplaying Game, 4th Edition — easier to understand and faster to get into. Get ready to expand your imagination, roll some dice, and battle dragons and other magical monsters.

About This Book

We originally wrote this book to make our favorite hobby game more accessible to every fantasy and gaming fan, from the novice who enjoys fantasy novels or films such as *The Lord of the Rings* trilogy and has a passing curiosity about the DUNGEONS & DRAGONS game, to the seasoned D&D player who goes to every convention and has been playing since Gary Gygax and Dave Arneson published the White Box version of the game. Whether you have yet to play your first game or have been in a regular gaming group for years, our mission is to measurably increase the fun you have playing D&D and your proficiency with the game.

Moreover, Wizards of the Coast, Inc. just released the 4th Edition of the DUNGEONS & DRAGONS game, and with a new edition comes a whole new series of opportunities to get in on the fun. But there are also changes to help you navigate through, new concepts to explain, and new challenges to help you overcome. We figured the best time to update *Dungeons & Dragons For Dummies* was in conjunction with the new edition of the game.

As a new player, you discover the basics of the game. You end up with a character to play and enough understanding to confidently take your place at any gaming table. Read this book today, grab a copy of the D&D *Player's Handbook*, and you can play tomorrow without worry or confusion. D&D is a game. Games are fun. We hope to make learning to play fun, too.

As experienced players, we help you immediately get up to speed on the new systems. We provide lots of hints and tips to elevate your level of play. Character creation, character advancement, combat and encounter strategies, game mastering — we cover it all. It doesn't matter if you've played once or a hundred times; you can find something in this book to make you a better D&D player or game master (called a Dungeon Master in D&D lingo).

Why You Need This Book

Novices need *Dungeons & Dragons 4th Edition For Dummies* because it's written by D&D experts to serve as the most comprehensive introduction to the D&D game. In this book, you can find out things about D&D and fantasy role-playing that many seasoned gamers still haven't discovered. Do you know the ins and outs of opportunity attacks? What the best class and race combos are? How to make the most of your character's key abilities? Which monsters can be brought down by which powers and weapons? You can find the answers to all kinds of D&D questions within these pages. And what if you already know a lot about the game? Get ready to discover a good deal more. We've filled this book with inside tips and behind-the-curtain details that you rarely encounter outside the hallowed walls of Wizards of the Coast.

We believe that DUNGEONS & DRAGONS speaks to and feeds the human condition. D&D is a game of the imagination, building on the myths and fantasies that have shaped our culture. D&D is a game of endless possibilities, where the only limit on what can happen is what you can imagine. D&D is a social experience, a fun and exciting activity that combines group storytelling and fantasy iconology with strategic challenges and dice rolling. Nothing else — no computer game, no board game, no movie — comes close to delivering the interactive and unlimited adventure of the D&D experience.

From the days of telling stories around a campfire about trolls and dragons and knights in shining armor to the high-tech equivalent that involves computers and high-speed Internet connections, make-believe has advanced along with society. Today, one of the purest expressions of the game is DUNGEONS & DRAGONS. No other outlet for the adventures of armored warriors and powerful wizards is as versatile, creative, or fun as D&D. So get out there and explore some dungeons and bash some monsters!

How to Use This Book

There's no right or wrong way to use this book. Read it from cover to cover or glance at the Table of Contents and dive into the sections that most interest you. If you're a new player, we suggest starting with Part I. You also want to become intimately familiar with the glossary and refer to it often as you explore these pages. If you have a few games under your belt and you're looking to become a better player, check out Parts II and III. Experienced players will want to look at Part III for insights into the nuances of the game. And if you like to be Dungeon Master (or you aspire to this position), you should dive into Part IV. Longtime players and folks who are new to the world of DUNGEONS & DRAGONS can find something fun and interesting in the Parts of Tens.

Much of this book is written with the assumption that you have a D&D *Player's Handbook*. We don't replace the D&D game rules in this book; instead, we try to make them clearer and help you navigate your way through them with inside tips and advice. In addition, you need a set of dice (see Chapter 1 for details) to use the practice sessions presented in later chapters.

How This Book Is Organized

Dungeons & Dragons 4th Edition For Dummies consists of five parts. The chapters within each part cover specific topics in detail. In each chapter, we start with the basics and build from there. Whenever a point needs further clarification, we cross-reference the appropriate chapter so you can immediately find any additional information you need. In addition, whenever it comes up, we refer you to the appropriate chapter in the D&D *Player's Handbook* or, if necessary, one of the other two books that make up the core rules of the game, the *Dungeon Master's Guide* and the *Monster Manual*.

Part 1: D&D Crash Course

This is your character and these are the dice you roll. We start out with a basic overview of the D&D game, assuming that you're a brand-new player who's looking to join an existing gaming group. We give you a little history on how the game began and how it developed, and we provide you with ready-to-play characters (called *pregenerated characters*) so you can join a game right now. We finish off this section with a discussion on starting your own game, just in case you don't currently know anyone who plays.

Part 11: Building a D&D Character

Using a pregenerated character is fine, but eventually you'll want to build a character of your very own. In this part, we explain the fine points of character creation and go behind the scenes to discuss character advancement. After all, where your character ends up might be more important than where he or she started. This part of the book is for the player who wants to become more invested in the D&D game. We help you navigate the *Player's Handbook* so that you can make solid, informed decisions about what kind of character you want to build and play.

Part III: Playing Your Best Game

Even expert players should find something new and informative in this part of the book. From effective combat tactics to powerful character combinations, from the basics of adventuring-party teamwork to advice on good roleplaying, we offer insights into the mechanics of the game and how to be the best D&D player you can be.

Part IV: The Art of Dungeon Mastering

The earlier parts of the book spend a lot of time offering advice and tactics to players. Here's where we provide tips and tricks to that select and important individual who makes every D&D game come alive — the Dungeon Master. It's good to be the DM, and this section of the book starts with the basics of DMing and builds to provide insights that should give even experienced DMs something to think about when running their own games.

Part V: The Part of Tens

No *For Dummies* book is complete without this section of top ten lists. Helpful and interesting collections of the best powers, monsters, and resources abound throughout these short chapters.

And finally, perhaps the most important part of this book, the glossary helps you navigate and understand the terms and jargon that pervade the D&D game. Use the glossary often as you use this book and the core D&D rulebooks.

Be sure to check out the color pages in this book. They feature fantastic, full-color artwork of several different D&D monsters and races.

Icons Used in This Book

To guide you along the way and to point out information you really need to know, this book uses the following icons:

This icon points to tips and tricks that make some aspect of the D&D game easier or faster.

Remember these important nuggets and you'll be a better player or DM.

If you see this icon, read and follow the accompanying directions. This information can prevent you (or your character) from having a very bad day.

Whenever you see this icon, you know we're directing you to more detailed information in one of the core D&D rulebooks — the *Player's Handbook, Dungeon Master's Guide,* or *Monster Manual.*

This takes you to the D&D Insider Web site, where you can get more information, use interactive tools and demos, and talk to other D&D players via message boards to find out more about the game.

Where Do I Go From Here?

If you're a new player, get a copy of the D&D *Player's Handbook.* If you aspire to be a Dungeon Master, you also need the *Dungeon Master's Guide* and the *Monster Manual.* But don't read them yet! Start by digging into the chapters in Part I of this book. We wrote that section specifically to help new players enter the D&D game.

If you've played a time or two (or two hundred!), check out Parts II, III, and IV for D&D gaming advice that anyone interested in the game can use. Part IV is especially relevant to you if you want to be the Dungeon Master or improve your already-formidable DMing skills.

Our last bit of advice before you move on (and see all the other advice we've packed between these yellow covers) is this: Have fun! D&D is a game. The basics of D&D are straightforward and relatively easy to grasp. Don't let all the details beyond that frighten or confuse you. We're here to help with that, so trust us and let us do our job. For the majority of D&D players around the world, those added details are what make D&D one of the greatest ways they know for spending their leisure time. Explore those details with us, and we think you'll come to the same conclusion.

Part I
D&D Crash Course

The 5th Wave   By Rich Tennant

In this part . . .

In this part of the book, we assume that you're a brand-new player to DUNGEONS & DRAGONS 4th Edition. We start out with a bit of background about the D&D game, and then we dive in and show you how to join an ongoing gaming group. With ready-to-play characters and an overview of the basic rules of play, you can get up to speed quickly and start bashing monsters with the best of them. Near the end of this part, we also offer advice on starting your own gaming group, providing you with every opportunity for getting into the D&D experience!

Chapter 1

Preparing for Adventure

. . . .

In This Chapter

▶ Exploring the origins and objectives of DUNGEONS & DRAGONS

▶ Looking at the components of the game

▶ Explaining the role of the Dungeon Master

▶ Examining the things you need to play

▶ Understanding the different expressions of the game

▶ Joining a 1st-level game

. . . .

*E*veryone played make-believe during childhood. Whether you played cops and robbers, cowboys and Indians, superheroes, or firefighters, you opened up your imagination and pretended to be something other than yourself. DUNGEONS & DRAGONS is a game of the imagination, a roleplaying game where players take on the roles of amazing heroes in a medieval fantasy setting. It's just like make-believe, only more sophisticated, grown up, and fun. D&D gives form and structure to your imagination, creating a leisure activity that's more interactive and open-ended than any movie, novel, or computer game.

The backdrop for D&D is a mythological world of fairy tales, epic adventures, and monsters, where heroes gain power and magic to win against all kinds of challenges and villains. This backdrop owes much to fantasy novels, including *The Lord of the Rings* trilogy by J.R.R. Tolkien, but also to a sort of collective consciousness consisting of material from comic books, TV shows, movies, and other fantasy-related influences. Over the course of more than 30 years, D&D has, in turn, influenced such media and helped set the stage for the computer game industry. This chapter provides an overview of the game and explores some of the topics that we discuss in greater detail throughout the book.

What Is D&D?

The DUNGEONS & DRAGONS Roleplaying Game is full of fantastic locations, strange creatures, magic items, treasure, and lots of monsters. Imagine an ancient place and time. Imagine a world much like our own, long ago, where armored warriors use swords and bows, castles sit atop wooded hills, and thatched cottages clump together here and there across the countryside.

The origin of D&D

It started with wargames, a popular pastime in which participants re-create famous battles on a tabletop using metal figures. In the mid-1960s, Gary Gygax formed a small group of wargamers who met regularly and set out to publish new wargames. This led to the development of the *Chainmail* miniatures rules, and by 1971, Gygax added supplemental rules that expanded the game to include fantastic creatures such as elves, dwarves, and monsters.

In 1972, Dave Arneson came to Gygax with a new take on the traditional wargame. Gone were the massive armies. Each player had a single character like the "hero" characters in *Chainmail*. A storyteller ran the game, unfolding a narrative in which the players were free to choose their own courses of action for their characters. This was a cooperative experience, not a competitive wargame, in which the players joined forces to defeat villains and gain rewards.

This combination of miniatures gaming and player imagination created a totally new experience. Gygax and Arneson collaborated on a set of rules, but they weren't able to find a publisher. So in 1974, Gygax formed a company (that eventually was called TSR, Inc.) and published DUNGEONS & DRAGONS himself.

In 1977, the rules were totally rewritten, and the original *DUNGEONS & DRAGONS Basic Set* was released. Sales rose rapidly, and the game became a phenomenon. A year later, a new version of the game, *Advanced DUNGEONS & DRAGONS* (AD&D), was introduced, published in a series of high-quality hardcover books.

The 1980s continued to see remarkable growth for the game, and new initiatives started during this decade. D&D novels were introduced, a cartoon series debuted on Saturday morning TV, and new fantasy worlds (called *campaign settings*) for D&D such as DRAGONLANCE and FORGOTTEN REALMS appeared. In 1989, the second edition of AD&D hit the shelves, and the 1990s saw the birth of even more campaign settings, including RAVENLOFT, DARK SUN, and PLANESCAPE.

In 1997, TSR changed hands. Wizards of the Coast, makers of the phenomenal trading card game MAGIC: THE GATHERING, purchased the company and moved most of the creative staff to its offices in Washington State. In 2000, the 3rd edition of the DUNGEONS & DRAGONS game was released.

In 2008, D&D 4th Edition hit the shelves. The newest edition concentrates on making a great game even better, ratcheting up the fun and speed of play, as well as adding online components via the D&D Insider Web site (www.dndinsider.com). Today the game is more popular than ever. Some 5 million people play D&D every month, using their imaginations and having fun with their friends.

D&D: It's good for you

A few times over the long history of the DUNGEONS & DRAGONS game, some people have tried to knock it as something silly or even harmful. Nothing could be further from the truth. D&D promotes teamwork and socialization. It teaches math and reading skills. It encourages creativity and imaginative problem solving. It's uplifting, inspirational, and thought provoking. And it's fun, too! You sit in the same room with other people, socialize, and create amazingly deep fantasy worlds in which good battles evil on a regular basis — and good usually wins out in the end. What could be better than that?

Imagine that in this ancient time magic really works, and that humans aren't the only intelligent species roaming the land.

D&D lets you explore this imaginary world. With the game, some willing friends, and your imagination, you strike out on epic quests set in this long-ago place that never existed but is as familiar as your own recollections. The D&D game lets you participate in the ultimate interactive story. In this story, you and the other players determine what happens next. How does the adventure end? That's the best part — the ending isn't determined until you and your character get there!

For a number of reasons, D&D is different from other games you may have played:

- **The play keeps on going.** Like an ongoing television series, your game continues from play session to play session.

- **Your character grows as the game goes on.** You play a character that grows and develops with every adventure in which he or she participates.

- **The only limit is your imagination.** The game offers endless possibilities and a multitude of choices because your character can do whatever you can imagine.

- **Everyone wins.** Because the game is really a series of stories told collectively by the players and the Dungeon Master, D&D is a game where everyone wins. If your character survives and wins the day (or dies spectacularly and memorably) and everyone has a good time, then the adventure ends in a win for the group.

Objectives of the D&D Game

D&D is a cooperative game, not a competitive one. In other words, you don't compete against the other players and you don't win by beating them. Instead, there are a lot of different ways to "win" the game. The common denominator in every victory condition is *fun*. If you and the other players have fun, everyone wins a game of D&D.

Storytelling

One way to "win" a D&D game is to help the group tell a fun and exciting story. Whether you successfully complete your adventure or fail miserably, if everyone has a good time and you contribute to creating a story that everyone is going to remember, the group wins.

Unlike other games, each D&D adventure that you play is just one tale in the continuing saga of your player character and the other characters in your group. Of course, you can play a single game session and have a great time, but the real excitement and power of the D&D game comes from the continuing story as your character improves and develops from one adventure to the next. A continuing storyline means that events have consequences. If you find a magic weapon or a potion in one adventure, for example, you can use it in the next. And that evil necromancer that got away? Watch out! He is likely return in a future adventure to cause more trouble, just like villains in novels, TV series, and movies.

Adventure goals

Every adventure contains its own set of victory conditions. Sometimes it's as simple as surviving the dungeon and escaping, or defeating the boss villain at the heart of the fortress of evil. Other times, you might have a specific goal to accomplish (take the evil ring and toss it in the volcano) or a specific monster to beat (stop the werewolf before it rampages through the town again). If you achieve the objective of the adventure, the group wins.

Character victories

When you begin playing D&D, your character starts out at 1st level — the lowest experience level. Your character wins each time he or she defeats monsters and gains experience points and treasure. With each new level your character gains, he or she increases in power and reputation. Each increase in wealth, power, and equipment is a win for your character.

Looking at the Components of the Game

You need three distinct components to play a DUNGEONS & DRAGONS game:

- ✔ **Players:** You need players, usually two to six of them, to take on the roles of adventurers in the fantasy world. The adventurers controlled by the players are also called *heroes* or *player characters* (PCs, for short).

- ✔ **A Dungeon Master:** The *Dungeon Master* (DM) controls all the *nonplayer characters* (NPCs) — the monsters, villains, and other incidental characters that inhabit the fantasy world. The DM sets the pace of the story and referees the action as the adventure unfolds.

- ✔ **An adventure:** An adventure is the activity that the player characters participate in. An adventure usually consists of a basic plot and a number of encounters. As the players (through their characters) interact with the plot and resolve the encounters, they help the DM tell a story. The cool thing is that every action the player characters perform affects the twists and turns of the plot, so that the outcome of the adventure winds up surprising everyone.

The following sections give more details about all the various parts of the D&D experience.

Players and characters

The action revolves around the characters in a D&D game just as it does around the protagonists of a novel or the heroes of a movie. Each player creates a character (or selects a ready-to-play character, such as the ones presented in Chapters 3 through 6), a heroic adventurer who is part of a team that regularly delves into dungeons and battles monsters. These characters include mighty fighters, brave clerics, cunning rogues, and powerful wizards. You get to play the game while your character takes all the risks.

Playing a D&D character is kind of like acting, except everything happens around the gaming table. You don't have to deliver lines or perform stunts. Just find a comfortable seat, explain what your character is doing, and roll some dice to determine the outcome. The scene plays out in your imagination and in the imaginations of the other players.

The Dungeon Master

One player has a special role in a D&D game. This player, the *Dungeon Master* (or DM), controls the pace of the story and referees the action along the way. Every D&D game needs a Dungeon Master — you can't play the game without one.

The cool thing about Dungeon Masters is that they allow the game to be totally interactive and open-ended. Players can have their characters attempt anything they can imagine because there's a real, live person sitting in the DM's chair, coordinating the action and determining how every event adds to the story. The game rules and the dice help, but the DM must use his or her imagination to make the world unfold.

The player who decides to take on the role of the Dungeon Master becomes a member of a select group. Not everyone has the dedication and creativity to be a DM, but those who do have a great outlet in the D&D game. The DM defines the game his or her group is going to play, and a good DM results in a great game of D&D.

Some groups use multiple DMs so that everyone gets to run a player character at some point, and all who want to try their hands at DMing get the opportunity. Other groups go for years with the same player serving as DM for every game session. It all depends on the desires of the group and the personalities involved.

The adventure

The player characters are the stars of your D&D game, just like the heroes in books or movies. They are adventurers, and adventurers need adventures. A D&D adventure features action, combat, mystery, challenges, and lots and lots of monsters. Adventures come in three forms: full-length adventures published specifically for D&D, adventure hooks in published products that DMs can turn into full-length adventures, and adventures that DMs create for themselves.

Adventures can be as simple as a basic dungeon crawl or as complex as a murder mystery. An adventure can last for a single game session or stretch out over a number of sessions of play. One adventure might take place in a haunted castle, another in a crime-ridden village, a third in the catacombs beneath an ancient graveyard. What makes D&D different from your typical board game is that each adventure is just a single tale in the continuing saga of your player characters. Adventures provide the stage upon which your player characters perform heroic deeds and resolve legendary quests. Anything is possible in a D&D game, and it is through adventures that the possibilities come alive.

Supplies you need

Players and characters, a Dungeon Master, and an adventure — these are the basic components of any DUNGEONS & DRAGONS game. However, you need a few supplies to get the most out of the experience. These supplies include the following items, which we explain in more detail shortly:

- ✔ The D&D game itself
- ✔ Special dice
- ✔ Character sheets
- ✔ *D&D Miniatures* and *D&D Dungeon Tiles*
- ✔ Pencils and lots of paper
- ✔ An Internet connection, if you want to use the tools and game aids available at www.dndinsider.com

You can find a selection of D&D rulebooks and supplements at most bookstores. But for the miniatures, dice, *D&D Dungeon Tiles*, and other items, your best bet is a hobby game store. You can also find many sources for gaming supplies online, such as www.amazon.com, www.chessex.com, or www.gamestation.net.

The D&D game

This *For Dummies* book is a great place to start, but eventually you'll need other products and books to get the most from the DUNGEONS & DRAGONS Roleplaying Game. Beginners should pick up the DUNGEONS & DRAGONS *Roleplaying Game Starter Set*, which includes the basic rules, dice, and many of the other components discussed in this section, all in one convenient box.

If you want to progress beyond the basics, you need the three 4th Edition core books, all published by Wizards of the Coast, that make up the full D&D game:

- ✔ *Player's Handbook:* Presents the rules of the game from the player's point of view and provides details on creating characters, outfitting adventurers, and playing the game.

- ✔ *Dungeon Master's Guide:* Presents the rules of the game from the Dungeon Master's point of view and provides detailed advice on running games, creating adventures, sustaining campaigns, and awarding experience to player characters.

- ✔ *Monster Manual:* Presents hundreds of creatures to use in any D&D game. From low-level to high-level, friendly to hostile, each creature has an illustration, game tactics, and statistics for ease of use.

The DM needs all three books, but players can get by with just a copy of the *Player's Handbook.*

Dice

You roll dice to determine the outcome of actions in the game. If you want your character to try something — such as attack the ogre, disarm the trap, or search for clues — you use the dice whenever the result isn't a sure thing. The D&D game uses dice of different shapes. Each player should have his or her own set of dice with which to play the game. Players get possessive and protective of their dice, and having your own set means you can customize it. (Dice come in all kinds of styles and colors.) Game play also proceeds more smoothly when you don't have to pass the dice around for sharing among players.

A set of dice for the D&D game includes at least the following (see Figure 1-1):

✔ One four-sided die (referred to as a d4)

✔ One six-sided die (d6)

✔ One eight-sided die (d8)

✔ One ten-sided die (d10)

✔ One twelve-sided die (d12)

✔ One twenty-sided die (d20)

Figure 1-1: The basic dice for D&D.	

The d20 determines character success at any given action, and the other dice determine what happens if an action succeeds.

Character sheets

Your D&D character is defined by a series of key statistics, as well as by the background story you create for the character. These statistics and other key information are contained on a character sheet. As your character participates in adventures, these statistics change.

This book contains a series of basic character sheets that provide ready-to-play characters. You can find these in Chapters 3 through 6.

Wizards of the Coast provides blank character sheets in the form of PDF files that you can download and print (at www.dndinsider.com).

D&D Miniatures and D&D Dungeon Tiles

Although most of the action of D&D occurs in the imaginations of the participants, it's often very helpful to display certain information where everyone can see it. Combat situations, for example, work better when the players and DM know where all the participants are (characters and monsters) in relation to one another. D&D uses a grid of one-inch squares to represent where the action takes place. To represent the characters and monsters, the players and DM place miniatures or other markers on the grid.

Look for official *D&D Dungeon Tiles*, high-quality cardstock tiles that you can configure to create any dungeon you can imagine. These make a great play surface for the game. When these are combined with official *D&D Miniatures*, which present heroic characters and monsters right out of the *Monster Manual* in detailed, prepainted plastic, every adventure you have comes to life.

You can find other play surfaces in the *D&D Roleplaying Game Starter Set,* in D&D adventures, and online at www.dndinsider.com.

Pencils, paper, and graph paper

You need a means for keeping notes and recording important information during game play, so have a lot of pencils, scrap paper, and graph paper available. Use the scrap paper for notes about the adventure. (Write down the names of NPCs and places, any treasure your character acquires, and any other details that you might forget or think may be important later.)

One player might take the role of note keeper, or each player may want to take his or her own notes. Use the graph paper to sketch a map of the area the PCs are exploring — players want to map the dungeon as they explore it, and the DM uses graph paper to design the whole dungeon before the adventurers enter it.

One Game Rule to Rule Them All

The DUNGEONS & DRAGONS game is built around a core mechanic. This core mechanic is used to resolve all actions in the game, keeping play fast and intuitive.

Expressions of D&D

The primary expression of DUNGEONS & DRAGONS takes the form of the D&D roleplaying game (RPG). This is where the whole thing started, and the RPG is still going strong after more than 30 years. This expression is presented in the three 4th Edition core rulebooks (*Player's Handbook, Dungeon Master's Guide,* and *Monster Manual*) and a plethora of supplements and accessories that expand the world of D&D. This *For Dummies* book focuses on the RPG experience and tries to make it clearer and easier to get into. But other expressions of D&D exist. Here are a few that you might want to check out:

✔ **DUNGEONS & DRAGONS Miniatures:** Official D&D prepainted plastic miniatures are available for use with the RPG. From hero characters to monsters such as bugbears, mind flayers, beholders, and more, a wide selection of the most popular and iconic D&D creatures can be found in randomly assorted booster packs. These miniature figures can also be used for a more competitive experience, a head-to-head skirmish game where players create warbands of D&D characters and creatures to throw against each other. If this concept (which goes back to D&D's roots) interests you, look for the *D&D Miniatures Starter Set* and *Booster Packs*.

✔ **DUNGEONS & DRAGONS novels:** Wizards of the Coast publishes fantasy novels set in the worlds of DUNGEONS & DRAGONS. Some of the most popular series include novels set in the FORGOTTEN REALMS and EBERRON settings and in the young adult PRACTICAL GUIDE series for younger readers.

✔ ***Dragon Magazine* and *Dungeon Magazine*:** Wizards of the Coast publishes two online magazines dedicated to the DUNGEONS & DRAGONS game. *Dragon Magazine* provides a player's perspective on the hobby, offering loads of new options to add to your game. Consider it to be an ongoing supplement full of new feats, powers, and magic items, as well as new player character races and classes, and tons of roleplaying and tactical advice to make any player better at the game. The companion periodical, *Dungeon Magazine*, is the definitive resource for D&D Dungeon Masters. It features DM advice, dungeon lairs, and ready-to-play adventures that can be dropped into any D&D campaign. Together, these magazines are required reading for serious D&D players and DMs everywhere. You can discover more about these magazines and find subscription information on the Web at www.dndinsider.com.

✔ **Computer and console games:** You might be more familiar with DUNGEONS & DRAGONS through the computer and video games that have been released over the years. The computer game industry grew out of the paper RPGs created by D&D, and today Atari continues to publish licensed games set in the worlds of DUNGEONS & DRAGONS.

The core game mechanic: Whenever your character attempts an action that has a chance of failure associated with it, roll a twenty-sided die (d20). The higher the roll, the better the character's chances of succeeding in that action.

Character actions boil down to three basic types:

- ✔ **Attack rolls:** A roll to determine whether your character succeeds at attacking a monster or other opponent. Using a longsword against a monster, for example, requires an attack roll.

- ✔ **Skill checks:** A roll to determine whether your character uses a skill successfully. Using the Athletics skill to climb a wall, for example, requires a skill check.

- ✔ **Ability checks:** A roll to determine whether your character succeeds at attempting to do something to which no specific skill really applies. Attempting to bash open a dungeon door, for example, requires a Strength ability check.

To determine whether any of these actions are successful, follow these steps:

1. **Roll a d20.**

2. **Add any relevant modifiers.**

3. **Compare the result to a target number.**

   If the result equals or exceeds the target number, the action succeeds. A result less than the target number indicates that the action fails.

Modifiers are determined by your character's level, ability scores, and other factors. You record modifiers on your character sheet for easy reference when you're playing. *Target numbers,* also called the Difficulty Class (DC) for a particular task or action, come from a variety of places. Some are set by the action itself and are defined in the rules, and other times the target numbers are determined by the Dungeon Master. For more details on modifiers and target numbers, see Chapter 7.

Joining a D&D Game

The best way to learn how to play DUNGEONS & DRAGONS is to jump right in. If you know other players who have a regular game, this book provides you with everything you need to join an existing game. The ready-to-play characters in Chapters 3 through 6 are 1st-level characters, completely built and outfitted for their first adventure. If you want to join a higher-level game, Chapter 9 presents one of these characters at greater levels of experience — specifically, at 4th level and at 8th level — giving you a little more latitude in where to start.

The best place to start

Other than this nifty *For Dummies* book, where's the best place to start learning the DUNGEONS & DRAGONS game? Well, we wrote this book to be a great starting point as well as a perfect companion to the full D&D game. Don't be afraid to just start out using the material in this book.

At some point, however, you need to get one of the D&D games. If you're brand new to the concept of roleplaying games, we urge you to buy the *DUNGEONS & DRAGONS Roleplaying Game Starter Set*. This jam-packed box includes dice, versatile dungeon tiles, character and monster tokens, and ready-to-play characters. This *For Dummies* book makes a great companion for learning to play with the *Starter Set*.

If you have some knowledge and experience with D&D or games like it, you might be ready to leap right into the 4th Edition core rulebooks. This trinity of knowledge comes in the form of the *Player's Handbook*, *Dungeon Master's Guide*, and *Monster Manual*. These volumes are available at fine hobby game stores and bookstores, and with this *For Dummies* book at your side, you should have no trouble navigating your way through them. If you go this route, you'll need to buy a set of dice, too, because the books don't come with them.

If you don't have an existing game group to join, you'll have to start your own. Chapter 9 discusses organizing your own game group.

Whether you join an existing group or start your own, we urge you to get moving. Every day you wait means one less day of getting in on the fun and excitement of D&D.

Chapter 2

Your First Character

In This Chapter

▶ Examining the D&D player character

▶ Playing a character

▶ Selecting the type of character you want to play

*Y*our interface with the fantastic adventures of the DUNGEONS & DRAGONS game is your *player character* (also called a *PC*). Like the hero of a novel, the star of a movie, or the character in a computer game, your player character (along with the other player characters in your adventuring party, run by other players) is at the center of all the action. Unlike the heroes of novels, movies, or even computer games, however, a D&D player character has no script to follow. *You* determine the course of every adventure through the actions you have your character take — and the only limit is your own imagination.

In this chapter, we examine the basics of what makes a D&D player character tick. From game statistics to race and class powers, this chapter provides an overview so that you can get a handle on the character you're going to play. This is all in preparation for selecting one of the ready-to-play characters presented in Chapters 3 through 6. In those chapters, we've done the work of creating characters so that you can spend time getting familiar with all the game concepts.

In Part II of this book, we walk you through the process of character creation using the *Player's Handbook* so that you can make your very own player character from scratch.

Defining Your Character

A DUNGEONS & DRAGONS player character lives in a world much like ours was in medieval times, when knights rode forth on charging warhorses and castles dotted the land. Now imagine this place, where magic really works and dragons and monsters roam in the dark beyond the firelight. Your character might be a strong fighter or a nimble rogue, a wise cleric or a mysterious wizard. Every day, your character explores the unknown places of the world, seeking monsters to slay and treasure to win. Every adventure that your character survives makes him or her a little more powerful, a little more famous, and a little richer.

D&D is a game, and so you need some way to express and describe your character in the context of the game world. Your fighter, for example, might be "extremely strong but not too bright," and those characteristics need to be translated into game terms. The following sections provide an overview of the things you find on your *character sheet,* a record of your character's game statistics.

Name

Every great character has a great name. You may have a name all picked out from the moment you conceive your character, or you may figure it out after you've determined all your character's game statistics. Great names are evocative. They fit the mood of the story and world in which the character adventures. John Savage is a great name for a character in a spy thriller set in the modern world, but it doesn't work so well for a character in a D&D fantasy world.

The characters presented for your use in Chapters 3 through 6 in this book have names already assigned to them. Chapter 3 of the *Player's Handbook* also lists sample names based on race. Those are good places to start when you decide to create your own character from scratch (which we discuss in Part II in this book).

Race

In the fantasy world of Dungeons & Dragons, humans aren't the only intelligent race walking around. Other intelligent races share their adventures, and your character can belong to any of these. To start, we present a few of the possible races you can choose from. The D&D *Player's Handbook* has additional races that make great player characters.

These races are drawn from myth and legend, and they're similar to the imaginary races that populate many popular fantasy worlds. For D&D, the races we begin with are *humans, dwarves, elves,* and *halflings.* You can find more detailed information on these character races in Chapter 12. Here's a quick rundown on the benefits of each:

✔ **Humans:** These are people just like you and us. They're adaptable, flexible, and extremely ambitious. Compared with the other races, humans are relatively short-lived. In game terms, humans get a +2 adjustment to one ability score, a bonus at-will power, a bonus feat, a bonus skill, and a +1 bonus to their Fortitude, Reflex, and Will defenses to reflect their natural tendencies.

✔ **Dwarves:** The members of this race are hearty and steadfast, standing about four-and-a-half-feet tall and powerfully built and extremely broad. They have a strong connection to mountains and rocky places. They can live to be more than 200 years old. In game terms, dwarves receive a +2 to Constitution and a +2 to Wisdom (see the "Ability scores" section, later in this chapter). They also receive a bonus to saves against poison; they can use their Second Wind (a self-heal) as a minor action (other characters need to use a standard action); and they are resistant to pull-push-slide effects, moving 1 square less than the effect calls for. Dwarves can also see in low-light conditions.

✔ **Elves:** Elves have a strong connection to the natural world, especially woodlands. They can live to be more than 200 years old. They are quick and quiet, slender and athletic. They stand about as tall as humans, with long, pointed ears, and vibrant eyes. Elves receive a +2 to Dexterity and a +2 to Wisdom (see the "Ability scores" section). Elves have low-light vision, a speed of 7, and a racial bonus on Nature and Perception checks (see the "Skills" section, later in this chapter). They provide their allies with a bonus to Perception checks, can ignore difficult terrain when they shift over squares, and have a racial power that allows them to reroll an attack roll once per encounter.

✔ **Halflings:** The members of this race are clever and capable — much more so than their small size might indicate. Standing about four feet tall, with slim, muscular builds, halflings are athletic and outgoing. Curious to a fault and usually with the daring to match, halflings love to explore. Halflings receive a +2 Dexterity and a +2 Charisma. They also receive bonuses to Acrobatics and Thievery checks (see the "Skills" section), as well as a bonus to saving throws against fear effects. They receive a bonus to AC against opportunity attacks, and they can use a racial power to force an enemy to reroll an attack against them once per encounter.

Class

In addition to your character's name and race, your character is most easily identified by his or her class. A *class* is kind of like a profession or vocation. It determines what role the character plays in the adventuring party. For example, your character might be Regdar, the human fighter. In this book, we present four of the most popular D&D classes for your use. You can find more classes in the 4th Edition D&D *Player's Handbook*.

The four basic classes are *fighter, rogue, wizard,* and *cleric.* You can find more detailed information on the character classes in Chapter 11. Here's a quick overview of each class:

- ✔ **Fighters:** These characters are warriors with exceptional combat capabilities and weapon skills. Nobody kills monsters and stands at the front of an adventuring party as well as the fighter.

- ✔ **Rogues:** Members of this class rely on tricks, cunning, and stealth to get through a dungeon and save the day. Rogues are great at getting past locked doors, scouting, spying, and attacking from the shadows.

- ✔ **Wizards:** These are spellcasters, calling on powerful magic spells to fight monsters and protect their teammates. Wizards need to stay out of direct combat, but the power they bring to the adventure makes them worthy members of any party.

- ✔ **Clerics:** These characters focus the might of divine magic to cast healing and protective spells. A good second-line warrior as well, a cleric might be one of the most versatile members of an adventuring party.

Each class fills a particular role in the party. For more details, see the "Roles" section later in this chapter.

Level and XP

Level is a description of your character's relative degree of power. A 10th-level character, for example, is more powerful and able to take on tougher challenges than a 5th-level character. With each new level your character attains, he or she becomes more powerful and capable. Your character begins play at 1st level.

Experience points (XP) are the numerical measure of your character's personal achievements. Your character earns experience points by defeating opponents and overcoming challenges. When your character's XP total reaches various milestones, he or she gains new levels. At 0 XP, for example, your character is 1st level. At 1,000 XP, your character attains 2nd level. More information on XP and levels can be found in Chapter 18.

Ability scores

The primary expression of your character in game terms starts with his or her ability scores. Every D&D character is defined by six abilities: Strength, Dexterity, Constitution, Intelligence, Wisdom, and Charisma. (See Chapter 13 for more information about ability scores.) Each ability gets a score, a number that determines how good your character will be at different tasks in the game.

The average score for everyday people in a D&D world is 10 or 11. Player characters are heroes, and so they have better ability scores than everyday folk. The average ability score for a player character is 12 or 13.

During character creation, you can assign numbers between 3 (a terrible score) and 18 (an excellent score) or higher. The characters presented for your use in Chapters 3 through 6 already have their ability scores and other statistics figured out, so you can start playing immediately.

Special abilities

If it hasn't been made clear yet, your player character is special. He or she stands above the normal people and becomes a hero in the world. As such, your character has special abilities. These might be based on your character's class or race or tied to certain feats you have selected.

For example, Regdar the fighter has the *spinning sweep* attack power. This provides him with a special encounter power that deals damage and knocks an enemy off its feet. Another example is Kathra the wizard's *cloud of daggers* at-will spell.

Key statistics

Your character has a number of key statistics that you'll refer to over and over throughout the course of play. These appear right at the top of the ready-to-play character sheets presented in Chapters 3 through 6. You can find more details on how to use these statistics in Chapter 7. Here's a quick rundown on the statistics:

- ✔ **Initiative modifier:** This modifier is used to determine who goes first in a combat round.

- ✔ **Speed:** This value shows how far your character can move (measured in squares) in a round.

- ✔ **Attack modifiers and damage:** These numbers are associated with your character's weapons of choice and powers. They show what you must roll to successfully attack opponents and how much damage your character does if the attack succeeds.

- ✔ **Defenses:** These values show what opponents need to roll to hit your character during combat. The four defenses are Armor Class (AC), Fortitude, Reflex, and Will.

✔ **Hit points (or hp):** This number defines how much damage your character can withstand in combat. When your character runs out of hit points, he or she is knocked unconscious — and may even be killed if he or she sustains more damage. Other important numbers derived from your character's hit points are his or her bloodied value (half of his or her total hit points) and healing surge value (one-quarter of your character's total hit points). The number of healing surges per day shows how many times you can restore hit points during a given day of adventuring.

Feats

Feats provide special bonuses or capabilities for your character, usually improving powers your character already has. The ready-to-play characters in Chapters 3 through 6 have already had feats selected for them. For more information about selecting your own feats, see Chapter 15.

Skills

Skills represent the training and education your character has beyond the combat and powers inherent to his or her class. Depending on your character's class, your character will have a greater or lesser number of skills to call upon. Rogues, for example, begin play trained in the use of six skills. Fighters, on the other hand, just don't go in much for studying and so start out with only three trained skills.

Skills have already been selected for the ready-to-play characters presented in Chapters 3 through 6. You can find additional information on skills in Chapter 16.

Gear

Every D&D player character must be well prepared for adventuring life. This is reflected not only in the class, skills, and feats the character has, but in the gear the character carries — the weapons, armor, rations, sleeping rolls, rope, torches, flint and steel, and the backpack to carry it all in. No adventurer goes naked into a dungeon!

Equipment has already been selected for the ready-to-play characters presented in Chapters 3 through 6. You can find additional information on adventuring gear in Chapter 17.

Powers

All player characters have powers. Powers are defined as either attack powers or utility powers. Some powers can be used all the time (at-will powers). Others are more powerful and have limits (encounter powers and daily powers). Powers are based on a character's class and the power source associated with it.

Fighters and rogues, for example, are martial characters. Their powers are called *exploits.* These come from the training and experience these characters have endured, and they can sometimes appear almost magical in nature to the less-initiated.

Clerics are divine characters. Their powers are called *prayers.*

Wizards are arcane characters. Their powers are called *spells.*

Powers have already been selected for the ready-to-play characters presented in Chapters 3 through 6. You can find additional information on powers in Chapter 14.

Playing Your Character

As stated earlier in this chapter, the way you interface with the D&D world is through your player character. Your character acts as your eyes and ears in the fantasy world, as well as your hands and feet. You can interact with the world your Dungeon Master presents in any way you want through your character. The only limit is your imagination — and sometimes how well you roll the dice. The following sections tell you how to get the most out of your player character.

Taking turns

When you're caught up in a game, it's easy to care only about whose turn it is during combat and other dramatic situations (such as when dealing with a trap or obstacle). Try not to forget that other people are playing the game with you. When you really get into your character and the fantasy, you might have a tendency to hog all the DM's attention. Resist that urge! Let every player have a turn talking to the DM, asking questions, or describing what his or her character tries to do. It's only fair, and it makes the game work much better. Besides, much of the fun is in seeing what the other players are thinking and how they're reacting to their characters' actions.

Players are not characters

Always keep in mind that you and your character are two different people. You have knowledge as a player that your character doesn't have. Your character shouldn't know what die rolls have been made or other things that don't make up his or her "character knowledge." Characters never talk about Armor Class or hit points or ability scores. They can discuss the quality of their armor, their general health, and their comparative strengths and weaknesses, but never the game mechanics behind those things.

Be sure to let the DM and the other players know when you're speaking as your character or as yourself, if there's any confusion. When you remember the difference between you the player and your character, everyone can have more fun roleplaying.

A good Dungeon Master may say during the game "You don't know that" or "You wouldn't think of that," meaning that you're confusing player knowledge with character knowledge. Good players learn to avoid this type of problem by keeping the two separate.

Players don't swing swords, cast spells, disarm traps, or die fighting monsters. Characters, on the other hand, do all this and more over the course of a typical adventure.

During combat situations, everyone makes an initiative roll to determine the order of play. We cover initiative and game play in greater detail in Chapter 7.

Roleplaying

D&D is a roleplaying game. That means that your character is much more than just a collection of game statistics (though those have their place). Take those game statistics and build a personality for your character. Remember that your character is a hero and is part of a team, but otherwise let your imagination be your guide. The quirks and mannerisms you bring to the role are what set your character apart.

D&D is a game. Have fun with it. You don't have to use funny voices or accents or anything like that. Just determine how your character would act in any given situation and remain true to the character as the adventure unfolds. Soon, your character will develop a personality all his or her own, and the game, in turn, will take on a fantastic life that makes each session fun to play.

Your imagination is the limit

In addition to attacking, casting spells, and using skills, characters can do all sorts of things. The only limit to what a character can do is the player's imagination and the rulings of the Dungeon Master. Depending on the situation, your character might bash apart a cabinet to find a secret compartment, make a rope out of bed sheets, or try to build a trap out of spare parts in an evil wizard's workshop. The DM decides whether an idea works or not, sometimes calling for die rolls to help determine the outcome.

Character Roles

Think of the adventuring party as you would a sports team. Every member of the team fills a position and performs a role. These roles aren't designed to restrict your character, but rather help define his or her usual place on the team. Just as a baseball team needs a pitcher and a catcher, or a basketball team needs a center and a point guard, so too does a D&D adventuring party need characters to fill specific roles.

The four roles that define a D&D adventuring party are

- ✔ **Controller:** A controller deals with large numbers of enemies at the same time, either dishing out damage over a wide area or hindering enemies in some other, less overt way. The wizard fills the role of controller.

- ✔ **Defender:** A defender, as the name implies, has the best defenses in the game. Defenders usually handle one enemy at a time, using close-combat offense to form a party's first line of defense. It's tough to ignore a defender when he or she wades into battle. The fighter fills the role of defender.

- ✔ **Leader:** A leader inspires, heals, and otherwise aids the rest of the adventuring party. A leader isn't necessarily the boss of the party, but he or she motivates and leads by example, making the rest of the party operate better thanks to the leader's presence. The cleric fills the role of leader.

- ✔ **Striker:** A striker deals a lot of damage to one target at a time. Strikers are highly mobile, with the ability to set up spectacular attacks and get away before they can take too much punishment in return. The rogue fills the role of striker.

Choosing Your Character

The earlier sections in this chapter cover the basics. After you have a handle on the basic stuff, select your own character from those presented over the next four chapters. There's no right or wrong way to choose a character. You might really want to play a specific class and/or race. Of course, you should read through all the material, but in the end, go with your gut and choose the character that most appeals to you. Here are some recommendations:

- ✔ **Fighters:** You want to play a fighter if being in the thick of combat appeals to you. Fighters always have something to do, no matter what challenge appears before them. Fighters are masters of many weapons, and have a diverse array of martial powers (called *exploits*) to choose from. If you want to play a fighter, turn to Chapter 3 and select one of the ready-to-play fighters presented therein.

- ✔ **Rogues:** You want to play a rogue if being sneaky and cunning appeals to you. Rogues have powers (also called *exploits*) that enhance their mobility and damage-dealing capability, excel at making sneak attacks, and master many skills. Rogues are a good choice for people who are new to the game and the concepts of D&D. If you want to play a rogue, go to Chapter 4 and take a look at the ready-to-play rogues it has to offer.

- ✔ **Wizards:** You want to play a wizard if using flashy arcane powers (called *spells*) appeals to you. Wizards cast spells that deal damage or hinder the enemy. Wizards are harder to play than fighters or rogues due to the slight complexity of spellcasting, but the rewards for playing a wizard well can be very satisfying. If you want to play a wizard, Chapter 5 has some ready-to-play wizards for you.

- ✔ **Clerics:** You want to play a cleric if spellcasting, up-close combat, and helping others appeal to you. Clerics have defensive and helpful divine powers (called *prayers*) that give the entire party a boost. In addition, they have the ability to fight alongside fighters when the monsters charge in fast and furiously. If you want to play a cleric, check out the ready-to-play clerics presented in Chapter 6.

Chapter 3

Starting Out as a Fighter

· ·

In This Chapter

▶ Understanding the fighter class

▶ Exploring who should play a fighter

▶ Discovering how to play a fighter

▶ Meeting three ready-to-play fighters

· ·

*T*he fighter is the quintessential DUNGEONS & DRAGONS player character. As the name of the class implies, the fighter has the best all-around fighting capabilities. A fighter usually has a good Strength score to better use melee weapons, such as swords and axes. Fighters can use most weapons and most kinds of armor and shields without penalty. They are trained in close-combat fighting.

Whether a fighter receives formal training in an army or local militia or is self-taught but battle tested, he or she stands at the front of any adventuring party. A fighter provides combat prowess, high hit points, and good defense to the party. In return, the fighter seeks magical support, healing, and scouting skills from comrades. As part of a team, the fighter is the defender — protecting the other party members and wading in to lock down the tough opponents. In other words, the fighter's job is to fight.

In this chapter, we provide a bit of advice on who might want to play a fighter character and how to play a fighter character if that's the route you decide to go. The rest of the chapter features three ready-to-play fighter characters that you can use to kick-start your adventuring career.

Who Should Play a Fighter?

The fighter is among the easiest, most straightforward classes to play. Anyone brand new to the concept of D&D and roleplaying might want to start out with a fighter character. If you think that being in the center of most combat encounters will appeal to you, or if you like the idea of playing a physically powerful character, then the fighter is the class for you.

Every adventuring party needs at least one fighter. In a party of four, a solid fighter is essential to success. In a party of five or six, two fighters really provide a lot of durability and make adventuring that much easier.

See Chapter 7 for details on how to read the description for each fighter's powers.

How to Play a Fighter

Your character can take any approach to the fighter class. He might be a questing knight, a king's champion, or an elite foot soldier. She might be a mercenary, a raider, or a thug. Some fighters use their expertise for the greater good, whereas others are interested only in personal gain.

Fighters should be brave and stalwart, gutsy and heroic. Later, you can play with the baselines and portray any kind of fighter you want, but to start out, go with the tried-and-true basics. Fighters live for the thrill of combat and the excitement of adventure. And woe to any evil that happens to cross their paths!

Have fun with the idea of being a physical powerhouse, a combat expert, and a master of weapons. That's the fighter's portfolio, and you should play it for all it's worth. That doesn't mean you shouldn't play smart, however. If your fighter blindly rushes into combat and gets killed, the rest of your team will be in real trouble. Be cautious, but not too cautious. Above all, be a hero.

Fighter builds

Fighters come in two basic builds: the Great Weapon Fighter and the Guardian Fighter. A Great Weapon Fighter uses two-handed weapons to fight hard instead of smart. A Guardian Fighter uses a one-handed weapon and a shield to increase his or her already formidable defenses even more. All fighters want to get up close and personal with the enemy and usually want to take on the toughest opponent personally.

The fighter's role

Just as each player has a position on a sports team, every character has a role in the adventuring party. For the fighter, that role is defender. As a defender, it falls to the fighter to form the front line of any battle, to protect the more fragile members of the team from excessive harm, to soak up attacks thanks to a high Armor Class and high hit points, and to contain monsters with the combat challenge class feature.

Selecting a Fighter

The rest of this chapter features three ready-to-play 1st-level fighter characters:

- ✔ **Regdar** is Great Weapon Fighter who is a champion of good, pledging his mighty greatsword to the cause of justice. He adventures to put down evil and to gain skill and experience that he can use in his ongoing crusade. Regdar's job on an adventuring team is defender, killing the monsters and protecting his teammates by forming the front line in battle.

- ✔ **Tordek** is a Guardian Fighter who quests to prove himself to his warclan. He refuses to return to his dwarven homeland until he has made a name for himself that his clan can be proud of. He believes the best way to accomplish this is through battle and adventuring. Tordek uses a warhammer and shield in combat. Tordek's job on an adventuring team is defender, killing the monsters and protecting his teammates by forming the front line in battle.

- ✔ **Calia** is a Guardian Fighter who has taken to the life of adventuring to satisfy her wanderlust. She believes in setting her own pace and wandering freely from dungeon to dungeon in search of adventure and glory. Calia never goes into a battle without her trusty longsword and shield at the ready. Calia's job on an adventuring team is defender, killing the monsters and protecting her teammates by forming the front line in battle.

Any one of these characters makes a great fighter and a worthy member of any adventuring party. Pick the one that most appeals to you and then turn to Chapter 7 for a quick overview of game play.

Regdar, 1st-Level Human Fighter

Hit Points: 29 _____ Bloodied: 14

Healing Surge: 7   Surges per Day: 11

Initiative: +1   Speed: 5 squares

Alignment: Good

Ability Scores

	Score	Bonus*
STRENGTH	18	+4
CONSTITUTION	14	+2
DEXTERITY	13	+1
INTELLIGENCE	10	+0
WISDOM	12	+1
CHARISMA	11	+0

* Bonuses and penalties have already been calculated into your statistics and powers.

Defenses

AC 17   Fortitude 15   Reflex 12   Will 12

Basic Attacks

Melee Basic Attack (Greatsword)
    d20 + 8   1d10 + 4 damage

Ranged Basic Attack (Longbow)
    d20 + 3   1d10 damage

Class Features

Combat Challenge: Every time you attack an enemy, whether the attack hits or misses, you can choose to mark that target. The mark lasts until the end of your next turn. While a target is marked, it takes a –2 penalty to attack rolls if its attack doesn't include you as a target. A creature can be subject to only one mark at a time. A new mark supersedes a mark that was already in place.

In addition, whenever an enemy that is adjacent to you shifts or makes an attack that doesn't include you as a target, you can make a melee basic attack against that enemy as an immediate interrupt.

Combat Superiority: You gain a +2 bonus to opportunity attacks.

Fighter Weapon Talent: You gain a +1 bonus to attack rolls when using two-handed weapons (already included in stats).

Feats

Action Surge: You gain a +3 bonus to attack rolls you make during any action you gained by spending an action point.

Power Attack: When making a melee attack, you can take a –2 penalty to the attack roll. If the attack hits, you gain a +3 bonus to the damage roll.

Skills

Acrobatics	**d20 + 1**
Arcana	**d20 + 0**
Athletics (trained)	**d20 + 9**
Bluff	**d20 + 0**
Diplomacy	**d20 + 0**
Dungeoneering	**d20 + 1**
Endurance (trained)	**d20 + 7**
Heal	**d20 + 1**
History	**d20 + 0**
Insight	**d20 + 1**
Intimidate (trained)	**d20 + 5**
Nature	**d20 + 1**

Perception	d20 + 1
Religion	d20 + 0
Stealth	d20 + 1
Streetwise (trained)	d20 + 5
Thievery	d20 + 1

Powers

Cleave　　　　　　　　　　Fighter Attack 1

You hit one enemy and then cleave into another.

At-Will ♦ Martial, Weapon

Standard Action　　　　　　Melee weapon

Target: One creature

Attack: d20 + 8 versus AC

Hit: 1d10 + 4 damage, and an enemy adjacent to you other than the target takes 4 points of damage.

Reaping Strike　　　　　　Fighter Attack 1

You punctuate your scything attacks with wicked jabs and small cutting blows that slip through your enemy's defenses.

At-Will ♦ Martial, Weapon

Standard Action　　　　　　Melee weapon

Target: One creature

Attack: d20 + 8 versus AC

Hit: 1d10 + 4 damage

Miss: 4 points of damage

Sure Strike　　　　　　　Fighter Attack

You trade power for precision.

At-Will ♦ Martial, Weapon

Standard Action　　　　　　Melee weapon

Target: One creature

Attack: d20 + 10 versus AC

Hit: 1d10 damage

Spinning Sweep　　　　　Fighter Attack 1

You spin beneath your enemy's guard with a long, powerful cut and then sweep your leg through his an instant later to knock him head over heels.

Encounter ♦ Martial, Weapon

Standard Action　　　　　　Melee weapon

Target: One creature

Attack: d20 + 8 versus AC

Hit: 1d10 + 4 damage, and you knock the target prone.

Brute Strike　　　　　　Fighter Attack 1

You shatter armor and bone with a ringing blow.

Daily ♦ Martial, Reliable, Weapon

Standard Action　　　　　　Melee weapon

Target: One creature

Attack: d20 + 8 versus AC

Hit: 3d10 + 4 damage

Miss: This is a reliable power. If you miss, you don't expend its use for the day.

Armor, Weapons, and Gear

Regdar wears scale mail armor. He carries a greatsword, a longbow, 20 arrows, a backpack, two sunrods, a bedroll, 50 feet of rope, and flint and steel. He has 10 gp.

Tordek, 1st-Level Dwarf Fighter

Hit Points: 29 _____ Bloodied: 14

Healing Surge: 7   Surges per Day: 11

Initiative: +1   Speed: 5 squares

Alignment: Lawful Good

Ability Scores

	Score	Bonus*
STRENGTH	**16**	**+3**
CONSTITUTION	**14**	**+2**
DEXTERITY	**13**	**+1**
INTELLIGENCE	**10**	**+0**
WISDOM	**16**	**+3**
CHARISMA	**11**	**+0**

* Bonuses and penalties have already been calculated into your statistics and powers.

Defenses

AC 18   Fortitude 14   Reflex 11   Will 13

Basic Attacks

Melee Basic Attack (Warhammer)
       d20 + 6   1d10 + 4 damage

Ranged Basic Attack (Throwing Hammer)
       d20 + 3   1d6 + 1 damage

Class Features

Combat Challenge: Every time you attack an enemy, whether the attack hits or misses, you can choose to mark that target. The mark lasts until the end of your next turn. While a target is marked, it takes a –2 penalty to attack rolls if its attack doesn't include you as a target. A creature can be subject to only one mark at a time. A new mark supersedes a mark that was already in place.

In addition, whenever an enemy that is adjacent to you shifts or makes an attack that doesn't include you as a target, you can make a melee basic attack against that enemy as an immediate interrupt.

Combat Superiority: You gain a +2 bonus to opportunity attacks.

Fighter Weapon Talent: You gain a +1 bonus to attack rolls when using one-handed weapons (already included in stats).

Racial Traits

Cast-Iron Stomach: +5 racial bonus to saving throws against poison.

Dwarven Resilience: You can use your second wind as a minor action.

Stand Your Ground: When an effect forces you to move — through a pull, a push, or a slide — you move 1 square less than the effect specifies. In addition, when an attack would knock you prone, you can make an immediate saving throw to avoid falling prone.

Feats

Weapon Focus: You gain a +1 feat bonus to damage rolls when using hammers (already included in the stats).

Skills

Acrobatics	**d20 + 1**
Arcana	**d20 + 0**
Athletics (trained)	**d20 + 8**
Bluff	**d20 + 0**
Diplomacy	**d20 + 0**
Dungeoneering	**d20 + 3**

Endurance (trained)	**d20 + 9**
Heal	**d20 + 3**
History	**d20 + 0**
Insight	**d20 + 3**
Intimidate (trained)	**d20 + 5**
Nature	**d20 + 3**
Perception	**d20 + 3**
Religion	**d20 + 0**
Stealth	**d20 + 1**
Streetwise	**d20 + 0**
Thievery	**d20 + 1**

Powers

Sure Strike   Fighter Attack 1

You trade power for precision.

At-Will ♦ Martial, Weapon

Standard Action   Melee weapon

Target: One creature

Attack: d20 + 8 versus AC

Hit: 1d10 + 1 damage

Tide of Iron   Fighter Attack 1

After each mighty swing, you bring your shield to bear and use it to push your enemy back.

At-Will ♦ Martial, Weapon

Standard Action   Melee weapon

Requirement: You must be using a shield.

Target: One creature

Attack: d20 + 6 versus AC

Hit: 1d10 + 4 damage, and you push the target 1 square if it is Large size or smaller. You can shift into the space that the target occupied before you pushed it.

Covering Attack   Fighter Attack 1

You launch a dizzying barrage of thrusts at your enemy, compelling him to give you all his attention. Under the cover of your ferocious attack, one of your allies can safely retreat from that same foe.

Encounter ♦ Martial, Weapon

Standard Action

Melee weapon

Target: One creature

Attack: d20 + 6 versus AC

Hit: 2d10 + 4 damage, and an ally adjacent to the target can shift 2 squares.

Comeback Strike   Fighter Attack 1

A timely strike against a hated foe invigorates you, giving you the strength and resolve to fight on.

Daily ♦ Healing, Martial, Reliable, Weapon

Standard Action   Melee weapon

Target: One creature

Attack: d20 + 6 versus AC

Hit: 2d10 + 4 damage, and you can spend a healing surge.

Miss: This is a reliable power. If you miss, you don't expend its use for the day.

Armor, Weapons, and Gear

Tordek wears scale mail armor and uses a light shield. He carries a warhammer, 3 throwing hammers, a backpack, two sunrods, a bedroll, 50 feet of rope, and flint and steel. He has 10 gp.

Calia, 1st-Level Elf Fighter

Hit Points: 27 _____ Bloodied: 13

Healing Surge: 6   Surges per Day: 10

Initiative: +2   Speed: 6 squares

Alignment: Good

Ability Scores

	Score	Bonus*
STRENGTH	**16**	**+3**
CONSTITUTION	**12**	**+1**
DEXTERITY	**15**	**+2**
INTELLIGENCE	**10**	**+0**
WISDOM	**16**	**+3**
CHARISMA	**11**	**+0**

* Bonuses and penalties have already been calculated into your statistics and powers.

Defenses

AC 18   Fortitude 13   Reflex 12   Will 13

Basic Attacks

Melee Basic Attack (Longsword)
    d20 + 7   1d8 + 4 damage

Ranged Basic Attack (Longbow)
    d20 + 4   1d10 damage

Class Features

Combat Challenge: Every time you attack an enemy, whether the attack hits or misses, you can choose to mark that target. The mark lasts until the end of your next turn. While a target is marked, it takes a –2 penalty to attack rolls if its attack doesn't include you as a target. A creature can be subject to only one mark at a time. A new mark supersedes a mark that was already in place.

In addition, whenever an enemy that is adjacent to you shifts or makes an attack that doesn't include you as a target, you can make a melee basic attack against that enemy as an immediate interrupt.

Combat Superiority: You gain a +2 bonus to opportunity attacks.

Fighter Weapon Talent: You gain a +1 bonus to attack rolls when using one-handed weapons (already included in stats).

Racial Traits

Group Awareness: You grant non-elf allies within 5 squares of you a +1 racial bonus to Perception checks.

Wild Step: You ignore difficult terrain when you shift.

Elven Accuracy: You can use *elven accuracy* as an encounter power.

Elven Accuracy   Elf Racial Power

With an instant of focus, you take careful aim at your foe and strike with the legendary accuracy of the elves.

Encounter

Free Action   **Personal**

Effect: Reroll an attack roll. Use the second roll, even if it's lower.

Feats

Weapon Focus: You gain a +1 feat bonus to damage rolls when using heavy blades (already included in the stats).

Skills

Acrobatics	**d20 + 2**
Arcana	**d20 + 0**
Athletics (trained)	**d20 + 8**
Bluff	**d20 + 0**
Diplomacy	**d20 + 0**
Dungeoneering	**d20 + 3**
Endurance (trained)	**d20 + 7**
Heal (trained)	**d20 + 8**
History	**d20 + 0**
Insight	**d20 + 3**
Intimidate	**d20 + 0**
Nature	**d20 + 5**
Perception	**d20 + 5**
Religion	**d20 + 0**
Stealth	**d20 + 2**
Streetwise	**d20 + 0**
Thievery	**d20 + 2**

Powers

Sure Strike   Fighter Attack 1

You trade power for precision.

At-Will ♦ Martial, Weapon

Standard Action   **Melee** weapon

Target: One creature

Attack: d20 + 9 versus AC

Hit: 1d8 + 1 damage

Tide of Iron   Fighter Attack 1

After each mighty swing, you bring your shield to bear and use it to push your enemy back.

At-Will ♦ Martial, Weapon

Standard Action   **Melee** weapon

Requirement: You must be using a shield.

Target: One creature

Attack: d20 + 7 versus AC

Hit: 1d8 + 4 damage, and you push the target 1 square if it is Large size or smaller. You can shift into the space that the target occupied before you pushed it.

Steel Serpent Strike   Fighter Attack 1

You stab viciously at your foe's knee or foot to slow him down. No matter how tough he is, he's going to favor that leg for a time.

Encounter ♦ Martial, Weapon

Standard Action   **Melee** weapon

Target: One creature

Attack: d20 + 7 versus AC

Hit: 2d8 + 4 damage, and the target is slowed and cannot shift until the end of your next turn.

Comeback Strike   Fighter Attack 1

A timely strike against a hated foe invigorates you, giving you the strength and resolve to fight on.

Daily ♦ Healing, Martial, Reliable, Weapon

Standard Action   **Melee** weapon

Target: One creature

Attack: d20 + 7 versus AC

Hit: 2d8 + 4 damage, and you can spend a healing surge.

Miss: This is a reliable power. If you miss, you don't expend its use for the day.

Armor, Weapons, and Gear

Calia wears scale mail armor and uses a light shield. She carries a longsword, a longbow, 20 arrows, a backpack, two sunrods, a bedroll, 50 feet of rope, and flint and steel. She has 10 gp.

Chapter 4

Starting Out as a Rogue

In This Chapter

▶ Understanding the rogue class

▶ Exploring who should play a rogue

▶ Discovering how to play a rogue

▶ Meeting three ready-to-play rogues

*T*he rogue has been part of the DUNGEONS & DRAGONS game experience from the beginning. In the early days, this class was called the thief, but as player characters, rogues can and should be so much more than that title implies. A rogue is an expert in the use of all kinds of skills, excelling at sneaking around, scouting, and disarming traps. A rogue needs a high Dexterity score to improve his or her success with many of the class's primary skills, as well as to bolster his or her Armor Class and ranged attacks.

In this chapter, we provide a bit of advice on who might want to play a rogue character and how to play a rogue character. The rest of the chapter features three ready-to-play rogue characters that you can use to kick-start your adventuring career.

Who Should Play a Rogue?

The rogue isn't as dedicated to a single mode of play as the fighter, but this class makes a good starting point for new players who aren't afraid of making a few decisions during the game. If you like to solve puzzles or want to play a character that is equal parts skillful, cunning, and stealthy while dealing tons of damage, then the rogue is the class for you.

Every adventuring party needs one rogue. In a party of four, a skillful rogue is essential to success. In a larger party, a single rogue still provides the abilities to avoid or overcome traps and hazardous obstacles. More than one rogue might be overkill, and you could be sacrificing other skill sets that the party might desperately need.

See Chapter 7 for details on how to read the description for each rogue's powers.

How to Play a Rogue

The rogue has a number of skills and abilities that make him or her an essential part of any adventuring team. Stealth and cunning are the rogue's tools of trade, so if you play a rogue, you have to be ready for anything. One of the rogue's functions is to deal lots of damage to a single opponent with his or her sneak attack. In addition, the rogue scouts for party, uses skills to deal with traps and locked doors, and usually has enough other skills to be a jack-of-all-trades. Rogues wear cloth and leather armor, and they use daggers, hand crossbows, shuriken, slings, and short swords. A rogue's relatively low hit points and Armor Class means he or she needs to choose opponents carefully in melee combat.

Your character can take any approach to the rogue class. He might be a stealthy thief, a silver-tongued trickster, or an elite scout. She might be a spy, a thug, or a diplomat. All rogues are versatile, adaptable, and resourceful. Later, you can play with the baselines and portray any kind of rogue you want; but to start out, go with the tried-and-true basics. You live for the thrill of adventure. You seek challenges to overcome, and you just have to open that locked door to see what's waiting on the other side. And if you can pick up some gold along the way, so much the better!

Have fun with the idea of being a skilled expert who's dexterous and stealthy. Use your skills and abilities often, and the rewards will come to you. Although all rogues have a little bit (or a lot) of thief in them, the code of the adventuring party urges you not to steal from your teammates. Be curious and a little reckless, but not too reckless. Above all, be a hero.

Rogue builds

Rogues come in two basic builds: The Brawny Rogue and the Trickster Rogue. Brawny Rogues prefer powers that deal a huge amount of damage. Dexterity and Strength are the Brawny Rogue's most important abilities. Trickster Rogues favor powers that deceive and misdirect their foes. Dexterity and Charisma are their most important abilities.

The rogue's role

Just as every player has a position on a sports team, every character has a role in the adventuring party. For the rogue, that role is striker. As a striker, it falls to the rogue to provide the offense in most battles, darting in to deal massive damage to one opponent at a time. In addition, the rogue has skills and class features that make him or her invaluable for exploring a dungeon and dealing with all kinds of skill challenges.

Selecting a Rogue

The rest of this chapter features three ready-to-play rogue characters:

- ✔ **Jax** is a Trickster Rogue who is a good-hearted and has a thirst for adventure. He sees every quest as a challenge to do his best and help his companions — and if he earns some gold along the way, so much the better. Jax's weapon of choice is the short sword, and the blade sings in his skilled hands. Jax's job on an adventuring team is striker, dealing massive damage and handling locked doors and traps.

- ✔ **Shadow** is a Brawny Rogue who slips through every adventure with quiet determination and impressive skill. She wants to overcome every challenge and is fond of treasure. She is a gifted athlete, highly skilled in climbing and jumping, and she uses this to the benefit of herself and her team. Shadow's job on an adventuring team is striker, dealing massive damage and handling locked doors and traps.

- ✔ **Lidda** is a Trickster Rogue, and like all halflings, she stands about half as tall as a human. She's sneaky, curious, and extremely fond of shiny objects. Her career as a rogue began when she left her home to wander in search of adventure. Lidda's job on an adventuring team is striker, dealing massive damage and handling locked doors and traps.

Any of these characters make a great rogue and a worthy member of any adventuring party. Pick the one that most appeals to you and then turn to Chapter 7 for a quick overview of game play.

Jax, 1st-Level Human Rogue

Hit Points: 24 _____ Bloodied: 12

Healing Surge: 6   Surges per Day: 7

Initiative: +4   Speed: 6 squares

Alignment: Good

Ability Scores

	Score	Bonus*
STRENGTH	**13**	**+1**
CONSTITUTION	**12**	**+1**
DEXTERITY	**18**	**+4**
INTELLIGENCE	**10**	**+0**
WISDOM	**11**	**+0**
CHARISMA	**14**	**+2**

* Bonuses and penalties have already been calculated into your statistics and powers.

Defenses

AC 16   Fortitude 12   Reflex 17   Will 13

Basic Attacks

Melee Basic Attack (Short Sword)
        d20 + 4   1d6 + 1 damage

Ranged Basic Attack (Dagger)
        d20 + 8   1d4 damage

Class Features

First Strike: At the start of an encounter, you have combat advantage against any creatures that have not yet acted in that encounter.

Rogue Tactics, Artful Dodger: You gain a +2 bonus to AC against opportunity attacks.

Rogue Weapon Talent: You gain a +1 bonus to attack rolls when using a dagger (already included in stats).

Sneak Attack: Once per round, when you have combat advantage against an enemy and you're using a light blade, crossbow, or sling, you deal +2d8 damage if the attack hits.

Feats

Backstabber: The extra damage dice from your Sneak Attack class feature increases from d6s to d8s (already included).

Human Perseverance: You gain a +1 feat bonus to saving throws (already included).

Skills

Acrobatics (trained)	**d20 + 9**
Arcana	**d20 + 0**
Athletics	**d20 + 1**
Bluff (trained)	**d20 + 7**
Diplomacy	**d20 + 2**
Dungeoneering	**d20 + 0**
Endurance	**d20 + 1**
Heal	**d20 + 0**
History	**d20 + 0**
Insight (trained)	**d20 + 5**
Intimidate	**d20 + 2**
Nature	**d20 + 0**
Perception (trained)	**d20 + 5**
Religion	**d20 + 0**
Stealth (trained)	**d20 + 9**
Streetwise (trained)	**d20 + 7**
Thievery (trained)	**d20 + 9**

Powers

Deft Strike   Rogue Attack 1

A final lunge brings you into an advantageous position.

At-Will ◆ Martial, Weapon

Standard Action   **Melee or Ranged** weapon

Requirement: You must be wielding a crossbow, a light blade, or a sling.

Target: One creature

Special: You can move 2 squares before the attack.

Attack: d20 + 7 versus AC (with short sword) or d20 + 8 versus AC (with dagger)

Hit: 1d6 + 4 damage (short sword) or 1d4 + 4 damage (dagger)

Piercing Strike   Rogue Attack 1

A needle-sharp point slips past armor and into tender flesh.

At-Will ◆ Martial, Weapon

Standard Action   **Melee** weapon

Requirement: You must be wielding a light blade.

Target: One creature

Attack: d20 + 7 versus Reflex

Hit: 1d6 + 4 damage

Sly Flourish   Rogue Attack 1

A distracting flourish causes the enemy to forget the blade at his throat.

At-Will ◆ Martial, Weapon

Standard Action   **Melee or Ranged** weapon

Requirement: You must be wielding a crossbow, a light blade, or a sling.

Target: One creature

Attack: d20 + 7 versus AC (with short sword) or d20 + 8 versus AC (with dagger)

Hit: 1d6 + 6 damage (short sword) or 1d4 + 6 damage (dagger)

Positioning Strike   Rogue Attack 1

A false stumble and a shove place the enemy exactly where you want him.

Encounter ◆ Martial, Weapon

Standard Action   **Melee** weapon

Requirement: You must be wielding a light blade.

Target: One creature

Attack: d20 + 7 versus Will

Hit: 1d6 + 4 damage, and you slide the target 2 squares.

Trick Strike   Rogue Attack 1

Through a series of feints and lures, you maneuver your foe right where you want him.

Daily ◆ Martial, Weapon

Standard Action   **Melee or Ranged** weapon

Requirement: You must be wielding a crossbow, a light blade, or a sling.

Target: One creature

Special: You can move 2 squares before the attack.

Attack: d20 + 7 versus AC (with short sword) or d20 + 8 versus AC (with dagger)

Hit: 3d6 + 4 damage (short sword) or 3d4 + 4 damage (dagger), and you slide the target 1 square.

Effect: Until the end of the encounter, each time you hit the target you slide it 1 square.

Armor, Weapons, and Gear

Jax wears leather armor. He carries a short sword, 5 daggers, a backpack, two sunrods, a bedroll, 50 feet of rope, thieves' tools, and flint and steel. He has 25 gp.

Shadow, 1st-Level Human Rogue

Hit Points: 29 _____ Bloodied: 14

Healing Surge: 7   Surges per Day: 7

Initiative: +4   Speed: 6 squares

Alignment: Unaligned

Ability Scores

	Score	Bonus*
STRENGTH	**14**	**+2**
CONSTITUTION	**12**	**+1**
DEXTERITY	**18**	**+4**
INTELLIGENCE	**10**	**+0**
WISDOM	**11**	**+0**
CHARISMA	**13**	**+1**

* Bonuses and penalties have already been calculated into your statistics and powers.

Defenses

AC 16   Fortitude 13   Reflex 17   Will 12

Basic Attacks

Melee Basic Attack (Short Sword)
        d20 + 5   1d6 + 2 damage

Ranged Basic Attack (Hand Crossbow)
        d20 + 6   1d6 damage

Class Features

First Strike: At the start of an encounter, you have combat advantage against any creatures that have not yet acted in that encounter.

Rogue Tactics, Brutal Scoundrel: You gain a +2 bonus to your Sneak Attack damage (already included).

Rogue Weapon Talent: You gain a +1 bonus to attack rolls when using a dagger.

Sneak Attack: Once per round, when you have combat advantage against an enemy and you're using a light blade, crossbow, or sling, you deal 2d8 + 2 damage if the attack hits.

Feats

Backstabber: The extra damage dice from your Sneak Attack class feature increases from d6s to d8s (already included).

Toughness: You gain an additional 5 hit points.

Skills

Acrobatics	**d20 + 4**
Arcana	**d20 + 0**
Athletics (trained)	**d20 + 7**
Bluff	**d20 + 1**
Diplomacy	**d20 + 1**
Dungeoneering (trained)	**d20 + 5**
Endurance	**d20 + 1**
Heal	**d20 + 0**
History	**d20 + 0**
Insight	**d20 + 0**
Intimidate (trained)	**d20 + 6**
Nature	**d20 + 0**
Perception (trained)	**d20 + 5**
Religion	**d20 + 0**
Stealth (trained)	**d20 + 9**
Streetwise (trained)	**d20 + 6**
Thievery (trained)	**d20 + 9**

Powers

Deft Strike   Rogue Attack 1

A final lunge brings you into an advantageous position.

At-Will ♦ Martial, Weapon

Standard Action   **Melee or Ranged** weapon

Requirement: You must be wielding a crossbow, a light blade, or a sling.

Target: One creature

Special: You can move 2 squares before the attack.

Attack: d20 + 7 versus AC (with short sword) or d20 + 6 versus AC (with hand crossbow)

Hit: 1d6 + 4 damage (short sword) or 1d6 + 4 damage (hand crossbow)

Piercing Strike   Rogue Attack 1

A needle-sharp point slips past armor and into tender flesh.

At-Will ♦ Martial, Weapon

Standard Action   **Melee** weapon

Requirement: You must be wielding a light blade.

Target: One creature

Attack: d20 + 7 versus Reflex

Hit: 1d6 + 4 damage

Riposte Strike   Rogue Attack 1

With a calculated strike, you leave your foe vulnerable to an adroit riposte should he dare attack you

At-Will ♦ Martial, Weapon

Standard Action   **Melee** weapon

Requirement: You must be wielding a light blade.

Target: One creature

Attack: d20 + 7 versus AC

Hit: 1d6 + 4 damage. If the target attacks you before the start of your next turn, you make your riposte against the target as an immediate interrupt: d20 + 5 versus AC, 1d6 + 2 damage.

Torturous Strike   Rogue Attack 1

If you twist the blade in the wound just so, you can make your enemy howl in pain.

Encounter ♦ Martial, Weapon

Standard Action   **Melee** weapon

Requirement: You must be wielding a light blade.

Target: One creature

Attack: d20 + 7 versus AC

Hit: 2d6 + 6 damage

Easy Target   Rogue Attack 1

You deal a staggering blow to your enemy, setting it up for future attacks.

Daily ♦ Martial, Weapon

Standard Action   **Melee or Ranged** weapon

Requirement: You must be wielding a crossbow, a light blade, or a sling.

Target: One creature

Attack: d20 + 7 versus AC (with short sword) or d20 + 6 versus AC (with hand crossbow)

Hit: 2d6 + 4 damage (short sword) or 2d6 + 4 damage (hand crossbow), and the target is slowed and grants combat advantage to you (save ends both).

Miss: Half damage, and the target grants combat advantage to you until the end of your next turn.

Armor, Weapons, and Gear

Shadow wears leather armor. She carries a short sword, a hand crossbow, 20 bolts, a backpack, two sunrods, a bedroll, 50 feet of rope, thieves' tools, and flint and steel. She has 25 gp.

Lidda, 1st-Level Halfling Rogue

Hit Points: 24 _____   Bloodied: 12

Healing Surge: 6   Surges per Day: 7

Initiative: +4   Speed: 6 squares

Alignment: Good

Ability Scores

	Score	Bonus*
STRENGTH	**13**	**+1**
CONSTITUTION	**12**	**+1**
DEXTERITY	**18**	**+4**
INTELLIGENCE	**10**	**+0**
WISDOM	**11**	**+0**
CHARISMA	**16**	**+3**

* Bonuses and penalties have already been calculated into your statistics and powers.

Defenses

AC 16   Fortitude 11   Reflex 16   Will 13

Basic Attacks

Melee Basic Attack (Short Sword)
    d20 + 4   1d6 + 1 damage

Ranged Basic Attack (Dagger)
    d20 + 8   1d4 damage

Class Features

First Strike: At the start of an encounter, you have combat advantage against any creatures that have not yet acted in that encounter.

Rogue Tactics, Artful Dodger: You gain a +2 bonus to AC against opportunity attacks.

Rogue Weapon Talent: You gain a +1 bonus to attack rolls when using a dagger (already included in stats).

Sneak Attack: Once per round, when you have combat advantage against an enemy and you're using a light blade, crossbow, or sling, you deal 2d8 damage if the attack hits.

Racial Traits

Skill Bonus: +2 Acrobatics, +2 Thievery (already included).

Bold: +5 racial bonus to saving throws against fear.

Nimble Reaction: +2 racial bonus to AC against opportunity attacks.

Second Chance: You can use *second chance* as an encounter power.

Second Chance   Halfling Racial Power
Luck and small size combine to work in your favor as you dodge your enemy's attack.
Encounter
Immediate Interrupt   **Personal**
Trigger: You are hit by an attack.
Effect: Force the attacker to reroll the attack and use the new result.

Feats

Backstabber: The extra damage dice from your Sneak Attack class feature increases from d6s to d8s (already included).

Skills

Acrobatics (trained)	**d20 + 9**
Arcana	**d20 + 0**
Athletics	**d20 + 1**
Bluff (trained)	**d20 + 8**

Diplomacy	**d20 + 3**
Dungeoneering	**d20 + 0**
Endurance	**d20 + 1**
Heal	**d20 + 0**
History	**d20 + 0**
Insight (trained)	**d20 + 5**
Intimidate	**d20 + 3**
Nature	**d20 + 0**
Perception (trained)	**d20 + 5**
Religion	**d20 + 0**
Stealth (trained)	**d20 + 9**
Streetwise	**d20 + 3**
Thievery (trained)	**d20 + 9**

Powers

Deft Strike   Rogue Attack 1
A final lunge brings you into an advantageous position.

At-Will ♦ Martial, Weapon

Standard Action   **Melee or Ranged** weapon

Requirement: You must be wielding a crossbow, a light blade, or a sling.

Target: One creature

Special: You can move 2 squares before the attack.

Attack: d20 + 7 versus AC (with short sword) or d20 + 8 versus AC (with dagger)

Hit: 1d6 + 4 damage (short sword) or 1d4 + 4 damage (dagger).

Sly Flourish   Rogue Attack 1
A distracting flourish causes the enemy to forget the blade at his throat.

At-Will ♦ Martial, Weapon

Standard Action   **Melee or Ranged** weapon

Requirement: You must be wielding a crossbow, a light blade, or a sling.

Target: One creature

Attack: d20 + 7 versus AC (with short sword) or d20 + 8 versus AC (with dagger)

Hit: 1d6 + 7 damage (short sword) or 1d4 + 7 damage (dagger)

Positioning Strike   Rogue Attack 1
A false stumble and a shove place the enemy exactly where you want him.

Encounter ♦ Martial, Weapon

Standard Action   **Melee** weapon

Requirement: You must be wielding a light blade.

Target: One creature

Attack: d20 + 7 versus Will

Hit: 1d6 + 4 damage, and you slide the target 3 squares.

Trick Strike   Rogue Attack 1
Through a series of feints and lures, you maneuver your foe right where you want him.

Daily ♦ Martial, Weapon

Standard Action   **Melee or Ranged** weapon

Requirement: You must be wielding a crossbow, a light blade, or a sling.

Target: One creature

Special: You can move 2 squares before the attack.

Attack: d20 + 7 versus AC (with short sword) or d20 + 8 versus AC (with dagger)

Hit: 3d6 + 4 damage (short sword) or 3d4 + 4 damage (dagger), and you slide the target 1 square.

Effect: Until the end of the encounter, each time you hit the target you slide it 1 square.

Armor, Weapons, and Gear

Lidda wears leather armor. She carries a short sword, 5 daggers, a backpack, two sunrods, a bedroll, 50 feet of rope, thieves' tools, and flint and steel. She has 25 gp.

Chapter 5

Starting Out as a Wizard

In This Chapter

▶ Understanding the wizard class

▶ Exploring who should play a wizard

▶ Discovering how to play a wizard

▶ Meeting three ready-to-play wizards

*T*he wizard is an arcane spellcaster who uses magic for attack, defense, and a myriad of other uses. A wizard approaches magic as a science, using training and study to cast spells. A wizard requires a good Intelligence score because this ability determines how powerful the wizard can ultimately become. Good Wisdom and Dexterity scores also help the wizard cast spells when trouble appears.

Wizards adventure to improve their abilities, to discover hidden knowledge and new sources of information. A wizard's role in an adventuring party is controller, damaging large groups of enemies at the same time while exerting control over the battlefield. As part of a team, the wizard uses his or her spells on behalf of the party, all the while seeking to master arcane magic and learn new spells.

See Chapter 7 for details on how to read the description for each wizard's powers.

Who Should Play a Wizard?

Spellcasting can be tricky, but every party needs a spellcaster, and the rewards for playing one can be high. If you want to play a character with a mysterious nature and a selection of powerful spells at the ready, then the wizard is the class for you.

Every adventuring party should have a wizard for the magical might the class provides. An arcane spellcaster has access to magical spells that can complement or enhance the natural abilities of nonspellcasters such as fighters and rogues. In a party of five, the wizard's offensive magic can be every bit as important as the fighter's greatsword or a rogue's sneak attack.

How to Play a Wizard

The wizard is not a melee combatant. When a battle breaks out, the wizard wants to be at a distance, casting spells from down range. A wizard can't stand up to a lot of physical damage and so must rely on other team members to provide defense. What the wizard has is a selection of spells that he or she can cast over the course of a battle. A wizard with damage-dealing spells can become a primary source of a party's offensive punch. A wizard with more control-based spells, on the other hand, warps the battlefield with amazing effects.

Wizards are proficient only with daggers and quarterstaffs. They lack training in the use of armor, so wizards usually avoid anything heavier than cloth armor.

Your character can take any approach to the wizard class. Most wizards believe that their power comes from the arcane forces that flow through the world, power they unlock through extensive study, hidden knowledge, and intricate preparation. Through arcane magic, wizards seek to control the world around them.

Wizards should be confident and a little mysterious. They are highly knowledgeable about many arcane matters and strong-willed. As a wizard, you adventure to test the limits of your power — and by testing them, to surpass them.

Have fun playing an enigmatic, mysterious spellcaster. Cast powerful spells at opportune times to help your party and then stand back and use your at-will spells to supplement the offensive melee capabilities of the fighter and rogue. Test yourself and your team often, for in the test is perfection. Above all, be a hero.

Wizard builds

Wizards come in two basic builds: the Control Wizard and the War Wizard. Control Wizards like powers that restrict enemies with effects such as poisonous gas clouds and encasing ice. Intelligence and Wisdom are the Control

Wizard's most important abilities. War Wizards choose powers that dish out lots of damage by gouts of fire or bursts of lightning. Intelligence and Dexterity are their most important abilities.

The wizard's role

Just as every player has a position on a sports team, every character has a role in the adventuring party. For the wizard, that role is controller. As a controller, the wizard uses spells to attack multiple enemies at the same time while exerting arcane control over the battlefield. As a Control Wizard, you turn the landscape against your enemies or render them unable to fight effectively for a short time. As a War Wizard, you delight in powers that deal lots of damage. Either way, when you step into a battle, you control every aspect of the fight.

Selecting a Wizard

The rest of this chapter features three ready-to-play wizard characters:

- ✔ **Beryn** is a Control Wizard who studied in the great towers of arcane knowledge before striking out to become an adventurer. Beryn's job on an adventuring team is controller, standing back to restrict enemies and deal damage to hostile areas when the need arises.

- ✔ **Dreggu** is a War Wizard who learned the arcane arts of battle as a student to a powerful and ancient mage. Dreggu's job on an adventuring team is controller, standing back to restrict enemies and deal damage to hostile areas when the need arises.

- ✔ **Telsa** is a wizard who combines offense with a strong defense. She learned her skills by studying with the eladrin arcane masters of the Feywild. Telsa's job on an adventuring team is controller, standing back to restrict enemies and deal damage to hostile areas when the need arises. Her powers favor the War Wizard build.

Any of these characters makes a great wizard and a worthy member of any adventuring party. Pick the one that most appeals to you and then turn to Chapter 7 for a quick overview of game play.

Beryn, 1st-Level Human Wizard

Hit Points: 21 _____   Bloodied: 10

Healing Surge: 5   Surges per Day: 6

Initiative: +5   Speed: 6 squares

Alignment: Good

Ability Scores

	Score	Bonus*
STRENGTH	10	+0
CONSTITUTION	11	+0
DEXTERITY	13	+1
INTELLIGENCE	18	+4
WISDOM	14	+2
CHARISMA	12	+1

* Bonuses and penalties have already been cal-culated into your statistics and powers.

Defenses

AC 14   Fortitude 11   Reflex 15   Will 13

Basic Attacks

Melee Basic Attack (Quarterstaff)
    d20 + 2   1d8 damage

Ranged Basic Attack (Magic Missile)
    d20 + 4   2d4 + 4 force damage

Class Features

Orb of Imposition: Once per encounter as a free action, you can choose to extend the duration of an effect created by a wizard at-will spell that would oth-erwise end at the end of your current turn. Instead, the effect ends at the end of your next turn.

Ritual Casting: You can master and per-form rituals of your level or lower.

Spellbook: You possess a spellbook in which you store your rituals and spells. It contains two daily spells; you can choose which daily spell to prepare for use each day, after an extended rest.

Feats

Human Perseverance: You gain a +1 feat bonus to saving throws.

Improved Initiative: You gain a +4 feat bonus to initiative checks (already included).

Skills

Acrobatics	d20 + 1
Arcana (trained)	d20 + 9
Athletics	d20 + 0
Bluff	d20 + 1
Diplomacy (trained)	d20 + 6
Dungeoneering	d20 + 2
Endurance	d20 + 0
Heal	d20 + 2
History (trained)	d20 + 9
Insight (trained)	d20 + 7
Intimidate	d20 + 1
Nature (trained)	d20 + 7
Perception	d20 + 2
Religion	d20 + 4
Stealth	d20 + 1
Streetwise	d20 + 1
Thievery	d20 + 1

Powers

Ghost Sound   Wizard Cantrip

With a wink, you create an illusory sound that emanates from somewhere close by.

At-Will ♦ Arcane, Illusion

Standard Action
Ranged 10

Target: One object or unoccupied square

Effect: You cause a sound as quiet as a whisper or as loud as a yelling or fighting creature to emanate from the target. You can produce non-vocal sounds such as the ringing of a sword blow, jingling armor, or scraping stone. If you whisper, you can whisper quietly enough that only creatures adjacent to the target can hear your words.

Light — Wizard Cantrip

With a wave of your hand, you cause a bright light to appear on the tip of your staff, upon some other object, or in a nearby space.

At-Will ♦ Arcane

Minor Action — **Ranged** 5

Target: One object or unoccupied square

Effect: You cause the target to shed bright light. The light fills the target's square and all squares within 4 squares of it. The light lasts for 5 minutes. Putting out the light is a free action.

Special: You can have only one light cantrip active at a time. If you create a new light, your previously cast light winks out.

Cloud of Daggers — Wizard Attack 1

You create a small cloud of whirling daggers of force that relentlessly attack creatures in the area.

At-Will ♦ Arcane, Force, Implement

Standard Action — **Area** 1 square within 10 squares

Target: Each creature in square

Attack: d20 + 4 versus Reflex

Hit: 1d6 + 4 force damage

Effect: The power's area is filled with sharp daggers of force. Any creature that enters the area or starts its turn in the area takes 2 force damage. The cloud remains in place until the end of your next turn. You can dispel the cloud earlier as a minor action.

Magic Missile — Wizard Attack 1

You launch a silvery bolt of force at an enemy.

At-Will ♦ Arcane, Force, Implement

Standard Action — **Ranged** 20

Target: One creature

Attack: d20 + 4 versus Reflex

Hit: 2d4 + 4 force damage

Special: You can use this power as a ranged basic attack.

Thunderwave — Wizard Attack 1

You create a whip-crack of sonic power that lashes up from the ground.

At-Will ♦ Arcane, Implement, Thunder

Standard Action — **Close** blast 3

Target: Each creature in blast

Attack: d20 + 4 versus Fortitude

Hit: 1d6 + 4 thunder damage, and you push the target 2 squares.

Icy Terrain — Wizard Attack 1

With frosty breath, you utter a single arcane word that creates a treacherous patch of ice on the ground, hampering your foes.

Encounter ♦ Arcane, Cold, Implement

Standard Action — **Area** burst 1 within 10 squares

Target: Each creature in burst

Attack: d20 + 4 versus Reflex

Hit: 1d6 + 4 cold damage, and the target is knocked prone.

Effect: The power's area is difficult terrain until the end of your next turn. You can end this effect as a minor action.

Freezing Cloud — Wizard Attack 1

A pellet shoots from your hand and explodes into a cloud of icy mist at the point of impact.

Daily ♦ Arcane, Cold, Implement

Standard Action — **Area** burst 2 within 10 squares

Target: Each creature in burst

Attack: d20 + 4 versus Fortitude

Hit: 1d8 + 4 cold damage

Miss: Half damage

Effect: The cloud lasts until the end of your next turn. Any creature that enters the cloud or starts its turn there is subject to another attack. You can dismiss the cloud as a minor action.

Sleep — Wizard Attack 1

You exert your will against your foes, seeking to overwhelm them with a tide of magical weariness.

Daily ♦ Arcane, Implement, Sleep

Standard Action — **Area** burst 2 within 20 squares

Target: Each creature in burst

Attack: d20 + 4 versus Will

Hit: The target is slowed (save ends). If the target fails its first saving throw against this power, the target becomes unconscious (save ends).

Miss: The target is slowed (save ends).

Armor, Weapons, and Gear

Beryn wears cloth robes. He carries a quarterstaff, an orb, a backpack, two sunrods, a bedroll, 50 feet of rope, a spellbook, and flint and steel. He has 23 gp.

Dreggu, 1st-Level Dwarf Wizard

Hit Points: 24 _____ Bloodied: 12

Healing Surge: 6 Surges per Day: 8

Initiative: +6 Speed: 5 squares

Alignment: Unaligned

Ability Scores

	Score	Bonus*
STRENGTH	**10**	**+0**
CONSTITUTION	**14**	**+2**
DEXTERITY	**14**	**+2**
INTELLIGENCE	**16**	**+3**
WISDOM	**15**	**+2**
CHARISMA	**11**	**+0**

* Bonuses and penalties have already been calculated into your statistics and powers.

Defenses

AC 13   Fortitude 12   Reflex 13   Will 14

Basic Attacks

Melee Basic Attack (Quarterstaff)
    d20 + 2   1d8 damage
Ranged Basic Attack (Magic Missile)
    d20 + 3   2d4 + 3 force
                       damage

Class Features

Ritual Casting: You can master and perform rituals of your level or lower.

Spellbook: You possess a spellbook in which you store your rituals and spells. It contains two daily spells; you can choose which daily spell to prepare for use each day, after an extended rest.

Wand of Accuracy: Once per encounter as a free action, you gain a +2 bonus to a single attack roll. You must wield your wand to gain this benefit.

Racial Traits

Cast-Iron Stomach: +5 racial bonus to saving throws against poison.

Dwarven Resilience: You can use your second wind as a minor action.

Stand Your Ground: When an effect forces you to move — through a pull, push, or slide — you move 1 square less than the effect specifies. In addition, when an attack would knock you prone, you can make an immediate saving throw to avoid falling prone.

Feats

Improved Initiative: You gain a +4 feat bonus to initiative checks (already included).

Skills

Acrobatics	**d20 + 2**
Arcana (trained)	**d20 + 8**
Athletics	**d20 + 0**
Bluff	**d20 + 0**
Diplomacy	**d20 + 0**
Dungeoneering (trained)	**d20 + 7**
Endurance	**d20 + 2**
Heal	**d20 + 2**
History (trained)	**d20 + 8**
Insight	**d20 + 2**
Intimidate	**d20 + 0**
Nature	**d20 + 2**
Perception	**d20 + 2**
Religion (trained)	**d20 + 8**
Stealth	**d20 + 2**
Streetwise	**d20 + 0**
Thievery	**d20 + 2**

Powers

Ghost Sound   Wizard Cantrip

With a wink, you create an illusory sound that emanates from somewhere close by.

At-Will ♦ Arcane, Illusion

Standard Action   **Ranged** 10

Target: One object or unoccupied square

Effect: You cause a sound as quiet as a whisper or as loud as a yelling or fighting creature to emanate from the target. You can produce non-vocal sounds such as the ringing of a sword blow, jingling armor, or scraping stone. If you whisper, you can whisper quietly enough that only creatures adjacent to the target can hear your words.

Light   Wizard Cantrip

With a wave of your hand, you cause a bright light to appear on the tip of your staff, upon some other object, or in a nearby space.

At-Will ◆ Arcane

Minor Action   **Ranged** 5

Target: One object or unoccupied square

Effect: You cause the target to shed bright light. The light fills the target's square and all squares within 4 squares of it. The light lasts for 5 minutes. Putting out the light is a free action.

Special: You can have only one light cantrip active at a time. If you create a new light, your previously cast light winks out.

Magic Missile   Wizard Attack 1

You launch a silvery bolt of force at an enemy.

At-Will ◆ Arcane, Force, Implement

Standard Action   **Ranged** 20

Target: One creature

Attack: d20 + 3 versus Reflex

Hit: 2d4 + 3 force damage

Special: You can use this power as a ranged basic attack.

Scorching Burst   Wizard Attack 1

A vertical column of golden flames burns all within.

At-Will ◆ Arcane, Fire, Implement

Standard Action   **Area** burst 1 within
                                           10 squares

Target: Each creature in burst

Attack: d20 + 3 versus Reflex

Hit: 1d6 + 3 fire damage

Burning Hands   Wizard Attack 1

A fierce burst of flame erupts from your hands and scorches nearby foes.

Encounter ◆ Arcane, Fire, Implement

Standard Action   **Close** blast 5

Target: Each creature in blast

Attack: d20 + 3 versus Reflex

Hit: 2d6 + 3 fire damage

Acid Arrow   Wizard Attack 1

A shimmering arrow of green, glowing liquid streaks to your target and bursts in a spray of sizzling acid.

Daily ◆ Acid, Arcane, Implement

Standard Action   **Ranged** 20

Primary Target: One creature

Attack: d20 + 3 versus Reflex

Hit: 2d8 + 3 acid damage, and ongoing 5 acid damage (save ends). Make a secondary attack.

Secondary Target: Each creature adjacent to the primary target.

Secondary Attack: d20 + 3 versus Reflex

Hit: 1d8 + 3 acid damage, and ongoing 5 acid damage (save ends).

Miss: Half damage, and ongoing 2 acid damage to primary target (save ends), and no secondary attack.

Freezing Cloud
Wizard Attack 1

A pellet shoots from your hand and explodes into a cloud of icy mist at the point of impact.

Daily ◆ Arcane, Cold, Implement

Standard Action   **Area** burst 2 within
                                           10 squares

Target: Each creature in burst

Attack: d20 + 3 versus Fortitude

Hit: 1d8 + 3 cold damage

Miss: Half damage

Effect: The cloud lasts until the end of your next turn. Any creature that enters the cloud or starts its turn there is subject to another attack. You can dismiss the cloud as a minor action.

Armor, Weapons, and Gear

Dreggu wears a cloth mantle. He carries a quarterstaff, a wand, a backpack, two sunrods, a bedroll, 50 feet of rope, a spellbook, and flint and steel. He has 23 gp.

Telsa, 1st-Level Elf Wizard

Hit Points: 22 _____   Bloodied: 11

Healing Surge: 5   Surges per Day: 7

Initiative: +7   Speed: 7 squares

Alignment: Unaligned

Ability Scores

	Score	Bonus*
STRENGTH	10	+0
CONSTITUTION	12	+1
DEXTERITY	16	+3
INTELLIGENCE	16	+3
WISDOM	15	+2
CHARISMA	11	+0

* Bonuses and penalties have already been calculated into your statistics and powers.

Defenses

AC 14   Fortitude 11   Reflex 13   Will 14

Basic Attacks

Melee Basic Attack (Quarterstaff)
    d20 + 2   1d8 damage

Ranged Basic Attack (Magic Missile)
    d20 + 3   2d4 + 3 force
                      damage

Class Features

Ritual Casting: You can master and perform rituals of your level or lower.

Spellbook: You possess a spellbook in which you store your rituals and spells. It contains two daily spells; you can choose which daily spell to prepare for use each day, after an extended rest.

Staff of Defense: The staff of defense grants you a +1 bonus to AC (already included). In addition, once per encounter as an immediate interrupt, you gain a +1 bonus to defense against one attack. You must wield your quarterstaff to gain these benefits.

Racial Traits

Group Awareness: You grant non-elf allies within 5 squares of you a +1 racial bonus to Perception checks.

Wild Step: You ignore difficult terrain when you shift.

Elven Accuracy: You can use *elven accuracy* as an encounter power.

Elven Accuracy   Elf Racial Power

With an instant of focus, you take careful aim at your foe and strike with the legendary accuracy of the elves.

Encounter

Free Action   **Personal**

Effect: Reroll an attack roll. Use the second roll, even if it's lower.

Feats

Improved Initiative: You gain a +4 feat bonus to initiative checks (already included).

Skills

Acrobatics	d20 + 3
Arcana (trained)	d20 + 8
Athletics	d20 + 0
Bluff	d20 + 0
Diplomacy	d20 + 0
Dungeoneering (trained)	d20 + 7
Endurance	d20 + 1
Heal	d20 + 2
History (trained)	d20 + 8
Insight (trained)	d20 + 7
Intimidate	d20 + 0
Nature	d20 + 2
Perception	d20 + 2
Religion	d20 + 3
Stealth	d20 + 3
Streetwise	d20 + 0
Thievery	d20 + 3

Powers

Ghost Sound   Wizard Cantrip

With a wink, you create an illusory sound that emanates from somewhere close by.

At-Will ◆ Arcane, Illusion

Standard Action   Ranged 10

Target: One object or unoccupied square

Effect: You cause a sound as quiet as a whisper or as loud as a yelling or fighting creature to emanate from the target. You can produce non-vocal sounds such as the ringing of a sword blow, jingling armor, or scraping stone. If you whisper, you can whisper quietly enough that only creatures adjacent to the target can hear your words.

Light   Wizard Cantrip

With a wave of your hand, you cause a bright light to appear on the tip of your staff, upon some other object, or in a nearby space.

At-Will ◆ Arcane

Minor Action   Ranged 5

Target: One object or unoccupied square

Effect: You cause the target to shed bright light. The light fills the target's square and all squares within 4 squares of it. The light lasts for 5 minutes. Putting out the light is a free action.

Special: You can have only one light cantrip active at a time. If you create a new light, your previously cast light winks out.

Cloud of Daggers   Wizard Attack 1

You create a small cloud of whirling daggers of force that relentlessly attack creatures in the area.

At-Will ◆ Arcane, Force, Implement

Standard Action   Area 1 square within 10 squares

Target: Each creature in square

Attack: d20 + 3 versus Reflex

Hit: 1d6 + 3 force damage

Effect: The power's area is filled with sharp daggers of force. Any creature that enters the area or starts its turn in the area takes 2 force damage. The cloud remains in place until the end of your next turn. You can dispel the cloud earlier as a minor action.

Magic Missile   Wizard Attack 1

You launch a silvery bolt of force at an enemy.

At-Will ◆ Arcane, Force, Implement

Standard Action   Ranged 20

Target: One creature

Attack: d20 + 3 versus Reflex

Hit: 2d4 + 3 force damage

Special: You can use this power as a ranged basic attack.

Burning Hands   Wizard Attack 1

A fierce burst of flame erupts from your hands and scorches nearby foes.

Encounter ◆ Arcane, Fire, Implement

Standard Action   Close blast 5

Target: Each creature in blast

Attack: d20 + 3 versus Reflex

Hit: 2d6 + 3 fire damage

Acid Arrow   Wizard Attack 1

A shimmering arrow of green, glowing liquid streaks to your target and bursts in a spray of sizzling acid.

Daily ◆ Acid, Arcane, Implement

Standard Action   Ranged 20

Primary Target: One creature

Attack: d20 + 3 versus Reflex

Hit: 2d8 + 3 acid damage, and ongoing 5 acid damage (save ends). Make a secondary attack.

Secondary Target: Each creature adjacent to the primary target.

Secondary Attack: d20 + 3 versus Reflex

Hit: 1d8 + 3 acid damage, and ongoing 5 acid damage (save ends).

Miss: Half damage, and ongoing 2 acid damage to primary target (save ends), and no secondary attack.

Sleep   Wizard Attack 1

You exert your will against your foes, seeking to overwhelm them with a tide of magical weariness.

Daily ◆ Arcane, Implement, Sleep

Standard Action   Area burst 2 within 20 squares

Target: Each creature in burst

Attack: d20 + 3 versus Will

Hit: The target is slowed (save ends). If the target fails its first saving throw against this power, the target becomes unconscious (save ends).

Miss: The target is slowed (save ends).

Armor, Weapons, and Gear

Telsa wears a cloth mantle. She carries a quarterstaff, a backpack, two sunrods, a bedroll, 50 feet of rope, a spellbook, and flint and steel. She has 28 gp.

Chapter 6

Starting Out as a Cleric

* *

In This Chapter

▶ Understanding the cleric class

▶ Exploring who should play a cleric

▶ Discovering how to play a cleric

▶ Meeting three ready-to-play clerics

* *

*N*o fantasy world is complete without a pantheon of mythical gods to add flavor, color, and background to the setting. And no DUNGEONS & DRAGONS adventuring party is complete without a servant of the gods — the cleric. A cleric uses divine magic and decent combat abilities to aid a party. A cleric needs a good Wisdom score to bolster his or her divine spells. A good Strength score improves a cleric's melee attack ability so he or she can wade into battle when called upon, and a good Charisma score improves the class's powers (called prayers).

An adventuring cleric devotes his or her life to a god's service from a young age. A cleric wields divine magic to aid the party, using prayers that provide healing, offense, and defense to best advantage. Having decent combat skills, the cleric provides melee support and often wades in to stand beside the fighter in battle. The cleric's job is to defend and heal with spells and to fight when battle rages.

Who Should Play a Cleric?

The cleric can be somewhat complex to play due to the class's proficiency in both combat and divine magic. However, this combination makes the cleric not only necessary for any adventuring team, but a lot of fun to play, too. If you think that playing a supporting role, helping your teammates, and occasionally mixing it up in battle sounds like the kind of character you want to play, then the cleric is the class for you.

Every adventuring party needs at least one cleric. In a party of four, a cleric is essential to success. In a party of five or six, two clerics can provide a lot of healing and defense, making adventuring easier.

See Chapter 7 for details on how to read the description for each cleric's powers.

How to Play a Cleric

In an adventuring party, the cleric is everybody's friend. Through the use of divine magic, a cleric can make a fighter stronger or a rogue quicker for a short period of time, for example, and everyone can benefit from a timely healing spell in the middle of a grueling battle.

Clerics can use cloth, leather, hide, or chainmail armor, and they can use simple melee and ranged weapons without penalty. To use weapons that fall into other categories without penalty, such as longswords and warhammers, a cleric needs to select the appropriate feat.

Clerics adventure to support the causes of their gods, to help those in need, and to work to improve the reputation of their deities and temples. You can find descriptions of mythical deities for the DUNGEONS & DRAGONS game beginning on page 21 of the *Player's Handbook*. In addition to following their faith, clerics might have any common motivation for adventuring as well. Clerics can seek fame, treasure, and power, just like any other class.

Clerics should be brave and helpful, faithful and heroic. Later, you can play with the baselines and portray any kind of cleric you want, but to start out, go with the tried-and-true basics. You live to help others and serve your god. You hate evil in all its forms, and you have a special loathing for the undead.

Have fun with the idea of being the one that the rest of the party counts on for healing and defense. Don't be afraid to pick up your mace, but melee should take second place to providing divine support for the team. Be devoted to your cause and your teammates. Above all, be a hero.

Cleric builds

Clerics come in two basic builds: The Battle Cleric and the Devoted Cleric. Battle Clerics like to mix it up in melee combat and favor powers that smite their enemies. Strength and Wisdom are the Battle Cleric's most important abilities. Devoted Clerics favor powers that aid the party by healing and providing bonuses. Wisdom and Charisma are their most important abilities.

The cleric's role

Just as the positions on a sports team, every character has a role in the adventuring party. For the cleric, that role is leader. As a leader, you should be shielding your allies with your prayers, healing hurt friends, and using prayers that bolster your allies' attacks. By leader, we don't necessarily mean that you're the boss — but you do motivate, encourage, and inspire your teammates to greatness.

Selecting a Cleric

The rest of this chapter features three ready-to-play cleric characters, all of which combine healing and defensive magic with good combat skills:

- ✔ **Thomm** is a cleric of Bahamut, the god of justice, honor, and protection. His training included the healing arts, battle prayers, and melee combat. He adventures to defeat evil and to promote the tenets of his faith. Thomm's job on an adventuring team is leader, inspiring his teammates and bolstering them with prayers during battle. He uses the Battle Cleric character build.

- ✔ **Chenna** is a cleric of Melora, the god of wilderness and the sea. Her training included the healing arts, healing prayers, and inspiring leadership. She adventures to defeat evil and to promote the tenets of her faith. Chenna's job on an adventuring team is leader, inspiring her teammates and bolstering them with prayers during battle. Chenna uses the Devoted Cleric build.

- ✔ **Eberk** is a cleric of Moradin, the god of creation and artisans, and special patron to the dwarves. His training included the healing arts, battle prayers, and inspiring leadership. He adventures to defeat evil and to promote the tenets of his faith. Eberk's job on an adventuring team is leader, inspiring his teammates and bolstering them with prayers during battle. Eberk favors the Battle Cleric build.

Any of these characters makes a great cleric and a worthy member of any adventuring party. Pick the one that most appeals to you and then turn to Chapter 7 for a quick overview of game play.

Thomm, 1st-Level Human Cleric

Hit Points: 24 _____ Bloodied: 12

Healing Surge: 6   Surges per Day: 8

Initiative: +1   Speed: 5 squares

Alignment: Lawful Good

Ability Scores

	Score	Bonus*
STRENGTH	**18**	**+4**
CONSTITUTION	**12**	**+1**
DEXTERITY	**10**	**+0**
INTELLIGENCE	**11**	**+0**
WISDOM	**14**	**+2**
CHARISMA	**13**	**+1**

* Bonuses and penalties have already been calculated into your statistics and powers.

Defenses

AC 16   Fortitude 15   Reflex 12   Will 14

Basic Attacks

Melee Basic Attack (Mace)
      d20 + 6   1d8 + 5 damage

Ranged Basic Attack (Crossbow)
      d20 + 2   1d8 damage

Class Features

Channel Divinity: You can use one of these special divine powers once per encounter.

Channel Divinity: Cleric Feature
Divine Fortune

In the face of peril, you hold true to your faith and receive a special boon.

Encounter ♦ Divine

Free Action   **Personal**

Effect: You gain a +1 bonus to your next attack roll or saving throw before the end of your next turn.

Channel Divinity: Cleric Feature
Turn Undead

You sear undead foes, push them back, and root them in place.

Encounter ♦ Divine, Implement, Radiant

Standard Action   **Close** burst 2

Target: Each undead creature in burst.

Attack: d20 + 2 versus Will

Hit: 1d10 + 2 radiant damage, and you push the target 4 squares. The target is immobilized until the end of your next turn.

Miss: Half damage, and the target is not pushed or immobilized.

Healer's Lore: When you grant healing with a cleric power that has the Healing keyword, add +2 to the number of restored hit points (already included).

Healing Word: Twice per encounter as a minor action, you can use the *healing word* power.

Healing Word   Cleric Feature

You whisper a brief prayer as divine light washes over your target, helping to mend its wounds.

Encounter (Special) ♦ Divine, Healing

Special: You can use this power twice per encounter, but only once per round.

Minor Action   **Close** burst 5

Target: You or one ally

Effect: The target can spend a healing surge and regain an additional 1d6 + 2 hit points.

Feats

Action Surge: You gain a +3 bonus to attack rolls you make during any action you gained by spending an action point.

Weapon Focus: You gain a +1 feat bonus to damage rolls with maces (already included).

Skills

Acrobatics	d20 − 1
Arcana	d20 + 0
Athletics	d20 + 3
Bluff	d20 + 1
Diplomacy (trained)	d20 + 6
Dungeoneering	d20 + 2
Endurance	d20 + 0
Heal (trained)	d20 + 7
History (trained)	d20 + 5
Insight (trained)	d20 + 7
Intimidate	d20 + 1
Nature	d20 + 2
Perception	d20 + 2
Religion (trained)	d20 + 5
Stealth	d20 − 1
Streetwise	d20 + 1
Thievery	d20 − 1

Powers

Righteous Brand Cleric Attack 1

You smite your foe with your weapon and brand it with a ghostly, glowing symbol of your deity's anger. By naming an ally when the symbol appears, you add divine power to that ally's attacks against the branded foe.

At-Will ♦ Divine, Weapon

Standard Action Melee weapon

Target: One creature

Attack: d20 + 6 versus AC

Hit: 1d8 + 5 damage, and one ally within 5 squares of you gains a +4 power bonus to melee attack rolls against the target until the end of your next turn.

Priest's Shield Cleric Attack 1

You utter a minor defensive prayer as you attack with your weapon.

At-Will ♦ Divine, Weapon

Standard Action Melee weapon

Target: One creature

Attack: d20 + 6 versus AC

Hit: 1d8 + 5 damage, and you and one adjacent ally gain a +1 power bonus to AC until the end of your next turn.

Sacred Flame Cleric Attack 1

Sacred light shines from above, searing a single enemy with its radiance while at the same time aiding an ally with its beneficent power.

At-Will ♦ Divine, Implement, Radiant

Standard Action Ranged 5

Target: One creature

Attack: d20 + 2 versus Reflex

Hit: 1d6 + 2 radiant damage, and one ally you can see chooses either to gain 1 temporary hit point or to make a saving throw.

Wrathful Thunder Cleric Attack 1

Your arm is made strong by the power of your deity. When you strike, a terrible thunderclap smites your adversary and dazes him.

Encounter ♦ Divine, Thunder, Weapon

Standard Action

Melee weapon

Target: One creature

Attack: d20 + 6 versus AC

Hit: 1d8 + 5 thunder damage, and the target is dazed until the end of your next turn.

Avenging Flame Cleric Attack 1

You slam your weapon into your foe, who bursts into flame. Divine fire avenges each attack your enemy dares to make.

Daily ♦ Divine, Fire, Weapon

Standard Action Melee weapon

Target: One creature

Attack: d20 + 6 versus AC

Hit: 2d8 + 5 damage, and ongoing 5 fire damage (save ends).

Miss: Half damage, and no ongoing fire damage.

Special: If the target attacks on its turn, it can't attempt a saving throw against the ongoing damage.

Armor, Weapons, and Gear

Thomm wears chain mail armor. He carries a mace, a crossbow, 20 bolts, a holy symbol of Bahamut, a backpack, two sunrods, a bedroll, 50 feet of rope, and flint and steel. He has 10 gp.

Chenna, 1st-Level Halfling Cleric

Hit Points: 24 _____ Bloodied: 12

Healing Surge: 6   Surges per Day: 8

Initiative: +1   Speed: 5 squares

Alignment: Good

Ability Scores

	Score	Bonus*
STRENGTH	**13**	**+1**
CONSTITUTION	**12**	**+1**
DEXTERITY	**13**	**+1**
INTELLIGENCE	**10**	**+0**
WISDOM	**16**	**+3**
CHARISMA	**16**	**+3**

* Bonuses and penalties have already been calculated into your statistics and powers.

Defenses

AC 16   Fortitude 11   Reflex 11   Will 15

Basic Attacks

Melee Basic Attack (Mace)
    d20 + 3   1d8 + 1 damage

Ranged Basic Attack (Crossbow)
    d20 + 3   1d8 damage

Class Features

Channel Divinity: You can use one of these special divine powers once per encounter.

Channel Divinity: Cleric Feature
Divine Fortune

In the face of peril, you hold true to your faith and receive a special boon.

Encounter ♦ Divine

Free Action   **Personal**

Effect: You gain a +1 bonus to your next attack roll or saving throw before the end of your next turn.

Channel Divinity: Feat Power
Melora's Tide

Melora sends a tide of healing energy to aid you or a bloodied friend.

Encounter ♦ Divine, Healing

Minor Action   **Ranged** 5

Target: You or one ally; bloodied target only.

Effect: The target gains regeneration 2 until the end of the encounter or until he or she is no longer bloodied.

Channel Divinity: Cleric Feature
Turn Undead

You sear undead foes, push them back, and root them in place.

Encounter ♦ Divine, Implement, Radiant

Standard Action   **Close** burst 2

Target: Each undead creature in burst.

Attack: d20 + 3 versus Will

Hit: 1d10 + 3 radiant damage, and you push the target 6 squares. The target is immobilized until the end of your next turn.

Miss: Half damage, and the target is not pushed or immobilized.

Healer's Lore: When you grant healing with a cleric power that has the Healing keyword, add +3 to the number of restored hit points (already included).

Healing Word: Twice per encounter as a minor action, you can use the *healing word* power.

Healing Word
Cleric Feature

You whisper a brief prayer as divine light washes over your target, helping to mend its wounds.

Encounter (Special) ♦ Divine, Healing

Special: You can use this power twice per encounter, but only once per round.

Minor Action
Close burst 5

Target: You or one ally

Effect: The target can spend a healing surge and regain an additional 1d6 + 3 hit points.

Racial Traits

Skill Bonus: +2 Acrobatics, +2 Thievery (already included).

Bold: +5 racial bonus to saving throws against fear.

Nimble Reaction: +2 racial bonus to AC against opportunity attacks.

Second Chance: You can use *second chance* as an encounter power.

Second Chance   Halfling Racial Power

Luck and small size combine to work in your favor as you dodge your enemy's attack.

Encounter

Immediate Interrupt   **Personal**

Trigger: You are hit by an attack.

Effect: Force the attacker to reroll the attack and use the new result.

Feats

Melora's Tide: You can invoke the power of your deity to use *Melora's tide.*

Skills

Acrobatics	**d20 + 2**
Arcana (trained)	**d20 + 5**
Athletics	**d20 + 0**
Bluff	**d20 + 3**
Diplomacy	**d20 + 3**
Dungeoneering	**d20 + 3**
Endurance	**d20 + 0**
Heal (trained)	**d20 + 8**
History (trained)	**d20 + 5**
Insight	**d20 + 3**
Intimidate	**d20 + 3**
Nature	**d20 + 3**
Perception	**d20 + 3**
Religion (trained)	**d20 + 5**
Stealth	**d20 + 0**
Streetwise	**d20 + 3**
Thievery	**d20 + 2**

Powers

Lance of Faith   Cleric Attack 1

A brilliant ray of light sears your foe with golden radiance. Sparkles of light linger around the target, guiding your ally's attack.

At-Will ♦ Divine, Implement, Radiance

Standard Action   **Ranged 5**

Target: One creature

Attack: d20 + 3 versus Reflex

Hit: 1d8 + 3 radiant damage, and one ally you can see gains a +2 power bonus to his or her next attack roll against the target.

Sacred Flame   Cleric Attack 1

Sacred light shines from above, searing a single enemy with its radiance while at the same time aiding an ally with its beneficent power.

At-Will ♦ Divine, Implement, Radiant

Standard Action   **Ranged 5**

Target: One creature

Attack: d20 + 3 versus Reflex

Hit: 1d6 + 3 radiant damage, and one ally you can see chooses either to gain 3 temporary hit points or to make a saving throw.

Divine Glow   Cleric Attack 1

Murmuring a prayer to your deity, you invoke a blast of white radiance from your holy symbol. Foes burn in its stern light, but your allies are heartened and guided by it.

Encounter ♦ Divine, Implement, Radiant

Standard Action   **Close blast 3**

Target: Each enemy in blast

Attack: d20 + 3 versus Reflex

Hit: 1d8 + 3 radiant damage

Effect: Allies in the blast gain a +2 power bonus to attack rolls until the end of your next turn.

Beacon of Hope   Cleric Attack 1

A burst of divine energy harms your foes and heals your allies. The radiant energy lingers around your holy symbol and improves your healing powers for the rest of the battle.

Daily ♦ Divine, Healing, Implement

Standard Action   **Close burst 3**

Target: Each enemy in burst

Attack: d20 + 3 versus Will

Hit: The target is weakened until the end of its next turn.

Effect: You and all allies in the burst regain 5 hit points, and your healing powers restore +5 hit points until the end of the encounter.

Armor, Weapons, and Gear

Chenna wears chain mail armor. She carries a mace, a crossbow, 20 bolts, a holy symbol of Melora, a backpack, two sunrods, a bedroll, 50 feet of rope, and flint and steel. She has 10 gp.

Eberk, 1st-Level Dwarf Cleric

Hit Points: 26 _____ Bloodied: 13

Healing Surge: 6   Surges per Day: 9

Initiative: +0   Speed: 5 squares

Alignment: Lawful Good

Ability Scores

	Score	Bonus*
STRENGTH	**16**	**+3**
CONSTITUTION	**14**	**+2**
DEXTERITY	**11**	**+0**
INTELLIGENCE	**10**	**+0**
WISDOM	**16**	**+3**
CHARISMA	**13**	**+1**

* Bonuses and penalties have already been calculated into your statistics and powers.

Defenses

AC 17   Fortitude 13   Reflex 11   Will 15

Basic Attacks

Melee Basic Attack (Warhammer)
    d20 + 5   1d10 + 3 damage

Ranged Basic Attack (Crossbow)
    d20 + 0   1d8 damage

Class Features

Channel Divinity: You can use one of these special divine powers once per encounter.

Channel Divinity:	Cleric Feature
Divine Fortune	

In the face of peril, you hold true to your faith and receive a special boon.

Encounter ♦ Divine

Free Action   **Personal**

Effect: You gain a +1 bonus to your next attack roll or saving throw before the end of your next turn.

Channel Divinity:	Cleric Feature
Turn Undead	

You sear undead foes, push them back, and root them in place.

Encounter ♦ Divine, Implement, Radiant

Standard Action   **Close** burst 2

Target: Each undead creature in burst.

Attack: d20 + 3 versus Will

Hit: 1d10 + 3 radiant damage, and you push the target 6 squares. The target is immobilized until the end of your next turn.

Miss: Half damage, and the target is not pushed or immobilized.

Healer's Lore: When you grant healing with a cleric power that has the Healing keyword, add +3 to the number of restored hit points (already included).

Healing Word: Twice per encounter as a minor action, you can use the *healing word* power.

Healing Word	Cleric Feature

You whisper a brief prayer as divine light washes over your target, helping to mend its wounds.

Encounter (Special) ♦ Divine, Healing

Special: You can use this power twice per encounter, but only once per round.

Minor Action   **Close** burst 5

Target: You or one ally

Effect: The target can spend a healing surge and regain an additional 1d6 + 3 hit points.

Racial Traits

Skill Bonus: +2 Dungeoneering, +2 Endurance (already included).

Cast-Iron Stomach: +5 racial bonus to saving throws against poison.

Dwarven Resilience: You can use your second wind as a minor action instead of a standard action.

Stand Your Ground: When an effect forces you to move — through a push, a pull, or a slide — you can move 1 square less than the effect specifies. In addition, when an attack would knock you prone, you can immediately make a saving throw to avoid the effect.

Feats

Weapon Proficiency: You gain proficiency in the warhammer.

Skills

Acrobatics	**d20 − 1**
Arcana	**d20 + 0**
Athletics	**d20 + 2**
Bluff	**d20 + 1**
Diplomacy (trained)	**d20 + 6**
Dungeoneering	**d20 + 5**
Endurance	**d20 + 3**
Heal (trained)	**d20 + 8**
History	**d20 + 0**
Insight (trained)	**d20 + 8**
Intimidate	**d20 + 1**
Nature	**d20 + 3**
Perception	**d20 + 3**
Religion (trained)	**d20 + 5**
Stealth	**d20 − 1**
Streetwise	**d20 + 1**
Thievery	**d20 − 1**

Powers

Righteous Brand   Cleric Attack 1

You smite your foe with your weapon and brand it with a ghostly, glowing symbol of your deity's anger. By naming an ally when the symbol appears, you add divine power to that ally's attacks against the branded foe.

At-Will ♦ Divine, Weapon

Standard Action   **Melee** weapon

Target: One creature

Attack: d20 + 5 versus AC

Hit: 1d8 + 3 damage, and one ally within 5 squares of you gains a +3 power bonus to melee attack rolls against the target until the end of your next turn.

Priest's Shield   Cleric Attack 1

You utter a minor defensive prayer as you attack with your weapon.

At-Will ♦ Divine, Weapon

Standard Action   **Melee** weapon

Target: One creature

Attack: d20 + 5 versus AC

Hit: 1d8 + 3 damage, and you and one adjacent ally gain a +1 power bonus to AC until the end of your next turn.

Wrathful Thunder   Cleric Attack 1

Your arm is made strong by the power of your deity. When you strike, a terrible thunderclap smites your adversary and dazes him.

Encounter ♦ Divine, Thunder, Weapon

Standard Action   **Melee** weapon

Target: One creature

Attack: d20 + 5 versus AC

Hit: 1d8 + 3 thunder damage, and the target is dazed until the end of your next turn.

Avenging Flame   Cleric Attack 1

You slam your weapon into your foe, who bursts into flame. Divine fire avenges each attack your enemy dares to make.

Daily ♦ Divine, Fire, Weapon

Standard Action   **Melee** weapon

Target: One creature

Attack: d20 + 5 versus AC

Hit: 2d8 + 3 damage, and ongoing 5 fire damage (save ends).

Miss: Half damage, and no ongoing fire damage.

Special: If the target attacks on its turn, it can't attempt a saving throw against the ongoing damage.

Armor, Weapons, and Gear

Eberk wears chain mail armor and carries a light shield. He carries a warhammer, a crossbow, 20 bolts, a holy symbol of Moradin, a backpack, two sunrods, a bedroll, 50 feet of rope, and flint and steel. He has 10 gp.

Chapter 7

Playing the Game

In This Chapter

▶ Understanding the D&D game

▶ Exploring the dungeon

▶ Determining who goes first in combat

▶ Examining what you can do in a fight

▶ Discovering how to move, attack, and use powers

▶ Understanding damage, saving throws, and character death

Although the heart of the DUNGEONS & DRAGONS game is imagination and adventure and your character can attempt to do anything you can think of, the best way to learn how to apply the game mechanics is by examining D&D combat. So in this chapter, we show you how to play the game from the perspective of beating up the monsters — which happens in almost every D&D adventure.

Refer to one of the ready-to-play character sheets from Chapters 3 through 6 when reading this chapter.

Understanding the D&D Game

Every DUNGEONS & DRAGONS game is an adventure. From an epic quest to a humble dungeon crawl, an adventure breaks down into three basic types of encounters:

✔ **Social encounters:** These encounters present players with situations in which they can roleplay their characters and interact with each other and with those characters controlled by the Dungeon Master (known as *nonplayer characters,* or NPCs). Trading, negotiating, or simply talking to locals are among the types of social encounters you may participate in. You'll often employ skills like Bluff, Diplomacy, and Intimidate during these encounters, but sometimes no dice rolls are necessary at all. Social encounters can lead to challenge or combat encounters, or they can be self-contained discussions between characters. Some social encounters (also called noncombat encounters) involve skill challenges (see the later section, "Facing Skill Challenges").

✔ **Challenge encounters:** Encounters of this type revolve around characters struggling against natural or man-made hazards, such as trying to cross a lake of fire or dealing with a poison-needle trap on a locked chest. These encounters require skill checks or ability checks to navigate. Often, challenge encounters (also called noncombat encounters) involve skill challenges (see the "Facing Skill Challenges" section, later in this chapter).

✔ **Combat encounters:** These encounters make up the heart of many D&D adventures. When no other option presents itself for dealing with monsters or other opponents (such as brigands, thugs, raiders, or pirates), the D&D character hefts sword, staff, or axe and wades into battle. Combat encounters are the most rigidly structured times in the game, where most of the core rules come into play. When most people talk about playing D&D, this is the part of the game they envision. We show you how to play the game using the combat encounter structure throughout the rest of this chapter.

Rolling Dice

To provide tension, suspense, and an element of luck, the DUNGEONS & DRAGONS game uses dice to determine the outcome of actions where failure has a consequence. Fighting a monster, picking a lock, disarming a trap, leaping over a pit of molten lava — the game provides a method for determining success or failure based on a character's skills and abilities and adding a touch of luck for drama and excitement. Rolling dice is fun, and D&D allows for plenty of dice-rolling action in every adventure.

Remember the Core Game Mechanic: Whenever your character attempts an action that has a chance of failure associated with it, roll a twenty-sided die (d20). The higher the roll, the better the chance of success.

These character actions boil down to attack rolls, skill checks, and ability checks. To determine whether any of these actions are successful, follow these steps:

1. **Roll a d20.**

2. **Add any relevant modifiers.**

3. **Compare the result to a target number.**

If the result equals or exceeds the target number, the action succeeds. A result of less than the target number indicates that the action fails. For any task or action, target numbers, also called the *Difficulty Class* (or DC), come from a variety of places. Some are set by the action itself and are defined in the rules, and others are determined by the Dungeon Master. An opponent's Armor Class or Reflex defense, for example, is the target number you need to equal or exceed to make a successful attack.

Exploring the Dungeon

Outside of combat, D&D play can be very casual. The Dungeon Master tells the players what their characters see (and hear, and smell, and so on) and asks them what they do. Players don't have to act in any particular order, though the DM may impose some structure just so everyone gets to do what they want to do. If you use the battle grid during these casual periods, it's probably just to see where the characters are in relation to each other. Here's an example of dungeon exploration:

Dungeon Master: "The 10-foot-wide corridor you've been following ends in a locked wooden door. What do you want to do?"

Lidda's player: "I try to unlock the door."

Dungeon Master: "Okay. Make a Thievery check."

Lidda's player: *Rolls a d20 and adds 8 (her Thievery modifier) to the result.* "I got an 18."

Dungeon Master: "The lock clicks open."

Regdar's player: "Now that the door is unlocked, I step past Lidda and open the door."

Dungeon Master: "The doors swings open with a slight creak. Inside, you see a small gold statue sitting atop a waist-high pedestal in the center of the room."

Lidda's player: "I walk up and take a look."

Telsa's player: "So do I."

Eberk's player: "I'll stand in the doorway in case something goes wrong."

Regdar's player: "Lidda's always getting into trouble. I'll step into the room but stand back, ready to move if Lidda and Telsa set off a trap."

Dungeon Master: "Okay. Telsa and Lidda look at the statue. It appears to be made of gold. It seems heavy, even if it isn't more than a foot and a half tall. It's carved in the shape of a dragon, and there is some kind of writing near the base that you can't read."

Telsa's player: "I want to see if I know anything about this."

Dungeon Master: "Okay. Make an Arcana check. Everyone else make a Perception check."

Telsa's player: *Rolls a d20 and adds 8 (her Arcana modifier) to the result.* "That's a 12."

All other players: *All of the other players roll d20s and add their Perception skill modifiers. Regdar's player lucks out and gets the highest result, an 18.*

Dungeon Master: "While the rest of you stare at the golden statue, Regdar notices that a panel in the far wall has swung aside. Beyond, Regdar sees a dark opening. Something has begun to emerge from that opening, but only Regdar sees it. What are you going to do?"

What happens next? That depends on the Dungeon Master and the actions of the players!

What can you do while exploring?

While exploring a dungeon or other adventure location, characters can do any of the following actions:

- Search the walls for secret doors.
- Listen at doors.
- Check doors to see if they're locked.
- Force open or unlock a door.
- Search rooms for treasure.
- Manipulate levers or push statues.
- Use the Intimidate skill to frighten a kobold, for example, into telling the party what waits around the bend.
- Do anything else you can think of!

Characters can do all sorts of things as they explore an adventure location. They might break apart a cabinet to locate a secret compartment, gather sand into a pouch, try to build a makeshift bridge out of a table, or do whatever else the players can imagine.

The Dungeon Master decides whether or not something the characters try actually works. Some things are easy and characters can succeed automatically. It doesn't take any special skill or luck to fill a pouch with sand, for example.

Some actions are impossible. No character can smash through a 12-inch thick, solid stone wall by hitting it with his or her fist.

When there's a possibility of either success or failure, and the task doesn't relate to any particular skill, the DM calls for an ability check.

Ability checks

To make an ability check, a player rolls a d20 and adds his or her character's bonus associated with the ability that best fits the action. If the DM decides that the result is high enough, using the sample DCs provided in the D&D rulebooks as a guide, the character succeeds. Here are some examples of ability checks and the DCs required to succeed:

- ✔ Trying to break down a strong wooden door requires a DC 20 Strength check.

- ✔ Attempting to thread a needle requires a DC 5 Dexterity check.

- ✔ Holding your breath for a long time requires a DC 10 Constitution check.

- ✔ Navigating a challenging maze requires a DC 20 Intelligence check.

- ✔ Recognizing the NPC rogue who was following your character at the market requires a DC 10 Wisdom check.

- ✔ Making sure your character gets noticed in a crowd requires a DC 15 Charisma check.

Combat Basics

As characters adventure into mysterious forests or dark dungeons, they often encounter monsters of all shapes and sizes. In the inevitable battles that ensue, you use dice and your character's statistics to determine the course of combat. Players roll dice for their characters. The Dungeon Master rolls dice for the monsters (or whatever opponents the player characters are facing).

In a combat encounter, you put miniature figures for each character and monster on a battle grid. Players take turns in order, one after the other, moving their figures on the battle grid to show where their characters are moving in the battle, placing the figures next to or within sight of the monsters that their characters are attacking. (See Chapter 8 for more about using the battle grid.) You roll a die to see if an attack hits. If it hits, you roll dice to determine how much damage the attack deals.

Determining who goes first

Every character and monster has an *initiative modifier*. This is a bonus or penalty added to a d20 roll called an *initiative check*. Everyone makes an initiative check at the start of a combat encounter. This sets the order of play for the entire encounter, as follows:

1. **Players make initiative checks for their characters by making a d20 roll and adding initiative modifiers.**

2. **The Dungeon Master makes an initiative check for the monsters, one roll for each type of opponent.**

   For example, if an encounter features two bugbear warriors and three goblin slingers, the DM makes one initiative check for the bugbears and one initiative check for the goblins.

3. **The DM notes all the results on a piece of paper to establish an initiative order, from highest result to lowest result.**

4. **The character or creature with the highest initiative result goes first and takes a turn, followed by the next highest result, and so on.**

5. **When everyone has had a turn, the round ends.**

   The second round uses the same order, starting with the character with the highest initiative result. Continue until the battle ends.

The DM's initiative log for a combat encounter might look like this:

Lidda	25
Goblin slingers	21
Telsa	17
Regdar	10
Bugbear warriors	7
Eberk	4

This indicates the order in which each character and monster will act in each round of the encounter. Notice that the DM makes one roll for all monsters of the same type in the encounter.

Taking your turn

Your turn has three parts:

- ✔ **The start of your turn:** Before you can perform any actions, you have to keep track of certain effects that may or may not be applied to your character. These include ongoing damage and effects that end on the start of your turn.

  Ongoing damage of the same type isn't added together; only the higher number applies.

- ✔ **Actions on your turn:** You perform actions on your turn to help yourself, help your allies, or harm the monsters. These actions are described in the next section.

- ✔ **The end of your turn:** After you complete your actions, you have to keep track of certain effects that may or may not be applied to your character. You can make saving throws at this time to attempt to put an end to ongoing damage. Also note that some effects end on the end of your turn.

Actions on your turn

On your turn in combat, your character can perform actions. The main action types are

- ✔ **Standard action:** Attacking and charging are examples of standard actions. Most attack powers require a standard action. You can take one standard action on your turn.

- ✔ **Move action:** Move actions involve moving from one place to another. Walking, running, and shifting are examples of move actions. Most powers that allow you to move in some way are move actions.

- ✔ **Minor action:** Minor actions enable you to get ready to perform a more substantial and exciting action (such as a standard or a move). Pulling an item from a pouch, unsheathing a weapon, opening a door, and picking up an item are examples of minor actions.

- ✔ **Free action:** Free actions take almost no time and have little effect. You can take as many free actions as you want, though the DM may restrict how many you perform on your turn. Yelling a battle cry, speaking a couple of sentences, and dropping an item are examples of free actions.

You can take your actions in any order you want, and you don't have to perform every action you are entitled to. You can also substitute actions. You can always take a move action or a minor action in place of a standard action, and you can take a minor action instead of a move action. So, on your turn, you can do any one of the following sets of actions, in any order:

- ✔ Standard action, move action, minor action
- ✔ Standard action, two minor actions

✔ Two move actions, minor action

✔ Move action, two minor actions

✔ Three minor actions

Actions on other turns

You can take some actions on another character's turn, but some actions can be taken only during your own turn:

✔ **Opportunity action:** You can take one opportunity action on each combatant's turn. An opportunity action must be triggered by an enemy's action. The most common opportunity action is an *opportunity attack* (an attack you make when an enemy leaves a square adjacent to you or uses a ranged or area power while adjacent to you).

✔ **Immediate action:** You can take one immediate action per round, either an immediate interrupt or an immediate reaction triggered by an event or the action of another combatant.

✔ **Free action:** You can take any number of free actions on other combatants' turns, as allowed by your DM.

Engaging in Combat

Combat encounters break out when the player characters run into an opposing force. That force could be a powerful solo monster, a group of terrifying creatures, or a gang of villainous nonplayer characters. The chaos of combat is organized into a cycle of rounds and turns:

✔ **Round:** In a round, every combatant takes a turn. A round represents about six seconds in the game world.

✔ **Turn:** On your turn, you take actions in any order you want.

Combat sequence

A combat encounter follows this sequence:

✔ **Establish positions.** The DM decides where the combatants start out on the battle grid. The DM shows the players where they can set up their characters and then places the monsters.

✔ **Roll initiative.** Everyone involved in the encounter rolls initiative (roll a d20 and add your initiative modifier, as shown on your character sheet). This determines the order of battle for the entire encounter.

✔ **Take turns.** In initiative order, highest result starting first, every combatant takes a turn.

✔ **Repeat.** Start a new round and repeat the initiative order. Continue until one side or the other flees or is defeated.

✔ **End the encounter.** After one side or the other flees or is defeated, the encounter ends when the remaining side takes a short or an extended rest.

Attacking with a weapon

In the D&D game, the two basic ways to attack with weapons are as follows:

✔ **Melee attacks:** These attacks require the use of a melee weapon (such as a sword or mace), and your character must be adjacent to an enemy to make a melee attack.

✔ **Ranged attacks:** Attacks of this sort require the use of a ranged weapon (such as a shortbow or crossbow). You must be able to draw an imaginary line between your character and the enemy target. If walls or other obstacles completely block the path between your character's square and the target's square, you can't make a ranged attack because your character doesn't have a clear line of sight. If you're adjacent to an enemy when you make a ranged attack, that enemy can make an opportunity attack against you.

The attack and damage rolling process is as follows:

1. **Decide which weapon your character is using to make the attack.**

2. **Roll a d20 and add the bonus listed for that weapon.**

3. **If the result of the roll and modifier is equal to or higher than the monster's Armor Class, your attack hits.**

4. **If the attack hits, roll the type of die indicated for the weapon's damage and add the listed modifier (if any).**

5. **Damage reduces the monster's hit points; if the monster's hit points drop to 0, it's defeated.**

Other defenses

In addition to Armor Class, player characters and monsters all have three other defenses that come into play during combat. These defenses are Fortitude, Reflex, and Will. Like Armor Class, these defenses provide the target number for certain attacks. Different powers, for example, target different defenses.

Attacks and damage

If you successfully attack an enemy with a basic attack or power, you deal damage. Roll the damage dice as specified on your character sheet. Damage reduces a character's hit points.

Some powers deal ongoing damage on the turns after the initial attack. See the earlier section, "Taking your turn," for more information about how to deal with such effects at the start and end of your turn.

Critical hits

When you roll a 20 on the die when making an attack roll, you score a critical hit. Instead of rolling damage, you deal the maximum amount of damage possible for the attack when you score a critical hit.

For example, Regdar scores a critical hit with his basic melee attack. The damage for this attack is 1d10 + 4. So, maximum damage for this attack is 14 points of damage (10 + 4 =14).

Flanking

Flanking provides a simple combat tactic for you and an ally to use against an enemy. To flank an enemy, you and an ally must be adjacent to the enemy and on opposite sides of the enemy's space. You and your ally must be able to attack the enemy (with a melee or ranged weapon or with an unarmed attack). If there's a barrier between your enemy and either you or your ally, you don't flank. If you're affected by a condition that prevents you from taking actions, you don't flank. Be careful, though — two monsters working together can flank you!

You have combat advantage against an enemy you flank (see the next section).

Combat advantage

When a defender can't give full attention to defense, it grants combat advantage to its attacker. This usually occurs when the defender is flanked, stunned, or otherwise caught off guard. When you have combat advantage, you gain +2 bonus to attack rolls.

You must be able to see the target to gain combat advantage against it.

Other actions in combat

In addition to making a basic attack, you have a few other options in combat. These include

- ✔ **Use your second wind.** As a standard action, you can spend a healing surge to regain hit points. When you do, you regain one-quarter of your maximum hit points (rounded down). You also gain a +2 bonus to all defenses until the start of your next turn. You can use your second wind once per encounter.

- ✔ **Use a power.** Most powers are standard actions. Refer to your character sheet to see what powers you have access to.

Using Powers in Combat

In addition to basic melee and basic ranged attacks, all characters have access to powers they can use during combat. Powers include attack powers (used to harm enemies) and utility powers (used to overcome obstacles in or out of combat). Powers are restricted by how often you can use them:

- ✔ **At-will powers** are powers you can use as often as you want. They represent easy attacks or simple magical effects that don't tax your resources.

- ✔ **Encounter powers** are powers that you can use once per encounter. These are more powerful and dramatic than at-will powers. You need to take a short rest to recharge encounter powers.

- ✔ **Daily powers** are powers that you can use once per day. These are the most powerful effects you can produce, and using them puts a significant strain on your resources. You need to take an extended rest to recharge daily powers.

Types of powers used in combat

Powers range from the spells of arcane characters to the prayers of divine characters to the exploits of martial characters. The use of most powers requires a standard action and an attack roll against an opponent's defense (either Armor Class, Fortitude, Reflex, or Will).

- ✔ **Divine prayers:** Clerics cast divine prayers. The ready-to-play clerics (see Chapter 6) can use each of their listed powers as defined in the power descriptions.

How to read a power

The powers in the *Player's Handbook* are a little dense to read through at first. In this sidebar, we show you how to read a power's description using *freezing cloud* as an example. (This applies to powers in the *Player's Handbook* and to the powers for the sample characters in Chapters 3 through 6 in this book.)

The superscript numbers in parenthesis (such as [1]) correspond to the numbers in the following list that describes each part of the power. (Note that these numbers don't appear in regular power descriptions.)

Freezing Cloud [1]   Wizard Attack 1 [2]

A pellet shoots from your hand and explodes into a cloud of icy mist at the point of impact. [3]

Daily [4] ◆ **Arcane, Cold, Implement** [5]

Standard Action [6]   **Area** burst 2 within 10 squares [7]

Target: Each creature in burst [8]

Attack: [9] d20 + 4 versus Fortitude [10]

Hit: 1d8 + 4 cold damage [11]

Miss: Half damage [12]

Effect: The cloud lasts until the end of your next turn. Any creature that enters the cloud or starts its turn there is subject to another attack. You can dismiss the cloud as a minor action. [13]

The following list breaks down each numbered part of the power block. (Note that not all powers have all these entries — for example, most powers don't have a Miss effect.)

[1] **The power's name:** The name of the power. *Freezing cloud,* in this case.

[2] **The power's class, type, and level:** The class indicated which classes can use the power (wizard, for this example). The type indicated what type of power it is, such as an attack or utility power. The level indicates the minimum level your character has to be to choose the power, and also how powerful or weak the power is.

[3] **Flavor text:** A description of what the power does and how it looks when used.

[4] **Usage:** This describes how often you can use the power — at will, once per encounter, or once per day. *Freezing cloud* is a daily power, so you can use it once, and then it's expended until the next time your character can take a long rest.

[5] **Keywords:** These tell you what rules apply to this power. *Arcane* means that this power is derived from the arcane power source — magic. *Cold* means that it's a cold effect. *Implement* means that your character delivers this attack with a wizardly implement such as a wand or staff, as opposed to a weapon like a longsword.

[6] **Action required:** This tells you whether the power is a minor, move, standard, immediate, or free action.

(7) **Range:** All powers are melee, close, area, ranged, or personal. In the case of area powers, the power description tells you the size of the area affected and from how far away you can use the power.

(8) **Target:** The creatures or area you can affect with the power.

(9) **Attack modifier:** The die and modifier you roll when you attack.

(10) **Defense targeted:** Which of the enemy's defenses (Fortitude, Reflex, Will, or Armor Class) this power attacks.

(11) **Hit:** The power's effect on a hit. For this example, if *freezing cloud* hits, you deal some cold damage to the target.

(12) **Miss:** Some powers also have effects even if you miss.

(13) **Effect:** Other effects of using the power. Anything explained here happens whether you hit or miss the target with your attack roll.

- **Arcane spells:** Wizards cast arcane spells. The ready-to-play wizards (see Chapter 5) can use each of their listed powers as defined in the power descriptions. (During the preparation that accompanies an extended rest, the wizard decides which of his or her daily and utility powers are available for that day of adventuring.)

- **Martial exploits:** Fighters and rogues use martial exploits. The ready-to-play fighters and rogues (see Chapters 3 and 4) can use each of their listed powers as defined in the power descriptions.

Power attack types

Powers come in a four attack types:

- **Melee attack:** A power that uses a melee attack usually uses a weapon and targets one enemy within reach (which is usually an enemy in an adjacent square). If a power attacks multiple enemies, you make a separate attack and damage roll for each target.

- **Ranged attack:** A power that uses a ranged attack strikes against a single distant target. If a power attacks multiple enemies, you make a separate attack and damage roll for each target. Making a ranged attack provokes opportunity attacks from adjacent enemies.

- **Close attack:** A power that uses a Close attack is an attack that comes directly from you. A Close attack creates an area of effect, usually a blast or burst:

- A *Close burst* uses your square as its origin space and extends in all directions out to the number of spaces specified in the power. Unless a power description notes otherwise, a close burst that you create does not affect you.

- A *Close blast* fills an area adjacent to you that is a specified number of squares on a side. The blast must be adjacent to its origin square, which is your space. It does not affect the origin square.

When you make a Close attack, make a separate attack roll for each target in the area of effect, but make only one damage roll that affects all the targets.

✔ **Area attack:** A power that uses an Area attack creates an area of effect, usually a burst. Choose a square within range of the power to serve as the origin square.

An *Area burst* uses the square you designate as its origin space and extends in all directions out to the number of spaces specified in the power. Unless a power description notes otherwise, an area burst that you create does affect you.

When you make an Area attack, make a separate attack roll for each target in the area of effect, but make only one damage roll that affects all the targets.

If you use an Area power while adjacent to an enemy, that enemy can make an opportunity attack against you.

Movement in Combat

You can use a move action to walk your speed in a turn. If you use two move actions (substituting a move for a standard action), you can walk your speed twice on your turn.

Move actions

These activities require the use of a move action.

✔ **Walk:** Move up to your speed.

✔ **Shift:** Move 1 square without provoking opportunity attacks. You can't normally shift into difficult terrain.

✔ **Run:** Move up to your speed +2 squares and grant combat advantage.

Forced movement

Certain powers and effects allow you to pull, push, or slide a target:

- ✔ **Pull:** When you pull a creature, each square you move it must bring it nearer to you.

- ✔ **Push:** When you push a creature, each square you move it must place it farther away from you.

- ✔ **Slide:** When you slide a creature, there's no restriction on the direction you can move it.

The following rules govern all forced movement:

- ✔ **Distance:** The power specifies how many squares you can move a target. You can choose to move the target fewer squares or not to move the target at all.

- ✔ **Specific destination:** Some powers instead specify a destination, such as any square adjacent to you.

- ✔ **No opportunity attacks:** Forced movement does not provoke opportunity attacks.

- ✔ **Difficult terrain:** Forced movement isn't hindered by difficult terrain.

- ✔ **Not a move:** Forced movement doesn't count against a target's ability to move on its turn.

- ✔ **Valid space:** Forced movement can't move a target into a space it couldn't enter by walking.

For more information on pull, push, slide, and forced movement, see page 285 of the *Player's Handbook.*

Distance and movement

To measure distance on a battle grid, simply count squares. You can move your speed in squares as a move action, in any direction, across squares or across diagonals.

Occupied squares

In general, you can't move through an occupied square.

✔ **Ally:** You can move through a square occupied by an ally.

✔ **Enemy:** You can't move through an enemy's space unless that enemy is helpless. (Unconscious foes are normally helpless.)

✔ **Ending movement:** You can't end your movement in an occupied square unless it's an ally's square and the ally is prone, or it's an enemy's square and the enemy is helpless.

Difficult terrain

Rubble, undergrowth, shallow bogs, steep stairs, and other types of difficult terrain hamper movement. It costs 1 additional square of movement to enter a square of difficult terrain. If you don't have enough movement remaining, you can't enter a square of difficult terrain. You can't shift into a square of difficult terrain unless you have a power that allows you to do so.

Obstacles

You can't enter a square with an obstacle that fills the square, such as a wall or pillar. When an obstacle fills a square, you can't move diagonally across the corner of that square.

Spending and Gaining Action Points

Once per encounter, you can spend an *action point,* which is a special advantage that player characters (and some monsters) have to represent their heroic (or formidable) nature. An action point allows you to take an extra action on your turn. When you spend an action point, it's gone. You earn more action points by adventuring.

✔ Player characters start with 1 action point. Only some monsters have action points, as shown in a monster's stat block.

✔ Player characters gain 1 action point when they reach a milestone in the adventure. A milestone occurs at the end of every two encounters that the PCs complete in the same day (without taking an extended rest, see the later section, "Rest and Recovery"). So, if the PCs complete five encounters before deciding to take an extended rest, they would earn a milestone at the end of the second and fourth encounters that day.

✔ After an extended rest (described in the "Rest and Recovery" section), player characters lose any unspent action points, but start fresh with 1 action point.

Most often, you spend an action point to take an extra action during your turn. Sometimes you might spend an action point because you have some other special benefit for doing so because of your paragon path or feat selection. You decide whether the extra action is a standard action, a move action, or a minor action.

Facing Skill Challenges

In a skill challenge, your character makes skill checks to accumulate a number of successes before accumulating too many failures and ending the encounter. For example, if Lidda is trying to disable a complicated trap, she needs to attain six successes before accruing three failures.

A skill challenge plays out like a combat encounter, with player characters taking turns to help overcome the challenge. They PCs might use the same skills, or they might each use different skills to approach the problem from different directions.

Hit Points, Healing, and Dying

Over the course of a battle, characters take damage from attacks. Damage reduces a character's hit points.

- ✔ **Maximum hit points:** PCs and monsters have a maximum number of hit points, as determined by class, level, and Constitution score. A character's current hit points can't exceed this number.

- ✔ **Bloodied:** When your current hit points drop to one-half your maximum hit points or lower, your character is bloodied. Certain powers work only (or work better) against a bloodied target.

- ✔ **Dying:** When a PCs current hit points drop to 0 or lower, the PC falls unconscious and is dying. Any damage the PC takes continues to reduce the PC's current hit points until the character dies. When a monster's hit points drop to 0, it is defeated.

- ✔ **Death saving throw:** When a PC is dying, the player makes a saving throw at the end of his or her turn each round. If the save succeeds (roll 10 or better), there is no change in the PC's condition. If the save fails (roll lower than 10), the PC slips one step closer to death. If the save fails three times, the character dies.

- ✔ **Death:** When a PC takes damage that reduces his or her current hit points to a negative number that's the same as the PC's bloodied number, or if the PC fails the death save three times, the character dies. Monsters simply die when they are reduced to 0 hit points.

Healing in combat

Even as the battle rages, characters can heal. A PC can heal himself by using his second wind (see page 291 in the *Player's Handbook*). An ally can use the Heal skill or power on a PC (see the following section). Monsters have limited ways to heal, as described in the encounters and the monster stat blocks, when appropriate.

When a power heals a PC, the PC doesn't have to take an action to spend a healing surge. Even when a PC is unconscious, the power uses the PC's healing surge to restore hit points. And some powers don't require a character to spend a healing surge at all.

Healing the dying

If a player character is dying and receives healing, the PC goes to 0 hit points and then regains hit points from there. As soon as the PC's current hit point total is higher than 0, he or she becomes conscious and is no longer dying.

Rest and Recovery

Outside of encounters, player characters can take one of two types of rest:

- ✔ **Short rest:** A short rest allows PCs to renew their encounter powers and use healing surges to regain hit points. It lasts about five minutes. PCs can take as many short rests per day as they want. During a short rest, PCs have to rest; no strenuous activity, no interruptions.

- ✔ **Extended rest:** Once per day, PCs can take an extended rest. It must last at least six hours to gain the benefits. PCs have to rest or sleep during this period. At the end of the rest, they regain any hit points they lost and any healing surges they spent, their daily powers are renewed, and they lose any unspent action points and gain 1 fresh action point.

Conditions That Affect Combat

Powers, monsters, traps, and the environment can all apply conditions to a character. A *condition* imposes a penalty or other effect until it is removed by a successful saving throw or it ends naturally.

Conditions that can affect a character are as follows:

Blinded: You can't see any target (your targets have total concealment), you take a –10 penalty to Perception checks, and you grant combat advantage. Furthermore, you can't flank an enemy.

Dazed: You grant combat advantage and you can't flank an enemy. You can take a standard action, a move action, *or* a minor action on your turn, rather than one of each. (You can also take free actions.) You can't take immediate actions or opportunity actions.

Deafened: You can't hear anything, and you take a –10 penalty to Perception checks.

Dominated: You're dazed, and the dominating creature chooses your one action. The only powers it can make you use are at-will powers.

Dying: You're unconscious because you're at 0 or negative hit points. You make a death saving throw every round.

Helpless: You grant combat advantage. *Note:* Usually you're helpless because you're unconscious.

Immobilized: You can't move from your space, although you can teleport and can be forced to move by a pull, a push, or a slide.

Marked: You take a –2 penalty to attack rolls if your attack doesn't include the creature that marked you.

Petrified: You have been turned to stone. You can't take actions, but you gain resist 20 to all damage. You are unaware of your surroundings; you don't age.

Prone: You're lying on the ground. (If you're flying, you safely descend a distance equal to your fly speed. If you don't reach the ground, you fall.) You grant combat advantage to enemies making melee attacks against you, but you get a +2 bonus to all defenses against ranged attacks from nonadjacent enemies. You take a –2 penalty to attack rolls.

Restrained: You're immobilized; you can't be forced to move by a pull, a push, or a slide. You grant combat advantage, and you take a –2 penalty to attack rolls.

Slowed: Your speed becomes 2. This speed applies to all your movement modes, but it does not apply to teleportation or to a pull, push, or slide. You can't increase your speed above 2, and your speed doesn't increase if it was lower than 2. If you're slowed while moving, stop moving if you have already moved 2 or more squares.

Stunned: You can't take actions; you grant combat advantage. When stunned, you can't flank an enemy.

Surprised: You grant combat advantage; you can't take actions, other than free actions. When surprised, you can't flank an enemy.

Unconscious: You're helpless; you fall prone, if possible. You can't take actions, and you take a –5 penalty to all defenses. This probably won't surprise you, but you can't flank an enemy while unconscious.

Weakened: Your attacks deal half damage. Ongoing damage you deal is not affected.

Chapter 8

Practice Session

. . . .

In This Chapter

▶ Using a battle grid and character markers

▶ Testing player characters against monsters

▶ Adding story elements to make an adventure

. . . .

*I*n the preceding chapters, we present an overview of the basics of the DUNGEONS & DRAGONS game; we introduce a group of ready-to-play characters; and we show you how to make attack rolls, damage rolls, and skill checks. After going over the basics, you can actually roll some dice and see how it all comes together at the gaming table.

This chapter takes you on a tour of a sample play session of DUNGEONS & DRAGONS. Note that you need a set of D&D dice to participate in this practice session. You can get a set of D&D dice at your local game store or bookstore, or you can buy a set from any online game seller. When you get your dice, continue with this practice session.

The Battle Grid and Markers

The DUNGEONS & DRAGONS game uses three-dimensional components to help players visualize scenes and work through tactics and strategy in combat. Miniatures and a battle grid provide the best way to visualize the action. A sample battle grid can be downloaded at www.dummies.com/ cheatsheet/dungeonsdragons4thedition. One side has an open grid that can be used to replicate any dungeon scene. The other side is set up as a portion of a dungeon and can be used with the sample adventure presented in Chapter 24.

A battle grid consists of 1-inch squares. You count distances in squares (though you can convert to the game world dimensions of 1 square equals 5 feet if you want). For example, Regdar has a speed of 5, meaning that he can move 5 squares when he uses a move action to walk or a standard action to charge and attack.

You use the battle grid and miniatures or other markers (see the following section, "Markers") to show the marching order of your group of adventurers or the relative location of characters and monsters in any given encounter.

The best use for the battle grid is when the characters stumble or charge into combat. When you can see how far away or how close the monster is, as well as where other player characters are in relation to it and your character, you can plan better moves and make full use of the environment during combat encounters.

A larger version of the battle grid can be found in the *Dungeon Master's Guide*. You might also want to use *D&D Dungeon Tiles*, which provide cardstock tiles that you can arrange in any configuration. You can purchase more durable battle grids made of vinyl at game and hobby stores or from online game sellers.

Markers

The battle grid works only if you use something to represent player characters and monsters. If you're ambitious, you can gather a bunch of DUNGEONS & DRAGONS miniatures to use instead of the markers.

Most characters and many monsters are considered to be Medium in size. A Medium character occupies a single square on the battle grid. Large creatures occupy a 2 x 2 area, or 4 squares. Only one character or creature can occupy a square. Characters can move through squares occupied by friendly characters, but they can't move through squares occupied by enemies. Characters can't stop moving in an occupied square (whether the occupant is a friend or an enemy doesn't matter).

Moving on the battle grid

To move, your character must use an action. Usually, you use the Walk action, which allows your character to move a number of squares equal to his or her speed. Walk requires your character to use a move action; normally, your character can use a standard action, a move action, and a minor action each turn. That means your character can move up to his or her speed on the Battle Grid with a move action, and then attack an enemy with a standard action. (You can also choose to spend a standard action as another move action and walk again, so you can move twice in a turn if you don't use any other actions.) For example, Regdar has a speed of 5. On his turn, he can walk 5 squares (his move action), and then use his *sure strike* power (a standard action) to attack an enemy, as shown in Figure 8-1.

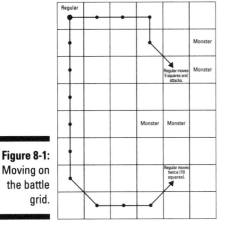

Figure 8-1:
Moving on
the battle
grid.

A Practice Combat

Now it's time for a practice combat involving player characters and monsters. This is very much like a real combat encounter that you would have in any D&D adventure. You need players; say there are four of you, one to play a character of each class described in this book. You need a Dungeon Master to run the monsters. Have each player select a character to play. (You can use the sample characters in Chapters 3 through 6 or create your own.) You can use any battle grid — each player should pick a character marker or miniature, and the DM should use two orc and two kobold markers or miniatures. (These are the monsters that the four player characters will face in this practice session.) Note that both orcs have the same statistics and the same number of hit points, and the same is true of the kobolds.

Placing characters on the battle grid and rolling initiative

Set the battle grid on the table and make sure the players and DM can comfortably sit around the play area with room for character sheets and dice rolling. The four player characters start on one end of the battle grid. The DM places the two orc and two kobold markers anywhere in the middle of the battle grid.

Next, everyone rolls initiative. Roll the d20 and add your character's initiative modifier. The DM makes a roll that covers both orcs, and a roll that covers both kobolds. (The orc and kobold statistics can be found in the nearby side-bars.) The DM jots down each character's result, in order, from highest to lowest. That sets the order of play for this combat encounter.

For example, Redgar gets a result of 11. Shadow gets a result of 20. Telsa gets a result of 18. Eberk gets a result of 2. The DM rolls and gets results of 5 and 10 for the orcs and kobolds. So, the initiative order for this combat looks like this:

Shadow	20
Telsa	18
Regdar	11
Kobolds	10
Orcs	5
Eberk	2

What to do on a turn

Each turn, a creature in combat can spend a standard action, a move action, and a minor action. Standard actions are most important: All attacks are standard actions. Move actions mean that the creature actually moves on the battle grid — for example, by using the Walk action (move up to the creature's speed) or by using the Shift action (move one square). Minor actions are good for using powers or abilities that only require a minor action, such as a cleric's *healing word* prayer. A creature can spend its standard action as a move action instead, if it wants. What that all means is this: On a typical turn, you can move and attack, you can attack and move, or you can move twice.

Remember that to make an attack, you roll a d20 and add the modifier for the weapon or power your character is using. If an attack hits (you get a result that's equal to or higher than your opponent's Armor Class or other appro-priate defense), roll the die or dice listed for the weapon's damage. Damage reduces a character's (or monster's) hit points.

If the characters reduce both orcs and both kobolds to 0 hit points, the char-acters win the combat. If the monsters reduce all the characters to 0 hit points, the monsters win the combat.

Orc fighter

Orcs are aggressive humanoids with gray skin, coarse hair, and boar-like faces. They hate adventurers and seek to destroy them on sight.

Initiative: +2   **Senses:** Perception +0; low-light vision

HP: 28; **Bloodied:** 14

AC: 16; **Fortitude:** 15; **Reflex:** 12; **Will:** 12

Speed: 6

Club (standard; at-will) ◆ **Weapon**

    +8 versus AC; 1d6 + 2 damage

Alignment: Chaotic evil   **Languages:** Common, Giant

Str: 16 (+3)   **Dex:** 10 (+0)   **Wis:** 10 (+0)

Con: 14 (+2)   **Int:** 8 (–1)   **Cha:** 9 (–1)

Equipment: hide armor, club

The Dungeon Master

The presence of a Dungeon Master turns D&D from a board game into a role-playing game where anything can happen. You can run this practice session with the DM simply controlling the actions of the monsters, or you can let the DM practice his or her DMing skills. A Dungeon Master isn't competing against the players (even though he or she controls their opponents in an adventure). The DM sets the scene, describes the action, and calls for skill checks and other rolls when necessary.

Example of player versus monster combat

Here's how the first round of this combat encounter might play out:

> **Turn 1 — Shadow:** Shadow goes first (she had the highest initiative result). She draws her hand crossbow and fires at the orc on the right. She rolls a 4 on the d20 and adds her modifier of +6 for a result of 10. That's not enough to hit the orc's Armor Class of 16, and the hand crossbow bolt whizzes past the orc's head.

> **Turn 1 — Telsa:** Telsa acts next. She uses a move action to get closer to the monsters and then for her standard action she casts her *burning hands* spell. This produces a Close blast 5 effect, which is a large enough

area to target all the monsters. She rolls separate attacks against each monster, getting 23 (a critical hit!) and 10 against the orcs, and 16 and 11 against the kobolds. These attacks are against the monsters' Reflex defenses, so the attack hits one of the orcs and one of the kobolds. The orc takes maximum damage because Telsa rolled a crit; 15 points of damage reduces the orc to 13 hit points. The orc is bloodied! The kobold takes 10 points of damage and is reduced to 17 hit points.

Turn 1 — Regdar: Regdar acts next. He uses a move action to get close to the same orc that Telsa damaged, and he uses a standard action to make an attack. He uses his *reaping strike* attack. He gets an 18 on his attack (a hit) and deals 12 points of damage to the orc! The orc has 1 hit point left! Plus, the orc is marked, meaning that it needs to include Regdar as a target in its next attack.

Kobold skirmisher

Kobolds are cowardly and small lizard creatures. They revere dragons as gods.

Initiative: +5   **Senses:** Perception +0; darkvision

HP: 27; **Bloodied:** 13

AC: 15; **Fortitude:** 11; **Reflex:** 14; **Will:** 13

Speed: 6

Spear (standard; at-will) ♦ **Weapon**

   +6 versus AC; 1d8 damage; see also *mob attack*

Combat Advantage

   The kobold skirmisher deals an extra 1d6 damage on melee and ranged attacks against any target it has combat advantage over.

Mob Attack

   The kobold skirmisher gains a +1 bonus to attack rolls per kobold ally adjacent to the target.

Shifty (minor; at-will)

   The kobold shifts 1 square.

Alignment: Evil   **Languages:** Common, Draconic

Skills: Acrobatics +7, Stealth +9, Thievery +9

Str: 8 (−1)   **Dex:** 16 (+3)   **Wis:** 10 (+0)

Con: 11 (+0)   **Int:** 6 (−2)   **Cha:** 15 (+2)

Equipment: hide armor, spear

Turn 1 — Kobolds: The kobolds get to act now. They move to flank Regdar. They are both adjacent to the target, so their *mob attack* ability comes into play. The DM rolls a d20 and adds the kobold's modifier of +7 (+6 plus +1 due to mob attacks) for a result of 14 for the first kobold (a miss) and 21 for the second. The 21 is a hit! The kobold also has combat advantage against Regdar since it's flanking him; it deals 9 points of damage to Regdar, leaving the fighter with 20 hit points.

Turn 1 — Orcs: The orcs get to act now. The orc on the left swings his club at Regdar. The DM rolls a d20 and adds the orc's modifier of +8 for a result of 18. That's a hit! The orc deals 4 points of damage to Regdar, leaving the fighter with 16 hit points. The second orc, the one with 1 hit point remaining, attempts to run away. When it leaves the square adjacent to Regdar, the fighter gets to make an opportunity attack against it. Regdar hits, and the orc drops to the ground.

Turn 1 — Eberk: Eberk has a turn now. He uses a minor action to cast a *healing word* spell, healing some of Regdar's damage. Then he moves up to a kobold and attacks. He rolls a 12, which misses the kobold, who hisses at the dwarf.

The first round of the combat has ended. Will the adventurers beat the monsters and win the day? Roll some dice and find out by playing through this scenario yourself!

Adding Story Elements

The DUNGEONS & DRAGONS game provides a platform for players to tell exciting stories in a medieval fantasy world. It's easy for the Dungeon Master to add story elements to an encounter and for the players to imagine what kinds of things their characters will do. In this section, we take the orc battle example and add some story elements to it.

Use a dungeon battle grid. Pick any room and place the markers for the monsters anywhere within it. Let the player characters start outside the room, somewhere down the corridor. The DM decides that the monsters have recently raided a human village, and now they're inside this dungeon room dividing their spoils. Maybe the orcs have a sack of ten silver pieces, a rusty sword, a scrawny dog tied to a table leg, and a scroll they stole from an empty farmhouse. The orcs are laughing and congratulating themselves in their coarse language when the player characters reach the corridor beyond.

Now the DM calls for Perception skill checks. The DM decides that it isn't too hard to hear the monsters and sets a target of 10 (called the Difficulty Class or DC) for the check. If any of the characters get a result of 10 or better on their check, they hear the noise coming from the room.

If the characters all fail to hear the noise, the DM can see whether the orcs hear the approaching characters. Because the orcs are laughing and talking, the DM decides that the monsters have a harder time hearing the player characters and sets the DC at 15.

Now, maybe the characters know that something is in the room, maybe they don't. Maybe the orcs and kobolds know the characters are coming, maybe they don't. The DM can use this information to build tension and drama as the characters move closer to the room.

When the characters finally reach the room and look in, they see the two orcs, the two kobolds, a table, and the spoils from the village. Can the adventurers defeat the monsters? Will the monsters try to fight or beg for their lives? What about the spoils? Is the rusty sword enchanted with magic power? Did the scroll belong to a wizard or does it have some important message scrawled upon its surface? Maybe it's a map to another dungeon and some fantastic treasure.

Story isn't hard, and the elements it brings to the game are fun! Give it a try after you've had some combat practice.

Chapter 9

Finding a D&D Game to Join

In This Chapter

▶ Joining someone else's game

▶ Starting your own game

▶ Joining a high-level game

▶ Playing as Regdar, 4th-level human fighter

▶ Playing as Regdar, 8th-level human fighter

D UNGEONS & DRAGONS is a cooperative game; you need at least one other person to play with, and preferably as many as five or six people altogether. One person is the Dungeon Master, the player who runs the monsters, presents the dungeon or adventure, and generally keeps the game moving. Everybody else controls a *player character* — a single hero in the DM's adventure.

In this chapter, we take a look at finding a game to play in, organizing your own game if you can't (or don't want to) find another game to play in, and joining a high-level game. We also provide you with a ready-to-play character at 4th level and at 8th level — Regdar, the human fighter.

A Typical Game Session

You might wonder what a D&D game session looks like. What do people wear, what do they bring, how long do they play, and where do they play? The best comparison for a D&D game is a regular Friday night poker game. People dress casually, they usually meet at somebody's house, they bring some snacks or drinks and what they need to play, and the game usually runs three or four hours — sometimes longer, sometimes shorter.

When you get invited to join a D&D game, it's a good idea to ask or check about the following:

- ✔ When is the game? Make sure you're punctual!

- ✔ Where is the game? Make sure you get good directions to the host's house or the hobby store, library, community center, or such place where the game is taking place. Get a street address and use MapQuest (www.mapquest.com) if you need to, or arrange to ride to the game with a friend.

- ✔ Who's the Dungeon Master? As a new player, the DM is your best friend. Get in touch with the DM a day or two before the game and find out what he or she expects of you.

- ✔ Ask what game materials you should bring. Most players show up for a game with the *Player's Handbook,* a set of D&D dice, something to write with and on, and their character sheet. Bring this *For Dummies* book if you expect to play one of the ready-made characters presented in Chapters 3 through 6.

- ✔ Ask if you can bring food and beverages. Bring some cash so you can pitch in for a pizza or something.

- ✔ Don't assume it's okay to bring children. Older children may very well want to play in the game with you, and that's something you need to clear with the people you will be playing with. Younger children demand your time and attention, and they will probably make things difficult for you and for everybody else. D&D night is probably a good time to get a babysitter.

The first few times you play, it's a good idea to do a lot of listening and watching and not so much talking. As you're learning your character's abilities and figuring out how the game works, pay attention to how the other players conduct themselves at the table. You can take your cues from them.

Finding Someone to Play With

So, say that you bought the *Player's Handbook*, flipped through the book you're holding in your hands, and have generally decided you'd like to play some D&D. How do you go about finding a game to play in? You have two basic choices: Find someone else's game to join or organize your own game.

Joining someone else's game

This is probably the easiest way to go if you're a novice at D&D. Find an existing group of players who are willing to make some room for you at the table and begin playing with those folks. Every week, hundreds of thousands of people gather for regular D&D games with friends or strangers, just like people fall into regular poker games, bowling leagues, or bingo nights. All you have to do is identify an existing group somewhere near you and let the members know you're interested.

So where do you find a D&D group meeting in your town? Try the following:

- ✔ **Friends and family:** Ask people you know to find out if somebody is in a game or if that person knows somebody who's in a game.

- ✔ **Gaming clubs:** Many high schools and colleges have active gaming clubs. If you're a student, see whether your school has a club or organization that sponsors regular games.

- ✔ **The friendly local gaming store:** People looking for players to join their game, or people looking for games to join, often post messages in local hobby stores. You won't find this sort of "player corkboard" at a big bookstore that carries D&D books — you need to find local hobby stores for this kind of search. The best hobby stores often sponsor games right on-site, which is a great way to meet people you might want to game with.

- ✔ **The Internet:** Some popular Web sites or message boards frequented by D&D fans include "players seeking players" posts. A good site for this sort of thing is `www.wizards.com/community`. If you're under 18, please check with your parents before you start trying to meet strangers online.

- ✔ **The RPGA:** This stands for Roleplaying Gamers Association, a worldwide network of D&D fans. Contact the RPGA at `www.wizards.com/rpga` and ask them if there are any RPGA chapters in your hometown.

Now, here's the hard part: Most gamers understand that it can be difficult to find a game to play in, but you need to show some courtesy when you ask to join a gaming group of strangers. Try something like, "I understand you run a regular D&D game. I'm interested in trying it out. Are you looking for new players?" Don't take it too personally if the answer is no; it's not unusual for Dungeon Masters to decline to add new players if they're already running a game with a lot of players in it.

Organizing your own game

If you can't locate an existing game to join, you'll need to organize your own game. Most players expect a D&D game to be an ongoing, regularly scheduled event — just like that weekly poker night we were talking about.

Your first order of business is finding a Dungeon Master (DM). Chances are good that you know someone — or know someone who knows someone — who's played D&D before and can serve as the game master. If at all possible, you want an experienced player to be your group's DM. Failing that, you'll need to choose a DM for your new game. Because you're trying to organize the thing, you might as well take a stab at it.

After you've determined who's going to be the DM, you need to round up a group of reliable and interested players. Ideally, you'd like to start with three to five players and one Dungeon Master. To find players, ask friends first. Family members are okay, but we suggest siblings or cousins — if you bring a parent or child to a game where most other people are about your age, you may create an awkward social dynamic for everybody else. (Of course, if *everybody* at the table is in your immediate family, that's not a problem.)

If you can't find enough players by asking people you know, you can try fishing for fellow gamers in your town. Post notices at your local hobby store or look for school gaming clubs (if you're a student, that is).

After you've gathered enough people to play, choose a place and a time to meet. In the long run, you'd like to find a good game night that could be regularly scheduled for everybody in your game, but when you're just starting it, there's no reason you can't schedule your games one at a time. Find a place where you can put half-a-dozen people around a good-sized table and not bother other folks by making a lot of noise. If you play at a house where there will be small children around, make sure that somebody (preferably someone who's not trying to play D&D with you) will be able to pay attention to the kids and keep them entertained.

The D&D Roleplaying Game Starter Set

If you're a novice and everyone you're playing with is a novice too, we highly recommend that you get your hands on the *D&D Roleplaying Game Starter Set* and start there. This starter set includes dice, character and monster tokens, ready-to-play characters, dungeon tiles, and ready-to-run dungeon scenarios. It's the best starting place for people who have never played the game before, and you'll have a much easier time learning the ropes with the *D&D Roleplaying Game Starter Set* than you will with the *Player's Handbook* and *Dungeon Master's Guide*.

Starting Off with a High-Level Character

When you join a gaming group that's been playing for a while, there's an excellent chance that their characters are well past 1st level. For example, you might be told something like, "Great, glad you can join the game — bring a 4th-level character on Saturday!"

Most Dungeon Masters have some ground rules for how new characters can join the game, so you should ask ahead of time who's going to be the Dungeon Master and find out from that person how you should build a character to suit. Don't be afraid to ask for help getting ready. But sometimes you might be joining a game blind, without any knowledge of who's DMing, what sort of game they're running, or how to get a character ready to play fast. For those circumstances, we provide you with a 4th-level and 8th-level version of Regdar, the fighter. (See Chapter 3 for Regdar at 1st level.) As a new player, you'll find that the easiest character class to play at higher levels is the fighter. When you get to your new game, tell the Dungeon Master that you're ready to play a 4th-level fighter or an 8th-level fighter out of this book, if it's okay by him or her.

If you want to play a fighter with Regdar's stats but don't like the name, change it to something you like. If you prefer a female character, you need only change the name.

Regdar, 4th-Level Human Fighter

Hit Points: 57 _____ Bloodied: 28

Healing Surge: 14   Surges per Day: 11

Initiative: +4   Speed: 5 squares

Alignment: Good

Ability Scores

	Score	Bonus*
STRENGTH	**19**	**+4**
CONSTITUTION	**14**	**+2**
DEXTERITY	**14**	**+2**
INTELLIGENCE	**10**	**+0**
WISDOM	**12**	**+1**
CHARISMA	**11**	**+0**

* Bonuses and penalties have already been calculated into your statistics and powers.

Defenses

AC 20   Fortitude 17   Reflex 14   Will 14

Basic Attacks

Melee Basic Attack (Greatsword)
        d20 + 12   1d10 + 6 damage

Ranged Basic Attack (Longbow)
        d20 + 6   1d10 damage

Class Features

Combat Challenge: Every time you attack an enemy, whether the attack hits or misses, you can choose to mark that target. The mark lasts until the end of your next turn. While a target is marked, it takes a –2 penalty to attack rolls if its attack doesn't include you as a target. A creature can be subject to only one mark at a time. A new mark supersedes a mark that was already in place.

In addition, whenever an enemy that is adjacent to you shifts or makes an attack that doesn't include you as a target, you can make a melee basic attack against that enemy as an immediate interrupt.

Combat Superiority: You gain a +2 bonus to opportunity attacks (+5 total with blade opportunist and combat reflexes feats).

Fighter Weapon Talent: You gain a +1 bonus to attack rolls when using two-handed weapons (already included in stats).

Feats

Action Surge: You gain a +3 bonus to attack rolls you make during any action you gained by spending an action point.

Blade Opportunist: You gain a +2 bonus to opportunity attack rolls with a heavy blade or a light blade.

Combat Reflexes: You gain a +1 bonus to opportunity attack rolls.

Power Attack: When making a melee attack, you can take a –2 penalty to the attack roll. If the attack hits, you gain a +3 bonus to the damage roll.

Skills

Acrobatics	**d20 + 4**
Arcana	**d20 + 2**
Athletics (trained)	**d20 + 11**
Bluff	**d20 + 2**
Diplomacy	**d20 + 2**
Dungeoneering	**d20 + 3**
Endurance (trained)	**d20 + 9**
Heal	**d20 + 3**
History	**d20 + 2**
Insight	**d20 + 3**
Intimidate (trained)	**d20 + 7**
Nature	**d20 + 3**

Perception   **d20 + 3**
Religion   **d20 + 2**
Stealth   **d20 + 4**
Streetwise (trained)   **d20 + 7**
Thievery   **d20 + 4**

Powers

Cleave   Fighter Attack 1

You hit one enemy, and then cleave into another.

At-Will ◆ Martial, Weapon

Standard Action   **Melee** weapon

Target: One creature

Attack: d20 + 12 versus AC

Hit: 1d10 + 6 damage, and an enemy adjacent to you takes 4 points of damage.

Reaping Strike   Fighter Attack 1

You punctuate your scything attacks with wicked jabs and small cutting blows that slip through your enemy's defenses.

At-Will ◆ Martial, Weapon

Standard Action   **Melee** weapon

Target: One creature

Attack: d20 + 12 versus AC

Hit: 1d10 + 6 damage

Miss: 4 points of damage

Sure Strike   Fighter Attack 1

You trade power for precision.

At-Will ◆ Martial, Weapon

Standard Action   **Melee** weapon

Target: One creature

Attack: d20 + 14 versus AC

Hit: 1d10 + 2 damage

Spinning Sweep   Fighter Attack 1

You spin beneath your enemy's guard with a long, powerful cut and then sweep your leg through his an instant later to knock him head over heels.

Encounter ◆ Martial, Weapon

Standard Action   **Melee** weapon

Target: One creature

Attack: d20 + 12 versus AC

Hit: 1d10 + 6 damage, and you knock the target prone.

Dance of Steel   Fighter Attack 3

Weaving your weapon in a graceful figure-eight, you lash out with a sudden attack.

Encounter ◆ Martial, Weapon

Standard Action

Melee weapon

Target: One creature

Attack: d20 + 12 versus AC

Hit: 2d10 + 6 damage, and the target is immobilized until the end of your next turn.

Brute Strike   Fighter Attack 1

You shatter armor and bone with a ringing blow.

Daily ◆ Martial, Reliable, Weapon

Standard Action

Melee weapon

Target: One creature

Attack: d20 + 12 versus AC

Hit: 3d10 + 6 damage.

Miss: This is a reliable power. If you miss, you don't expend its use for the day.

Unstoppable   Fighter Utility 2

You let your adrenaline surge carry you through the battle.

Daily ◆ Martial

Minor Action   **Personal**

Effect: You gain 2d6 + 2 temporary hit points.

Armor, Weapons, and Gear

Regdar wears *black iron scale mail armor +1* (which resists 5 fire and 5 necrotic damage). He carries a *+2 greatsword* (+2d6 damage on a crit), a longbow, 20 arrows, a backpack, two sunrods, a bedroll, 50 feet of rope, and flint and steel. He has 100 gp.

Regdar, 8th-Level Human Fighter

Hit Points: 82 _____ Bloodied: 41

Healing Surge: 20   Surges per Day: 13

Initiative: +6   Speed: 5 squares

Alignment: Good

Ability Scores

	Score	Bonus*
STRENGTH	**20**	**+5**
CONSTITUTION	**15**	**+2**
DEXTERITY	**14**	**+2**
INTELLIGENCE	**10**	**+0**
WISDOM	**12**	**+1**
CHARISMA	**11**	**+0**

* Bonuses and penalties have already been calculated into your statistics and powers.

Defenses

AC 24   Fortitude 19   Reflex 16   Will 16

Basic Attacks

Melee Basic Attack (Greatsword)
    d20 + 16   1d10 + 8 damage

Ranged Basic Attack (Longbow)
    d20 + 8   1d10 damage

Class Features

Combat Challenge: Every time you attack an enemy, whether the attack hits or misses, you can choose to mark that target. The mark lasts until the end of your next turn. While a target is marked, it takes a –2 penalty to attack rolls if its attack doesn't include you as a target. A creature can be subject to only one mark at a time. A new mark supersedes a mark that was already in place.

In addition, whenever an enemy that is adjacent to you shifts or makes an attack that doesn't include you as a target, you can make a melee basic attack against that enemy as an immediate interrupt.

Combat Superiority: You gain a +2 bonus to opportunity attacks (+5 total with blade opportunist and combat reflexes feats).

Fighter Weapon Talent: You gain a +1 bonus to attack rolls when using two-handed weapons (already included in stats).

Feats

Action Surge: You gain a +3 bonus to attack rolls you make during any action you gained by spending an action point.

Blade Opportunist: You gain a +2 bonus to opportunity attack rolls with a heavy blade or a light blade.

Combat Reflexes: You gain a +1 bonus to opportunity attack rolls.

Durable: Increase your number of healing surges by 2 (already included).

Fast Runner: You gain a +2 bonus to speed when you charge or run.

Improved Initiative: +4 to initiative checks, already calculated into statistics

Power Attack: When making a melee attack, you can take a –2 penalty to the attack roll. If the attack hits, you gain a +3 bonus to the damage roll.

Skills

Acrobatics	**d20 + 4**
Arcana	**d20 + 2**
Athletics (trained)	**d20 + 11**
Bluff	**d20 + 2**
Diplomacy	**d20 + 2**
Dungeoneering	**d20 + 3**
Endurance (trained)	**d20 + 9**
Heal	**d20 + 3**
History	**d20 + 2**
Insight	**d20 + 3**
Intimidate (trained)	**d20 + 7**
Nature	**d20 + 3**
Perception	**d20 + 3**
Religion	**d20 + 2**
Stealth	**d20 + 4**
Streetwise (trained)	**d20 + 7**
Thievery	**d20 + 4**

Powers

Cleave   Fighter Attack 1

You hit one enemy, and then cleave into another.

At-Will ♦ Martial, Weapon

Standard Action   Melee weapon

Target: One creature

Attack: d20 + 16 versus AC

Hit: 1d10 + 8 damage, and an enemy adjacent to you takes 4 points of damage.

Reaping Strike   Fighter Attack 1

You punctuate your scything attacks with wicked jabs and small cutting blows that slip through your enemy's defenses.

At-Will ♦ Martial, Weapon

Standard Action   Melee weapon

Target: One creature

Attack: d20 + 16 versus AC

Hit: 1d10 + 8 damage

Miss: 5 points of damage

Sure Strike   Fighter Attack 1

You trade power for precision.

At-Will ♦ Martial, Weapon

Standard Action   Melee weapon

Target: One creature

Attack: d20 + 18 versus AC

Hit: 1d10 + 3 damage

Spinning Sweep   Fighter Attack 1

You spin beneath your enemy's guard with a long, powerful cut and then sweep your leg through his an instant later to knock him head over heels.

Encounter ♦ Martial, Weapon

Standard Action

Melee weapon

Target: One creature

Attack: d20 + 16 versus AC

Hit: 1d10 + 8 damage, and you knock the target prone.

Dance of Steel   Fighter Attack 3

Weaving your weapon in a graceful figure-eight, you lash out with a sudden attack.

Encounter ♦ Martial, Weapon

Standard Action

Melee weapon

Target: One creature

Attack: d20 + 16 versus AC

Hit: 2d10 + 8 damage, and the target is slowed until the end of your next turn.

Come and Get It   Fighter Attack 7

You call your opponents toward you and deliver a blow they will never forget.

Encounter ♦ Martial, Weapon

Standard Action   **Close** burst 3

Target: Each enemy in burst you can see

Effect: You pull each target 2 squares to a space adjacent to you. You cannot pull a target that cannot end adjacent to you. You then make a close attack targeting each adjacent enemy.

Attack: d20 + 16 versus AC

Hit: 1d10 + 8 damage.

Brute Strike

Fighter Attack 1

You shatter armor and bone with a ringing blow.

Daily ♦ Martial, Reliable, Weapon

Standard Action   **Melee** weapon

Target: One creature

continued on next page

Attack: d20 + 16 versus AC

Hit: 3d10 + 8 damage.

Miss: This is a reliable power. If you miss, you don't expend its use for the day.

Dizzying Blow   Fighter Attack 5

You crack your foe upside the head.

Daily ◆ Martial, Reliable, Weapon

Standard Action   **Melee** weapon

Target: One creature

Attack: d20 + 16 versus AC

Hit: 3d10 + 8 damage, and the target is immobilized (save ends).

Miss: This is a reliable power. If you miss, you don't expend its use for the day.

Unstoppable   Fighter Utility 2

You let your adrenaline surge carry you through the battle.

Daily ◆ Martial

Minor Action   **Personal**

Effect: You gain 2d6 + 2 temporary hit points.

Unbreakable   Fighter Utility 6

You steel yourself against a brutal attack.

Daily ◆ Martial

Immediate Reaction   **Personal**

Trigger: You are hit by an attack.

Effect: Reduce the damage from the attack by 7.

Armor, Weapons, and Gear

Regdar wears *scale mail armor +3*. He carries a *+3 greatsword* (+3d6 damage on a crit), a longbow, 20 arrows, a backpack, two sunrods, a bedroll, 50 feet of rope, and flint and steel. He has 1,000 gp.

Part II

Building a D&D Character

The 5th Wave   By Rich Tennant

"So, tell me about this new refinement to your encounter power."

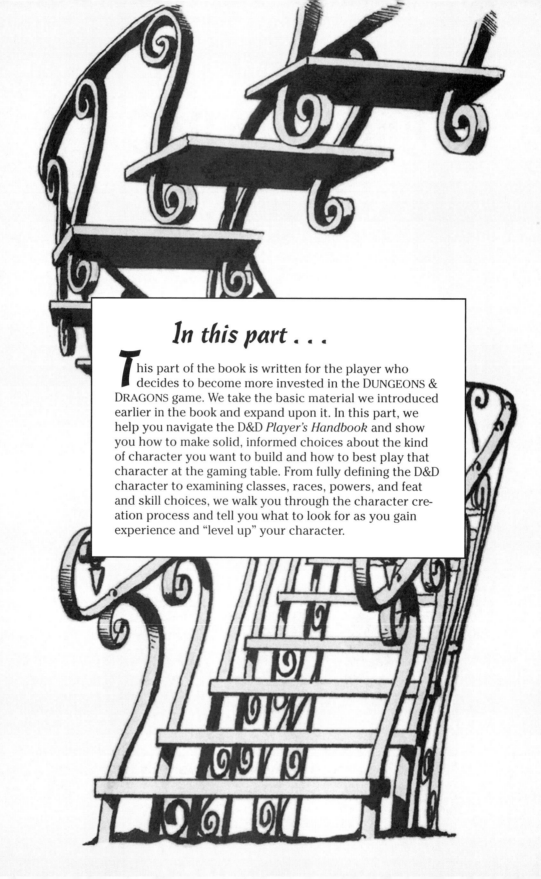

In this part . . .

This part of the book is written for the player who decides to become more invested in the DUNGEONS & DRAGONS game. We take the basic material we introduced earlier in the book and expand upon it. In this part, we help you navigate the D&D *Player's Handbook* and show you how to make solid, informed choices about the kind of character you want to build and how to best play that character at the gaming table. From fully defining the D&D character to examining classes, races, powers, and feat and skill choices, we walk you through the character creation process and tell you what to look for as you gain experience and "level up" your character.

Chapter 10

Defining Your Character

. . . .

In This Chapter

▶ Understanding the D&D character sheet

▶ Creating your own characters

▶ Defining D&D game statistics

. . . .

*T*his is the part of the book where you move on from basic game concepts and dive headfirst into the full DUNGEONS & DRAGONS rules experience. Don't worry, we help you through it. And when you're done, you'll see that even the advanced rules aren't that tough or scary. Just keep the basics from Part I in mind, and we'll handle the rest.

At this point, we figure that you've used one of the ready-to-play characters from Part I to play a game or two of D&D. Now you're ready to create your own character from the ground up. After all, creativity is one of the most compelling aspects of roleplaying, and it all starts with your player character.

In this chapter, you take a more detailed look at the D&D character. We go over all the basic statistics again, but this time we delve into all the possible things you can do with them. This chapter helps you navigate the rest of Part II, explaining the parts of a full D&D character sheet and then pointing you to the information you need to fill out each section as you create your own character.

Your Character Sheet

A D&D character record sheet contains all the pertinent information and game statistics for your player character. A character sheet can be as simple as a blank piece of paper upon which you've written down all your character's statistics. Or you can get a premade, blank character sheet and fill it in. Blank character sheets are available online at www.dndinsider.com. You can also photocopy the two-page character sheet in the D&D *Player's Handbook* (see Figure 10-1). Yet another option is to pick up a pack of D&D *Character Sheets* at your local game or hobby store. Use whichever version of the character sheet that you feel most comfortable with. The information that follows pertains to all versions of D&D character sheets.

Figure 10-1:
The
character
sheet from
the *Player's*
Handbook.

You can approach the creation of a D&D character in many different ways. Some people start out knowing exactly the kind of character they want to play, from race and class to specific roleplaying quirks and background information. Others build their characters around the ability scores they generated. Then there are those who know one aspect of the character they want to play (the race or class, for example) and then decide on the rest after they see how their scores line up. These are all good ways to approach character creation. Throughout the chapters in this part of the book, we provide details to help you make informed decisions, no matter which approach you take.

Filling Out the Character Sheet

You can fill out your character sheet in any order that makes sense to you. We discuss the various sections of the character sheet in the order they appear, however, so you can more easily reference the material.

Names

There's a place on the front of the character sheet for your name and your character's name. A cool, evocative character name helps set the personality of your character and contributes to the tone of the campaign, so choose your character's name wisely. A campaign with characters named Elfy,

Sugarplum, Bennie, and Toejam has a very different feel than one that features Regdar, Lidda, Wellyn, and Jerek. Talk with your Dungeon Master and the other players to decide what kind of names (and what kind of campaign) you all want to play, and then name your character accordingly. A good, solid name is important, and even though the space for a name appears at the top of your character sheet, this is the piece of information you'll probably record last, after you see how the rest of your character's statistics turn out and you've had a chance to think about it.

The D&D *Player's Handbook* provides lists of sample names by character race in Chapter 3. Feel free to use one of these names or to draw inspiration from them as you craft your own name for your character.

Class and level

Out of all the characteristics, class has the most profound effect on your character's adventuring career. Class determines a character's role in the adventuring party and provides a character with special qualities that set him or her apart from the rest of the team. You can select a class and then apply your ability scores appropriately, or you can determine your ability scores and select a class that takes best advantage of your results. Most people choose their class first and then assign ability scores as appropriate for that class.

Character level is usually easy when you're creating a starting character: All characters start at 1st level — unless the Dungeon Master gives you different instructions. (Sometimes a DM has characters start at a level more suitable for the campaign he or she plans to run, such as 3rd level if the DM wants the characters to have a little experience prior to the start of the campaign, or 11th level if the DM wants to run a paragon-tier campaign right out of the gate.)

Chapter 11 provides detailed information on choosing a class. Chapter 18 discusses levels and character advancement for when you're ready to improve your character.

Level modifier

In many places on the character sheet, you can find a reference to "1/2 LVL." This is your level modifier, which is a bonus to the most important things you do: attack, defend, and use skills. It's equal to half your character level (round down). For example, a 5th-level character adds a modifier of +2 to the character's attack rolls, skill checks, and defense scores. When you're playing a 1st-level character, your level modifier is +0.

Path and destiny

When your character reaches 11th level, you get to select a *paragon path*. A paragon path is a sort of advanced class that lets you specialize your character; for example, paragon paths available to the fighter class include the iron vanguard, kensei, pit fighter, and swordmaster. Your character doesn't stop gaining levels in his or her original class when you choose a paragon path; instead, you gain the benefits of both your character's paragon path and class as your character reaches levels 11 through 20.

Epic destiny takes over when you finish up your paragon path. At 21st level, you get to choose your character's path to immortality. At the highest levels of the game, your character transcends the merely mortal and becomes a hero of mythological proportions such as an archmage, a demigod, or an eternal seeker. As with the paragon path, your character continues to advance in his or her class, but you gain access to abilities of incredible power. After all, your character is contending with cosmic catastrophes and evil gods by the time he or she reaches epic level!

If you're confused by all these decision points, here's the good news about your paragon path and epic destiny: You don't have to pick them for a long, long time. Leave these lines blank for now. Play your character for a few adventures and make your decision about your paragon path when the character gets closer to 11th level.

Race and size

Another key defining aspect of a D&D character is the fantasy race the character belongs to. In addition to humans, the fantasy worlds of D&D are inhabited by all kinds of amazing, intelligent beings. Want to play an enigmatic elf? How about a dour dwarf? Maybe a dangerously curious halfling? Race provides more than a colorful hook for roleplaying. Each race has ability adjustments and special abilities to help set it apart from the others. After you've decided on a race for your character, record it on the character sheet.

Most of the character races, including dwarves, elves, and humans, are Medium in size. That's the standard, and there are no special bonuses or penalties associated with characters of this size. Both Medium and Small characters occupy a single square on the battle grid. However, Small characters can't use weapons that would be two-handed weapons for Medium characters. For more details about Small characters, see the halfling entry in Chapter 13.

Chapter 13 discusses the core D&D races in more detail and provides the information you need to choose the best race for the character you want to play.

Alignment, deity, and personality

Where does your character fit into the ongoing struggle between good and evil? It's a big question, but the answer to it (or at least the trip to discover the answer) pervades every fantasy epic from *The Lord of the Rings* to the *Tales of King Arthur and the Knights of the Round Table*. The same is true of any DUNGEONS & DRAGONS campaign. In the D&D game, your character's general moral attitude is represented by the character's *alignment*. Whether you choose to be lawful good or chaotic evil, alignment is a tool for developing your character's identity in the game. Alignment isn't designed to be restrictive, and characters can always behave inconsistently from time to time. Your alignment choices are described on page 19 of the *Player's Handbook,* and include

- ✔ **Good:** Aiding people in need is the right thing to do. Laws or systems that keep you from doing that need to be changed.

- ✔ **Lawful good:** Just laws and honorable codes of conduct are the best way to protect the weak from oppression. Laws or systems that aren't working should be reformed, not abandoned.

- ✔ **Unaligned:** You're willing to help others, but you do so with the expectation of some reward.

✔ **Evil:** Evil characters don't care if they hurt other people as long as they get ahead. They believe that the purpose of law and order is to protect the privileged few and keep the weak oppressed. Check with your DM before you choose this alignment!

✔ **Chaotic evil:** Chaotic evil characters take anything they want from anyone who can't stop them. The only law they respect is simply "might makes right." Check with your DM before you choose this alignment!

The thing to remember with alignment is that players should talk about their choices before setting anything in stone. For example, your Dungeon Master may have a particular type of campaign in mind, one that works best if the characters all have complementary alignments. Sometimes the tension generated by having a chaotic evil character in with a group of lawful good ones can be fun, but often such deviations lead to troublesome play and hard feelings. Better to all move in compatible directions than in competitive ones when playing D&D.

Another thing to consider when choosing your character's alignment is that D&D is really about heroes. The game works best when player characters choose alignments that aren't evil in outlook. Antiheroes and villains have their place in fantasy stories, but the most memorable, long-lasting D&D campaigns focus on the good guys.

Along with alignment, a character's choice of deity can help create a background and an allegiance that give you more opportunities for roleplaying. Is your fighter a casual follower of Avandra, the goddess of luck and adventure? Or is he a committed servant of Bahamut, the god of honor and justice? A character's deity is a personal choice; each deity description in the *Player's Handbook* offers suggestions for character races or classes that might favor that deity. Now, every campaign is different and may have a different selection of deities. Your Dungeon Master will tell you if you should select a deity from the list in the *Player's Handbook* or from some other source (such as the *Forgotten Realms Campaign Guide*). Your choice of deity is more important if you're playing a cleric; see Chapter 15 for information on the cleric's Channel Divinity feats.

Finally, the last component of your character's roleplaying characteristics is personality. The concept of choosing personality traits may seem pedestrian compared to electing to fight for good or evil or deciding which mythological deity your character follows, but it's also the place where you can put your own completely unique stamp on your character. Is your human fighter a glum, skeptical fellow who expects the worst at every turn, or is he a charming and reckless rake who laughs in the face of danger?

Chapter 2 of the *Player's Handbook* offers some advice for picking out personality traits that might surface in social encounters, in discussions of decisions with other characters in the party, or when deadly peril threatens.

In the end, alignment, patron deity, and personality traits are mostly for flavor. They're here to help you roleplay your character better. Use them as much or as little as you like.

Character description

The next section of the character sheet provides a place to record information that helps describe your character but has little effect on game play. Age, height, and weight for your character are determined by personal choice (although your DM has the right to veto really unusual choices such as characters 11 feet tall, heroes who are very young children, and so on). The racial descriptions in Chapter 3 of the *Player's Handbook* provide guidance on the average height and weight of various character races, and you can assume that most characters begin their adventuring careers as young adults.

What you put in the Gender is a personal choice that has almost no effect in the game. Male and female characters are totally equal. Chapter 3 in the *Player's Handbook* talks about the general appearance of each of the races, and you can use the descriptions there as a starting point if you want to go into more details about how your character appears.

Check out the D&D Character Visualizer at www.dndinsider.com. It allows you to choose your character's race and gender and then create the look of your character. You add armor and weapons, decide on hair styles and colors, and generally create a cool-looking D&D character that you can print out and use on your character sheet. It's a fun way to design the look of your character.

Ability scores

In addition to class, race, and level, a character's ability scores provide the base upon which your character grows and develops. Consider ability scores the frame upon which the rest of your statistics are hung. Every character has six ability scores: Strength, Constitution, Dexterity, Intelligence, Wisdom, and Charisma. These scores provide modifiers that affect everything from attacks and damage rolls to skill checks and saving throws.

Chapter 13 provides more information about ability scores and how they're used.

Hit points and healing surges

When combat begins, your character's hit points (hp) are literally all that stands between the character and certain death. Class and level determine your character's hit point total, adjusted by your character's Constitution score. Lose a few hit points in battle? No problem! Your character continues to function without any ill effects as long as he or she has at least 1 hit point remaining. That's heroic and fantastic, and that's pure D&D.

Your character class determines how many hit points your character has at 1st level. For example, a 1st-level fighter has a number of hit points equal to 15 + Constitution score, whereas a 1st-level wizard has 10 + Constitution score. If your fighter character has a Constitution score of 14, you have 29 hit points at 1st level. Your character class also dictates how many hit points you gain when you reach 2nd level and each time you go up a level after that. (In the case of the fighter, it's 6 hit points per level.)

Two important numbers are derived from your hit point score:

- **Bloodied number:** Your bloodied number is simply half your normal maximum hit points; this is the "halfway" point to falling unconscious. Many characters and monsters have special powers or abilities that trigger when they become bloodied or when the opponent they're fighting becomes bloodied.

- **Healing surge value:** Your healing surge value is one-quarter of your normal maximum hit points. Most healing effects in the game restore a number of hit points equal to your healing surge value. For example, if your character has 17 hit points, his bloodied number is 8, and his healing surge value is 4.

    The number of times each day you can use a healing surge is determined by your character class. For example, a fighter has a number of healing surges equal to 9 + Constitution modifier. The fighter with a 14 Constitution (+2 Con modifier) can use 11 healing surges per day.

When your character takes damage in battle or through some other method (such as a trap or a natural hazard), that damage reduces your character's hit point total. When your character's hit point total reaches 0, he or she falls unconscious and is dying. When your hit points reach a negative number equal to your bloodied number, your character dies.

Healing can restore lost hit points back up to your original total. However, most healing effects require you to spend a healing surge. When your character is out of healing surges, that's it — no more healing effects requiring a surge can work on that character. It's time to call it quits and retreat from the dungeon for the day before someone gets killed!

Senses

Your character sheet calls out two senses-related skills, Insight and Perception. Insight is used to counter Bluff checks and to give you a sense of another character's motives and attitudes. Perception describes your character's ability to spot, hear, or otherwise sense danger and notice things that aren't obvious. Insight and Perception are Wisdom skills, but even if you character isn't trained in these skills, you need to know what your modifiers are. Your modifier is equal to your level modifier plus your Wisdom modifier, plus 5 if you character is trained in the skill.

Sometimes you don't know whether you should be making an Insight or a Perception check, so the Dungeon Master will instead check for you. This is handled using your passive score. Your *passive perception* score, for example, represents how hard it is for someone to escape your notice when you're alert but not looking for anything in particular. It's equal to 10 + your Perception modifier.

See Chapter 16 for more information on skills.

Initiative

Initiative is a Dexterity check. It determines the order in which characters and monsters act in combat. Your character's initiative modifier is equal to his level modifier plus his Dexterity modifier. You can improve your character's initiative even more by selecting the Improved Initiative feat. (See Chapter 6 of the *Player's Handbook* for this and other feat descriptions.)

Defenses

There are more dangers in D&D worlds than simply being attacked by sword, bow, or claw. Environmental hazards, magical attacks, poisons, and mental attacks are among the numerous other dangers adventurers face on a daily basis.

Your character has four defenses: Armor Class, Fortitude defense, Reflex defense, and Will defense. Each monster attack or villain power your character encounters in the game strikes at one of those four defenses. Your character's defense score is the attack roll result — the target number — that an opponent needs to achieve to hit your character with an attack targeting that particular defense:

 ✔ **Fortitude defense:** This measures your character's ability to withstand attacks against his health or physical endurance, such as poison, disease, and effects that might knock him down or shove him around.

 ✔ **Reflex defense:** This reflects your character's ability to react quickly enough to avoid area attacks such as breath weapons and *fireball* spells, or to evade attacks such as pit traps and falling boulders.

- ✔ **Will defense:** This defense measures your character's resistance to mental influence and mental-attacking magical effects, such as psionic attacks and illusion spells.

- ✔ **Armor Class (AC):** This represents how hard it is for opponents to hit your character in physical combat.

Each of your character's defense scores begins at 10 and is improved by your level modifier and an ability score modifier relevant to that type of defense, like so:

> Defense = 10 + 1/2 level + ability modifier (+ armor bonus for Armor Class)

The abilities that apply vary for each of your character's defenses. Each defense allows you to add the *better* ability modifier of two different abilities, as follows:

- ✔ **Fortitude defense:** Add the better of your Strength or Constitution modifiers

- ✔ **Reflex defense:** Add the better of your Intelligence or Dexterity modifiers

- ✔ **Will defense:** Add the better of your Wisdom or Charisma modifiers

- ✔ **Armor Class:** Add the better of your Intelligence or Dexterity modifiers (but only if you aren't wearing heavy armor)

For example, Regdar is a 1st-level fighter with Strength 18 (+4), Constitution 14 (+2), Dexterity 13 (+1), Intelligence 10 (+0), Wisdom 12 (+1), and Charisma 11 (+0). He wears scale armor (+7 armor bonus) but doesn't carry a shield, because he prefers to fight with a greatsword, which requires both hands. His defenses are

- ✔ **Fortitude defense:** 14 (10 + 4 for his Strength modifier)

- ✔ **Reflex defense:** 11 (10 + 1 for his Dexterity modifier)

- ✔ **Will defense:** 11 (10 + 1 for his Wisdom modifier)

- ✔ **Armor Class:** 17 (10 + 7 for his scale armor; he doesn't add his Dexterity modifier because scale armor is heavy armor)

Fighters gain a +2 bonus to Fortitude defense, so Regdar's Fortitude defense is a little better than shown here. (It goes up to 16.) Most classes grant a bonus to one or more defenses. Your race and feat selection may influence your defenses, too. For example, humans have a racial ability that adds +1 to Fortitude, Reflex, and Will defense, so Regdar's defenses are actually a bit higher than shown in the preceding list when the final calculation is made — counting the class and racial bonuses, they're Fort 17, Ref 12, Will 12, AC 17. Finally, as your character defeats monsters and wins treasures, he may find magic items that improve his defenses even more!

Speed

A character's speed shows how far the character can move (as measured in 5-foot squares on a battle grid) in a single move action. Your character's speed is determined by his or her race and by the type of armor that he or she is wearing. Most characters have a speed of 6, or 5 if they wear heavy armor. Elves have a speed of 7 (they're quick!), and dwarves have a speed of 5 — but dwarves aren't slowed down by wearing heavy armor.

Action points

Action points are special resources that you can spend to gain an extra action in your turn. For example, you might move, use an attack power, and then spend an action point to use another attack power — all in the same round! Normally you begin each day with 1 action point. When you spend it, it's gone for the day, but as you adventure, you may earn additional action points.

Basic attacks

Your character sheet provides space to record your character's basic attack options — the attacks he or she uses when he or she isn't using a specific attack power. Most characters carry one or two melee weapons and a ranged weapon of some kind. Record the attack bonus for each weapon your character might use. Remember that, when attacking, you make an attack roll with a d20 and add your attack bonus to try to get a result that's equal to or greater than your target's AC.

Your character's attack bonus and damage dealt with a melee weapon is determined as follows:

> Attack bonus (melee weapon) = level modifier + Strength modifier + weapon proficiency bonus + class or feat bonuses (if any)

> Damage (melee weapon) = base weapon damage + Strength modifier + class or feat bonuses (if any)

The weapon proficiency bonus and base damage are characteristics of the weapon; see the weapon chart in Chapter 7 of the *Player's Handbook*. For example, Regdar's basic attack bonus with his greatsword is +8 = level modifier +0, Strength modifier +4, +3 for being proficient with the greatsword, and +1 for the fighter class feature Weapon Talent. The greatsword deals 1d10 damage, + 4 for Regdar's Strength bonus.

You can calculate your character's attack bonus with a ranged weapon as follows:

> Attack bonus (ranged weapon) = level modifier + Dexterity modifier + weapon proficiency bonus – range penalty

The *range penalty* exists only when your character is attacking at long range for that ranged weapon; it's simply a –2 on your attack roll. The weapon chart in Chapter 7 of the *Player's Handbook* shows the long range and maximum range for all ranged weapons.

For example, Lidda's attack bonus with her shortbow is +6 = level modifier +0, Dexterity modifier +4, and +2 for being proficient with the shortbow. The shortbow has a range of 15/30 squares; if Lidda shoots at a target 16 to 30 squares (80 to 150 feet) away, she takes a –2 penalty on her attack.

Every weapon brings its own statistics to the table, and you should record these on your character sheet as well. A weapon has a damage rating that tells you what die (or dice) to roll to deal damage after a successful attack. In general, high-accuracy weapons deal a little less damage than low-accuracy weapons, so when choosing your character's weapons, you should decide whether you want to hit more often or hit harder.

Usually, you'll use an attack power instead of a basic attack. Basic attacks tend to come up in three common circumstances: when you use the charge action, when you make an opportunity attack, and when enabled by another character's use of a power that grants extra attacks.

Skills

Every character has some amount of aptitude in talents ranging from Acrobatics to Thievery. (You can find the complete list of skills on your character sheet.) Skills aren't often very useful in combat, but they're great for solving other types of challenges — for example, climbing a cliff, bluffing your way past a guard, or puzzling out an arcane mystery.

Depending on your character class, your character begins play with *training* in three to six skills. In addition, humans begin with one extra skill. The class description provides a list of skills you can choose from. In addition, your class may specify one or more skills that your character is automatically trained in. For example, wizards are automatically trained in Arcana, and they choose three other trained skills from the following list: Diplomacy, Dungeoneering, History, Insight, Nature, and Religion.

Every skill is based on one of your character's six ability scores. For example, the key ability for the Acrobatics skill is Dexterity, whereas the key ability for Heal is Wisdom. Your character's skill check bonus for each skill is

> Skill bonus = level modifier + ability modifier (+5 if trained) – armor check penalty (if any)

The armor check penalty applies only to a few skills such as Acrobatics or Stealth, and only if your character wears armor that actually imposes a penalty; see Chapter 17 for details. It's harder for your character to be stealthy when wearing 40 pounds of iron!

For more information on skills, see Chapter 16.

Feats

Feats provide characters with special edges or improve existing abilities in meaningful ways. A character gains a feat at 1st level and at every even-numbered level as he or she advances. Human characters gain a bonus feat at 1st level, so you get to select two feats when creating a human character. In addition, certain classes gain bonus feats.

Jot down the name of the feat or feats you select on your character sheet, as well as a brief description of the benefit it provides or the page number of the *Player's Handbook* where you can look up the details when you need to.

For more details about feats, see Chapter 15.

Race and class features

Your character's race and class provide certain special abilities. Record these in the appropriate section on the character sheet.

For more information on racial features, see Chapter 12. For more information about class abilities, see Chapter 11.

Powers

The powers section of the character sheet is where you record the various powers your character knows. After character class, your selection of powers is the most important part of your character — these are what you use to defeat monsters and overcome obstacles. You can get by with basic attacks, but pretty much any power you know is better than a basic attack.

Powers come in four basic varieties:

- **At-will powers:** These are weak attacks that are never exhausted. A 1st-level character begins with two at-will powers.

- **Encounter powers:** These powers are stronger than at-will powers, but you can use each encounter power only once per fight. Once you've used it, it's not available for the rest of that encounter. A 1st-level character begins with one 1st-level encounter power.

- **Daily powers:** These are the best attack powers, but you have to choose the right moment to use them — when you expend a daily power, you don't get it back for the rest of the day. If your character still has a lot of dungeon-delving to do before he or she can rest, you might regret using up daily powers too early. A 1st-level character begins with one 1st-level daily power.

- **Utility powers:** These powers aren't attacks but can often be quite useful in a fight. Utility powers may be defensive tactics or spells, special tricks for getting around the battlefield, opportunities to call on your healing surges, or generally useful things like being able to turn invisible. Depending on the specific power, you might be able to use it in every fight as an encounter power, or you might be able to use it only once per day as a daily power. Your character doesn't gain any utility powers until he or she reaches 2nd level.

Magic items

Record the magic items your character owns in the magic items section of the character sheet. Most magic items fill body slots, and you can use only one item in each slot at a time. For example, characters have a neck slot that can be filled by either an amulet or a cloak. If you wear both an amulet and a cloak, you must choose which one provides its magical benefits. (For more about magic items, see Chapter 20.)

Some magic items contain powers that you can use. For items with daily powers, you're restricted in how many of those you can use in a day, depending on your character's level.

Making informed choices

The rest of Part II walks you through the various components of your character and gives you the information and advice you need to make decisions about character creation. Which class is right for you? How should you distribute ability scores? What feats and skills should you select? What kind of gear should your character carry around? These questions and more are examined in Chapters 11 through 18. Take the chapters one at a time, and by the end, you'll be ready to make informed choices throughout the character-creation process.

For more about magic items, see Chapter 20 in this book and Chapter 7 in the *Player's Handbook*.

Other equipment

Characters need equipment, and adventuring gear of all kinds is available to get your character through the toughest dungeons. List the equipment your character hauls around in the spaces provided on the character sheet.

For more information about adventuring gear, see Chapter 17.

Chapter 11

Choosing a Class

* *

In This Chapter

▶ Choosing your character's role

▶ Exploring the fighter class

▶ Examining the rogue class

▶ Understanding the wizard class

▶ Understanding the cleric class

▶ Finding out about other classes in the game

* *

Characters in a DUNGEONS & DRAGONS game all share a thirst for excitement and a need to adventure. They just have to explore the dark places of the world and find increasingly difficult challenges with which to test themselves. Where characters differ is in the way they approach each adventure and what knowledge and abilities they bring to the table. A character's class, in large part, determines this approach.

Your character's class is his or her profession or vocation. The class you select determines much of what your character can do in the game. Your character's combat prowess, powers, special abilities, skills, and other qualities are defined and given boundaries by his or her class.

When you're creating a character, the class you want to play suggests where you should assign ability scores and even hints at which races are most appropriate to play. In all cases, however, these are only suggestions. D&D is a game about choices and options, not restrictions. You can always play against type if that better fits the concept you have for the character you want to play.

Chapter 4 of the *Player's Handbook* goes into greater depth on character classes and benefits. Check it out after you read through this chapter.

Bring what your friends need

When you're choosing the class of your next character, ask whether any of the four roles (controller, defender, leader, and striker) aren't yet represented in the adventuring party your character is joining. If the party currently includes no defenders, you can help out everyone by creating a fighter or a paladin. Does the party already have two leaders? Maybe you should create something other than a cleric or a warlord. If the party mix is well-balanced already, you can create a character for whichever role you think you'd like the most. Defenders and strikers are good choices for beginning players.

Character Roles

Each character class in the game is designed to fit into one of four general combat roles: controller, defender, leader, or striker. Battling fearsome monsters and evil villains is one of the most common (and dangerous) challenges your character faces in the DUNGEONS & DRAGONS game, so every character needs to be able to contribute to victory in a combat encounter. Characters can do a variety of interesting things outside of combat too, of course, but fighting is the bread and butter of most fantastic heroes.

Much like the players filling positions for a team sport, characters of different roles have different jobs in combat. A baseball team wouldn't be very good if every player on the field were a catcher; similarly, an adventuring party isn't all that effective if every character is a wizard. An adventuring party needs tough characters who can take damage and keep monsters away from less robust party members and characters who can heal and protect their friends, or else the wizards will get chopped to pieces by the monsters.

The controller

Controllers affect large numbers of enemies at the same time and usually attack them from long range. They often hit several enemies at once with powers dealing average damage — when you add it all up, controllers deal the most damage of any character in the game. Controllers also excel at hindering enemies by creating effects that slow them down, weaken them, confuse them, or box them in behind dangerous obstacles. The wizard is an example of a controller.

Because controllers are so good on offense, they have to pay for it in other ways — in this case, their defense. Controllers have low hit points, lower defenses, and can't stand up to a lot of punishment.

Play a controller if you like the idea of blasting several enemies at a time from a distance.

The defender

Defenders are tough. They have the highest defenses in the game and loads of hit points. Their job is to stand at the front of the party and keep enemies from getting to the rest of the characters. Wizards and other less-armored characters might think of defenders as "meat shields," but they don't dare set foot into a dungeon without one or more defenders around.

To make sure monsters don't ignore them or move by them, defenders usually have special abilities that keep monsters close by and punish enemies that ignore them to attack other characters. Defenders don't have much ability to attack at range, but their melee attacks are quite good. The fighter is an example of a defender, as is the paladin.

Play a defender if you like being the toughest character at the table and standing toe-to-toe with fearsome monsters. You'll take a pounding in many fights, but you'll usually still be standing when the dust settles. Any other character with a different role trying to handle that job would be toast — or maybe even dinner for the monsters.

The leader

Leaders help the other characters to stay on their feet and fight better. They inspire, heal, and support the rest of the party. All leaders have innate healing abilities and can give other characters opportunities to regain hit points lost to enemy attacks. Leaders also have many powers that provide additional healing and protection to their allies. Sometimes the healing ability of a leader is all that stands between a party of adventurers and certain death. Clerics and warlords are examples of leaders.

Leaders are reasonably tough and can stand shoulder-to-shoulder with the party's defenders, but leaders have the weakest offense of any characters; their attack powers tend to serve as "target designation" that help other characters to hit affected enemies even harder.

Leaders don't get to tell other players what to do; in the context of this character role, "leader" really means "healer, protector, and targeter." Leader powers support those functions.

Play a leader if you like helping out other players and like the idea of being the glue that holds the rest of the party together.

How many of each?

The D&D roleplaying game is built around the idea that the typical adventuring party consists of five characters of different roles. So, four of the positions on the team are filled by a controller, a defender, a leader, and a striker. The fifth position we recommend is a second defender. If your DM decides to run a six-character party, we recommend that a second striker fill the sixth position. Larger parties are possible, but they require a lot more work on the part of the DM. In general, the game works best with four to six players (each playing a different character) and a DM.

The striker

Strikers excel at focused damage; no other character can deal out damage to single targets as fast as a striker can. They're highly mobile and extremely deadly. Strikers cooperate with defenders to take down enemies fast, or they slip through enemy lines to take out important targets before disappearing back into the shadows. Rogues, rangers, and warlocks are all examples of strikers.

Strikers need to get close to deal their damage, but they pay for it with weaker defenses and fewer hit points. Sometimes strikers find themselves fighting alone — if you're going to slip through the lines to take down the enemy boss, you'll usually wind up with the monsters standing between you and the safety of your friends. Consequently, strikers have abilities that allow them to evade and escape from monsters they don't want to fight so that they can focus on the high-value targets.

Play a striker if you like hit-and-run tactics and dishing out lots of damage to a single target at a time.

Class Descriptions

Each class description in the *Player's Handbook* provides key information about the class. Where should you put your best ability scores? How many hit points does a character of this class have? What skills can this character select? What weapons and armor can characters with this class use? What powers are available to this class? What special class features do members of this class possess?

All these questions are covered in the class descriptions. In the rest of this chapter, we explore some of the answers as they relate to the four iconic D&D classes — fighter, rogue, wizard, and cleric — so that you can decide which one you want to play.

Character builds

Your character's particular combination of ability scores, class, power selection, and feat selection is sometimes referred to as a *build*. The idea behind a build is to choose things complementary to each other; for example, you don't want to set Strength as your highest ability score and then choose a lot of powers that use Wisdom as the key ability. Fortunately, the 4th Edition *Player's Handbook* provides you with two suggested builds for each character class to help you avoid mistakes like that. For example, the *Player's Handbook* provides guidance for creating a Great Weapon Fighter or a Guardian Fighter. There are plenty of other ways to build fighter characters, but these are very easy builds that have a lot of support throughout the game rules. You can find plenty of powers and feats that work well with these two fighter builds.

Your character's build influences the way you allocate ability scores and your selections for race, powers, feats, skills, and arms and armor. We touch on these builds throughout Part II of this book; but in this chapter, we concentrate on the four basic classes (fighter, rogue, wizard, and cleric).

The fighter is the best class

Characters of the fighter class have the best all-around melee capability — they can take damage and they can dish it out in close combat. Deciding to play a fighter means that your character is going to have a lot of hit points for his or her level, good melee attack powers, and a direct approach to game play. That makes the fighter class particularly attractive to new players and players who don't want to deal with the intricacies of magic and rituals.

The fighter fills the defender role. Good armor, high hit points, and a high number of healing surges allow the fighter to absorb punishment that other characters have little hope of withstanding for very long. Fighters are proficient in all simple and military weapons and most armor types, including heavy armors like chainmail and scale. The fighter's power choices are almost all melee attacks, so the fighter is well suited to take the battle right to the monsters.

The two fighter builds described in the *Player's Handbook* are

- ✔ **Great Weapon Fighter:** You want to deal the most damage in melee that you can. You disdain a shield and use the biggest two-handed weapon you can find — usually a greatsword, greataxe, or maul. Powers that deal a lot of damage are good for you.

- ✔ **Guardian Fighter:** You want to be the toughest defender you can be. You use a heavy shield and fight with a one-handed weapon such as a longsword. Your powers deal decent damage but are really good for boosting your own defense and hindering your enemies' actions.

Characters of any race can be successful fighters, although the best race choices for a fighter character are those that offer a bonus to Strength or Constitution. Of the races described in this book, humans and dwarves make the best overall fighters (although elves and halflings can be good Guardian Fighters).

The *Player's Handbook* offers additional player character races. Of the additional races, the dragonborn really takes to the fighter class thanks to a good Strength adjustment. If you want to play a powerful melee-oriented fighter, you might want to consider playing a dragonborn.

Abilities

If you decide to play a fighter, you should put your highest ability score in Strength. Most fighter powers are based on Strength. A good Constitution gives your character extra hit points and provides access to good feats for big weapons such as axes or hammers. Dexterity helps your character's Reflex defense and gives you access to feats for swords, flails, shields, and spears. Finally, a high Wisdom score helps your Will defense and boosts your Combat Superiority class feature.

Fighter class features

Class features are generally intended to provide a character with some built-in ability to meet his or her role in an adventuring party. The fighter has three class features:

- ✔ **Combat Challenge:** You can choose to mark enemies your fighter attacks, whether or not the attack is successful. When an enemy is marked, he takes a penalty if he attacks anyone other than your character. You can also make an attack when an adjacent enemy shifts away from your fighter or attacks someone else. Combat Challenge, therefore, makes enemies fight you instead of your friends. Because your character is a defender, this is exactly what you want the monsters to do.

- ✔ **Combat Superiority:** Your opportunity attacks are especially dangerous. You can add your Wisdom modifier to any opportunity attacks you make, so this class feature rewards you for having a high Wisdom score.

- ✔ **Weapon Talent:** Choose whether your character is a one- or two-handed weapon user. (Usually, Great Weapon Fighters favor two-handed weapons, and Guardian Fighters prefer one-handed weapons so they can use a shield.) You gain a +1 to attacks with weapons of the type you choose. Because your fighter will almost always attack that way, this ability is pretty much a free +1 on every attack roll you ever make.

Hit points and healing surges

The fighter begins with hit points equal to 15 + his or her Constitution score. Every level thereafter, the fighter gains 6 more hit points. If you like to play a character with a lot of hit points, you can't do better than the fighter class. The fighter also has a lot of healing surges available (9 + Constitution modifier), which means the fighter can be healed over and over again in the course of a day of adventuring.

Skills

You won't be playing a scholar when you play a fighter. Fighters have a small selection of class skills. The class skills most important to a fighter are Athletics, Endurance, and Intimidate. Athletics includes climbing, jumping, and swimming — the day may come when your character's life depends on making a spectacular leap or scaling a cliff.

Fighter powers

Fighter powers are called *exploits*. A 1st-level fighter knows two 1st-level at-will exploits, one 1st-level encounter exploit, and one 1st-level daily exploit. All these are melee attacks. As your fighter gains levels, he gains the opportunity to learn a few powers that aren't melee attacks, but melee attacks remain the fighter's bread and butter throughout his career.

A number of higher-level fighter exploits feature special effects based on the weapon your character uses, so keep your eyes peeled for power choices that reward your character's weapon choice. For example, the 3rd-level encounter exploit *crushing blow* allows you to add your Constitution modifier to damage if your character is wielding an axe, a hammer, or a mace.

The rogue is the best class

The rogue relies on stealth, sneak attacks, and mastery of skills to get to the center of a dungeon and back again. Rogues come in all varieties, from the swashbuckler to the expert spy who uses craftiness and a silver tongue to accomplish the nearly impossible. Although quite capable in combat, a rogue's job in any adventuring group is to also be versatile and resourceful. A rogue usually has a trick up his or her sleeve to get the team out of any jam. Need a lock opened? Need a trap disarmed? Need to sneak past the sleeping dragon? The rogue is the character for the job.

In combat, rogues are strikers. They're very, very good at dealing a lot of damage to one enemy at a time. As you might expect, they don't have the staying power of fighters in pitched battles — but rogues have a knack for getting out of scrapes and choosing their moment to shine. They prefer to make opportunistic strikes from the shadows, use hit-and-run attacks, or rely on ranged weapons to attack without exposing themselves to undue danger.

Rogues favor light armor and light weapons. They're proficient in leather armor and place their trust in agility and wits instead of shields or iron. Their weapons are small, easy to hide, and quick to draw — the dagger, the short sword, the hand crossbow. Precision is more important than power.

The two rogue builds in the *Player's Handbook* are

- ✔ **Brawny Rogue:** You prefer offensive powers and are willing to trade some defense in order to deal more damage. You rely on your sneak attack class feature and favor powers that reward a good Strength score.

- ✔ **Trickster Rogue:** You prefer powers that misdirect and deceive your foes. You can deal plenty of damage, but you prefer powers that leave you with an easy escape route; striking and moving away is better than dishing out a little more damage. Powers that reward a good Charisma score work well for you.

All races make decent rogues, so a rogue character can be created using any of the D&D races. Of the races described in this book, halflings and elves make the best rogues due to their natural Dexterity bonus. Humans also make decent rogues, especially because of the extra skill that human characters begin play with. (See Chapter 12 for more on races.)

The *Player's Handbook* offers additional player character races. Of the additional races, the tiefling makes an excellent Trickster Rogue due to her bonus to Charisma and her racial skill bonuses to Bluff and Stealth.

Abilities

If you decide to play a rogue, you should put your highest ability score in Dexterity. Almost all your powers use Dexterity attacks, and a high Dexterity score also helps out your character's Reflex defense and Armor Class. A good Strength score helps your character's Fortitude defense and improves many of the powers important to the Brawny Rogue build. Likewise, a high Charisma score provides your character with a good Will defense and is very useful for many powers in the Trickster Rogue build.

Rogue class features

A rogue's class features boost his or her damage output, as you would expect from a striker. These include

- ✔ **First Strike:** At the start of each encounter, a rogue has combat advantage against any enemy who hasn't acted yet. This means that you get your sneak attack bonus damage (see the Sneak Attack bullet in this list) against enemies whose initiative you beat. (This means that the Improved Initiative feat is very good for you!)

- ✔ **Rogue Tactics:** Choose whether you want to add your Strength bonus to sneak attack damage (see the Sneak Attack bullet), or your Charisma bonus to Armor Class against opportunity attacks. The Brawny Rogue build prefers the former, and the Trickster Rogue build prefers the latter.

- ✔ **Rogue Weapon Talent:** Your rogue is especially good with daggers and shuriken, weapons that otherwise aren't very dangerous. You gain a +1 bonus on attacks with daggers, and you deal 1d6 damage with shuriken instead of 1d4 damage.

- ✔ **Sneak attack:** The rogue is naturally a master of *sneak attacks* (attacks made from hiding or when the rogue's opponent has his or her attention focused elsewhere). If you have combat advantage over your foe and you're using a light blade, a crossbow, or a sling, you deal 2d6 bonus damage on a successful attack, in addition to the attack's normal damage. The easiest way to gain combat advantage over a foe is to beat his initiative roll at the start of the fight (see the preceding First Strike bullet) or to flank an enemy with the help of one of your friends (defenders are especially good at this).

Hit points and healing surges

A 1st-level rogue begins with a number of hit points equal to 12 + his or her Constitution score. Each level after 1st, the rogue gains 5 more hit points. A rogue doesn't have very many healing surges — only 6 + Constitution modifier. When playing a rogue, remember that you're not a defender, and you'd rather not be around when the monsters get their turn.

Skills

As a rogue, you're a jack-of-all-trades. You have more skills at your disposal than any other character, and those skills are often useful in dangerous situations. All rogues are trained in Stealth and Thievery. In addition, a rogue begins play with skill training in four additional skills. Want to be an expert dungeon delver? Choose Acrobatics, Athletics, Dungeoneering, and Perception. Want your rogue to be the man (or woman) of a thousand faces, a master impersonator? Then choose Bluff, Insight, Perception, and Streetwise instead. If you like to play a character with a lot of skills, you can't do better than the rogue class.

Rogue powers

Rogue powers are called *exploits*. (Like the fighter's powers, they're derived from the martial power source.) A 1st-level rogue knows two 1st-level at-will exploits, one 1st-level encounter exploit, and one 1st-level daily exploit. The powers available to you are a mix of melee and ranged attacks; it's a good idea to make sure you choose at least one of each. Many rogue powers require your character to wield specific weapons (usually light blades), so keep that in mind before you decide to abandon the dagger or short sword in favor of something bigger.

The wizard is the best class

Select the wizard class for your character if you want to play an arcane spell-caster. If calling forth magical energy, shaping it into powerful spells, and unleashing those spells upon monsters and villains appeals to your sense of play, the wizard class is the one for you.

The wizard is a controller. Wizards can deal with multiple enemies at a time because most of their powers cover a broad area or target several foes at once. Want to be an offensive powerhouse? Select spells that deal damage. Want to be more subtle in your spellcasting? Choose spells that hinder enemy movement or trap your foes in dangerous terrain. Almost all of a wizard's spells deal some amount of damage, so even if you decide to specialize in keeping the monsters immobilized through magic, you'll still be contributing to wearing down their hit points. The wizard has outstanding ranged attack ability and hits monsters hard from a long ways off — which is good, because the wizard has low hit points and mediocre defenses. You don't want to let the monsters get close!

Wizards are proficient only in cloth armor — the weakest armor there is. They avoid damage by staying away from attackers and using defensive powers such as *shield* or *invisibility* when they can't quite stay out of reach. Their weapons are an afterthought — the dagger and the quarterstaff. Wizards disdain physical attacks and use their arcane powers in all but the most desperate of circumstances.

The two wizard builds in the *Player's Handbook* are

✔ **Control Wizard:** You prefer powers that hinder enemies first and damage them as a secondary function. For your arcane implement (see the "Wizard class features" section, later in this chapter), you prefer the orb or the staff.

✔ **War Wizard:** You like powers that deal as much damage as possible. If they happen to inflict some controlling effects on your enemies, so much the better, but that's not your priority. For your arcane implement, you should choose the wand or the staff.

Wizards come from all character races, but some races are renowned for their arcane inclination. Of the races described in this book, humans make the best wizards, especially if they choose to take their ability score bonus in Intelligence. (See Chapter 12 for more on races.) Elves don't have an Intelligence bonus, but they do gain Dexterity and Wisdom bonuses, which are useful secondary scores for wizards.

Of the character races in the *Players Handbook* not discussed in this book, eladrins and tieflings also make exceptional wizards due to their favorable ability score modifiers.

Abilities

If you decide to play a wizard, you should put your highest ability score in Intelligence. Almost all your wizard powers use Intelligence attacks, and wizards are offensively minded characters; hitting with your powers is absolutely crucial. A good Intelligence score also helps improve your Reflex defense and Armor Class. Other important abilities for wizards include Dexterity, which is useful for the War Wizard build and for powers that are about dealing damage; Wisdom, which helps your Will defense and is useful for the Control Wizard build; and Constitution, which improves your Fortitude defense and hit points and offers defensive advantages for either build.

Wizard class features

Most of the wizard's ability to function as a controller in combat lies in the various powers available to him. The wizard's class features are really about flavor more than function. These include

✔ **Arcane implement mastery:** Just like a fighter wields a sword, axe, or flail, a wizard uses arcane implements — the orb, staff, or wand. Choose one of these implements. The orb works well for the Control Wizard build because it makes conditions you inflict with your wizard's powers last longer or makes it harder for saving throws to overcome these conditions. The staff improves your defense and is good for either build. The wand is best for the War Wizard because it increases your wizard's accuracy with damaging attacks.

✔ **Cantrips:** You gain several minor at-will spells you can use any time you like: *ghost sound, light, mage hand,* and *prestidigitation*. None of these are very useful in combat, but they're handy for dungeon exploration.

✔ **Ritual Caster:** You gain the Ritual Caster feat as a bonus feat. The wizard automatically has access to the ritual magic system, which includes a variety of useful magical effects that mostly come into play outside of combat.

✔ **Spellbook:** Unlike other characters, a wizard actually *knows* more powers than he or she can use. A 1st-level wizard knows two daily spells; at the beginning of each day, the wizard picks which of those spells he or she will be able to use during the day. As the wizard gains levels and new utility and daily powers, he or she can continue to add "extra" powers to the spellbook, increasing the number of options available for the day's adventuring.

Hit points and healing surges

A 1st-level wizard begins with a number of hit points equal to 10 + his or her Constitution score. Each level after 1st, the wizard gains 4 more hit points. The wizard has a number of healing surges equal to 6 + Constitution modifier. As you can see, the wizard doesn't have a lot of staying power — it doesn't take many hits to make a wizard fall down.

The wizard in the 4th Edition DUNGEONS & DRAGONS roleplaying game is tougher than he used to be, but he still has the fewest hit points of any class in the game and very few powers that work well against enemies who are up close and personal. A wizard doesn't want to get into a prolonged melee battle with any monster. The best way to play a wizard during a battle is to stand back and use powers to attack from a distance. Let the defenders and strikers get in close so that your wizard can take control of the battlefield from a distance.

Skills

The wizard has a fair selection of skills, especially knowledge skills. All wizards automatically begin with training in the Arcana skill, and they can choose three others from a list including Diplomacy, Dungeoneering, History, Insight, Nature, and Religion. Arcana is your most useful skill because it's very useful for ritual magic (see Chapter 20). Dungeoneering, Nature, and Religion are useful for monster knowledge checks (see Chapter 16). The wizard is supposed to be the smartest character in the party, so your character ought to know something about nearly any monster or mysterious effect your group encounters.

Wizard powers

A wizard's powers are arcane in nature and are known as *spells*. A 1st-level wizard automatically knows two at-will 1st-level spells. *Magic missile* is an unusual spell in that it counts as a basic attack, so a wizard can use it any time he or she would be allowed to make a basic attack. It's one to look at when choosing your at-will spells. In addition, the wizard knows one 1st-level encounter spell and two 1st-level daily spells (but can use only one 1st-level daily spell per day; see the Spellbook bullet in the earlier section, "Wizard class features"). Most wizard powers are ranged or area attacks, but it's a good idea to select at least one power that's a Close attack — unlike ranged or area attacks, Close attacks don't provoke opportunity attacks when you make them. Someday, a Close attack might just save your bacon.

The cleric is the best class

The cleric is the class for you if you want to play a character who has a profound connection to a higher power. With divine powers, decent combat prowess, and the ability to repel undead monsters, the cleric bolsters any adventuring group. The cleric's powers revolve around healing damage and enhancing the abilities of other party members. These powers allow the cleric to make everybody around him or her better.

The cleric is a leader. The cleric's job in any adventuring group is to wield divine prayers that provide a mix of offense, healing, and defense. By using prayers on his or her teammates, a cleric can make a fighter more powerful, a rogue more deadly, and a wizard more effective. Prayers that are attack powers often serve as "target designation" effects, granting all the cleric's allies a bonus to attack or increased damage against the foe the cleric singles out.

Clerics are trained to use all simple weapons and leather, hide, or chain armor. They typically wield a mace in one hand and a holy symbol in the other, switching between melee attacks and ranged powers as the encounter demands.

The two cleric builds in the *Player's Handbook* are

- ✔ **Battle Cleric:** You prefer to lead from the front ranks, standing shoulder to shoulder with the party's defenders. Your powers include a number of good melee attacks and rely on Strength over Wisdom. Although you're a competent healer and have many ways to protect your allies with divine powers, you'd rather use your powers to punish villains and defeat monsters.

- ✔ **Devoted Cleric:** You're more defensively minded than the Battle Cleric and often use your powers from the rear ranks of the adventuring group. Your powers usually rely on Wisdom rather than Strength, and they include many ranged effects. You place a higher value on safeguarding your allies than beating the monsters down with your own attacks — you contribute to the party's offense by making everyone around you fight better and by protecting them with your divine magic.

All races have clerics, so a cleric character can be created using any of the D&D races. Of the races described in this book, humans make very good Battle Clerics because they can choose a bonus to their Strength score, whereas dwarves and elves make good Devoted Clerics because of their Wisdom bonuses. (See Chapter 12 for more on races.)

All clerics choose a patron deity, church, or faith to which they devote themselves. In the fantastic world of the DUNGEONS & DRAGONS roleplaying game, this usually means choosing a mythological god from a pantheon of imaginary deities. Clerics must choose deities compatible with their alignment; if you want to play a good-aligned cleric, you can't choose an evil or chaotic evil deity for your character to follow. A cleric doesn't automatically gain any special abilities or advantages for choosing a deity. However, the choice might affect how you spend your feats — some feats, known as divinity feats, are keyed to a character's patron deity.

The *Player's Handbook* features a selection of sample deities that can be used in any D&D campaign world. You can find these in Chapter 2. Pick a deity for your cleric that corresponds with your character's alignment. Check out the various divinity feats in Chapter 6 to see whether any seem especially good for your character.

Abilities

If you decide to play a cleric, you should set your highest ability score as either Strength or Wisdom. If you're creating a Battle Cleric build, choose Strength — many of the cleric powers you'll want to take are Strength attacks. If your character follows the Devoted Cleric build instead, choose Wisdom. Whichever way you go, the other ability should probably be your second highest score. Charisma is useful for your Channel Divinity class feature. Remember that your character needs a respectable Dexterity or Intelligence score for Reflex defense and Armor Class (if you don't wear heavy armor, anyway).

Cleric class features

Any leader needs to have access to potent healing powers, so the cleric class is built to provide good healing ability no matter what power selections you make for your character. This is reflected in the cleric's class features, which include

- **Channel Divinity:** A cleric begins with a bonus power known as *channel divinity.* Once per encounter, the cleric can use *channel divinity* to perform one of two special powers: *divine fortune* or *turn undead.*

- **Healer's Lore:** A cleric gets to add his or her Wisdom modifier to the number of hit points bestowed by any cleric power with the Healing keyword. For example, a cleric with a Wisdom score of 18 adds 4 points to the amount of damage cured by any of his or her healing powers.

- ✔ **Healing Word:** Twice per encounter, a cleric can use the *healing word* power. Basically, this power allows the recipient to use one of his or her healing surges. This is the power that gives the cleric the ability to keep allies on their feet and battling on against the monsters.

- ✔ **Ritual Casting:** Finally, the cleric gains the Ritual Caster feat as a bonus feat. Like the wizard, the cleric automatically has access to the ritual magic system, which includes a variety of useful magical effects.

Hit points and healing surges

A 1st-level cleric begins with a number of hit points equal to 12 + his or her Constitution score. Each level after 1st, the cleric gains 5 more hit points. Clerics have a good number of healing surges; they begin with 7 + Constitution modifier per day. Overall, a cleric's hit points are about as good as a rogue's.

Skills

All clerics begin with training in the Religion skill and then choose three others from the following: Arcana, Diplomacy, Heal, History, or Insight. The most important skills for a cleric are those with applications in ritual magic; Arcana, Heal, and Religion come up the most often.

Cleric powers

Cleric powers are known as *prayers* and are divine in origin. A 1st-level cleric knows two 1st-level at-will prayers, one 1st-level encounter prayer, and one 1st-level daily prayer. Of course, a cleric also has three additional encounter powers in the form of his or her class features: Two uses of his or her *healing word* power, and one use of a *channel divinity* power (either *turn undead* or *divine fortune*).

Other classes

The Dungeons & Dragons roleplaying game features eight core classes. We concentrate on the four most iconic classes for this book, but you should know that other choices are available. Chapter 4 in the *Player's Handbook* details all these classes. Here's a brief rundown so you know what else is out there:

- ✔ **Paladin:** The paladin is a divine defender who can stand in for the fighter.

- ✔ **Ranger** and **warlock:** These two classes are strikers, like the rogue. The ranger is very good with bows, whereas the warlock uses magical blasts and curses against his or her foes.

✔ **Warlord:** The warlord is a leader, like the cleric, but his or her powers are martial instead of divine.

When you're ready to try something different, take a look at these classes in the *Player's Handbook*. Additional classes such as bard, barbarian, druid, and swordmage will appear in upcoming D&D sourcebooks.

Chapter 12

Picking a Race

. . . .

In This Chapter

▶ Examining the fantasy races

▶ Picking the right race for the job

▶ Checking out other race options

. . . .

*N*o fantasy world is complete without a selection of mythical races to join humans in the struggle against monsters and Evil with a capital *E*. These distinct races usually have their own homelands, but everyone comes together in the larger towns and cities. There, those with adventurous spirits join up and head out to banish threats and undertake quests that might be personal or world-altering in nature.

In this chapter, we look at the fantasy races available for use as player characters in the DUNGEONS & DRAGONS game. We concentrate on four of those races — humans, dwarves, elves, and halflings — discussing the benefits each brings to the table and why you'd want to play a character of that race. You can play any race and class combination you want, but keep in mind that some races have natural tendencies that enable them to perform better in certain classes, as discussed in this chapter.

At the end of the chapter, we provide a quick overview of other races available in the D&D game.

Chapter 3 of the *Player's Handbook* goes into greater depth on character races and the benefits and disadvantages of each. Check it out after you read through this chapter.

Humans

Humans in D&D worlds are more or less just like humans in the real world, except stronger, more heroic and daring, and usually better looking. They come in all the usual human shapes, sizes, and colors. They range in height from about 5 feet to just over 6 feet tall. They reach adventuring age somewhere between their 16th and 20th birthdays. Human adventurers are adaptable, flexible, and extremely ambitious. They tend toward no particular alignment or deity, and they have a habit of championing causes and ideals over people or places.

Play a human character if you want a lot of maneuverability for your character as he or she advances in level. Humans gain an extra at-will power and an extra skill and feat to reflect their racial tendency toward versatility and capability for mastering new tasks.

Ability adjustments

A human character can excel in one ability score. After you've assigned the ability scores you generated to your abilities, add 2 points to the ability score of your choice. (It's usually a good idea to add this bonus to the ability that's most important for your character's class; see Chapter 13.)

Special traits

Humans have the following special traits:

- Humans start play with one extra feat at 1st level, choosing two feats to begin play instead of one.

- Humans begin play with training in one additional class skill. For example, a fighter normally begins with training in three skills, but a human fighter begins play with training in four.

- Humans are naturally resilient and begin with a +1 bonus to their Fortitude, Reflex, and Will defenses.

- Humans know one extra at-will power from their class. Normally characters know two at-will powers, but human characters know three at-will powers at the start of play.

A word about gender

Dungeons & Dragons characters can be either male or female. Many players make their characters the same gender they are in real life, but you're free to make a character of the opposite gender if you wish. Playing a male or female character is a personal choice, and to keep it that way, the game sees no difference in ability scores, class choices, powers, skills, equipment, and so on for characters of either gender. In D&D worlds, female and male adventurers are absolute equals.

Best class

Because humans can choose to add their racial ability score bonus to any ability, they do equally well with all the classes. Humans are good at any adventuring careers they set their minds to.

Dwarves

Dwarves are short and extremely broad, standing about 4½ feet tall and weighing about the same as much taller humans. Hailing from mountainous kingdoms, dwarves excel at warfare, mining, and construction. Longer lived than humans, dwarves have great patience and take pride in hard work done well. Dwarf adventurers often seek quests that will bring honor to their clans, respect from their friends, and treasure beyond their wildest imaginings.

Play a dwarf character if you want to focus on pure toughness. Dwarves are often more comfortable underground than folk of other races and make for good dungeon adventurers. If courage, loyalty, and a love of strong ale appeal to your sense of heroics, the dwarf race is a good choice for you.

Ability adjustments

After you've assigned the ability scores you generated to your abilities, make the following adjustments:

- ✔ Add 2 points to your dwarf's Constitution score. Dwarves are stout and tough.
- ✔ Add 2 points to your dwarf's Wisdom score. Dwarves are exceptionally strong-willed and observant.

Special traits

Dwarves have the following racial traits:

- ✔ Due to their size and build, dwarves have a base speed of 5 squares (1 square less than human speed). However, they retain this speed even when wearing armor or carrying a heavy load.
- ✔ Dwarves have low-light vision, which means that they see in dim light as well as humans see in bright light. They can't see in the dark, however.
- ✔ Dwarves gain a +2 racial bonus on Dungeoneering and Endurance skill checks.
- ✔ All dwarves are proficient with the throwing hammer and the warhammer.
- ✔ Dwarves are extremely stable. When an effect causes a dwarf to move — for example, a pull, push, or slide effect — a dwarf moves 1 square less than the effect specifies. If an attack would knock a dwarf prone, the dwarf can make an immediate saving throw to remain standing.
- ✔ Dwarves are hardy. They receive a +5 racial bonus on saving throws against poisons.
- ✔ Dwarves are extremely resilient. A dwarf can use his or her second wind as a minor action instead of a standard action (see Chapter 7).

Best class

Dwarves are especially suited to the cleric class, thanks in large part to their Wisdom bonus and their innate weapon training. The fighter class is also a very good choice for a dwarf character. However, dwarves can excel at any class. They are tough and competent wizards, although their lack of speed is a bit of a drawback for the rogue class.

Elves

Elves are slender and graceful, standing about 5½ to 6 feet tall, with tanned skin, hair that ranges from dark brown to mossy green, large, almond-shaped eyes, and pointed ears. Elven homelands lie deep in the forests and woodlands, where the elves learn archery and woodlore. With a love for nature and a talent for the arts, elves have a unique outlook on life. They are a people of deeply felt but short-lived passions, quick to laugh but also quick to anger. For elves, the call to adventure comes from an inborn wanderlust, though they can become focused and relentless when a particular quest catches their interest.

Play an elf character if you want to focus on quickness or ranged combat. Elves have special abilities that make them indispensable for wilderness adventuring. If playing a hauntingly beautiful, somewhat alien, and magically inclined character appeals to you, consider selecting the elf race for your character.

Ability adjustments

After you've assigned the ability scores you generated to your abilities, make the following adjustments:

- ✔ Add 2 points to your elf's Dexterity score. Elves are quick and graceful.

- ✔ Add 2 points to your elf's Wisdom score. Elves are highly perceptive and attuned to their surroundings.

Special traits

Elves have the following racial traits:

- ✔ Elves are fleet of foot and have a base speed of 7 squares.

- ✔ Elves have low-light vision, which allows them to see in dim light as well as a human sees in bright light.

- ✔ All elves are proficient with the longbow and shortbow.

- ✔ Elves have keen senses and are renowned for their woodcraft. They gain a +2 racial bonus on Perception and Nature checks.

- ✔ Elves help their allies to stay alert and tune in to their surroundings. They grant non-elf allies within 5 squares of them a +1 bonus to Perception checks.

✔ Elves have a knack for stepping in the exact right place. They ignore difficult terrain when they shift, which is often very helpful in moving around dangerous battlefields.

✔ Elves have a special racial power called *elven accuracy.* Once per encounter, as a free action, an elf can reroll one attack roll.

Best class

Elves make very good rogues and clerics, due to their Dexterity and Wisdom bonuses. They are competent fighters, especially with the Guardian Fighter build, and also do well as wizards — both the Battle Mage and Control Wizard builds are suited for elf characters.

Halflings

Halflings are about 4 feet tall, with slender, muscular frames and natural quickness. Many halflings are nomads, river-folk who migrate with the seasons, calling no land and all lands home. Clever and capable, cunning and resourceful, halflings constantly seek ways to avoid boredom and complacency. Although halflings often have a bit of thief in them, most follow their curiosity and have learned how to get into and out of trouble better than any of the other races.

Play a halfling character if you want to focus on stealth and skirmishing. Halflings have special abilities that let them excel at avoiding danger. If curious, fun-loving, good-hearted scoundrels appeal to your sense of adventure, consider selecting the halfling race.

Ability adjustments

After you've assigned the ability scores you generated for your abilities, make the following adjustments:

✔ Add 2 points to your halfling's Dexterity score. Halflings are quick, agile, and athletic.

✔ Add 2 points to your halfling's Charisma score. Halflings are plucky, likable, and friendly.

Special traits

Halflings have the following racial traits:

- ✔ Halflings are Small creatures. Due to their size, halflings can't use two-handed weapons such as greatswords and halberds.

- ✔ Halflings gain a +2 racial bonus on Acrobatics and Thievery checks.

- ✔ Halflings are naturally good at avoiding danger. They gain a +2 racial bonus to AC against opportunity attacks.

- ✔ Because they let their curiosity overpower their sense of fear, halflings gain a +5 racial bonus on saving throws against fear.

- ✔ Halflings have a special racial power called *second chance.* Once per encounter as an immediate action after being hit with an attack, halflings can force the attacker to reroll the attack. The attacker must use the second roll, even if it's lower than the first.

Best class

Halflings make outstanding rogues, especially Trickster Rogues. They are good clerics and wizards, and can do pretty well as fighters — although they make much better Guardian Fighters than Great Weapon Fighters.

More Races to Choose From

The *Player's Handbook* features additional races for player characters. These include the dragonborn (a big, strong race of warriors with draconic features), the eladrin (a race of high elves from the supernatural realm of the Feywild, and masters of arcane magic), the half-elf (a charismatic people who combine human versatility with elven intuition), and the tiefling (a race tainted by infernal influences long ago, but now free to choose their own destiny).

Beyond the core books, the D&D game is full of fantasy races suitable for use as player characters. The FORGOTTEN REALMS *Player's Guide*, for example, introduces two new races that offer additional options for creating cool player characters. Start by playing the races from the core books and then look for new options with which to expand your play experience.

Check out www.dndinsider.com for an ever-expanding collection of races to choose from. *D&D Insider* constantly previews material from upcoming products, including new races to add to your D&D campaign.

Chapter 13

Figuring Out Your Character's Ability Scores

In This Chapter

▶ Discovering the six ability scores

▶ Choosing a method for generating scores for your character

▶ Understanding the benefits and disadvantages of the random generation method

▶ Understanding the benefits and disadvantages of the elite array

▶ Exploring ability scores by character class

*E*very DUNGEONS & DRAGONS character consists of a number of key statistics that begin with the character's ability scores.

Class, race, and equipment help to refine and develop a character concept, but when you create a new character, you begin by determining that character's ability scores. The *Player's Handbook* describes several methods for generating ability scores. We discuss two methods for determining ability scores in this chapter: the standard array and the customizing scores approach.

In this chapter, we examine what the ability scores are used for and how to generate the best scores for the character you want to create. Afterward, we look at the choices available and help you best assign ability scores to create the character you envision — or at least make the character viable and fun to play.

You can find out more about ability scores and ability score generation methods in Chapter 2 of the *Player's Handbook*.

How the Ability Scores Work

Each character has six abilities — Strength, Constitution, Dexterity, Intelligence, Wisdom, and Charisma. *Ability scores* rate a character, painting a broad picture of how strong, dexterous, and intelligent (and so on) that character is. Ability scores form the foundation upon which a character of myth and legend grows.

Three of a character's abilities are physical (Strength, Constitution, and Dexterity) and three are mental (Intelligence, Wisdom, and Charisma).The following list describes each ability and gives advice on which classes need a high score in that ability:

- **Strength (Str):** This score gauges your character's physical might. How much equipment can he or she carry? Can he or she force open a heavy door? Arm-wrestle a bugbear? Swing a greatsword effectively? Bash open a locked chest? A strong character is better at melee combat than a weaker one. Any fighter wants a high score in this ability, as do rogues with the Brawny Rogue build and clerics using the Battle Cleric build.

- **Constitution (Con):** This number expresses your character's overall physical health and stamina. How long can he or she hold his or her breath? How well does his or her body deal with physical damage? How much punishment can he or she take before falling unconscious? These are the types of things measured by your character's Constitution score. All characters want at least a decent score in this ability because of its connection to hit points and healing surges, but it's especially useful to fighters using the Great Weapon Fighter build.

- **Dexterity (Dex):** This score measures your character's physical reflexes and agility. How good is he or she with a ranged weapon, such as a sling or bow? Can he or she use speed and coordination to avoid being hit and taking damage? Can he or she use skills that require a great deal of hand-eye coordination? A dexterous character is better at ranged combat than a less agile one. All rogues wants a high score in this ability, as do wizards with the Battle Mage build and fighters using the Guardian Fighter build.

- **Intelligence (Int):** This score gauges your character's ability to learn, use deductive reasoning, and predict enemy attacks. What does your character know about the monster he or she is facing? The history of the dungeon? The uses for the arcane ingredients found in the necromancer's vault? A smart character is better at finding answers than a less intelligent one. A character with the wizard class wants a high score in this ability.

- **Wisdom (Wis):** This score measures your character's perception and willpower. Does he or she notice the gnolls lurking in the shadows? Can he or she hear the dragon breathing in the dark cave ahead? Does he or she have the strength of will to withstand the vampire's hypnotic gaze? A wise character is better at taking advantage of insight and intuition than a less wise character would be. All clerics want a high score in this ability, and fighters with the Guardian Fighter build want a decent score.

- **Charisma (Cha):** This number represents your character's personal magnetism, self-confidence, and physical attractiveness. Can he or she get the castle guard to look the other way with convincing words or a well-timed bribe? A charismatic character is better at being suave or subtle when the situation calls for it than a less charismatic one is. A rogue who chooses the Artful Dodger class features benefits from a good Charisma score.

When you create a character, you generate ability scores and assign them to the abilities as you see fit. How you assign the scores depends on what kind of character you're creating. If you're making a wizard, for example, you would assign a high score to Intelligence, whereas if you're making a fighter, you would assign a high score to Strength. (See Table 13-3, later in this chapter, for more information.)

An average score is 10 or 11. Scores of less than 10 are below average, and scores of 12 or better are above average. In general, ability scores range from 8 to 18 when you first create a character. The score provides a modifier, either a bonus or a penalty that's tied to certain types of actions in the game, as described in Table 13-1. In general, ability scores relate to actions in the following way:

✔ Low ability scores (9 and lower) provide penalties to actions they're associated with.

✔ Middling scores (10 or 11) have no effect on actions they're associated with.

✔ High ability scores (12 and higher) provide bonuses to actions they're associated with.

Table 13-1		Ability Modifiers	
Score	*Modifier*	*Score*	*Modifier*
1	–5	12–13	+1
2–3	–4	14–15	+2
4–5	–3	16–17	+3
6–7	–2	18–19	+4
8–9	–1	20–21	+5
10–11	0	22–23	+6

Remember the Core Game Mechanic (described in Chapter 1):

✔ Roll a d20

✔ Add a modifier (bonus or penalty)

✔ Compare the result to a target number

So bonuses (such as +1) are always better, because they help make your d20 result higher and increase the chance for success at a given action. Penalties (such as –1) lower your d20 result and make the chance of failure more likely.

Pairing up defenses

You may have noticed that Fortitude defense, Reflex defense, and Will defense come up under *two* ability scores each. That's because you determine your character's defenses by using the *best* score in a pair of ability scores. Your character's Fortitude defense is improved by the better of the Strength or Constitution modifiers; your character's Reflex defense (and Armor Class, as long as he or she isn't wearing heavy armor) by the better of the Dexterity or Intelligence modifiers; and your character's Will defense by the better of the Wisdom or Charisma modifiers. For example, if your character is a brilliant but clumsy wizard with a Dexterity of 8 and an Intelligence of 20, you get to add +5 to the Reflex defense and Armor Class because the ability modifier for a score of 20 is +5. Clearly, your character is much better at analyzing enemy attacks than she is at leaping nimbly out of the way, but however the wizard does it, she's a slippery target!

A low score in a key ability for your character class means that the character faces difficult challenges doing what it is he or she is supposed to do; a high score for a key ability is often crucially important.

In the following list, we describe each of the six abilities and their effects on character actions in the game:

- **Strength (Str):** The modifier provided by the character's Strength score is applied to basic melee attacks and damage rolls, attack and damage rolls with Strength-based powers, Fortitude defense, and physical skill checks such as Athletics. Many fighter and cleric powers are based on Strength.

- **Constitution (Con):** The character's Constitution score is added to his or her 1st-level hit points (determined by character class). The Constitution modifier is also added to number of healing surges a character can use per day, Fortitude defense, and skill checks such as Endurance.

- **Dexterity (Dex):** The modifier provided by the character's Dexterity score is applied to basic ranged attacks and damage rolls, attack and damage rolls with Dexterity-based powers, Reflex defense, Armor Class (if not in heavy armor), and to Dexterity-based skill checks such as Acrobatics or Thievery. Many rogue powers are based on Dexterity.

- **Intelligence (Int):** The modifier provided by the character's Intelligence score is applied to attack rolls and damage rolls with Intelligence-based powers, Reflex defense, Armor Class (if not in heavy armor), and Intelligence-based skill checks such as Arcana. Most wizard powers are based on Intelligence.

- **Wisdom (Wis):** The modifier provided by the character's Wisdom score is applied to attack and damage rolls with Wisdom-based powers, Will defense, and Wisdom-based skill checks such as Heal and Perception. Many cleric powers are Wisdom-based.

- **Charisma (Cha):** The modifier provided by the character's Charisma score is applied to attack and damage rolls with Charisma-based powers, Will defense, and Charisma-based skill checks such as Bluff or Intimidate. A good Charisma modifier improves the effectiveness of some rogue and cleric powers.

Generating Ability Scores

Some people approach the game knowing exactly what kind of character they want to create and play. Others prefer to generate their ability scores first, see what they get in the way of bonuses and penalties, and then create the best character they can around those scores. Either way, at some point early in the process of creating your character, you need to figure out what your character's ability scores are. Check with your Dungeon Master to see whether he or she has a preferred method for determining ability scores. In the following sections, we examine two popular methods — the standard array and the customized score method — and we discuss how to get the most out of them when creating a new DUNGEONS & DRAGONS player character.

The standard array

You can use a standard array to generate ability scores. This method provides a solid group of set numbers that you can assign as you see fit. That's right — the standard array always uses the same numbers. You have more control with this method because you always know exactly what scores you're going to get. The standard array provides a set of numbers that combines decent bonuses with two average scores thrown in for good measure. The standard array looks like this:

16, 14, 13, 12, 11, and 10

The benefits of using the standard array are speed and consistency. This set of scores allows you to quickly create a character that has at least a decent score (a score that produces a bonus) in every ability important to the class you want to play. The disadvantages are that you don't have the possibility of generating a score of 17 or higher, as you do with the customizing scores method.

When you're in a hurry or when you want to guarantee a selection of bonuses so you can better create the character concept you have in mind, go with the standard array. We used the standard array to create all the ready-to-play characters in Part I.

The customizing scores method

Customizing your ability scores is more complicated than using the standard array, but it gives you a wider mix of scores while providing comparable results. With this method, you can build a character that's really good in one score at the cost of having average scores in the other five.

To use this method, start with these six scores:

8, 10, 10, 10, 10, and 10

You have 22 points to spend on improving these numbers. The cost to raise a number is shown in Table 13-2.

Table 13-2		Customizing Ability Scores	
Score	*Cost*	*Score*	*Cost*
9	*	14	5
10	*	15	7
11	1	16	9
12	2	17	12
13	3	18	16

* If your score is 8, you can pay 1 point to make it 9 or 2 points to make it 10. You must buy your score up to 10 before you can improve it further.

Racial ability adjustments

Every race provides a bonus to one or two ability scores. An elf, for example, gets a +2 Dexterity and a +2 Wisdom. Apply racial ability adjustments after you determine your charac-ter's scores using one of the methods described in the sections "The standard array" and "The customizing scores method."

Improving ability scores

Your character begins play with a heroic set of ability scores, and they get better as your character advances in level. When your character reaches 4th level, you can add +1 to two different scores of your choice. For example, if your character is a fighter, you might decide to increase his Strength score by 1 and Constitution score by 1. You get to do this again at 8th level, 14th level, 18th level, 24th level, and 28th level (pick the same or different scores — it's up to you). In addition, your character gains +1 to *all* ability scores when he or she reaches 11th level, and again at 21st level.

If you're playing a fighter created using the standard array, you may choose to advance his ability scores as follows:

1st level: 16 Str, 14 Con, 12 Dex, 11 Int, 13 Wis, 10 Cha

11th level: 19 Str, 17 Con, 13 Dex, 12 Int, 14 Wis, 11 Cha

21st level: 22 Str, 20 Con, 14 Dex, 13 Int, 15 Wis, 12 Cha

28th level: 24 Str, 22 Con, 14 Dex, 13 Int, 15 Wis, 12 Cha

As you can see, your character's ability scores improve dramatically over the course of his or her adventuring career.

Here are some sample scores generated using this method:

14, 13, 13, 13, 13, 13

15, 15, 13, 12, 11, 10

16, 16, 12, 11, 11, 8

17, 14, 12, 11, 10, 10

18, 14, 11, 10, 10, 8

Assigning Ability Scores by Class

For every class, certain abilities are more important than others and provide a key to a character's success. We define these important abilities for each class in Table 13-3. For each class, we show where to place the highest score (++), the second- and third-best scores (+), and the remaining scores (–). The two different recommendations for each class are based on the builds presented in the *Player's Handbook*. You don't have to arrange your scores this way, but it's the easiest way to create an effective character.

Table 13-3	Ability Scores by Class					
Class	*Str*	*Con*	*Dex*	*Int*	*Wis*	*Cha*
Fighter, great weapon	++	+	−	−	+	−
Fighter, guardian	++	−	+	−	+	−
Rogue, brawny	+	−	++	−	+	−
Rogue, trickster	+	−	++	−	−	+
Wizard, battle	−	+	+	++	−	−
Wizard, control	−	+	−	++	+	−
Cleric, battle	++	−	−	−	+	+
Cleric, devoted	+	−	−	−	++	+

Chapter 14

Choosing Powers

In This Chapter

▶ Sorting out types of powers

▶ Gaining new powers as your character levels up

▶ Selecting fighter powers

▶ Selecting rogue powers

▶ Selecting wizard powers

▶ Selecting cleric powers

*E*very DUNGEONS & DRAGONS character is basically a collection of powers. The powers your character knows define what he or she can do. A skilled fighter might know a deadly combination attack, a sweeping strike that threatens several enemies at once, or an upending strike that knocks down an enemy. A wizard might know spells that conjure up an icy blizzard, create a streaking ball of fire, or grant invisibility for a short time. Each character class has scores of powers available, but your character knows only a few of them; deciding which powers suit your character best is a challenging test of your character-building skills

In this chapter, we explain how your character learns powers. We tell you about the various options available to you when you choose your character's powers. We also show you how your character's build influences your selection of powers.

Each character class in the *Player's Handbook* includes two basic builds. You can choose any powers you like, so you don't have to follow the builds — but they are designed to be effective, iconic, and easy to use. Using a build helps to ensure that your character's ability scores, race selection, feat selection, and power choices are all working together. We cover builds in Chapter 11, and in this chapter we refer to them extensively.

Navigating through Powers

You can find a lot of different types of powers in the DUNGEONS & DRAGONS game. There are powers for fighters, powers for wizards, powers gained by belonging to a particular race, powers characters can use whenever they want, powers characters can use only once per day, powers that attack enemies at range, powers that attack enemies close up, powers that don't attack anybody at all but add to your character's defense or heal an ally instead . . . let's just say there are a lot of powers.

Fortunately, the powers aren't thrown at you willy-nilly. The game has powers organized in the following ways:

- ✔ **Character class:** The first organizing principle of powers is character class. If you're playing a fighter, you only have to worry about fighter powers. As your fighter character gains levels, he learns new fighter powers, not cleric or wizard or whatever powers. You need to concentrate only on a small part of the *Player's Handbook* at a time.

- ✔ **Level:** Powers are organized into levels, ranging from 1 to 29. As your character rises in level, he or she gains access to ever more impressive powers. For example, a 1st-level wizard can cast a selection of 1st-level spells, but a 9th-level wizard's best power is a 9th-level spell.

  You might notice that your character's level correlates to the level of powers he or she can access when he or she advances in experience level; when a character reaches 9th level, he or she gets to choose a 9th-level power. Powers don't "fill in" all available levels because there are levels your character advances to that don't give any new power choices. For example, there are no 4th-level powers anywhere in the game — characters don't get to pick any new powers when they reach 4th level. They instead gain other benefits for achieving 4th level.

- ✔ **Usage:** Powers are also organized by their usage: *at-will, encounter,* or *daily.* This refers to how often a character can employ that particular power. For example, *magic missile* is an at-will 1st-level wizard power. Any time your character spends a standard action, he or she can fire off a *magic missile.* Encounter powers work once per battle; they take five minutes to recharge, so as long as your character has a short break after a fight, his or her encounter powers are available for use again. Daily powers, on the other hand, work once per day. Your character must rest for several hours in order to recharge a daily power he or she has used.

- ✔ **Type:** Powers are divided into *attack* and *utility* powers. Most of the powers you choose as your character advances in level are attack powers, but you also gain a number of utility powers over time. The cleric's *cure light wounds* prayer, the rogue's *tumble* exploit, and the wizard's *fly* spell are all good examples of utility powers. Utility powers are set at different levels from attack powers, so you're never forced to choose between picking up some highly useful utility power or your next big attack power. Utility powers vary in usage: They can be at-will, encounter, or daily powers.

For more information on how powers are sorted and used in play, check out "Power Types and Usage," at the beginning of Chapter 4 in the *Player's Handbook.*

Powers you don't choose

In general, you get to choose from among several different powers each time your character gains the ability to pick a power. However, sometimes your character gains powers that you can't choose — they're just automatic for your character. These include the following:

✔ **Racial powers:** Some character races grant powers — for example, an elf character automatically knows the power *elven accuracy.* All elf characters can use that power.

✔ **Class powers:** Some character classes include powers. The best example is the cleric class, which includes the *healing word* power. All clerics gain *healing word* in addition to the powers they select normally.

✔ **Paragon path:** Your character's paragon path provides an 11th-level encounter power, a 12th-level utility power, and a 20th-level daily power. These are locked into your paragon path selection; for instance, if your character is a swordmaster, you get the swordmaster powers at those levels. We look at the paragon path more in Chapters 18 and 22.

✔ **Epic destiny:** Your character's epic destiny provides a 26th-level utility power. Again, this is locked into your choice of epic destiny; whatever the destiny offers at that level, you get.

Using powers

To use a power in game play, you simply tell the DM that your character is using a power. In combat, you have to wait for your character's turn to come up (although some powers can be used to interrupt an enemy's turn). When you use an encounter power, it's expended for the rest of that encounter. When you use a daily power, it's used up for the whole day. You can't refresh daily powers until your character has an opportunity to rest. Usually, this means retreating from the dungeon and circling the wagons for a time while your character recharges for the next day.

✔ **Magic items:** Many magic items that your character finds during the course of his or her adventuring career have powers, too. Depending on your Dungeon Master, you may have the ability to choose the magic items your character wields, or you might have to settle for whatever your character finds in treasure hoards.

Learning new powers

When creating a 1st-level character, you get to select the following class powers:

✔ Two 1st-level at-will powers (For a human character, pick three.)

✔ One 1st-level encounter power

✔ One 1st-level daily power

The powers you select are determined by your class. If your character is a rogue, you begin with rogue powers; if your character is a wizard, you begin with wizard powers; and so on. In addition, your character may have a racial power (such as *elven accuracy*) or additional powers determined by his or her character class (such as the cleric's *healing word* power). Human characters have the advantage of beginning with three 1st-level at-will powers instead of only two. (That's one of the human racial benefits.)

As your character gains experience levels, he or she gains additional powers. For example, at 2nd level, your character gains one 2nd-level utility power; at 3rd level, one 3rd-level encounter power; and at 5th level, one 5th-level daily power. Your character is gaining other benefits, too, but the opportunity to choose new powers is one of the most interesting and useful parts of gaining levels.

You can find character advancement and power acquisition in the table on page 29 of the *Player's Handbook*. Flag this page with a bookmark or sticky note; you're going to use it a lot!

Replacing powers

Eventually, you reach a point where instead of gaining a new power, you replace one of your character's old powers with a new one. For example, at 13th level, your character gains a new 13th-level encounter power, but you must also choose one old encounter power to discard. Usually this is the character's 1st-level encounter power because it's the lowest-level encounter power your character knows. Low-level powers aren't as good as higher-level powers, so it makes sense to replace your character's oldest powers first. Your 13th-level character would, therefore, know encounter powers of 13th, 11th (the paragon path power), 7th, and 3rd level (after discarding the 1st-level power), for a total of four known encounter powers.

Daily powers are also replaced in this fashion. However, at-will powers never get swapped out — there are only 1st-level at-will powers, and you never gain access to new bins of at-will powers to choose from. Utility powers don't get replaced, either. You just keep adding those each time you hit a level where you can choose one.

Choosing Fighter Powers

Fighter powers are derived from the martial power source, which means that they're the product of training, practice, and pure physical ability. (See the sidebar on page 54 of the *Player's Handbook* for more on power sources.) They're called *exploits.*

The great majority of fighter powers are melee attacks — attacks a fighter makes against one or more specific enemies within reach of his or her sword (or axe, or hammer, or some other melee weapon). Some fighter powers are close attacks. Close attacks affect an area; for example, a power whose area is listed as "Close burst 1" affects everything within 1 square of your character. If a fighter is surrounded by four goblins, he or she gets to attack each one with that power. However, if you want to attack monsters standing a long distance away, you must fall back to your basic ranged attack to shoot a bow or throw a javelin. It's not as effective as using a power, but sometimes that's the only way to get the job done.

Fighters care more about which weapons they're using than any other character. A number of fighter powers have special benefits for using particular weapons. That means you should decide which weapon your character uses most before you begin choosing powers. If you decide that your character favors axes, for example, you can keep an eye out for powers that reward axe users, such as *crushing blow* or *giant's wake.*

To begin choosing your fighter powers, the first thing you should do is settle on your fighter build:

- **Great Weapon Fighter:** This type of fighter prefers offense to defense, and so uses a two-handed weapon such as a greataxe, greatsword, or maul. Your best powers are ones that deal high damage to one target or attack multiple targets.

- **Guardian Fighter:** Your character prioritizes defense and crowd control over pure damage, so he or she uses a one-handed weapon such as a longsword, battleaxe, warhammer, flail, or spear, as well as a shield. Powers that slow, immobilize, restrain, or slide enemies are good for keeping your enemies close by you so they can't get to your friends.

To use the power selections in Tables 14-1 and 14-2, remember that your fighter knows every power listed on the table for his or her character level, plus the powers listed for previous levels. In other words, the lists are cumulative; if you're playing a 5th-level fighter, your character knows every exploit listed for levels 1 through 5. However, at 13th and 15th level, you replace your older powers with your new selections, as shown on the table.

Many fighter daily exploits have the special keyword of Reliable, which means that if you miss with the attack, you haven't actually expended the power — it's still available, and you can try it again in later rounds until you do hit with it.

The Great Weapon Fighter

This might be the simplest character to play in the DUNGEONS & DRAGONS game. All you have to do is move your character next to the monsters and hit them with the best attack you can. Repeat until no more monsters are standing. For purposes of choosing powers in Table 14-1, we assume that your character wields a greataxe. If you choose a different weapon, you might want to change a couple of your power selections.

Table 14-1	Great Weapon Fighter Build Powers
Level	*Fighter Exploits Known*
1st	At-will: *cleave, reaping strike* Encounter: *spinning sweep* Daily: *brute strike*
2nd	Utility: *boundless endurance* (daily)
3rd	Encounter: *crushing blow**
4th	(No new powers)
5th	Daily: *dizzying blow*
6th	Utility: *unbreakable* (encounter)
7th	Encounter: *reckless strike*
8th	(No new powers)
9th	Daily: *thicket of blades*
10th	Utility: *into the fray* (encounter)
11th	Encounter: (determined by paragon path)

Level	Fighter Exploits Known
12th	Utility: (determined by paragon path)
13th	Encounter: *giant's wake** (replaces *spinning sweep*)
14th	(No new powers)
15th	Daily: *dragon's fangs* (replaces *brute strike*)

* Keyed to your weapon choice; if you don't use a greataxe, try a different power.

Your character's 1st-level at-will powers are *cleave* and *reaping strike*. Both allow you to add extra damage based on your Strength modifier. Use *reaping strike* when you're fighting a single enemy or enemies that are hard to hit; even if you miss, you deal a little damage. *Cleave* is good when you're fighting multiple enemies, especially if those enemies aren't hard for you to hit.

Your character's encounter powers begin with *spinning sweep*. It doesn't deal a lot of damage, but if you hit, you knock your target prone — it's always handy to put your enemy on the ground. If you'd prefer more damage, choose *passing attack* instead. At 3rd level, your character can learn *crushing blow*. This power allows you to add your Constitution modifier to the damage you deal, so it's a great choice if you have a high Constitution score. Our recommendation for your 7th-level encounter power is *reckless strike*. You take a small penalty on your attack roll, but you deal excellent damage with this power. Try to save it until you have combat advantage in a fight, so that the attack penalty won't hurt so much.

Your character's 11th level encounter power is determined by the paragon path you choose; see page 53 of the *Player's Handbook* for more information on paragon paths. (Iron vanguard and pit fighter work well for the Great Weapon Fighter build.) When you gain your 13th level encounter power, you reach the "cap" of four encounter powers, so you have to choose one of your old encounter powers to replace. It's time to scratch off your 1st-level *spinning sweep* power and replace it with *giant's wake*. *Giant's wake* is like *crushing blow* on steroids; in addition to waling the tar out of the enemy you hit, you get to make a secondary attack against any enemies adjacent to the first foe you attacked.

Your daily powers are *brute strike* (1st), *dizzying blow* (5th), and *thicket of blades* (9th). *Brute strike* is just simple big damage against one target. *Dizzying blow* is the same, but it also immobilizes your target. *Thicket of blades* is similar, but its range is Close burst 1, so your fighter can attack every adjacent enemy. At 15th level, replace *brute strike* with the exploit *dragon's fangs* — it's just as good, and you can make two attacks instead of one.

Because you're mixing it up in just about every encounter, we recommend utility powers that help you shake off the damage your character inevitably collects. Save *boundless endurance* (2nd) until you're in a battle that you aren't sure you can win; it's a daily power, so after you use it, it's gone until your character can rest. On the other hand, *unbreakable* (6th) is an encounter power, so make sure you use it during every fight! You might as well use it the first time you get hit. At 10th level, *into the fray* doesn't help you avoid damage, but it's an extremely useful encounter power that lets you move a short distance as a minor action. Use this power to move up to a new enemy after you drop a foe. Keeping monsters and villains under the threat of your axe is what you're supposed to do!

The Guardian Fighter

The Guardian Fighter is the thinking player's fighter. Your Guardian Fighter is tough as nails, armored from head to toe, and no matter what the enemies do, they just can't seem to get away from your character. Your fighter's powers are good melee attacks, but more important, they control enemy movement and keep your foes from getting to your less protected allies.

Guardian Fighters are typically equipped with a heavy shield and a one-handed weapon. For the purposes of Table 14-2, we assume that your weapon of choice is the trusty longsword.

Table 14-2	Guardian Fighter Build Powers
Level	*Fighter Exploits Known*
1st	At-will: *sure strike, tide of iron* Encounter: *covering attack* Daily: *comeback strike*
2nd	Utility: *get over here* (encounter)
3rd	Encounter: *dance of steel*
4th	(No new powers)
5th	Daily: *crack the shell*
6th	Utility: *unbreakable* (encounter)
7th	Encounter: *come and get it*
8th	(No new powers)
9th	Daily: *shift the battlefield*
10th	Utility: *stalwart guard* (daily)

Level	Fighter Exploits Known
11th	Encounter: (determined by paragon path)
12th	Utility: (determined by paragon path)
13th	Encounter: *storm of blows* (replaces *covering attack*)
14th	(No new powers)
15th	Daily: *unyielding avalanche* (replaces *comeback strike*)

* Keyed to your weapon choice; if you don't like longsword, try a different power.

The Guardian Fighter's at-will strikes are *sure strike* and *tide of iron. Sure strike* provides a high-accuracy, low-damage attack for when you really need to get an enemy's attention. *Tide of iron* has the coolest power name ever, and it's also extremely useful. *Tide of iron* lets you push back an enemy and move into its square — a great way to get your foe out of a doorway, shove it away from an ally, or back it into a corner.

We recommend *covering attack* for your 1st-level encounter power. If you hit, one of your allies adjacent to the foe can immediately shift by 2 squares. It's perfect for getting a less-defended ally out of danger. At 3rd level, your character learns *dance of steel* (have we mentioned that the Guardian Fighter has some great power names?), which does decent damage and slows your enemy. *Come and get it,* your 7th-level encounter power, might be the best crowd-control power in the game; you pull all enemies within 3 squares adjacent to you, and whack each one when he, she, or it moves next to you. Your character's 11th-level encounter power is determined by your paragon path. For the 13th-level encounter power, *storm of blows* is a deceptively good attack. It doesn't deal much damage, but you can attack up to three enemies, shifting each time. It's very handy for moving by several squares through a furious battle to wind up exactly where you want to stand. However, if your character happens to be using a hammer, *anvil of doom* is probably a better choice. Either way, the 13th-level encounter power replaces *covering attack.*

For daily exploits, begin with *comeback strike* at 1st level. It's not a very strong attack for a daily power, but it lets you use a healing surge. The ability to trigger your own healing surge is extremely handy for those occasional battles when the party's leader is incapacitated and can't heal you. At 5th level, *crack the shell* is useful because it helps the rest of your party hit the creature you're fighting. Use this one on a tough solo monster if you get the chance. *Shift the battlefield* is your 9th-level daily exploit, and it's a tactician's dream; not only do you make a decent attack against every foe adjacent to you, you can then move each foe 1 square. Your 15th-level exploit replaces *comeback strike;* we recommend *unyielding avalanche.* It isn't much of an attack, but it increases your defense and your ability to exert control over the battlefield — and that is exactly what a Guardian Fighter is all about.

Speaking of battlefield control, your utility powers offer more opportunities for moving your allies out of dangerous situations. At 2nd level, *get over here* is a move action that lets you slide one willing ally up to 2 squares to get him or her out of harm's way and into a better defensible position. *Unbreakable* (6th level) is just as useful for the Guardian Fighter as it is for the Great Weapon Fighter; use it in every battle. Finally, for your 10th-level utility power, try *stalwart guard*. It's usable only once per day, but it's a minor action and it gives you the ability to directly protect all nearby allies by increasing their AC and Reflex defenses.

Choosing Rogue Powers

Like fighters, rogues have martial powers. Their powers (also called exploits) are acts of agility, training, and tricks they practice and study, with no magic involved.

Rogue powers mix melee and short-range attacks. Many powers also include some built-in mobility. Rogues can move around the battlefield like no one else, which makes it relatively easy to set up for their big damage boost: the sneak attack. The Sneak Attack class feature grants rogues bonus damage when they attack with combat advantage, and one of the simplest ways to gain combat advantage is to move to a flanking position against the target.

Weapon choice is almost as important to rogues as it is to fighters, although in the rogue's case, it's about meeting a requirement rather than choosing an advantage. Many rogue powers require the rogue to wield specific weapons — usually a crossbow or sling for ranged attacks, or a light blade for melee attacks. (Light blades include daggers, short swords, and rapiers.) No matter how much you might want to try out a dwarf rogue with a battleaxe, it's just a bad idea; too many of your powers won't work. Stick with the classic rogue weapons.

To choose your rogue exploits, first determine which rogue build you're aiming for. Many powers work well for any kind of rogue, but you want to make sure you don't pick powers really intended for the other build.

- ✔ **Brawny Rogue:** Your powers tend to deal lots of damage. You aren't particularly elusive, but you can be hard to corner simply because your powers often stun or immobilize your targets; they can't counterattack effectively after your turn is over. For Rogue Tactics (see page 117 of the *Player's Handbook*), choose brutal scoundrel; it improves your Sneak Attack damage. Choose rogue powers that your Strength modifier improves.

- ✔ **Trickster Rogue:** You're more mobile and elusive than the Brawny Rogue, but your powers tend to deal less damage. Many of your powers are enhanced by a good Charisma modifier. You should choose artful dodger for your Rogue Tactics class feature, which protects you against opportunity attacks.

Tables 14-3 and 14-4 show recommended power selections for your rogue build. The lists are cumulative, so you know each power listed for your character level and the powers of all previous levels (unless your character is high enough in level that you've actually replaced some of your old power selections).

The Brawny Rogue

All rogues like sneak attack, but you especially like it if you're playing the Brawny Rogue, because your Brutal Scoundrel class feature allows you to add your Strength bonus to sneak attack damage. Therefore, many of the powers in this build are intended to help you get or keep combat advantage. Make sure you choose Acrobatics as one of your trained skills because you need it for some of the powers in this build.

Table 14-3	Brawny Rogue Build Powers
Level	*Rogue Exploits Known*
1st	At-will: *piercing strike, riposte strike* Encounter: *torturous strike* Daily: *easy target*
2nd	Utility: *tumble* (encounter)
3rd	Encounter: *topple over*
4th	(No new powers)
5th	Daily: *deep cut*
6th	Utility: *ignoble escape* (at-will)
7th	Encounter: *cloud of steel*
8th	(No new powers)
9th	Daily: *knockout*
10th	Utility: *shadow stride* (at-will)
11th	Encounter: (determined by paragon path)
12th	Utility: (determined by paragon path)
13th	Encounter: *unbalancing attack* (replaces *torturous strike*)
14th	(No new powers)
15th	Daily: *slaying strike* (replaces *easy target*)

The Brawny Rogue begins with the at-will powers *piercing strike* and *riposte strike*. *Piercing strike* is a good general-purpose melee attack because it targets your enemy's Reflex defense. That's almost always several points lower than Armor Class, so it's a highly accurate attack. *Riposte strike* is useful because the creature you hit with it is strongly discouraged from attacking you on its next turn — if it does, you gain an immediate attack against it. Use *piercing strike* when the situation calls for offense, and *riposte strike* when you want to be attacked less often.

Your first recommended encounter power is *torturous strike,* which is a straightforward damaging attack. At 3rd level, you gain a power called *topple over.* You get to add your Strength modifier to your attack with this power, and a successful hit deals damage and knocks the target prone. The 7th-level power we like best for the Brawny Rogue is *cloud of steel.* It's a Close attack that affects a very large area, so you could easily catch three or four enemies with a single attack. Your character learns the encounter attack power for your chosen paragon path at 11th level (see page 53 of the *Player's Handbook* for more on paragon paths). At 13th level, you replace *torturous strike* with the *unbalancing attack* power. This power deals very good damage, improves your opportunity attacks against the target, and prevents the target from shifting out of its current square.

Easy target is your character's 1st-level daily exploit. It's especially useful because it guarantees that the target will continue to grant combat advantage to you (at least until it successfully saves). At 5th level, *deep cut* is a very damaging power that targets Fortitude defense; don't use it on very big or strong opponents if you can help it. Your 9th-level daily exploit is *deadly positioning.* It deals fine damage and gives you the ability to move your opponent just before attacking until the end of the encounter — again, an easy way to set up sneak attacks. At 15th level, replace your *easy target* exploit with *slaying strike.* This power deals good damage, but if the target is bloodied, it deals *extremely* good damage. In fact, it'll often kill a wounded enemy outright. Make sure you save this one for use against a bloodied opponent!

Although many interesting rogue utility powers are available, the Brawny Rogue is all about gaining combat advantage, so *tumble* (2nd) and *ignoble escape* (6th) are the first two recommendations. Both powers let you shift your position by multiple squares as a move action, which is extremely useful for flanking an opponent or getting away from enemies trying to box you in. *Shadow stride* (13th) is also good because it lets you move and hide at the same time.

The Trickster Rogue

The Trickster Rogue is happy to gain combat advantage and sneak attack damage, but he or she specializes in making enemies look bad. Many of the powers listed on Table 14-4 are designed to hinder or slow enemies; a rogue of this build can often move or lure an enemy right into the path of another character's attack. Make sure you choose Bluff as one of your trained skills if you're a Trickster Rogue, because several of your powers require it.

Table 14-4	Trickster Rogue Build Powers
Level	*Rogue Exploits Known*
1st	At-will: *deft strike, sly flourish* Encounter: *positioning strike* Daily: *trick strike*
2nd	Utility: *master of deceit* (encounter)
3rd	Encounter: *bait and switch*
4th	(No new powers)
5th	Daily: *walking wounded*
6th	Utility: *slippery mind* (encounter)
7th	Encounter: *cloud of steel*
8th	(No new powers)
9th	Daily: *knockout*
10th	Utility: *shadow stride* (at-will)
11th	Encounter: (determined by paragon path)
12th	Utility: (determined by paragon path)
13th	Encounter: *tornado strike* (replaces *positioning strike*)
14th	(No new powers)
15th	Daily: *bloody path* (replaces *trick strike*)

Rogue at-will powers are some of the best in the game, and you begin 1st level with two very good ones. *Deft strike* includes a move of 2 squares when you use the attack, which makes it easy to get into position. *Sly flourish* simply adds your Charisma modifier to the damage you deal with the attack, so it's the single most damaging rogue at-will power. Use *sly flourish* unless the extra movement of *deft strike* would give you the chance to move into a flanking position and gain combat advantage.

Your character's 1st-level encounter exploit is *positioning strike.* In addition to dealing decent damage, this power lets you slide the target a few squares. Try using this against an opponent that another character has dazed or slowed; the affected creature won't be able to get back into melee range and attack you back. We recommend *bait and switch* for your character's 3rd-level encounter exploit; this power lets you switch places with your target and shift several squares, which is extremely useful for getting out from behind enemy lines and back to the safety of the rest of the party. For 7th level, choose *cloud of steel.* It's the best area attack available to a heroic-tier rogue.

Your character's 11th-level encounter exploit is determined by your paragon path, just as it is for any other class. At 13th level, replace *positioning strike* with the encounter exploit *tornado strike.* It's similar to *positioning strike,* except you can attack at range or in melee, you can attack two targets instead of one, and you get a free 3-square move after making the attack.

At 1st level, we suggest *trick strike* for your character's daily exploit. You gain the ability to slide the target each time you hit it, which gives you the ability to set up your allies' attacks against that foe. At 5th level, *walking wounded* targets your foe's Fortitude defense, knocks him prone on a hit, and slows him for the duration of the encounter. Your 9th-level daily exploit is an extremely good power called *knockout;* you render your target unconscious with a successful hit. At 15th level, replace *trick strike* with *bloody path.* *Bloody path* is a little hard to use because you need to run by as many enemies as possible, but each enemy you run past swings at you and hits himself instead. That's worth the use of a daily power!

For utility powers, *master of deceit* (2nd level) allows you to re-roll a Bluff check you don't like. You can use Bluff checks to gain combat advantage or give yourself a chance to hide, both of which can be very useful. *Slippery mind* (6th level) is a useful defensive power that helps you boost your Will defense once an encounter. At 10th level, we recommend *shadow stride.* The ability to move and hide at the same time lets a rogue cause all sorts of trouble both in and out of combat, and that's what being a rogue is all about.

Choosing Wizard Powers

Wizards rely on arcane powers known as spells. These powers are extremely diverse compared with the selections available to characters of other classes. Want to play a fire wizard? Take a lot of fire spells. Want to play a mind-bending enchanter? Take a lot of spells dealing with psychic damage or that attack the targets' Will defense. It's really up to you.

Wizard spells fall into two basic groups: high-damage low-control, or low-damage high-control. All wizards can deal decent damage and hinder groups of enemies with at least some of their spells, so it's really a matter of which you'd like your wizard character to favor. In a perfect world, you'd like to have a few spells of each group in order to be ready for anything the Dungeon Master throws at your party.

First, decide which build your wizard character is pursuing:

- **War Wizard:** A wizard whose spell repertoire is geared toward dealing damage to enemies. The war wizard is the simpler wizard to play. Choose a lot of high-damage, low-control spells. Find the spells that deal the most damage and pick them.

- **Control Wizard:** A wizard who chooses spells that create general confusion and frustration for the enemy and deal damage as a secondary effect. Choose a lot of low-damage, high-control spells; any spells that carry conditions such as restrain, slow, stun, or daze are good choices.

To use the spell selections in Tables 14-5 and 14-6, all you have to remember is that your wizard knows every spell given on the tables here for his or her character level, plus all the spells for all previous levels. In other words, the lists are cumulative; if you're playing a 5th-level wizard, your character knows every spell in these tables for levels 1 through 5. (However, at level 13 and level 15 your new selections actually replace older spells.)

The wizard's Spellbook class feature means that you actually pick two daily spells when you get the opportunity to pick daily spells, and you acquire two utility spells when you get the opportunity to pick utility spells. Each day, you can decide which of those two powers your character prepares.

The War Wizard

The advantage of playing a War Wizard is that all your character's efforts directly contribute to the monster's defeat. Your character's spells (see Table 14-5) concentrate on reducing hit points, just like the fighter's sword and the rogue's sneak attack. Everyone in the party is working toward the same goal, which is to reduce the monster's hit points to zero as fast as possible. The disadvantage of playing a War Wizard is that you can't delay or hinder monsters, so you don't mitigate enemy attacks as well as the Control Wizard does.

Table 14-5	War Wizard Build Powers
Level	*Wizard Spells Known*
1st	At-will: *magic missile, scorching burst* Encounter: *burning hands* Daily: *acid arrow*, flaming sphere**
2nd	Utility: *expeditious retreat** (daily), *shield** (encounter)
3rd	Encounter: *shock sphere*
4th	(No new powers)
5th	Daily: *fireball*, stinking cloud**
6th	Utility: *dimension door ** (daily), *invisibility** (daily)
7th	Encounter: *spectral ram*
8th	(No new powers)
9th	Daily: *ice storm*, lightning serpent**
10th	Utility: *blur** (daily), *resistance** (daily)
11th	Encounter: (determined by paragon path)
12th	Utility: (determined by paragon path)
13th	Encounter: *prismatic burst* (replaces *burning hands*)
14th	(No new powers)
15th	Daily: *blast of cold*, prismatic beams** (replaces 1st-level daily)

* These powers are in your wizard's spellbook — you must choose which of the two listed powers at that level to prepare each day.

Your wizard begins with the *magic missile* at-will power. It's an accurate but weak long-range attack. For the War Wizard, we recommend *scorching burst* for your remaining at-will power. It lets you scorch a couple of enemies at range, provided they're standing next to each other.

Your recommended encounter spells are *burning hands* (1st), *shock sphere* (3rd), and *spectral ram* (7th). *Burning hands* is a Close attack; you generally don't want to be in melee if you're a wizard, but if you find yourself there anyway, it's important to retain good offensive options that won't get you killed. *Shock sphere* is a good medium-range attack power that covers a wide area and inflicts lightning damage. It's always a good idea to make sure your attacks dish out two or three different damage types, because you don't want to be shut down when your wizard runs into monsters resistant to fire (or whatever other energy your attack spells rely on). Likewise, *spectral ram* is a good 7th-level choice because it gives you an attack that targets your enemies' Fortitude defense. If you're fighting monsters with very high Reflex defenses, it's good to be able to strike at a different defense with your spells.

Your paragon path determines your 11th-level encounter power, but at 13th level, you get to replace your old 1st-level *burning hands* spell with *prismatic burst,* a long-range attack that also blinds the affected creatures for a short time.

Because of the wizard's Spellbook class feature, you get to pick two daily spells each time you reach a level where you pick daily spells. No other character class gets to do this. Your wizard knows two spells but must prepare one of them for your day of adventure. At 1st level, we recommend preparing *acid arrow;* it deals very good acid damage that can continue to sear the target for several rounds. The 5th-level daily spell *fireball* is one of the iconic spells in the game; it's a long-range attack that affects a big area, dealing moderate damage. Use it on large groups of weak monsters if you can. At 9th level, prepare *ice storm;* it covers a big area and deals less damage, but it has an excellent immobilize effect. When your character reaches 15th level, replace one of your 1st-level spells with *prismatic beams. Prismatic beams* lets you attack all three defenses of your targets at once, and it creates a variety of nasty effects for the bad guys.

Your utility spells work just like your daily spells; you get to pick two each time your character learns a utility spell, even though you have to choose which of the pair to prepare for use each day. We recommend *shield* (2nd level), *dimension door* (6th level), and *blur* (10th level). Your character is a War Wizard, after all, so you want to favor powers that have immediate uses in combat. *Shield* is a very good defense that boosts your wizard's Armor Class and Reflex defense once per encounter. *Dimension door* is one of several very good 6th-level powers, but we like it best because it's a "get out of jail free" card; if your character has a big, hungry monster right in his or her face, he or she can just teleport away. *Blur* is also a fine defensive power that works especially well in battles where you can hang back from your enemies; what they can't see, they can't hit.

The Control Wizard

Damage is great, but given the choice between a spell that deals 3d6 damage or another one that deals 2d6 and immobilizes your targets, you should choose the one that carries the potent side effect. The difference between 2d6 and 3d6 is only an average of 3.5 points of damage, but a monster that's stuck in its square is a monster that you can get away from, that your teammates can surround, or — if nothing else — that you can target again next round, because it's going to be exactly where you left it.

Table 14-6	Control Wizard Build Powers
Level	*Wizard Spells Known*
1st	At-will: *cloud of daggers, thunder wave* Encounter: *icy terrain* Daily: *freezing cloud*, sleep**
2nd	Utility: *expeditious retreat** (daily), *shield** (encounter)
3rd	Encounter: *color spray*
4th	(No new powers)
5th	Daily: *fireball*, web**
6th	Utility: *levitate* *(daily), *invisibility** (daily)
7th	Encounter: *winter's wrath*
8th	(No new powers)
9th	Daily: *ice storm*, wall of fire**
10th	Utility: *arcane gate** (daily), *mirror image** (daily)
11th	Encounter: (determined by paragon path)
12th	Utility: (determined by paragon path)
13th	Encounter: *prismatic burst* (replaces *icy terrain*)
14th	(No new powers)
15th	Daily: *Bigby's grasping hands*, prismatic beams** (replaces 1st-level daily)

* These powers are in your wizard's spellbook — you must choose which of the two listed powers at that level to prepare each day.

For your 1st-level at-will powers, we recommend *cloud of daggers* and *thunder wave. Cloud of daggers* offers good terrain control because the effect persists in the target square until your next turn — creatures that try to move through that square take extra damage. Use this power to block a doorway or narrow hall and keep your enemies at a safe distance. *Thunder wave* deals damage to multiple targets and pushes them away from you.

At 1st level, we recommend *icy terrain* for your encounter power. It knocks each creature you hit prone and creates a nice patch of ice that costs double to move through. When your wizard knocks enemies prone, it severely restricts their actions next turn — it costs a move action to stand up, so they can't move and attack with their remaining action. Choose *color spray* (3rd level) for your next encounter power. It's a Close attack spell, so you can use it even when your character is in the middle of melee, and it attacks Will defense. At 7th level, we recommend *winter's wrath;* it covers a wide area and inflicts good damage.

Your 11th-level encounter power is determined by your paragon path; Spellstorm Mage is the best option for a Control Wizard. At 13th level, you get to replace your 1st-level encounter spell with a 13th-level one. We like *prismatic burst* here because it's another attack against Will defense, and it blinds affected creatures. Monsters can't easily hit what they can't see!

For your character's daily powers, begin with *sleep* (1st level) and then choose *fireball* (5th) and *ice storm* (9th). At 15th level, replace *sleep* with *Bigby's grasping hands* (15th). *Sleep* is a very powerful 1st-level spell that can take several enemies out of the fight in one shot, even if it doesn't do any damage at all. *Fireball* may seem like an odd choice for a Control Wizard, but you do need some powers that apply damage downrange — your character is a controller, not a pacifist. *Ice storm* combines good damage and the ability to immobilize multiple enemies, which is the controller's dream.

Your utility spell choices are much like the War Wizard's. Unlike most other classes, a wizard's utility powers have little to do with his or her role; they're just weird, useful magical things the wizard can do. We recommend *shield* (2nd), *levitate* (6th), and *arcane gate* (10th). Trust us, you'll find plenty of ways to use them!

Choosing Cleric Powers

Cleric powers are called prayers. Clerics channel potent magical prayers, using the divine power source to create overtly supernatural effects; they're armed with the power of mythic deities, after all. Cleric prayers offer a mix of melee and ranged attacks, but they specialize in powers that protect, heal, and strengthen their comrades.

Before you pick out your cleric powers, you need to decide on your cleric build. It's important to pay attention to your ability scores for this — clerics have both Strength-based powers and Wisdom-based powers, so make sure that you choose the build that corresponds with your best ability score.

- ✔ **Battle Cleric:** This cleric favors prayers designed for use in melee and wields his or her powers from the front line. Look for powers that are melee attacks, Close attacks, or rely on Strength.

- ✔ **Devoted Cleric:** The Devoted Cleric supports his or her comrades from the second rank, staying out of melee and relying on ranged prayers. The best powers for this build are ranged attacks or area attacks and are based on Wisdom attacks.

Clerics and healing prayers

The classic job of the cleric in the D&D game is healing, and in previous editions, players with cleric characters had to make sure they loaded up on healing spells. In 4th Edition, you don't have to do that anymore — the game just gives clerics the *healing word* class feature, so your cleric is automatically armed with two uses of the *healing word* power per encounter. Using this power is only a minor action for you, so you can move and use your standard action to make an attack or activate some other power in the same round.

Although *healing word* provides your cleric character with an effective baseline healing ability, many of the cleric powers provide extra healing. It's up to you to decide how many more healing powers you want above the baseline afforded by your class features; we think it's a good idea to have at least one or two more than the minimum mandated by the class.

Take a look at Tables 14-7 and 14-8 in the following sections. If you want to use these recommendations, simply choose the prayers given for each character level. Your character knows all the powers for all previous levels.

The Battle Cleric

To keep it simple, we're steering the Battle Cleric toward hitting bad guys in melee and healing allies. The cleric prayers on Table 14-7 don't offer much ability to "designate targets" for the party or deal with enemies at range, but they let you hit the monsters hard and pour on the healing for your friends. If you want to play an easy cleric, this is the way to go.

Table 14-7	Battle Cleric Build Powers
Level	*Cleric Prayers Known*
1st	At-will: *righteous brand, priest's shield* Encounter: *wrathful thunder* Daily: *avenging flame*
2nd	Utility: *cure light wounds* (encounter)
3rd	Encounter: *command*
4th	(No new powers)
5th	Daily: *consecrated ground*
6th	Utility: *cure serious wounds* (daily)

Level	Cleric Prayers Known
7th	Encounter: *strengthen the faithful*
8th	(No new powers)
9th	Daily: *divine power*
10th	Utility: *mass cure light wounds* (daily)
11th	Encounter: (determined by paragon path)
12th	Utility: (determined by paragon path)
13th	Encounter: *inspiring strike* (replaces *wrathful thunder*)
14th	(No new powers)
15th	Daily: *holy spark* (replaces *avenging flame*)

The Battle Cleric's at-will power selections are *righteous brand* and *priest's shield*. *Righteous brand* is an outstanding offensive power, not because it lets you hit the monster all that hard, but because it confers a very significant attack bonus to an ally of your choice against the foe you attack. If your party is having a hard time hitting a monster, *righteous brand* can help to turn the tide.

For your character's 1st-level encounter power, we suggest *wrathful thunder*. It's an attack that dazes the target. As you advance in level, add the encounter prayers *command* (3rd) and *strengthen the faithful* (7th). *Command* is an effective and accurate ranged attack. While you don't use many ranged attacks, it's good to have a couple in your pocket for when you need one. *Strengthen the faithful* can potentially heal up multiple characters at once. Your 11th level encounter power depends on your paragon path, but at 13th level, replace your old *wrathful thunder* power with *inspiring strike*. It doesn't heal much damage, but the healing this power offers doesn't cost a healing surge — and conserving healing surges can be very important in long adventures.

For your 1st-level daily power, we recommend *avenging flame*. It's a solid attack power that discourages the target from attacking on its turn. *Consecrated ground* is an excellent 5th-level daily prayer. It doesn't make use of an attack roll; it simply establishes an area around your character where enemies take damage and your allies regain hit points every turn. Use it at the beginning of a battle to get the most out of its effects. Your best 9th-level prayer is *divine power,* a potent, close-range, area-effect attack. At 15th level, replace *avenging flame* with *holy spark*.

Cure light wounds is probably the simplest 2nd-level utility power, offering another way to patch up hit point damage. At 6th and 10th level, default to *cure serious wounds* and *mass cure light wounds.* You're not going to run out of healing oomph in this build — we guarantee it.

The Devoted Cleric

Compared with the Battle Cleric, the Devoted Cleric build includes many more powers that work at range, so your character can stand back out of the fray. The Devoted Cleric heals just as well as the Battle Cleric and also has more "target designation" powers — that is, powers that provide your allies with bonuses to attack the enemies you're affecting. Part of the leader role is helping the other players decide which bad guys their characters should be attacking!

Table 14-8	Devoted Cleric Build Powers
Level	*Cleric Prayers Known*
1st	At-will: *lance of faith, sacred flame* Encounter: *healing strike* Daily: *beacon of hope*
2nd	Utility: *shield of faith* (daily)
3rd	Encounter: *daunting light*
4th	(No new powers)
5th	Daily: *spiritual weapon*
6th	Utility: *bastion of health* (daily)
7th	Encounter: *searing light*
8th	(No new powers)
9th	Daily: *flame strike*
10th	Utility: *mass cure light wounds* (daily)
11th	Encounter: (determined by paragon path)
12th	Utility: (determined by paragon path)
13th	Encounter: *mantle of glory* (replaces *healing strike*)

Level	Cleric Prayers Known
14th	(No new powers)
15th	Daily: *seal of warding* (replaces *beacon of hope*)

The suggested at-will prayers for the Devoted Cleric are *lance of faith* and *sacred flame*. Both are ranged powers; if you find yourself in melee, your at-will "power" is simply a basic melee attack with your mace. *Lance of faith* is a good target-designation power because it grants one ally a bonus to attack the target you hit. *Sacred flame* is another ranged attack, but this one is an excellent healing power. When you use it, you can either grant temporary hit points to an ally or grant an ally the opportunity to make a saving throw. Temporary hit points aren't healing, but they help to mitigate the damage suffered by the ally you're protecting the next time he or she gets hit by an attack.

For your 1st-level encounter prayer, we recommend *healing strike*. It's a melee attack, but you need a couple of those. At 3rd level, take *daunting light*. It's a good ranged attack and also gives your allies combat advantage against the target, so it's another good target-designator prayer. At 7th level, *searing light* deals damage and blinds the target. Your 13th-level encounter prayer replaces *healing strike;* we recommend *mantle of glory*. This is a great Close attack that covers a big area, deals a lot of damage to enemies, and also triggers a healing surge for any of your allies who happen to be in the area of the effect.

The Devoted Cleric's 1st-level daily prayer is *beacon of hope,* a Close power that weakens all enemies around you while healing your allies and boosting your healing ability for the rest of the encounter. At 5th level, choose *spiritual weapon* for a decent ranged attack that gives your allies combat advantage against the target for as long as you keep the power going. *Flame strike* is a fine area attack at 9th level. It doesn't provide any healing or help out your allies, but sometimes you just need to toast the bad guys. When you reach 15th level, replace *beacon of hope* with *seal of warding*. This deals very high damage for a cleric power and adds a little bit of terrain control, too.

For your utility powers, we recommend *shield of faith* (2nd), *bastion of health* (6th), and *mass cure light wounds* (10th). The Devoted Cleric can afford to skip *divine aid* because the *sacred flame* at-will power lets you grant saving throws when you need to. The Devoted Cleric prefers *bastion of health* to *cure serious wounds* because *bastion of health* is a minor action, and it has a very good range. It might not provide as much healing, but it's extremely easy to use. *Mass cure light wounds* provides you with the ability to turn around a losing battle in a hurry because you can heal the whole party with one prayer.

If you choose to play a healing-heavy cleric, you may find that you have few discretionary actions in the course of the game. Many of your turns will be sucked up in tending to injured characters. Other players will often take it for granted that you're willing to give up your turn in order to keep their characters in the fight. If that doesn't sound like fun to you, avoid using your utility power selections for healing prayers that cost you standard actions.

Powers for other classes

One of the biggest innovations in DUNGEONS & DRAGONS 4th Edition game is that *every* character is a spellcaster . . . so to speak. The paladin, ranger, warlock, and warlord gain powers using the same master advancement table that the four classes we discuss in this chapter use. Here are a few quick tips on choosing powers when you create characters of one of these other classes:

✔ **Paladin:** *Righteous smite* is an excellent 3rd-level encounter prayer that deals good damage and provides temporary hit points to you and all your allies. The only drawback is that it's a Charisma attack, which probably lags behind your Wisdom attacks. *Benign transposition* (7th level) is an encounter prayer that lets you switch places with an endangered ally and make a good attack against any foe you're now next to.

✔ **Ranger:** Your choice of ranger powers depends on whether you decided to go with the archery style or two-weapon fighting style. Fortunately, many ranger powers work in both melee and at range, changing from Strength attacks to Dexterity attacks accordingly. Rangers also excel in reactive powers that you can use as interrupt actions; for example, at 3rd level, the encounter exploit *disruptive strike* lets you immediately attack an enemy who's taking a swing at you or one of your allies. If you hit, you deal damage and a big attack penalty on the attacking creature.

✔ **Warlock:** Warlocks are strikers, like rangers and rogues, but many of their daily spells also inflict substantial control effects. For example, the 5th-level daily spell *hunger of Hadar* is a small-area-effect attack that creates a zone of damaging darkness. Any creature in the zone — or that moves into the zone later — takes damage. This allows the warlock to deny an area to enemies who don't want to take damage.

✔ **Warlord:** Warlords have few powers that work well at range. They're all melee leaders, really. However, some of the most iconic warlord powers let the warlord grant an ally the opportunity to attack. Powers such as *hammer and anvil* (1st-level encounter power) or *surprise attack* (7th-level encounter power) don't allow the warlord to do much damage, but the ability to choose an ally to take a swing at the target as well means that these powers actually provide excellent offensive leadership.

Chapter 15

Selecting Feats

. . . .

In This Chapter

▶ Adding up your feat choices

▶ Understanding feat requirements

▶ Getting a handle on feat types

▶ Taking a shortcut: choosing feats for your character's build

. . . .

*E*very character has his or her own unique set of advantages, training, or special tricks. Even two characters who otherwise would appear to be very similar — say, two dwarves who are both 5th-level fighters — might choose different powers, acquire different magic items, and specialize in different weapons. *Feats* are one of the ways you can customize your character and differentiate him or her from similar characters. Feats are special advantages that represent your character's own unique training and combat style.

Fighter characters can choose feats that reward them for mastering specific weapons such as light blades, axes, or hammers. Wizard characters can gain feats that make them especially good at casting certain types of spells or using certain types of wizardly implements. Clerics and paladins can learn feats that give them new ways to use their Channel Divinity class features. And all characters can choose feats that give them training in new skills, make them especially observant or quick to react, or grant proficiency in armor or weapons they wouldn't normally be able to use.

In this chapter, we tell you how your character gains feats and how you can use feat selections to customize your character with special edges and hidden strengths. We also provide you with recommendations on how you should spend your feats for the basic builds of the fighter, rogue, wizard, and cleric classes. Feats can be a great way to fine-tune your character build, and we help you do it right.

What's a Feat?

Feats are specific bonuses or unusual advantages that customize your character's capabilities and performance. They range from relatively simple feats like Durable (which gives your character more healing surges per day) to spectacular combat options such as Lightning Arc (which allows you to convert a critical hit you score with a lightning power into a hit against another target altogether). Most feats simply grant your character a static, "always-on" benefit or adjustment that you don't have to track during play.

Over the course of your character's career, you eventually build up a collection of feats. Taken together, your character's feats form a suite or library of special edges, useful talents, and combat tricks that make him or her different from any other character of the same class and level. The higher your character's level, the more feats he or she knows, and the more feats known, the more unique and powerful your character becomes.

You can find the definitive word on feats in Chapter 6 of the *Player's Handbook*. Feats are organized into heroic tier, paragon tier, and epic tier. Your character must be at least 11th level to choose paragon feats and at least 21st level to choose epic feats.

Sample feats

Here are three quick examples of some feats you can find in the *Player's Handbook*. (You'll need to visit the *Player's Handbook* to find the definitions of the feats we mention throughout this book, as well as to see the entire range of feats available to characters.)

✔ **Improved Initiative**

Prerequisite: None.

Benefit: You get a +4 bonus on Initiative checks.

✔ **Power Attack**

Prerequisite: Strength 15.

Benefit: When making a melee attack, you can take a –2 penalty to the attack roll. If the attack hits, you gain a +2 bonus to the damage roll (or a +3 bonus to the damage roll with a two-handed weapon). This extra damage increases by level: At 11th level, you gain a +4 bonus to your damage roll (or +6 with a two-handed weapon); at 21st level, you gain a +6 bonus to your damage roll (or +9 with a two-handed weapon).

✔ **Surprise Knockdown [Rogue]**

Prerequisites: Str 15, Rogue class

Benefit: If you score a critical hit while you have combat advantage, you knock the target prone.

Most feats are general feats that any character can take, but some — like Surprise Knockdown — are restricted to characters of certain classes or races. You may notice that Power Attack and Surprise Knockdown also have an ability requirement: Your character must have a Strength score of 15 or better in order to choose either of these feats.

The Basics of Acquiring Feats

Here's the bad news about feats: They're great, but your character learns them slowly. Characters get one feat at 1st level, plus one feat for every even-numbered level they reach (which gives characters a total of two feats at 2nd level, three feats at 4th level, four feats at 6th level, and so on).

The two key exceptions to this rule are that

- ✔ Humans begin with one bonus feat at 1st level as a racial advantage.
- ✔ Some classes offer bonus feats as class features. For example, clerics and wizards gain the Ritual Caster feat as a bonus feat — they don't have to spend any of their feat selections on Ritual Caster.

As much as you might like to pick Heavy Blade Mastery for your character's first feat choice, you can't do it. Most feats have one or more requirements that your character must meet before you can add them to his or her arsenal. For example, your character must have a Strength score of 15 or better to take the Power Attack feat. The best feats require that your character first reach paragon or epic level, and then you have to meet challenging ability requirements. In the case of Heavy Blade Mastery, your character must have a Strength score of 21 or better, a Dexterity score of 17 or better, and be at least 21st level. Wow!

The good news for beginning characters is that many feats have requirements that are easily met by even a 1st-level character (or no requirements at all), so you're pretty much guaranteed of finding something your character can use right from day one.

Two tricky requirements are race and class. If your character isn't a dwarf, he or she can't pick dwarf feats. That's pretty straightforward. Similarly, you can't pick a rogue feat if your character isn't a rogue. (You can't get around the requirements for racial feats, but you can take a multiclass feat to gain access to another class's feats. See Chapter 22 for more information about multiclassing your character.)

Planning Your Feat Choices

Feats can be pretty daunting because there are so many to choose from. So, what we do here is provide you with a recommended set of feat selections for the two basic builds in each character class. It's a good idea to have a plan for which feats your character will select over the next few levels so that you can make sure you get the feats you want as quickly as possible.

If you're not sure which feats are the best choice for your character, you can use these feat packages as a basic plan for making a sound (if not particularly creative) set of feat choices for your character as he or she rises in level and gains more feat choices.

Try the following process when evaluating your feat choices:

1. **Choose your character's class (if you haven't already), and then decide which build you want your character to follow within that class.**

   A skillful Guardian Fighter, for example, needs to learn different feats from a muscle-bound, axe-wielding Great Weapon Fighter, even though they're both fighters.

2. **Consult the feat recommendations for your character's class and chosen build (for descriptions of how these work in each build, see the sections that follow), or design your own feat plan.**

   After you've played the game for a while and you've made up a few characters, experiment with building feat plans that exploit feat choices our recommendations here don't make use of.

3. **Make any extra feat selections you have coming to you, such as the bonus feat that human characters get at 1st level.**

4. **Record your feat selections on your character sheet.**

The feat recommendations presented in this chapter don't account for a human character's bonus feat. In most cases, you can use the bonus feat to climb your way up the list even faster, but watch out for feats with level requirements. For example, if you're following the Guardian Fighter build recommendations on Table 15-1, you simply can't buy the Mettle feat before your character reaches 11th level, because Mettle is a paragon feat. Try using your character's human bonus feat to pick up Alertness, Durable, Human Perseverance, or Skill Training. (The Perception skill is a very good choice.) These feats are good for any human character.

Choosing fighter feats

For the purpose of choosing feats, we're going to make you decide whether you want your fighter character to be a Great Weapon Fighter or Guardian Fighter. (See Chapter 11 for a description of these builds.)

Table 15-1	Fighter Feat Recommendations	
Level	*Great Weapon Fighter*	*Guardian Fighter*
1	Weapon Focus	Toughness
2	Toughness	Weapon Focus
4	Armor Proficiency (Plate)	Armor Proficiency (Plate)
6	Alertness	(racial feat)
8	(racial feat)	Blade Opportunist
10	Power Attack	Durable
11	Mettle	Mettle or Evasion
12	Devastating Critical	Shield Proficiency (Light)
14	Blood Thirst	Heavy Blade Opportunity

Great Weapon Fighter feat suggestions

The basic plan for a Great Weapon Fighter is to run up to the monsters and just beat the tar out of them with a big sword, axe, warhammer, or whatever implement of mayhem catches your fancy. If you ever find that you don't know what you want your character to do, have him or her *hit something!* You want your character to deal out terrific amounts of damage in the shortest time possible.

Your fighter character needs a Strength score of 15 or better to make this set of recommendations work. Your best weapon choices are the greataxe, greatsword, heavy flail, or maul. (Our power recommendations in Chapter 14 assume the greataxe, so keep that in mind.)

Start with the Weapon Focus feat to gain a bonus to damage with your chosen weapon. Then take Toughness to get more hit points — as a fighter, you can never have too many hit points. Armor Training is a good idea, because switching from scale armor to plate armor is worth +1 AC. A little bit of Armor Class improvement goes a long way on the front lines.

For your 8th level feat, we recommend choosing one of the feats offered by your character race — for example, Action Surge for a human, Lost in the Crowd for a halfling, and so on. Racial feats tend to be very good, and you'll want them. If you don't like any of these choices, Durable or Improved Initiative never go out of style.

The Power Attack feat doesn't do that much for your character early in his or her career, so wait until you approach the 11th-level threshold, where the damage boost offered by the feat improves.

In paragon tier, pick up Mettle as soon as you can; it's one of the best feats out there. After that, have fun maximizing your damage with Devastating Critical and Blood Thirst. You want to hit the bad guys hard, after all!

Guardian Fighter feat suggestions

A Guardian Fighter character is built to move to the exact spot where he or she can do the most good and then slice the enemy to pieces with panache. A Guardian Fighter is especially good at fighting defensively and exerting control over the battlefield, so he or she can lock down multiple enemies and keep them busy. Your character is willing to give up some damage-dealing potential in order to maximize defenses and keep many enemies under control.

These recommendations are a little more challenging than those for the Great Weapon Fighter because you need to have a good Dexterity score and a respectable Wisdom score, too. Your character needs a Dexterity of 13 early on, and 15 by paragon tier. And, because you're a fighter, you still need to have the best Strength score you can manage. For weapons and armor, your character should be a sword-and-shield fighter; the longsword is the best bet.

In your character's early career, your feat choices look a lot like the Great Weapon Fighter's. The first important point of divergence is Blade Opportunist. Hitting hard isn't terribly important to you, but making sure that your opportunity attacks are *extremely* dangerous is — that's one of your principle mechanisms for keeping the monsters under control.

In paragon tier, get Mettle early. Eventually, you'll want Evasion too, but first, we recommend Shield Specialization. It grants you an additional +1 to AC and Reflex defense for using a shield, which is very good. At 14th level, Heavy Blade Opportunity allows you to use an at-will power any time you make an opportunity attack. The *sure strike* and *tide of iron powers* are much more effective than a simple basic attack when your enemy gives you that opening you've been waiting for.

Choosing rogue feats

Rogues have access to a variety of interesting and sneaky feats. The two builds we show you in Table 15-2 are the Brawny Rogue and the Trickster Rogue. (See Chapter 11 for more on the rogue builds.)

Table 15-2	Rogue Feat Recommendations	
Level	*Brawny Rogue*	*Trickster Rogue*
1	Weapon Focus	Backstabber
2	Nimble Blade	Nimble Blade
4	Toughness	Improved Initiative
6	Improved Initiative	(racial feat)
8	(racial feat)	Press the Advantage
10	Armor Proficiency (Hide)	Toughness
11	Evasion	Evasion
12	Defensive Advantage	Combat Anticipation
14	(racial feat)	Danger Sense

Brawny Rogue feat suggestions

A rogue with this build is meant to get into a scrape and dish out as much sneak attack damage as he or she can. When one of your character's allies engages a foe in a toe-to-toe fight, your character gets behind the bad guy as quickly as possible to set up a flanking situation and then makes as many attacks as he or she can.

Your character needs a Dexterity of 15 or higher to optimize this strategy because that's what you need to select the Nimble Blade feat. (Then again, every rogue should have a Dex of at least 15, really.) By paragon tier, your character must have a Dexterity of 17 or better to be able to select Defensive Advantage.

Begin your feat selections with Weapon Focus (Light Blades) and Nimble Blade. Your character should be fighting with a short sword or dagger, and these feats help you to hit more often and deal more damage with those weapons. Toughness is useful because the Brawny Rogue is often in the middle of the melee, and despite your best efforts, your character is going to get hit. The extra hit points provided by Toughness really add up over time. Improved Initiative is key for any rogue because you want your character to go first in a fight in order to maximize opportunities for dealing sneak attack damage.

Eventually, you want to choose a feat restricted to your character race. These are some of the best feats in the game, and you don't want to miss out. Finish up your heroic tier feats by choosing Armor Proficiency (hide) to upgrade from leather armor to hide armor. It's worth a +1 bonus to your Armor Class.

In paragon tier, select Evasion early — if you have Evasion, Close, and Area attacks that would normally deal half damage on a miss against your AC or Reflex defense instead deal no damage at all. Powers that attack your Reflex defense include things like *fireball* spells cast by evil wizards or dragon breath attacks; trust us, it's useful. The Defensive Advantage feat helps you to survive once you get into a position where you have combat advantage over a foe. Finally, don't miss the opportunity to choose another racial feat at paragon tier.

If your character is a halfling, make sure you take the feat Halfling Agility. It's very, very good, as it provides a penalty to your enemies when you make them roll again using your *second chance* racial ability (described in Chapter 12).

Trickster Rogue feat suggestions

Characters who spend a lot of time in the middle of the group of bad guys get hurt, so the Trickster Rogue wants no part of that. A Trickster Rogue doesn't rely on flanking an enemy to gain combat advantage. Instead, he or she places more emphasis on going first each encounter. The class feature of First Strike grants your rogue combat advantage against enemies who haven't yet acted in the encounter, so beating enemy initiative rolls is the easiest way to gain your sneak attack bonus damage. After that first round, the Trickster Rogue relies on powers instead of positioning to set up additional sneak attacks.

You need a Dexterity score of 15 (for Nimble Blade) and a Charisma score of 15 (for Press the Advantage) to follow these feat recommendations, but a higher Dexterity is better. A high Dexterity helps your character to win initiative and makes him or her harder to hit, and both are highly desirable for any rogue.

Your first feat choices should be Backstabber, Nimble Blade, and Improved Initiative. Backstabber helps you to make up for the edge a Brawny Rogue gains on sneak attack damage. Nimble Blade gives you an attack bonus with light blades as long as you have combat advantage, which you're trying to get in almost every round anyway. Improved Initiative maximizes your initiative bonus — and you want to make sure you go first.

Press the Advantage is interesting. If you score a critical hit, you automatically retain combat advantage against the target for a round. It's a little situational; after all, you score critical hits only when you roll a 20. However, it's very useful for the Trickster Rogue because you would prefer to *not* have to flank the enemy in order to gain combat advantage. This feat works quite well for an elf rogue because *elven accuracy* (a racial power) gives you more opportunities to roll that 20.

As with the Brawny Rogue, Toughness and Evasion are smart investments. You don't need Toughness as much as the Brawny Rogue does (theoretically, you're not getting attacked as often), but you should pick it up eventually. Combat Anticipation is a very useful defensive feat that protects you against most attacks made from a distance. Because you hope to spend less time in melee than the Brawny Rogue, it's another good investment. Finally, we finish up our Trickster Rogue recommendations with Danger Sense. This feat lets you roll two dice and use the better result when you're rolling initiative, which translates to another big bonus on initiative checks. Rogues always want to go first.

Choosing wizard feats

You have an entirely different set of feat choices to weigh for a wizard character than for a fighter or rogue. You want to choose feats to enhance your character's magical prowess and to master useful spellcasting tricks, not study the arts of swordsmanship and archery. The two builds described in Table 15-3 are the War Wizard and Control Wizard (see Chapter 11).

Table 15-3	Wizard Feat Recommendations	
Level	*War Wizard*	*Control Wizard*
1	Improved Initiative	Expanded Spellbook
2	Astral Fire	Improved Initiative
4	Toughness	Burning Blizzard
6	(racial feat)	(racial feat)
8	Armor Proficiency (leather)	Toughness
10	Raging Storm	(racial feat)
11	Arcane Reach	Arcane Reach
12	Devastating Critical	Spell Focus
14	Evasion	Second Implement

War Wizard feat suggestions

The War Wizard's objective is pretty simple: Get as much damage downrange on as many targets as possible. All you need to do with this build is choose feats that provide damage bonuses, especially if you can match up those bonuses with the types of powers your character employs most often.

To make use of these feat suggestions, your War Wizard needs Constitution 13, Dexterity 15, and Charisma 13 or better. That may sound like a lot, but it's not that hard — and you want ability scores that can help out your Fortitude and Will defenses anyway. Dexterity is a little tougher, but it's important. First of all, your Wand of Accuracy class feature relies on it. Secondly, the Astral Fire and Arcane Reach feats require it, and those are feats you want.

Your initial feat selections include Improved Initiative, Astral Fire, and Toughness. Improved Initiative lets you usually go earlier in the combat so that you can cast your area spells without fear of accidentally catching your allies in the blasts. Astral Fire just gives you a straight damage bonus on fire and radiant powers, and you'll acquire plenty of those during your career. Toughness is a good idea, simply because wizards don't have many hit points and you never know when you might wish you had more.

At 6th level, pick up one of your racial feats. Then choose Armor Proficiency (leather) to upgrade your armor choices. When you reach 8th level, pick Raging Storm to boost spells with lightning or thunder damage.

For paragon tier feats, we like starting with Arcane Reach. It lets you begin a Close power up to two squares away from your actual location. This lets you include more enemies in the area of effect or steer your Close powers around your own allies more easily. Devastating Critical should be your next choice. Normally we're lukewarm on feats that work only when you roll a 20, but here's the deal: As a War Wizard, you make more attack rolls than any other character in the game because your powers affect multiple targets and you're usually rolling two or three attacks every time you take an action. You'll get plenty of chances for your extra damage. Finally, we recommend Evasion. Evasion is an excellent defensive feat that helps you to avoid damage from many Area and Close attacks.

Control Wizard feat suggestions

Your feat selection is a little scattershot, covering a mix of damage, defense, tactics, and utility. Ideally, you want to find feats that make your heavy-control spells hit more often or last longer . . . but feats like that are scarce, so you'll have to settle for feats that provide a little extra damage or boost your defense when you cast the spells you use most often.

To make use of our recommendations, your wizard character needs a minimum Intelligence 13, Wisdom 13, and Charisma 13. (Your Intelligence score should be *much* higher than that, though!) Wisdom 13 is required for your Expanded Spellbook and Burning Blizzard feats, and Charisma 13 is what you need for your Spell Focus feat — one of the most important feats to a Control Wizard.

Your early feat selections include Expanded Spellbook, Improved Initiative, and Burning Blizzard. Expanded Spellbook lets you learn even more daily attack spells, ensuring that you'll be able to customize your spell selection for specific adventures. Improved Initiative is helpful because as a Control Wizard your Dexterity score is probably marginal — a 13 is all you need for a long time — and you need the help. Establishing control over your enemy's movements works best if you get to throw your spell *before* your enemies get to move up next to your allies. Finally, Burning Blizzard is handy because many of the best control spells are cold-based, so you might as well hand out just a little more damage.

Pick up a good racial feat of your choice at 6th level (Action Surge or Human Perseverance are good if you're human) and then take Toughness at 8th level. Extra hit points never go out of fashion. For your 10th level feat, pick up another racial feat for good measure.

In the paragon tier, make sure you choose Arcane Reach and Spell Focus. Spell Focus is the Control Wizard's dream feat because many of your best powers last only until your targets succeed on their saving throws. Second Implement is good for any wizard and gives you more options for improving the effectiveness of your spells.

Choosing cleric feats

Clerics are interested in a variety of feats, ranging from feats that provide new weapon and armor choices to feats that improve the effectiveness of various prayers. The two builds of cleric we discuss here are the Battle Cleric and Devoted Cleric, described in Table 15-4. (See Chapter 11 for more information on character builds.)

Table 15-4	Cleric Feat Recommendations	
Level	*Battle Cleric*	*Devoted Cleric*
1	Weapon Proficiency	Channel Divinity (by deity)
2	Armor Proficiency (Scale)	Astral Fire
4	Channel Divinity (by deity)	(racial feat)
6	(racial feat)	Toughness
8	Toughness	Alertness
10	Weapon Focus	Skill Training
11	Mettle	Combat Anticipation
12	Devastating Critical	Iron Will
14	Astral Fire	Weapon Focus

Battle Cleric feat suggestions

The Battle Cleric likes mixing it up, and he or she wants to be a very good melee combatant. Your character is almost as good at melee combat as the fighter, and your powers have the added advantage of being able to strengthen friends and heal the wounded when needed.

To follow these suggestions, your cleric needs Strength 13, Constitution 13, Intelligence 13, and Charisma 13. The Strength and Constitution requirements let you acquire Armor Proficiency (Scale); in fact, if you have Strength and Constitution scores of 15 or better, you could actually train up to plate armor after you learn how to use scale armor. The Intelligence and Charisma requirements are for your Astral Fire feat.

The *Player's Handbook* suggests that Battle Clerics should begin with Weapon Focus, but we have a better idea: Choose Weapon Proficiency and learn how to use a bastard sword instead. Most simple weapons have a proficiency bonus of +2, but the bastard sword has a proficiency bonus of +3, so in effect you're getting +1 to hit. And its 1d10 damage is better than most simple weapons too, giving you an effective +1 to damage as compared to the mace. Wait on Weapon Focus until you've gained proficiency in a weapon better than the cleric's old standby.

Because you're going to be in melee, you should improve your armor choices as much as you can. Pick up Armor Proficiency (Scale); it's +1 AC compared to chain armor. At 4th level, choose the Channel Divinity feat appropriate for your character's patron deity; these are all very fun feats that make your Channel Divinity class feature useful in just about every encounter, not just encounters against undead.

Toughness is important for a Battle Cleric. (Once again, your character is in melee a lot, so he or she will get hit.) Make sure you pick up a racial feat when you can — racial feats are usually quite good.

In paragon tier, you'll find that Mettle is an excellent defensive feat that will save you a fair amount of damage in encounters against the right monsters. Evasion is better, but it requires a Dexterity of 15, so you probably can't meet the ability requirements. Devastating Critical may come up any time you make an attack. Finally, Astral Fire provides a nice damage boost because many cleric powers deal radiant or fire damage.

Devoted Cleric feat suggestions

Your Devoted Cleric is much less interested in melee combat than the Battle Cleric but should still be reasonably competent if the battle comes to close quarters. Most of your combat power comes in the form of decent direct-attack prayers that also enhance your companions' fighting abilities and defenses.

Key feats for other classes

Although these feat suggestions give you serviceable clerics, fighters, rogues, and wizards, you might wonder which feats you should consider if your character happens to be a member of one of the other classes in the game. Here's a quick set of suggestions for each of the classes we don't cover at length:

✔ **Paladin:** Choose Channel Divinity feats; pick the one appropriate to your deity early in your career. Weapon Focus is a good choice. Astral Fire is another good choice if your Intelligence is 13; many of your powers deal radiant damage. And don't forget Toughness!

✔ **Ranger:** The ranger's combat style class ability provides your character with a free feat. If you follow the archery path for your ranger, you gain Defensive Mobility for free; if you follow two-weapon combat, you gain Toughness. Make sure you pick up Weapon Focus, Two-Weapon Fighting, and Two-Weapon Defense if you're a melee ranger.

✔ **Warlock:** You can select feats that improve the effects of your pact boon: Improved Dark One's Blessing, Improved Fate of the Void, or Improved Misty Step. Energy damage feats such as Astral Fire, Burning Blizzard, and Dark Fury are also good choices. Consider improving your Armor Class by choosing Armor Proficiency (hide).

✔ **Warlord:** You should definitely invest in Shield Proficiency (light and heavy), Armor Proficiency (scale), and Toughness. Taking Weapon Proficiency in a superior melee weapon and Weapon Focus in that weapon is a good idea. Choose Inspired Recovery or Tactical Assault when you get the chance.

To use these suggestions, your character needs an Intelligence of 13 and a Charisma of 13 to acquire the Astral Fire feat. If you decide you want to improve your armor options, you also need Strength 13 and Constitution 13 in order to select Armor Proficiency (Scale).

For your first few feats, we recommend starting with the Channel Divinity feat appropriate to your character's deity choice. These feats significantly expand the ways you can use your Channel Divinity class feature. After that, learn the Astral Fire feat. Although you don't care all that much about inflicting damage, the great majority of prayers available to your character deal out radiant or fire damage. Don't forget to take a look at the racial feats available to your character early in your career.

To finish out the heroic tier, we recommend Toughness and Alertness. You may have noticed that we recommend Toughness for every single character. There's a reason; extra hit points help in every encounter. Alertness is more of a "flavor" choice that makes it harder for the monsters to surprise you. Because you're the party's primary healer, you want to make sure that you aren't taken out of the fight by a sudden ambush.

Multiclass feats

One last thing we should tell you about feats: Feats are how your character learns class features and powers from different character classes. This is referred to as "multiclassing," and it lets you create combinations such as a warlock/fighter, a cleric/ranger, or a paladin/ wizard. Multiclass feats are described at the end of Chapter 6 in the *Player's Handbook*. Multiclassing is an advanced technique for character creation, so we look at multiclass feats more closely in Chapter 22 in this book.

As you move into paragon tier, Combat Anticipation and Iron Will are good choices. Combat Anticipation is a good defensive feat, especially because the Devoted Cleric tries to stay out of the front lines; most of the attacks that come your way are Close, Area, or Ranged. Iron Will makes your Will defense even more formidable. Finally, take Weapon Focus to reinforce your melee attacks for the rare occasions when you do take out your mace.

Chapter 16

Picking Skills

In This Chapter

▶ Getting a handle on skills

▶ Choosing skills for your character

▶ Using skill packages

 egdar the fighter and Kerwyn the rogue are fleeing from a rampaging umber hulk when they come to a slender rope bridge swaying over a bottomless chasm. Kerwyn darts across the bridge with ease, but Regdar picks his way over the obstacle hand-over-hand, only one small slip away from a terrifying plunge. If you're wondering how Kerwyn made it look so easy, the answer is simple: skills. Kerwyn is trained in Acrobatics — balancing, tightrope walking, tumbling, and other such tasks. Regdar's training doesn't extend to such exercises — and at the moment, he kind of wishes it did.

In this chapter, we tell you how characters learn and use skills, and we show you a set of quick skill packages that will make choosing skills for your character fast, easy, and effective.

All about Skills

Skills represent your character's training in tasks that don't directly involve combat. The DUNGEONS & DRAGONS game has 17 distinct skills in the *Player's Handbook*, ranging from Acrobatics to Thievery.

All characters have some basic ability in any skill; for example, you can try an Acrobatics skill check even if your character doesn't have any special talent for it. In the example at the beginning of the chapter, Regdar's in exactly that position: He's taking his chances with that precarious rope bridge even though he doesn't have a knack for balancing. However, if you want your character to be good at a skill, your character must be *trained* in it. If you're trained, you gain a +5 bonus on checks you make with that skill, and (depending on the skill) you may be able to try things that untrained characters simply can't.

A sample skill

Here's an example of a skill description from the *Player's Handbook*, Chapter 5. (You can find descriptions of all the other skills in the game there.) This example shows the Thievery skill and one of its four basic functions — disabling traps.

THIEVERY (DEXTERITY)

Armor Check Penalty

Your character has picked up thieving abilities and can perform tasks that require nerves of steel and a steady hand: disabling traps, opening locks, picking pockets, and sleight of hand. The DM may decide that some uses of this skill are so specialized that your character is required to be trained in it to have a chance of succeeding.

Disable Trap

Make a Thievery check to prevent a trap from triggering. You need to be aware of a trap to try to disable it. Make a Perception check to find a hidden trap.

Disable Trap: Standard action in combat or as part of a skill challenge.

- ✔ *DC:* See the following table. You get a +2 bonus on the check if you use thieves' tools.

- ✔ *Delay Trap:* You get a +5 bonus on the check if you try to delay a trap rather than disabling it.

- ✔ *Success:* You disable or delay the trap. Disabling a trap makes it harmless until it resets. Delaying a trap makes the trapped area safe for passage until the end of your next turn.

- ✔ *Fail by 4 or less:* Nothing happens.

- ✔ *Fail by 5 or more:* You trigger the trap.

Trap	Thievery DC
Heroic tier	20
Paragon tier	30
Epic tier	35

The information following the name of the skill tells you that this is a Dexterity-based skill, so you make a Dexterity check to use Thievery. *Armor Check Penalty* means that you must add the armor check modifier for the armor your character wears to this check; it's hard to disable traps in plate armor. The information under *Disable Trap* tells you how to use Thievery to accomplish this specific task; there are similar sections for Open Lock and Pick Pocket, which we didn't include here. The table shows the average Difficulty Class for disabling traps found in adventures at the various adventuring tiers; this is the target number you have to hit with a roll of 1d20 + ½ your level + your Dex modifier (and + 5, if you're trained in Thievery) in order to disable a trap of that sort.

The number of skills your character is trained in and the skills he or she can choose from depend on his or her class, race, and level. Some character classes gain training in more skills than others — for example, rogues and rangers rely on their skills more than fighters or wizards do. We explain the skill selection process later in this chapter, in the "Choosing your character's skills" section.

Every skill is associated with a *key ability*. For example, Acrobatics is a Dexterity-based skill — the reasoning is that if a person has great Dexterity, he or she is good at balancing and tumbling, but a person who has a crummy Dexterity is terrible at them. Your *skill bonus* is your character's total modifier to checks made with that skill. This always includes your character's level modifier and your character's key ability modifier, and it may include modifiers for being trained in the skill, racial bonuses, feat bonuses, or magic item bonuses.

Sometimes a great ability score and a few experience levels can largely make up for a lack of training. For example, a 1st-level character with training in Acrobatics and a Dexterity score of 13 (+5 trained modifier, +1 ability modifier, for a total +6 skill check bonus) isn't quite as good at balancing as an untrained 6th-level character with a Dexterity score of 18 (+3 level modifier and +4 ability modifier, for a total +7 skill check bonus).

Using skills

To use one of your character's skills, you make a *skill check*. A skill check is a twenty-sided die (d20) roll adjusted by your level modifier (½ your level), the key ability score modifier for the skill, an additional +5 if you're trained in the skill, and any other bonus or special modifier. Some character races and feats confer additional bonuses on particular skill checks; for example, elves gain +2 on Nature and Perception checks. The most common special modifier is an *armor check penalty* — a negative modifier to certain skills for wearing heavy armor. If a skill is affected by the armor check penalty, the skill description will clearly state that. In addition, there may be various circumstance modifiers the DM decides to apply. So here's what the formula looks like:

> **Skill Check** = 1d20 + level modifier + ability modifier + 5 (if trained) + special modifiers (if any)

Your skill check yields a result that might range from less than 0 (if significant negative circumstances apply) to 30 or better (if you rolled well on a trained skill based on one of your character's higher ability scores).

The DM compares your skill check result to a *Difficulty Class (DC)* or target number appropriate to the task your character is trying to accomplish. Difficulty Class works a lot like Armor Class — it's a target number you're trying to reach or exceed by rolling a d20 and adding the appropriate modifiers. For something easy, the DC might be only 5 or 10. (Table 16-1 shows some sample DCs.) For something fiendishly hard, the DC might be 35, 40, or even higher. In fact, it might be completely impossible for your character to succeed at some tasks; no character can leap a 100-foot wide crevasse (a DC 201 Athletics check, DC 101 with a running start) without a lot of magical help.

The skill descriptions in the *Player's Handbook* list specific DCs for all sorts of things you might have your character try to do with that skill. The DM uses these skill descriptions to set the DC for any specific skill use you want your character to attempt. Sometimes the DM just has to take a best guess at how hard something is because you can try almost anything in a D&D game. If you want your character to leap down from a rooftop and land astride a galloping horse streaking by below, it's an Acrobatics or Athletics check of some kind, but you won't find "jump into the saddle of a galloping horse" on the DC tables in those skills. That's why you have a Dungeon Master — so someone can take a shot at adjudicating things the rules don't cover.

Table 16-1	Sample Skill DCs
DC	**Example of a Task**
5	Overhear normal conversation close by with the Perception skill
10	Climb a rope with the Athletics skill
15	Grant an ally a chance to make a saving throw with the Heal skill
20	Balance on a narrow or unstable surface with the Acrobatics skill
25	Recall lore only a master wizard might know with the Arcana skill
30	Learn secret information in a hostile settlement with the Streetwise skill
35	Recall the resistances and vulnerabilities of a pit fiend with the Religion skill

Chapter 5 of the *Player's Handbook* has long descriptions of every skill, including a number of sample DCs for tasks in each skill.

Choosing your character's skills

When you create a 1st-level character, you begin play with training in a certain number of skills. The number of skills you gain training in depends on your character's class and whether or not you're playing a human — humans begin with training in one extra skill as a racial benefit.

There's one more thing you need to know: The list of skills you can choose for your character is limited by his or her class. For example, a 1st-level fighter begins play with three trained skills, chosen from this list: Athletics, Endurance, Heal, Intimidate, and Streetwise. You might like to play a fighter who knows something about Religion or Thievery, but no such luck — to gain access to skills that aren't on your class list, you'll have to spend a feat.

Five key skills

Not all skills are created equal. Although skills such as Endurance or Heal *sound* like they should be pretty important in the game, in practice you'll fall back on your character's class abilities and spells to deal with most situations involving those skills. Here's a short list of five skills with key game effects that you shouldn't ignore:

✔ **Bluff:** Rogues can use the Bluff skill to manufacture sneak attack opportunities with the Gain Combat Advantage skill application. It's also a great skill for your character to use to talk his or her way past wary guards or getting into places he or she shouldn't be.

✔ **Diplomacy:** This is a great catch-all skill for convincing nonplayer characters (NPCs) or talkative monsters to help out your character, leave him or her alone, or give your character something he or she needs.

✔ **Stealth:** There's just one sneaking-up-on-people skill: Stealth. It covers hiding and stealing up on the bad guys without making a sound. If you're playing a rogue, you can use your character's Stealth skill to set up sneak attack opportunities (or avoid fights altogether, if you prefer).

✔ **Perception:** There's one I'm-hard-to-sneak-up-on skill: Perception. If you don't like monsters surprising your character, look for a way to gain training in Perception so your character will know they're coming.

✔ **Acrobatics:** It doesn't come up often, but when it does, it's *really* important. Acrobatics is the skill your character uses for balancing on things like narrow ledges above pits of molten lava. It also gives you the opportunity to escape from enemy grabs or restraints or land on your feet after a fall. If your character is trained in Acrobatics, you can even try to reduce falling damage with an Acrobatics check.

The feat for learning a skill you otherwise couldn't is Skill Training. If you have a feat to spare, picking up this feat to get trained in Acrobatics or Perception might be very worthwhile. However, as long as you're looking at spending a feat to pick up some training, take a look at the various multiclass feats at the end of Chapter 6 in the *Player's Handbook*. We talk about multiclassing more in Chapter 22.

Quick Picks: Using Skill Packages

Skills really aren't that complicated, but it may not be clear which ones your character needs and which he or she can ignore. To help you separate the useful from the distracting, the *Player's Handbook* offers a set of recommended skill packages for the two builds in each character class. We review these skill packages briefly and offer a few thoughts of our own on ways to get even more out of your character's skills.

Refer to Chapter 11 in this book for more information on the builds for each character class.

Fighter skill packages

A fighter is one of those characters who just doesn't care that much about skills. Your character depends on fighting ability, not skill training. However, your character does receive training in a few skills, and there's no reason not to choose those intelligently. Fighters don't start out with training in any skills by default. At 1st level, you can choose three skills that your fighter has trained in.

We recommend selecting the following skills for a fighter:

✔ **Great Weapon Fighter:** Athletics, Endurance, Intimidate

✔ **Guardian Fighter:** Heal, Intimidate, Streetwise

Fighters are good at Athletics checks because scale armor (the fighter's normal armor of choice) doesn't have any armor check penalty. Add training in Athletics, and your character will be very good at climbing, jumping, and swimming. Someday the ability to scale a cliff or leap a crevasse might save your character's life.

Intimidate is useful for fighters because it's the only interaction skill they can choose training in. You'd rather not approach every "talking" encounter by issuing threats, but sometimes a little display of, hmmm, *assertiveness* can help one of your more eloquent allies to make his or her point.

If you decide to add a skill by spending a feat, Perception is a very good choice. Perception is useful for avoiding ugly surprises, such as monster ambushes. It's one of the few skills that might actually mean the difference between life and death. Acrobatics or Stealth are good choices too, especially for fighters with decent Dexterity scores.

Rogue skill package

As a rogue, your character is the master of skills. They're essential to your success in playing a rogue character.

You should take some time and bone up on the skills descriptions in Chapter 5 of the *Player's Handbook* because your familiarity with your character's skills will directly impact how well you can play that character. You'd expect someone playing a wizard to know something about his character's spells — if you're playing a rogue, you should be just as conversant about your character's skills.

All rogues begin with training in Stealth and Thievery. At 1st level, you can choose four additional skills that your character is trained in.

We recommend selecting the following skills for a rogue:

- ✔ **Brawny Rogue:** Athletics, Dungeoneering, Intimidate, Stealth, Streetwise, Thievery
- ✔ **Trickster Rogue:** Acrobatics, Bluff, Insight, Perception, Stealth, Thievery

Because all rogues automatically have training in Stealth and Thievery, your rogue is going to be good at those skills whether you want to be or not. Thievery is especially useful because it allows rogues to do things that characters of other classes generally can't do: disable traps and open locked doors. You can save the whole party a great deal of aggravation by disabling or disarming traps and getting into places the bad guys don't want you to go.

After those two fixed skills, you have a lot more discretion in choosing which skills your character is trained in. We think Perception is a key skill no rogue should overlook — after all, you have to be able to *find* those traps in order to disable them! Acrobatics and Athletics are potential life-savers in some predicaments. Athletics serves as another "access" skill (or escape skill, as the case may be) because it may enable your character to climb or jump to places he or she otherwise couldn't get to. Acrobatics is important because it covers balancing, helps reduce falling damage, and also gives your character a very significant edge on escaping from grabs. Normally you make a Dexterity check to get out of a grab, but if you can make a trained Acrobatics check instead, you gain a +5 bonus on your roll. To be clear, that's just as valuable to your escape attempt as 10 more experience levels!

Finally, most rogues should pick up Bluff. It's a good idea for every character to have at least one interaction skill (a skill you use in "talking" encounters) in his or her back pocket, and Bluff is one of the more broadly useful interaction skills. In addition, Bluff has a good combat function — you can use Bluff to gain combat advantage, even though it takes a standard action. But sometimes you'd rather set up next round's attack than take a poor attack this round.

Wizard skill package

Skills? Bah! Wizards have magic. Skills are merely an afterthought for a wizard, with the exception of the Arcana skill (which all wizards automatically are trained in). At 1st level, a wizard starts with training in three more skills.

We recommend selecting the following skills for a wizard:

- ✔ **Control Wizard:** Arcana, Diplomacy, Insight, Nature
- ✔ **War Wizard:** Arcana, Dungeoneering, Nature, Religion

All wizards begin with training in Arcana. That's good, because it's really the only skill your wizard *has* to have. Arcana is important because it includes the Detect Magic skill function (available only to trained characters), which can often help you to unravel magical puzzles or identify dangerous magical effects. It's also the key skill for many magical rituals (see Chapter 20). A good Arcana check can significantly improve the results of a ritual.

The next most important skill that wizards can get training in is *monster knowledge*. If you don't know what a monster is or what it can do, you can attempt a check against the appropriate skill to see whether your character's deep lore and learning might supply an answer. It doesn't cost your character any actions to attempt a monster knowledge check — just ask your DM whether you can try one. Monster knowledge is divided among several skills, as shown in Table 16-2.

Table 16-2	Knowledge Skill Checks to Identify Monsters
Skill	*Knowledge of Creatures of These Types*
Arcana	Elemental, fey, or shadow origin (for example, demons)
Dungeoneering	Aberrant origin (for example, beholders)
Nature	Natural origin (for example, dragons)
Religion	Immortal origin (for example, devils)

Diplomacy and Insight are reasonable choices because they're useful in interaction encounters. Every wizard should have at least one interaction skill for successfully navigating challenges that don't involve blowing things up with fireballs.

If you find the opportunity to pick up new skills by spending a feat or two, consider Acrobatics or Perception. Acrobatics may save your neck someday because it's the skill that covers balancing, falling, and escaping from grabs — when you need it, you really need it. Perception is just as good for the wizard as it is for any character; no one likes to get surprised by the monsters.

Cleric skill package

Like the wizard, a cleric doesn't rely much on skills. A cleric prefers to use combat, prayers, or rituals to solve problems, and skills are just the finishing details of your character. Don't be afraid to spend some skill choices on things that just strike your fancy, because your cleric doesn't need to be good at very many skills. All clerics have training in the Religion skill. At 1st level, you can choose three additional skills that your cleric is trained in.

We recommend selecting the following skills for a cleric:

- ✔ **Battle Cleric:** Diplomacy, Heal, Insight, Religion
- ✔ **Devoted Cleric:** Arcana, Heal, History, Religion

All clerics automatically have training in Religion, as you might expect. It's not a terribly useful skill in gameplay, but it does give your character familiarity with monsters of the immortal origin — angels, devils, and immortal guardians such as nagas or sphinxes.

Your biggest priority in skill selection is the ritual magic system. Arcana, Heal, and Religion are the key skills for most of the rituals your character might eventually use, so make sure your skill checks with those skills are as good as you can make them. Training in Heal is also useful because the skill allows you to use your action to trigger another character's second wind or grant a saving throw. You'd rather not give up your action for another character if you can help it, but sometimes that's exactly what it takes to beat the monsters.

After that, you should have at least one skill useful in an interaction encounter (Diplomacy or Insight). Because clerics tend to have very high Wisdom scores, a cleric is a natural for covering Insight for the party. History is also on the list of cleric skills, but there are very few game reasons to choose it. Select it as one of your character skills if you think it suits your character concept to be knowledgeable about old wars and ancient empires.

If you use a feat to gain additional skill training, consider Acrobatics or Athletics. Most clerics wear heavy armor and don't have much in the way of a Dexterity score, which means that fairly easy balance checks are murderously hard for them. The consequences of a failed balance check or swim check might be catastrophic, so you may want to invest a feat against the day your character will need to make a key check or die horribly. As with any other character, you'll do well to pick up Perception if you can, but don't feel like you have to. Because your character probably has a high Wisdom score, you're pretty good at Perception checks even if you aren't trained in it.

Chapter 17

Choosing Armor, Weapons, and Gear

In This Chapter

▶ Choosing the optimal weapon

▶ Suiting up with the best armor

▶ Picking out adventuring gear

▶ Improving your character's weapons and armor

*Y*ou've picked out your character's race, class, feats, and skills. You know who your character is and what he or she can do. But there's one more component your character needs — stuff. Just because a character knows how to swing a spiked chain doesn't mean that he or she is going to walk around with one. All the training in the world won't do your character any good if you don't actually take a few minutes to equip him or her for adventuring.

In this chapter, we tell you about the considerations you should keep in mind when choosing your character's equipment, and we show you some quick optimal weapon and armor picks so that you can make good starting choices and begin playing right away.

 Chapter 7 in the *Player's Handbook* tells you everything you could possibly want to know about your choices in mundane adventuring gear, ranging from weapons and armor to handy things like rope, grappling hooks, lanterns, and tents. Magic items are defined later in the same chapter.

Money in D&D

The basic unit of currency in D&D is the gold piece, abbreviated as gp. When you see something that costs 15 gp, that's 15 gold pieces. Smaller in value than gold pieces are silver pieces (sp); 1 gp is worth 10 sp. Less in value than silver pieces are copper pieces (cp); 1 sp is worth 10 cp — but by that point, you really shouldn't care. Not many players actually keep track of how many copper pieces are in their characters' pockets. (An easy way to track money is to treat gold pieces like dollars, silver pieces like dimes, and copper pieces like pennies. So if your character has 4 gp, 6 sp, and 15 cp, it's like $4.75.)

Currency that's more valuable than gold pieces becomes the norm when your character reaches paragon or epic levels. Platinum pieces are worth 100 gold pieces apiece. Astral diamonds are worth 100 times that — each one is worth 10,000 gold pieces!

Going Shopping

Your 1st-level character begins with 100 gold pieces to outfit himself or herself for adventuring. To spend this money, you have to peruse the various tables in Chapter 7 of the *Player's Handbook*, deciding what you want. Frankly, picking out equipment can be a little tedious, and many of the minor details, such as rations and a bedroll, are things that are never going to matter in many normal DUNGEONS & DRAGONS games.

If possible, you should make sure that you buy the following equipment for your character:

✔ A melee weapon (for example, a sword, mace, or dagger)

✔ A ranged weapon (bow, crossbow, or thrown weapon)

✔ The best suit of class-appropriate armor you can afford

✔ A shield (if your character is proficient in shields)

✔ Class-specific items (a holy symbol, wizard implement, or set of thieves' tools)

✔ A light source such as torches, lantern and oil, or a sunrod

✔ A backpack with rope, rations, waterskin, and anything else you think your character would need

If you want to do all this the quick and easy way, just use the packages we put together for you in the "Sample starting gear" sidebar. If you decide to use weapons different from the ones we present in our samples, you may need to check the cost of the weapons you actually purchase for your character and add or subtract the difference from the money left over.

Sample starting gear

Want an easy way out of shopping? Just choose one of the packages here. We've already equipped your character for you!

- ✔ **Fighter, Great Weapon:** Scale mail (40 gp), greataxe (30 gp), standard adventurer's kit (15 gp), 2 javelins (total 10 gp), sling and 20 bullets (2 gp), 3 gp left over.

- ✔ **Fighter, Guardian:** Scale mail (40 gp), heavy shield (15 gp), longsword (15 gp), standard adventurer's kit (15 gp), 2 javelins (total 10 gp), sling and 20 bullets (2 gp), 3 gp left over.

- ✔ **Rogue (any):** Leather armor (25 gp), short sword (10 gp), 3 daggers (3 gp), standard adventurer's kit (15 gp), sling and 20 bullets (2 gp), thieves' tools (20 gp), 25 gp left over.

- ✔ **Cleric (any):** Chainmail (40 gp), mace (5 gp), crossbow and 10 bolts (26 gp total), stan-

dard adventurer's kit (15 gp), holy symbol (10 gp), 4 gp left over.

- ✔ **Wizard, Control:** Cloth armor (1 gp), quarterstaff (5 gp), orb (15 gp), spellbook (50 gp), standard adventurer's kit (15 gp), 14 gp left over.

- ✔ **Wizard, War:** Cloth armor (1 gp), dagger (1 gp), wand (7 gp), spellbook (50 gp), standard adventurer's kit (15 gp), 26 gp left over.

In case you're wondering, the standard adventurer's kit includes a backpack, bedroll, flint and steel, belt pouch, 2 sunrods (4 hours of illumination each), 10 days of trail rations, 50 feet of rope, and a waterskin. If you're really worried about getting caught in the dark, buy some extra sunrods (2 gp apiece) or torches (10 for 1 gp).

Choosing the Right Weapon

For most characters, choosing the right weapons is an important part of building your combat strategy and creating an unforgettable character. Weapons have five important characteristics, as follows:

- ✔ **Categories:** This characteristic describes how complex the weapon is to use. Weapons are organized into improvised, simple, martial, or superior categories:

  - *Improvised weapons* are things most characters don't train with — for example, rocks, chairs, candlesticks, or bare fists.

  - *Simple weapons* are weapons that characters of almost any class can use proficiently.

  - *Martial weapons* require some training (for example, being a fighter).

  - *Superior weapons* are weapons that no character is proficient in without taking a specific Weapon Proficiency feat to learn to use that weapon.

- ✔ **Type:** Type describes the weapon's basic role and use. Weapons are divided into melee weapons and ranged weapons; melee weapons are divided again into one- and two-handed weapons. A character can use a one-handed weapon and still use a shield, but your character can't use a shield and a two-handed weapon at the same time.

- ✔ **Proficiency:** If your character is proficient with a weapon, you get a bonus to attack rolls with that weapon — usually a +2 or +3. Some weapons are more accurate than others. Your class description lists the weapons your character is proficient with.

- ✔ **Group:** This is the weapon group to which the weapon belongs — for example, axe, flail, light blade, or bow. Some character powers (especially fighter and rogue powers) work only if you're using the right type of weapon.

- ✔ **Damage:** This is the fun part. The weapon's damage rating is expressed as a die range: for example, a dagger deals d4 damage (1 to 4 points per hit), but a greataxe deals d12 damage (1 to 12 points per hit). Bigger is better.

In general, superior weapons are better than martial weapons, which are better than simple weapons. And two-handed weapons deal out more damage than one-handed weapons. Table 17-1 sums up the best weapon choices, depending on your character's class, whether you're after a one-handed or two-handed weapon, and whether you're willing to spend a feat on a weapon proficiency.

Table 17-1	Optimal Melee Weapon Choices	
Class	*No feat*	*Feat*
Fighter, Great Weapon	Greataxe, greatsword	(same)
Fighter, Guardian	Longsword, battleaxe, warhammer	Bastard sword
Rogue	Short sword, dagger	Rapier
Wizard	Quarterstaff	Bastard sword
Cleric	Mace, spear	Bastard sword

Dwarves enjoy some special advantages with weapon choices. All dwarves are proficient with the throwing hammer and warhammer. A dwarf cleric might as well use a warhammer as use a mace; the warhammer deals more damage. Don't use the warhammer if you're playing a dwarf rogue, though — many rogue powers require a light blade, and a warhammer is most definitely not a light blade.

Elves also have an edge with weapon choices. All elves, regardless of class, are proficient with the longbow and shortbow. If you're playing an elf fighter, this doesn't help at all. But if you're playing an elf rogue or cleric, you should definitely choose longbow for your character's ranged weapon. It doesn't even cost a feat.

Fighter weapons

A fighter pretty much has the pick of weapons. Fighters are proficient with almost every weapon. If you don't spend a Weapon Proficiency feat, the best choices are the longsword (if you want your character to fight one-handed and keep another hand free for a shield or second weapon) or greatsword (if you want your character to deal more damage at the cost of some defense). The battleaxe and warhammer are good replacements for the longsword, if you prefer. The greataxe or falchion (a big two-handed scimitar, in case you're wondering) are reasonable substitutions for the greatsword.

If you're willing to spend a feat on weapon proficiencies, get Weapon Proficiency for the bastard sword or spiked chain. The bastard sword effectively gives +1 damage above the longsword. The spiked chain deals less damage than the greatsword, but your character will gain *reach* — the ability to strike foes who aren't standing next to him or her. That's a major tactical advantage. The spiked chain also can be used for a number of fancy maneuvers such as trip attacks.

For a ranged weapon, you should rely on thrown weapons — javelins, handaxes, or throwing hammers. These are all "heavy thrown" weapons, so they work as Strength attacks rather than Dexterity attacks.

Magic throwing weapons automatically come back to you after you throw them. By the time you're 4th or 5th level, you can probably afford to carry a *+1 handaxe* in your belt. It's a little insurance in case something happens to your preferred melee weapon, and you'll never be without the ability to attack an enemy who's just a few squares away.

You should also carry a longer-ranged projectile weapon such as a bow or sling for that very rare combat situation where you can't close with your enemies and have to attack from 20 squares off. Slings are cheap and light, but buy yourself a longbow when you can.

Rogue weapons

A rogue's weapon choices are limited compared to the fighter's choices, but that's okay. Whatever weapons rogues employ in battle aren't anywhere near as important as their sneak attack capability. When your character is dealing 10 or 15 points of damage from a sneak attack, the difference between a weapon that averages 3 points a hit or 4 points a hit just isn't that important.

If you don't want to spend a feat on your rogue's weapon choices, your melee options are pretty simple: short sword or dagger. The short sword deals more damage (d6), but the dagger is more accurate thanks to the Rogue Weapon Talent class ability. It's probably more important to score a hit than to deal a little extra damage, so make the dagger your weapon of choice. If you're willing to spend a feat on Weapon Proficiency, learn to use the rapier. It's the most damaging of the light blades.

For a ranged weapon, your choices are the hand crossbow, sling, or shuriken. The sling and hand crossbow are exactly the same, but the sling is much cheaper, so go with the sling. Rogue Weapon Mastery gives the shuriken just as much damage potential as the previous two weapons, but the shuriken has better accuracy. The shuriken's range is a little shorter, but many of the powers you'll use with the shuriken have ranges of 5 or less, so the shuriken's short range won't be a problem. Go with the shuriken (but carry a sling just in case).

Cleric weapons

Weapons are tough for clerics. As a cleric, your character wants to be handy in a fight, but he or she begins with proficiency only in simple weapons. A mace, morningstar, or spear just doesn't deal the same damage that a similarly sized sword or axe deals, so you're a little bit behind the eight-ball in your character's weapon selection. You should seriously consider using a feat so your cleric can become proficient in a better weapon.

If you don't want to spend a feat, choose the mace. It's traditional. If you choose to spend a feat on Weapon Proficiency, the bastard sword is your best choice. It'll give you a +1 accuracy boost over the mace, and it deals more damage too.

Take a sling or crossbow for your ranged weapon. The sling is dirt-cheap, but the crossbow has better range and deals more damage. Either way, don't expect to get much use out of your ranged weapon. Most clerics have better things to do in combat than take potshots with a crossbow.

Wizard weapons

Wizards are restricted to just two weapons: the dagger and quarterstaff. But you know what? You don't care if you're playing a wizard. Most of a wizard's actions will be taken up with casting spells, so toting around an effective melee weapon just isn't necessary for this class.

If you really want to, you can take a Weapon Proficiency feat to get your character's hands on a better weapon, but here's the deal: A wizard is hardly ever going to make melee attacks, so don't waste a feat on this. (If you happen to be playing a dwarf wizard, though, your character is proficient with the warhammer as a racial trait — so your character might as well carry one.)

You might have noticed that you have no ranged weapon options. If your character needs to attack an enemy at range, use your *magic missile* spell (or one of your other at-will powers). You never run out of at-wills, and it's just way more stylish to zap your enemies with glowing darts of magical energy than to fumble around with a crossbow you're no good at.

Choosing Armor

The other important decision you need to make in equipping your character is what sort of armor you intend him or her to wear. Each character class begins with proficiency in a different set of armor choices; for example, fighters are proficient in any armor up to and including scale mail, whereas wizards are only proficient in cloth armor.

Beyond the question of proficiency, there are two basic decisions you need to make when considering your choice of armor: shield or no shield, and light versus heavy.

Shield or no shield?

If you're playing a fighter, you need to decide whether you want your character to carry a shield. Shields are a great way to improve Armor Class by a couple of points, but by carrying a shield, your character is giving up some offense. Instead of carrying a shield, your character could be swinging a two-handed weapon that deals more damage. This is the difference between the Great Weapon fighter build and the Guardian fighter build.

There really isn't a right answer here. As they say, the best defense is a good offense; building your character to dish out damage instead of taking it means that he or she will kill enemies faster and give them fewer chances to put damage on him or her. On the other hand, you'll find that even 1 or 2 points of extra Armor Class often results in a disproportionate reduction in the amount of damage your character takes from enemy attacks. It's really up to you.

Characters of other classes have to spend a feat on Light Shield Proficiency to even think about picking up a shield. It's probably worthwhile for a melee-oriented cleric; +1 AC is worth a feat, after all. But don't buy up to the heavy shield, since you need to have a hand free to hold your holy symbol. With a light shield, you can do that, but with a heavy shield, you can't. You don't want your character to mess with spending actions to put away his or her mace and take out the holy symbol when you decide you want to use a power based on your divine implement rather than the weapon in your hand.

Light versus heavy

Here's an important nuance of the D&D armor system: If you wear light armor, you can add your character's Dexterity or Intelligence modifier to your Armor Class; if you wear heavy armor, you can't. But heavy armor offers an armor bonus that's much better than the one provided by light armor.

To get the best Armor Class possible, you have to decide whether your Dexterity or Intelligence score is high enough to overcome the difference between light armor AC bonuses and heavy armor AC bonuses. As it turns out, the best light armor available at low levels is hide armor (+3 armor bonus). The worst heavy armor at the same levels is chainmail (+6 armor bonus). So, if your ability score can add at least a +3 ability modifier to your armor class, you'll break even on AC. Therefore, if either your Dexterity score or your Intelligence score is at least 16, go with light armor. Otherwise, wear heavy armor — assuming, of course, that your character is proficient in some type of heavy armor.

In addition to negating your ability score modifier, heavy armor slows your character down and usually imposes a small penalty on physical skill checks such as Acrobatics or Athletics. When you're weighing armor choices, you need to decide whether you care about having your character's movement reduced by wearing heavy armor.

Table 16-2 provides an overview of the best armor choices by class (the first column) and the best armor choices if you invest a feat in Armor Training.

Table 16-2	Optimal Armor Choices	
Class	*No feat*	*Feat*
Fighter, Great Weapon	Scale armor*	Plate armor
Fighter, Guardian	Scale armor* + heavy shield	Plate armor + heavy shield
Rogue	Leather armor	Hide armor
Wizard	Cloth armor	Leather armor
Cleric	Chainmail**	Scale armor

* If your Dex or Int is 18+, wear hide armor instead.
** If your Dex or Int is 16+, wear hide armor instead.

If you're playing a dwarf, you don't care about the speed penalty of heavy armor. Dwarves get to ignore the movement penalty for wearing heavy armor, so unless you're playing a dwarf with a very high Intelligence or Dexterity score, your character might as well wear the heaviest armor he or she can afford.

Armor choices for other classes

Players who have characters of other classes have some different choices to weigh when picking out armor. Here are a few quick guidelines:

✔ **Paladin:** Invest in plate armor and a heavy shield. It's costly, but you should take advantage of the fact that you can use the best armor in the game.

✔ **Ranger:** Go with hide armor. You take a –1 penalty on a few skill checks, but the +1 AC as compared with leather armor is worth it.

✔ **Warlock:** You can wear leather armor, and you should. Later in your career, you can decide whether to spend feats to improve your armor options.

✔ **Warlord:** If your Intelligence or Dexterity score is 16 or better, wear hide armor; otherwise, wear chain armor. Take a light shield. You should think about using feats to gain heavy shield proficiency, or you should improve your chain armor to scale armor.

Everything Else Your Character Is Carrying

Your choices of armor and weapons are important, but they're not all that's involved in equipping your character. Dungeon exploration requires a lot of specialized gear, and you'll want to make sure that your character is carrying everything he or she will need to survive in the hostile environment of a monster-filled dungeon.

Watch out! You might not realize it, but your character class might demand specialized gear to accomplish its basic purpose. There are four prime examples of this:

- ✔ Rogues require thieves' tools (20 gp) to use the Thievery skill properly.

- ✔ Clerics require a holy symbol (10 gp) to better use many of their powers.

- ✔ Wizards require a spellbook to keep their daily spells, utility spells, and rituals. They also require an arcane implement (orb, staff, or wand; 15 gp, 12 gp, or 5 gp, respectively) to better cast their spells.

- ✔ Clerics and wizards require ritual components in order to make use of the rituals they know. For a 1st-level character, you can get by with 20 to 40 gold pieces' worth of arcane reagents, mystic salves, or sanctified incense. That will see you through the first couple of times your character uses a ritual.

At the very minimum, make sure your character's miscellaneous equipment includes the noted item if you're playing a member of that class.

Useful gear

These things won't make your character fight better, but they're darned useful for successful dungeon exploration. Every adventurer should carry a light source, a rope, and a useful tool or two such as a grappling hook, crowbar, hammer and pitons, flint and steel, and so on. Not everyone in the party needs to carry one of each of these things — divvy out these tools among the party.

A light source is particularly important because most races can't see a thing in complete darkness. You have four good, cheap choices at the beginning of your character's career: torch, lantern, sunrod, or magic (a wizard's *light* spell).

Magic is a good emergency measure, but you shouldn't rely on it exclusively. You don't want the whole party to be stranded in pitch blackness just because the wizard got eaten by a grick.

Of the nonmagical alternatives, torches are heavy and don't light up a very large area, but they're cheap. Lanterns are more expensive but provide better light and usually last longer. In addition, you can set all kinds of things on fire with a few flasks of lamp oil. Trust us; we've seen it done. Your best non-magical alternative is probably the sunrod. Sunrods are alchemical devices that provide a bright, long-lasting light without the need for oil. They're expensive (2 gp apiece) but give four hours of illumination at a time.

Oh, and one more thing: *Don't forget the rope.* Every member of the party should carry at least 50 feet, preferably 100 feet or more, of rope. Because so many dungeons feature difficult vertical obstacles, you just can't skimp on the rope. With enough rope, only one character in the party needs to be a good climber — everybody else can follow the best climber after he or she fixes a rope in place.

Write it down and forget it

Ever been camping? If so, you've probably got half an idea of what your character likely goes through every day when he or she is off exploring vast wildernesses or delving for weeks into a fearsome dungeon. Anybody going away from civilization for a few days carries something to sleep on or in, food, water, camp tools, and so on.

So, just for form's sake, you should probably write a few things on your character sheet, such as "backpack, bedroll, 3 days' rations, 2 waterskins, flint and steel." Or, better yet, just buy the standard adventurer's kit at the top of the Adventuring Gear list in Chapter 7 of the *Player's Handbook*. There. That's all it takes. The vast majority of Dungeon Masters will never challenge you on this, and you'll never actually concern yourself with this mundane gear again. But you'll be able to say that your character has it.

You might be tempted to write down a whole general store worth of tools, rations, special items, and miscellaneous junk, but remember — your character needs to carry everything. Check page 222 in the *Player's Handbook*, and you'll see that characters have a finite limit on how much weight they can carry. Again, not many DMs will think to enforce this rule, but some do, so don't be embarrassed by being caught with 860 pounds of gear on your 13-Strength rogue. (If you like the idea of carrying around the whole general store on your back, consider investing in magic items such as a *bag of holding* or a *handy haversack* later in your character's career.)

Improving Weapons and Armor

Your character's equipment at 1st level is nothing remarkable. Your character hasn't yet found the great piles of treasure that will let him or her buy really good armor or powerful magic weapons. But within a level or two, you're going to want to upgrade your character's weapons and armor to the best he or she can afford to own. In DUNGEONS & DRAGONS, your character doesn't *keep* treasure; he or she spends it to buy better weapons and armor so that he or she can find even bigger treasures and buy even better weapons and armor.

Masterwork armors

You may have noticed that the armor table in Chapter 7 of the *Player's Handbook* includes some very unusual entries — for example, dragonscale armor, warplate armor, or starweave armor. The cost for each is simply "special." All these unusual armor types are known as masterwork armor.

Equipping higher-level characters

If you're creating a higher-level character to join an existing game, you'll find that the agonizing decisions of the typical impoverished 1st-level character are simply a thing of the past. High-level characters typically have thousands of gold pieces worth of equipment, including magic weapons, armor, potions, and other such wondrous possessions.

To equip a higher-level character, you should ask your DM how much money your character has to spend. Then ask for the DM's help in picking out suitable magic items for your character. Remember, if your character doesn't have a magic weapon or magic armor, you'll need to pick out nonmagical gear to serve. Make sure that you review the bulleted list in the "Going Shopping" section of this chapter and equip your character with magical or nonmagical versions of everything on the list.

Masterwork armors have a "minimum magic bonus," which means you never just find a suit of warplate armor; the *least* valuable set of warplate armor you can ever have is *+4 warplate armor.* A suit of +4 armor is a 16th-level magic item worth 45,000 gp. Eventually your character may find a suit of master-work armor or amass enough wealth to buy some, but you have a lot of adventuring ahead of you first.

Magical arms and armor

The best way to improve your character's attack rolls and AC is to get his or her hands on a good magical weapon and a suit of magical armor. Magical weaponry is expensive stuff, but you'll find that you absolutely need it if your character is going to have a fighting chance of dealing with the game's more dangerous monsters. See Chapter 20 for more details.

Magical weapons carry a bonus to attack and damage rolls, ranging from +1 to +5 or more. So when you hear someone at the table boasting about his *+3 sword,* what he's saying is that his character has a sword that gives a +3 bonus on attack and damage rolls. That's a good sword. Similarly, magical armor carries a bonus to AC ranging from +1 to +5 or more. For example, a suit of chainmail normally provides an AC bonus of +6, but a suit of *+2 chain-mail* gives an AC bonus of 8. Magic weapons or armor with an enhancement bonus of +1 are 1st-level magic items and cost 360 gp each. Because you start with only 100 gp to spend as a 1st-level character, you can see that you'll have to liberate some monster-guarded treasure hoards if you want to arm yourself with magic armor and weapons.

Chapter 18

Advancing Your Character

●●●

In This Chapter

▶ Discovering how your character earns experience points

▶ Examining what happens when your character gains a level

▶ Exploring paragon paths and epic destinies

●●●

Characters in the DUNGEONS & DRAGONS game are not static. They grow and develop the longer you play the game. That's one of the key aspects of the game — like the heroes of a novel, movie, or television series, your characters learn, grow, and are influenced by past and present events.

In this chapter, we explore the concept of experience points (XP) and gaining levels, examining how and in what ways your character improves. We go over the process of "leveling up" and show you how to add your new goodies to your character. Finally, we look at paragon paths and epic destinies, the pinnacle that every character can strive to achieve.

The Character Advancement table in Chapter 2 of the *Player's Handbook* (page 29) is your one-stop reference for determining what your character gets at each and every experience level. Paragon paths for each character class are described in Chapter 4 at the end of each class section. Epic destinies for all character classes are found at the end of Chapter 4.

Gaining Experience Points

Experience points (XP for short) measure a character's accomplishments. They represent both training and learning by doing. In the fantasy worlds of D&D, experience has a direct correlation to power. Characters earn experience points by defeating opponents and otherwise overcoming the challenges that the Dungeon Master places before them. When a character has earned a specific number of XP, as detailed on the Character Advancement table on page 29 of the *Player's Handbook*, he or she gains a new level. Table 18-1 shows the first couple of stops on the path to greatness.

Table 18-1	XP and Your Character's First Few Levels
You Need This Many XP . . .	*. . . To Reach This Level*
0	1st level
1,000	2nd level
2,250	3rd level
3,750	4th level
5,500	5th level

Where do XP come from?

Every monster and opponent in the game comes with an XP award based on its level. A monster's level is a rating of how easy or difficult a monster is to overcome, and it roughly corresponds to the level of player characters who ought to be fighting it. For example, the roper is a level-14 monster, so it's intended to be a challenge when the adventuring party is around 14th level. It's way too tough for 4th-level characters, and it's a pushover for 24th-level characters. Traps, obstacles, other challenges, and quests are also assigned levels and award XP, as described in Chapters 5 and 7 of the *Dungeon Master's Guide*.

The DM decides when a challenge has been overcome. Usually, this means when a battle has been won or a trap disarmed, but clever players can come up with all kinds of ways for their characters to overcome the challenge of the moment. If the party successfully slips by the hobgoblins guarding the corridor by using stealth and clever distractions, the DM can determine that the characters have overcome this challenge and reward them experience points accordingly.

All characters that take part in an encounter gain XP for that encounter. Remember that encounters come in three forms: a challenge, combat, or role-playing encounter that is integral to the plot of the adventure. DMs usually award XP at the end of each encounter, although awarding XP at the end of a game session works too.

For the Dungeon Master

The DM usually awards experience points at the end of an encounter, but some DMs dole out awards at the end of a game session. Training and advancement, however, should still take place between game sessions or

What is monster level?

Every monster or obstacle the player characters have to deal with in an adventure has a level. Generally speaking, a good combat encounter consists of monsters equal in level to the level of the player characters, and equal in number to the number of characters in the party. In other words, with reasonable luck and a bit of skill, an average party should overcome a similar number of creatures or obstacles of their own level with some damage and expenditure of resources. A party of five 4th-level characters, for example, should be able to get through an encounter with five 4th-level standard monsters or traps with a few resources expended but without suffering any casualties.

at the beginning or end of a game session. If you have a good breakpoint in the action — for example, the PCs are planning to go back to town for a bit before returning to the dungeon — it's okay to let player characters level up in the middle of the game session.

To determine the XP award for an encounter, follow these steps (which are described more fully in Chapter 4 of the *Dungeon Master's Guide*):

1. **Determine the XP value of each monster, trap, or obstacle in the encounter.**

   In the case of monsters and traps, the XP award is right at the top of the monster stat block or trap description.

2. **Total the XP values of the monsters, traps, and obstacles in the encounter.**

3. **Divide the XP total by the number of characters in the party.**

   The result is the amount of XP that each character receives for helping to overcome the encounter. Round fractions normally.

Gaining Levels

Your character becomes more powerful as he or she rises in level. At higher levels, your character hits better, defends better, becomes harder to kill, and gains new and more powerful abilities. Using the *Player's Handbook*, you can advance your character from 1st level to 30th level over the course of a campaign. A character's level provides other benefits and essential information, as described in the next few sections.

Ability score increases

Characters increase their ability scores as they advance in level. A character can increase any two ability scores by 1 point every time he or she attains a level ending in 4 or 8. That means that Lidda, a halfling rogue, increases two of her ability scores by 1 point each at 4th, 8th, 14th, 18th, 24th, and 28th level. So, upon achieving 4th level, Lidda's player can increase her Dexterity score from 17 to 18 and her Charisma score from 14 to 15. In addition, when your character reaches 11th level and 21st level, you add 1 to *all* the character's ability scores. It's good to reach paragon or epic level! (For more on ability scores, see Chapter 13.)

Level modifier

Your character's level modifier represents the sheer skill his or her experience confers. It's a bonus equal to half the character's level, rounded down — so, in other words, +1 at 2nd level, +2 at 4th level, +3 at 6th level, and so on. You get to add the level modifier to every attack roll your character makes, to all your character's defenses, and to every skill check your character attempts.

New powers

Your character learns new powers as he or she gains levels, as shown on the Character Advancement table (page 29 of the *Player's Handbook*). For example, when Jozan, a human cleric, reaches 2nd level, he learns a 2nd-level utility power; when he reaches 3rd level, he learns a new 3rd-level encounter power; and when he reaches 5th level, he learns a new 5th-level daily power. Some levels — for example, 4th level — don't offer you the chance to learn new powers, but you gain other good stuff at those levels.

Unfortunately, you don't get to keep adding powers forever. Eventually you reach a point for encounter and daily powers where you gain access to a new level of power selections, but you don't gain any more "slots." You have to drop one of your old powers and replace it with your new selection. This comes at 13th level for encounter powers and 15th level for daily powers. Usually, you just drop your old 1st-level powers when you reach these points; you've outgrown them. Higher-level powers are usually much better than lower-level powers, so this isn't much of a hardship for your character. Chapter 14 in this book has more detail about powers.

Feats

Characters gain feats according to level. All characters start with one feat at 1st level. Each character can select a new feat every time he or she attains an even-numbered level. That means that Regdar, a human fighter, selects new feats at 2nd level, 4th level, 6th level, and so on.

In addition, all characters get to select a feat when they reach 11th level (welcome to paragon tier!) and again at 21st level (welcome to epic tier!). When you reach a new tier, you gain a whole new menu of feats to choose from because feats are organized into heroic, paragon, and epic feats. Naturally, paragon and epic feats are better than heroic feats. For more on feats, see Chapter 15.

Advancing a Level

Your character can advance to the next level when your XP total reaches the minimum amount needed according to the Character Advancement table in the *Player's Handbook*. Regdar, for example, can go from 1st to 2nd level when he accumulates at least 1,000 XP. Going up a level provides a number of immediate benefits that demonstrate that the character has learned and improved in some way.

Imagine that your character spends time between adventures training, studying, and practicing his or her skills. Even if your character achieves the necessary XP milestone, he or she can't go up a level in the middle of an encounter. In game terms, this means that you have to wait until the DM allows your character a brief respite before you can level up. The end of a game session is a great time to level up, but if your DM is willing to give your characters a break in the action, you might be able to level up immediately after winning the encounter that gave you the XP to get over the top. That's up to the DM and the kind of game he or she wants to run.

When your character has earned the necessary XP to go up a level, grab your character sheet and your *Player's Handbook* and follow these steps:

1. **Depending on the level your character gained, adjust his or her ability scores.**

   When your character attains 4th, 8th, 14th, 18th, 24th, and 28th level, choose two abilities and increase each by 1 point. When your character reaches 11th level, and again at 21st level, add 1 point to *all* your ability scores.

Check the Ability Modifier table (page 17 of the *Player's Handbook*) to see whether modifiers associated with any of your improved abilities need to be adjusted.

2. **Depending on the level your character gained, adjust your level modifiers for attack, defense, and skill bonuses.**

   Your character's level modifier is equal to half your level (rounded down), so each time you hit an even-numbered level, your level modifier goes up. Level modifier figures into your defenses, your attacks, and your skill checks. If your level modifier improves, modify your attack, defense, and skill bonuses accordingly.

3. **At 11th or 21st level, choose your paragon path or epic destiny, respectively.**

   If you just reached 11th level, you get to pick a paragon path for your character. Each character class description in Chapter 4 of the *Player's Handbook* includes several paragon paths to pick from. If you just reached 21st level, select an epic destiny. These are described at the end of Chapter 4 in the *Player's Handbook*. We take a look at paragon paths and epic destinies in Chapter 22 in this book.

4. **Increase your hit points.**

   Your class description tells you how many hit points your character gains each time he or she advances a level. For example, a fighter gains 6 hit points at each level.

5. **Update your class features.**

   Check your class description for class features that improve with level. For example, at 16th level, a cleric can use his or her *healing word* power three times per encounter instead of just twice.

6. **Depending on the level your character gained, choose your new feat.**

   When your character reaches an even-numbered level, you gain one feat of your choice. Make sure that your character meets any prerequisites the feat requires.

7. **Get your new power.**

   All characters learn additional powers as they advance. Check the Character Advancement table (page 29 of the *Player's Handbook*) to see what kind of power to add to your character's repertoire at his or her new level.

Part III
Playing Your Best Game

"I wouldn't waste a *righteous smite* power at this time. Save it for when we're driving home on the expressway."

In this part . . .

DUNGEONS & DRAGONS is a complex game that presents your character with an infinite variety of challenges. In this part of the book, you graduate from the basics of how to play and how to create a character into the study of how to play the game *well.* You can play the game at a basic level (see the monster, hit the monster) and have plenty of fun, but if you want to find out how to take on the toughest opponents and win, how to forge your adventuring party into a tight team of specialists who can take on any challenge, and how to immerse yourself in the imagination and fun of the game, this part is for you.

Chapter 19

Handling Yourself in a Fight

- -

In This Chapter

▶ Picking the right way to beat the monsters

▶ Managing your best powers

▶ Building a combat strategy

▶ Using advanced tactics

▶ Adapting your tactics to your foes

- -

The point of the DUNGEONS & DRAGONS game is to have fun, be creative, and engage in a little healthy escapism. But D&D is a game, and just like any game, you can play it well or you can play it poorly. Many people have a great time making bad choices and exploring those consequences, but we're guessing that you want to play to *win* — or at least do your best to maximize your character's impact on the game.

There are two good ways to play the game smart: Build effective characters (we talk more about that in Chapter 22), and fight your best fight. Any character can shine for a battle with some lucky combat rolls, but if you consistently select the best and most efficient actions for your character round after round, you won't need lucky die rolls to excel.

In this chapter, we tell you about the right way to approach battles and encounters, and we show you how to come up with a winning strategy for almost any fight.

Choosing the Right Weapon for the Job

Choosing the right weapon for the situation at hand doesn't mean carrying around a *bag of holding* full of magic weapons and pulling out the most effective one for each foe. It means finding your enemy's weakness and targeting it. This strategy goes all the way back to Sun Tzu: Don't throw strength at strength if there's a better option available. Your high-powered fighter might be able to cut his or her way through a roomful of hill giants, but melee combat is what hill giants do *best*. You would be better off to use powers that attack Will defense at a long range, because giants generally can stand up to a lot more physical abuse than mental attacks.

The four basic strategies for defeating foes in the D&D game are hit point attrition, action denial, maneuver, and diplomacy.

Killing 'em quickly: Attacking hit points

Use melee attacks, ranged attacks, and damage-causing powers such as *magic missile* or *flame strike* to reduce your opponents' hit points to zero as fast as possible. This strategy works best against foes with low hit points or foes who don't have much ability to hurt your character while the party goes through their hit points. It's a bad strategy to use against brutes and soldiers (big strong monsters who frankly are looking for a chance to mix it up with your party).

This is the default strategy for almost any monster: If you don't know what else to do, make attacks and knock down your enemy's hit points. Sooner or later, you'll win.

Playing for time: Action-denial powers

In this combat strategy, lead with powers that keep the monsters from acting effectively, such as *command* or *web*. Ultimately you defeat the monsters in pretty much the same way as before — you deplete their hit points — but the goal here is damage mitigation; you want to prevent the monsters from getting good shots on you while you're wearing them down. Ideally, you'll tie the monsters up so badly with effects that daze, stun, or immobilize them that they won't be able to lay a finger on you.

Good action-denial effects include

- ✔ Daze or stun
- ✔ Knock prone (especially when combined with push or slide against monsters without good ranged attacks)
- ✔ Weaken
- ✔ Slow or immobilize (best against monsters without good ranged attacks)
- ✔ Restrain
- ✔ Blind

Action denial works best in encounters where one or two of the monsters pose a much more serious threat than the other monsters. Don't waste an action-denial effect like *command* on a lowly goblin minion or a goblin skirmisher; use it on the goblin chieftain or the hobgoblin warcaster, the creatures in that encounter that can really hurt you. Action denial is especially effective against elite and solo monsters — monsters who are significantly tougher than normal monsters. Typically, an encounter with an elite or solo monster means that you're dealing with a smaller number of tougher monsters, so denying monsters actions has a bigger effect on the battle (although most elite and solo monsters have some special defense against action denial in the form of big saving throw bonuses).

Beating 'em with footwork: Maneuver

Many foes can be avoided through an artful maneuver, especially if your character or another in the party has useful ritual magic at hand. If nothing else, you might be able to maneuver your character into a position from which he or she can attack a foe with little chance of being hit back. For example, if the opponent is a powerful brute with no ranged attacks (say, an ogre warhulk), use flying magic and attack it safely with ranged weapons and powers.

The true coup of maneuver, of course, is to simply bypass a fight you don't need to fight. If the evil lord surrounds his castle with a moat of giant crocodiles, why would you slog your way through the monsters when you might go around, over, or through them without fighting? Powers such as *arcane gate* or *levitate* are obvious mechanisms for winning an encounter through maneuver, but don't overlook the rogue's knack for sneaking through dangerous places with the Stealth skill, or powers that disguise or hide you from your foes.

Maneuvering works best on enemies who are stuck in place. (There's not much point in avoiding a pack of hell hounds if they'll just follow the party to the next room and attack them there.) It's also the best way for dealing with enemies who are simply too dangerous to fight.

Winning with a smile: Negotiation

Sometimes you can simply talk your way past an obstacle. If your character is facing a roomful of orc warriors, he or she might be able to convince them that the adventuring party is far too dangerous to attack with a display of astounding bravado (and a good Bluff or Intimidate check). Or your character might persuade them that it's in their own best interests to let the party continue through the dungeon unmolested so that the party can deal with a rival gang of monsters the orcs might want out of the way — a good use of the Diplomacy skill.

Negotiation works best on intelligent adversaries, but don't rule out negotiation tactics against non-intelligent monsters. A character might use the Handle Animal function of the Nature skill to get a party of adventurers past a dangerous and ill-tempered creature such as a dire bear or giant crocodile. And, even if you're not particularly skilled in calming wild animals, throwing a big haunch of meat to the evil tyrant's dire wolf might serve as well as a bribe of gold would for an intelligent guardian.

Many Dungeon Masters require you to attempt skill checks in skills such as Bluff, Diplomacy, or Intimidate in order to carry off a negotiation strategy. However, some DMs deliberately avoid using the skill challenge rules to resolve these encounters: They want you, the player, to explain exactly what your character says, and then they'll decide if they think you were convincing enough for your character to succeed in his or her efforts to talk to the monsters. Other DMs combine skill checks with roleplaying, letting good rolls bolster weak roleplaying or vice-versa. Each method is a reasonable way for the DM to handle a negotiation — you'll just have to see which way your DM prefers to play encounters like this.

Bugging out: Knowing when to retreat

Even the best D&D players tend to forget that running away is an option. Very few challenges in the game are worth getting a player character killed. If the situation is so grim that it seems likely that one or more characters will die, extricate the party from the battle and come back to fight another day after your characters have healed up and made the right preparations for dealing with whatever dangerous adversary forced the retreat.

Warning signs that you should watch out for include

✔ One or more player characters are rendered helpless.

✔ Two or more player characters are bloodied, with no prospect of healing back up to full.

✔ Half the player characters are out of daily attack powers and encounter attack powers.

✔ Three straight rounds go by in a fight where no player character damages an adversary.

Whether or not you heed these warning signs is up to you. Sometimes, retreat simply isn't an option. Other times, you might need to fight on past the warning signs because you'll put your character at greater risk in trying to retreat than you would by trying to win the fight.

Managing Expendable Powers and Resources

All your character's abilities fall into three basic categories: things you can do at will, things you can do once per encounter, and things you can do once per day. Powers and abilities that can be used up — either in the encounter at hand or for the whole day's adventuring — are *expendable* resources. Usually, your expendable resources fall into three basic categories:

✔ Attack powers (encounter or daily)

✔ Utility powers (encounter or daily)

✔ Magic item powers (encounter or daily)

To play your best game, you want to meet each challenge or encounter you face with an appropriate use of your resources. You don't want your character to get killed because he or she was hoarding a resource for possible use later, and you don't want your character to get killed because he or she is out of resources that were spent too freely in earlier encounters. Knowing when to pull the trigger on a rare but powerful resource and when to save your big guns is one of the ways you can play the game well.

Fire away: Using encounter powers

Encounter powers are fairly easy to manage. Here's the deal: In *every* encounter your character meets, you want to use *all* your encounter powers. If your character finishes the fight with some encounter powers unused, you let the monsters off easy. Sometimes you can't help it, of course; your cleric can use *healing word* twice per encounter, but if the monsters happen to miss a lot in this fight, there might be no call for a healing prayer.

It's okay to be aggressive in using your encounter powers because you're expending them only for the encounter in which you're currently engaged. As soon as that battle is over, you regain all your used-up encounter powers with a short rest. The trick to managing your encounter powers is simply deciding *when* in the battle to use them. As your turn approaches each round, ask yourself: Is this the right round to use an encounter power?

Use an encounter power if . . .

✔ You want to do more damage than you would with your at-will powers, or you need to attack a defense that your at-will powers don't target.

✔ You have a perfect situation for it. (For example, you have a melee power that targets two enemies, and you have a couple of monsters in just the right place to use it.)

✔ It's early in the fight and you're not sure how tough this encounter is yet. (You want to use your encounter powers anyway, so you might as well get started.)

Don't use an encounter power if . . .

✔ The situation appears dire enough to warrant a daily power.

✔ Your available encounter powers are unsuited to the tactical situation. (For example, you can hit only one target with a power that normally could affect two or three targets.)

✔ You have an at-will power that will do the job as well as any of your encounter powers.

Hold on, there: Using daily powers

Daily powers are much harder to manage than encounter powers. You want to make sure that you use all your daily powers during each day of adventuring, but a day of adventuring might include one combat encounter or five combat encounters. All too often, you can't predict how many more encounters your character will battle through until you hit the last one and realize that you're really out of gas. You don't want to bring unused daily powers "back to the barn," but you *really* don't want to get into a battle where you desperately need daily powers you've already used up.

If the trick to using encounter powers is deciding which round of the fight deserves an encounter power, the trick to using daily powers is to decide which encounter of the day deserves a daily power. Don't use them up in easy encounters; if it looks like you can fight through just using at-will and encounter powers, hang on to your daily powers for later.

Remember, your daily powers are a *party* resource as well as a character resource. If the party has five characters with two daily attack powers each, you have ten daily powers to spend among yourselves. Normally, an adventuring party should shoot for getting through four to six encounters before the characters think about resting. That means the whole party should spend maybe one to three daily powers per encounter. If you've seen two or three other characters use their daily powers in a fight, it's time to hoard yours for the next battle — unless the situation is desperate and nothing less will do.

Here are a few good tips on pacing your daily powers:

✔ Don't use your daily powers in easy fights.

✔ The earlier in the fight you identify the need for a daily power, the better. Many daily powers have benefits that last for the duration of the en- counter, so it's better to use them early in the fight in order to maximize the effect they have on that battle.

✔ Unless you're desperate, make sure that you don't sell a daily power short by using it when conditions aren't favorable. For example, if you've got a daily power that might let you attack three or four monsters at once, don't use it to attack just one monster.

✔ If an encounter is going badly, use your daily powers freely. Better to run out of daily powers than to let the monsters defeat you while your best powers are still unused.

Putting It All Together: Developing Your Combat Strategy

Every time your character gets into a scrape, you should have an idea of what you're trying to accomplish and how you want to go about it. That means formulating a combat strategy early in the fight. Here's a quick and dirty primer on combat strategy:

Step 1: Define the situation

Identify what sort of fight you're facing by figuring out whether anyone is sur- prised and what sort of terrain you're fighting on.

The default management strategy

If managing your character's encounter and daily powers all seems pretty intimidating to you, here's an easy way to handle them that works well in most combat encounters: Begin the fight with an encounter power in your first round or two. You want to make sure you use them in most fights, and this gives you time to evaluate how dangerous the fight really is. If the encounter looks tough a couple of rounds in, it's time to bust out a daily power. On the other hand, if the fight looks to be under control after those first couple of rounds, save your daily powers and fall back to at-will attacks when your encounter powers run out.

When you're determining surprise, you must figure out who got the jump on whom. Do you even have a choice about this fight? Here are some guidelines to keep in mind:

- **We got ambushed.** The bad guys jumped out of the darkness and attacked your party without warning. Your first step should be to limit the damage the monsters are dealing to the party by drawing back or using defensive powers. Only when you're sure that your character or another player character in the party is not going to get killed do you turn to serious offense.

- **We just ran into them.** Neither side has an advantage. These situations are dangerous because you might not realize how much trouble the party is in until you're several rounds into the fight and you don't have any good escape options open. Fight defensively until you know that it's safe to shift over to offense.

- **They're in our way.** The monsters are obstacles the party has to get past, but you have time to get ready for a fair fight. This type of encounter presents the best maneuver or negotiation opportunities; if you decide to make it a fight, look for ways to stack the odds in your favor (or maybe even change it into an ambush; see the next bullet).

- **We ambushed them.** You have time to hide and set up a surprise attack of your own. Lay down as much hurt as you can as fast as you can so that the monsters don't get any real chance to fight back.

Where are you fighting? Does the ground favor your party or the other side? Does the party have an easy way to get out if things go bad? Terrain affects combat in myriad ways. Here are some guidelines:

- **Obstructed:** You're fighting in tight spaces or with little room to maneuver. Make sure that you control the battlefield by using walls and obstacles to keep enemies from getting around your character or other characters in the party.

- **Wide open:** There's no place to hide. If your party is faster than the monsters, don't let them close to the party until you're ready. If your party is slower, try to bog down your foes in melee combat or by using powers that slow enemies or create difficult terrain for them to cross.

- **Grossly unfair:** Your party is hanging on a cliff, fighting against harpies, rocs, or something else with wings. Back off and try it again when you've taken steps to make it a fair fight. For example, maybe the wizard can hit his spellbook to find a couple of utility powers that will help even the odds.

Step 2: Evaluate your foes

Study the monsters you're facing and determine each one's role: brute, soldier, lurker, artillery, controller, skirmisher, or minion. In many encounters, the monsters include representatives of two or three different monstrous roles. Don't forget to take a quick head count and determine whether your party is outnumbered. Take special note of the following roles:

- **Brutes and soldiers:** They're big, strong melee machines. Gangs of orc warriors, evil fighters, ogres or trolls, or physically powerful creatures such as dire bears all fall into this group. Brutes hit hard and have a lot of hit points but are usually easy to hit. Soldiers usually have higher defenses than brutes but not as many hit points.

- **Lurkers:** The lurker monsters are dangerous when they catch your party by surprise, but they aren't much for a stand-up fight.

- **Artillery:** These monsters prefer to attack at range, using either missile weapons, magical powers, or innate abilities. Goblin archers, flameskulls, or spined devils are all good examples.

- **Controllers:** These monsters have special attacks that inflicts various types of action denial against the heroes — for example, monsters that stun or slow their targets, or monsters that create difficult or dangerous terrain around their targets.

- **Skirmishers:** The skirmisher monsters are highly mobile and have good melee attack power, but their best defense against counterattack is moving away again. They have abilities that let them get around the party's front line and threaten rear-rank characters.

- **Minions:** These monsters are mostly cannon fodder, creatures that pose a threat in large numbers but are individually easy to eliminate.

- **No threat:** These monsters aren't a real threat to your party. They might outnumber you, but they're individually too weak to hurt anyone in the party.

Step 3: Choose the right tactic

Decide what method will give you the best odds of victory, depending on your foes, such as

- **Brutes and soldiers:** Maneuver and action denial are your best ploys. You don't want to give these monsters a fair fight at close range since that's what they excel at. Try to keep them immobilized at a short distance and soften them up with ranged attacks and powers.

- **Lurkers:** Assuming your party was ambushed, it's too late for maneuver or negotiation. Use action denial to slow down their attacks against you, and then lock them up in melee and deal damage.

- **Artillery:** Many artillery monsters are less effective in close combat. Maneuver to close the range, and reduce their hit points with melee attacks.

- **Controllers:** Like artillery, many controller monsters are less dangerous in melee. However, the control effects they use against you often keep you from getting close to them. Use ranged attacks and powers to deal damage from a distance if you can't get close to melee range.

- **Skirmishers:** You're not likely to out-maneuver skirmishers, so take away their mobility with action denial attacks. When you have them where you want them, you can keep them engaged in melee.

- **Minions:** Area attacks that deal damage on a hit are really good for taking out minions quickly.

- **No threat:** Save your daily powers and take out these monsters with at-will or encounter attacks. Don't bother with very weak monsters, however, until you've contained the threat of more powerful monsters in the encounter.

Step 4: Rethink your assumptions

At the end of every round, you should reassess the battle and figure out whether any of your basic assumptions about the fight have changed. Did the monsters get reinforcements? Have you found a spot of good terrain that gives your character an advantage? Were the monsters no real threat at all? Is this a fight you should run away from? Rethink your assumptions every round to make sure you're still fighting the right fight.

Using Advanced Tactics

If all you ever do is pick the right target for your character's powers, manage your expendable and daily powers well, attack efficiently, and consider the occasional tactical retreat, you're already better off than a significant number of experienced players. You might have noticed that the preceding advice is fairly generic. In this section, we talk about a few specific artifacts of the D&D rules that you can master in order to play your best game.

Flanking

Flanking is the first and easiest of the advanced tactics you should put to work. If your character and your allies are fighting the same foe, make sure that someone gets on the monster's opposite side. Now your character and your flanking buddy each gain *combat advantage* against that target, which means a +2 bonus to melee attacks. Better yet, if your character (or your friend's character) is a rogue, every attack he or she makes against that target deals sneak attack damage.

Flanking is described on page 285 of the *Player's Handbook*.

Powers that allow you to *shift* (move without provoking opportunity attacks) are a great way to slip around the monster to a flanking position without getting mauled by opportunity attacks (more about those later in this chapter).

Beating the initiative order

The novice player assumes that it's always better to take his or her turn as early as possible in the round. We're working on making you smarter than that. Sometimes you can manufacture significant tactical advantages by readying actions or delaying your character's actions.

Delaying or readying your action lets you change the initiative order and time your character's attacks for maximum effect.

Delaying and readying are described on pages 288 and 291 of the *Player's Handbook*.

Some specific examples of ways to use the ready and delay actions to your advantage include:

- **Waiting for a flank:** Your character is toe to toe with the ogre, but your buddy hasn't taken his turn yet. Delay your character's action until your friend's character moves up to flank the ogre. When your ally attacks, he gets the flanking bonus because your character is already in position. Then, your character attacks after your friend goes, and your character gets the flanking bonus also. If your character had attacked on your turn before your friend's character was in place on the other side of the monster, your character wouldn't have been flanking.

- **Waiting for a buff:** The party is facing a troll, and the player running the party's cleric tells you that he's going to use his *righteous brand* power and give your character the attack bonus if he hits. You can have your character make an attack right now without the benefit of the prayer — or, you can delay your character's action until after the cleric hits the troll and then make an attack with the bonus conferred by the cleric's prayer.

- **Fighting enemies your character can't reach:** If you're dealing with a flying monster that swoops in to attack your character and then finishes its turn well out of reach, ready an action to strike at the monster the instant it comes within sword-reach. When it attacks, so does your character, and you don't spend round after round with your character getting hit and not being able to strike back because the monster isn't nearby anymore when your turn comes up.

Charging

Most attack powers in the game are standard actions. If you're ever in a situation where a monster you want to attack isn't within range and you can't get him in range with your move action, you might think that you can't attack it. But you'd be wrong. The Charge action is a special combat action that, as a single standard action, enables your character to move up to his or her speed and make a basic melee attack at the end of the move. If you need to reach a foe and attack him fast, charging is a good answer. Your character also receives a +1 attack bonus when charging.

Charging is described on page 287 of the *Player's Handbook*.

The big disadvantage of using the Charge action is that most attack powers —
even at-will attacks — aren't usable in a charge. In other words, all you can
do when you charge is run up and make a single, relatively weak attack. But
if you had no other way to attack an enemy on your turn, it might be the best
you can do.

Charging is especially useful if you want to use a melee attack and

- You start your turn prone with no enemies next to you. Standing up takes
a move action, and then you can charge in order to move up to a monster
and make a melee attack.

- You start your turn dazed with no enemies next to you. Because you're
limited to a single action when you're dazed, the only way you can get to
an enemy and make a melee attack is to charge.

- The monster you want to hit is so far away you can't reach it in a single
move action, but you could reach it in two. Use your first move action to
get close and then charge with your standard action.

Avoiding opportunity attacks

Opportunity attacks are free, instant basic melee attacks anyone gets when an
adjacent foe undertakes a complicated or risky action. Things that provoke
opportunity attacks include using ranged or area attacks or powers or ignoring a foe in order to move out of a square adjacent to that foe.

You can read all about opportunity attacks on page 290 of the *Player's
Handbook*.

Basically, you don't want to provoke opportunity attacks. It's not smart to
give the monsters free extra attacks against your character because sometimes those attacks will hit, and your character will wind up taking more
damage than necessary. Worse yet, maybe the monster will get really lucky,
roll a critical hit, and take your character out of the fight with one swing —
when it's not even the monster's turn.

That said, sometimes players go to extreme lengths to avoid insignificant
opportunity attacks. If you're playing a cleric with an AC of 22 who's fighting
a goblin warrior with an attack bonus of +2, the goblin's only going to hit your
cleric on a roll of 20. Ninety-five percent of the time, you can safely disregard
the threat the goblin poses and ignore him or her. Be conservative in deciding when a foe can be ignored, though.

You have two good ways for your character to maneuver around monsters and foes without giving them opportunity attacks:

✔ **Shift:** You can limit your character's movement to a single square per move action. If your character uses the Shift action, he or she moves only 1 square but doesn't provoke opportunity attacks just for leaving a square adjacent to an enemy. Another good use for Shift is to step back from a foe in order to get room to use a ranged or area power safely.

✔ **Powers:** Many powers give you the ability to move without provoking. For example, the 6th-level wizard power *dimension door* allows you to teleport 10 squares. When you teleport, you just disappear and reappear — even if you "leave" a square adjacent to an enemy, your foe doesn't get an opportunity attack against you. Rogues have several powers that let them move around the battlefield safely, although none are as spectacular as teleportation.

Concentrating on defense

Most players believe that the best defense is a good offense; if you want to avoid getting hit, take down the monster so fast it doesn't get many chances to hurt you. However, sometimes your best move is to play for time.

Consider this scenario: Your character has used up his or her expendable powers and is badly bloodied. One more good hit from the hill giant you're fighting might take you out. But you're providing a flanking opportunity for the rogue, who happens to be in much better shape than you. Taking a mace swing at the hill giant is okay, but it won't make that much of a difference to the fight. However, as long as you stay on your feet, you're giving the rogue combat advantage.

In a situation like this, it might be better to concentrate on defense. Here are a few ways to do it:

✔ **Second Wind:** The Second Wind action lets you use a healing surge and also gives you +2 on all defenses until the start of your next turn. It takes a standard action, so normally you can't attack and use your Second Wind on the same turn. (However, dwarf characters can use Second Wind as a minor action.) You can find the full description of this action on page 291 of the *Player's Handbook*.

✔ **Total Defense:** If you don't want to use a healing surge (or you used your Second Wind already), use the Total Defense action. It costs you a standard action, so you can't have your character attack in the same round that you use total defense, but you gain a +2 bonus to all your character's defenses. In other words, Total Defense is just like Second Wind, except with no healing.

- ✔ **Aid Another:** You can use the Aid Another action with a melee attack. If you hit AC 10 (pretty easy, really) you can choose to grant an ally +2 to all defenses against the target creature's next attack. If you can't hurt the monster, you can at least help your ally defend himself or herself.

- ✔ **Using cover:** Try to put something big and solid between your character and the monster. Cover inflicts a –2 or –5 penalty on the attacker's attack roll, depending on whether it's normal cover (a pillar, a small tree, a large piece of furniture, a low wall) or superior cover (an arrow slit, a portcullis, or something similarly unfair). You may or may not suffer a penalty to attack the monster out of your own cover, depending on where your character is in relation to the monster and the object that's providing cover. Cover is described in detail on page 280 of the *Player's Handbook*.

Setting up opportunity attacks

Your single most precious commodity in the game is the number of turns you get in the course of the day. The typical D&D battle lasts about five rounds, and you can expect your character to be in about four to six battles per day of adventuring — so your character has only 20 to 30 turns per day to beat down bad guys and make a difference in the adventure. Getting the most out of every turn you take is absolutely vital.

If actions are your most valuable asset, then any tactic that lets your character get more opportunities to damage the enemy without costing any actions is worth a closer look. Opportunity attacks offer your character the chance to make extra attacks even when it isn't your turn; if you can manufacture even one opportunity attack per five rounds of combat, you're cramming six rounds of actions into five rounds of fighting. You'll be 20 percent more effective than the player who didn't position his or her character to take advantage of the opening when it came up.

The first thing you can do to maximize your opportunity attacks is to play a fighter; the fighter class has a couple of very potent abilities based on opportunity attacks. However, even if you're not playing a fighter, you can choose feats that maximize the effectiveness of opportunity attacks. Here are a few you should look at:

- ✔ Combat Reflexes provides a +1 attack bonus on opportunity attacks.

- ✔ Blade Opportunist provides a +2 attack bonus on opportunity attacks if you use a light blade or heavy blade.

- ✔ Potent Opportunity lets a fighter add his or her Con modifier to damage dealt in an opportunity attack.

- ✔ Heavy Blade Opportunity lets you use an at-will power when your character makes an opportunity attack.

- ✔ Tripping Chain knocks the target of your opportunity attack prone, if you're using a flail.

In addition to your feat selection, you can also use some hard-nosed tactical play to put your character in a position to gather up every opportunity attack that might come his or her way:

- ✔ **Controlling territory:** Put your character in a spot where the enemy has to go past your character to get at other party members (or to get away from other party members). Look for tactical chokepoints in the fight where your character can block a hallway or a door and get a free hack on anyone trying to go through.

- ✔ **Menacing everyone:** Move your character adjacent to as many foes as possible, especially if they aren't brutes or soldiers (monsters that are at their most dangerous in melee combat). This strategy is a little risky, because it's usually not a great idea to get your character surrounded, but the more enemies adjacent to you, the more likely it is that one of them will do something stupid and give you a free shot.

Adapting Your Tactics to Your Foes

The earlier sections of this chapter give you the medieval equivalent of a Ph.D. in Hurt. In the rest of the chapter, we show you some specific tactical situations that come up all the time in game play. It's rare that you participate in an adventure that doesn't feature at least one or more of the following scenarios.

Beating ranged controllers

Some of the most dangerous monsters and villains are controllers because they can either put damage on a number of party members at once (an evil wizard with a *fireball* spell, for example) or take out one of your comrades with a nasty effect like petrification, paralysis, or domination. Controllers who can attack effectively at range are especially frustrating because many player characters are built for melee combat. Fighters, rogues, and battle clerics often find themselves without a single attack power that works at range.

Fortunately, most ranged controllers tend to be soft targets (enemies with low Armor Class and poor hit points). You can beat them if you hit them fast and hard. Here are three basic tactics you can try the next time your party comes across an evil wizard:

- ✔ **Split up:** The best answer to area-effect attacks is to simply make sure that no two characters are close enough to each other to get caught in the same blast. If a controller's got a power that can affect two targets but you make sure he or she can catch only one target at a time, you've cut that enemy's effectiveness in half.

- ✔ **Box and menace:** The classic response to an enemy using ranged or area attacks is to put an angry fighter in his or her face. Charge or run past any obstacles in the way to reach the controller. If he or she uses a ranged power while your character is adjacent, he or she will have to shift away from your character in order to cast safely. If you can get an ally on the other side of the enemy, you can box him or her so that he or she can't use a ranged or area power without giving your character an opportunity attack.

- ✔ **Block line of sight:** Wizards (and warlocks) have access to powers that can block line of sight — for example, *stinking cloud, wall of fog,* or *wall of fire*. Although these are decent offensive spells, you can use them defensively by creating a "smoke screen" the enemy controller can't see through. The enemy will have to get on your side of the obscuring effect in order to attack, and that means moving to a place where you might be able to get at him or her.

Handling numerous foes

The good news about being badly outnumbered is that you're probably dealing with foes who are individually weaker than your character. D&D is heroic fiction, and in heroic fiction, you can mop the floor with whole gangs of numerous bad guys who can't hit the broadside of a barn. If you find your character outnumbered by foes who are as tough (or tougher) than your character, then *run!* Your character is going to get creamed.

The following list offers some helpful tactics to try when your character is outnumbered and surrounded by enemies:

- ✔ **Concentrate the damage:** Don't have your character hit one orc in one round and then attack a different orc in the next round. In D&D, enemies don't lose any offensive potential until they're knocked all the way down to 0 hit points, so slowly wearing down multiple foes at once simply means that you're giving more enemies opportunities to hurt your character before they go down. Pick on one or two foes at a time and drop them before starting on the next enemies.

- ✔ **Control the battlefield:** Look for ways to divide and conquer foes. Have your character retreat into a narrow passage where enemies can come at him or her only a couple at a time. Use terrain-altering spells such as *icy terrain* or *consecrated ground* to isolate some of your enemies from their pals. If nothing else presents itself, just move. When your character is standing still on open ground, you're making it easy for your foes to surround your character and attack from all sides. If you keep your character moving, you won't find your character in the middle of three or four bad guys all taking swings on him or her every round.

Fighting monsters your character can't hurt

Few monsters are really invulnerable, but sometimes you encounter opponents that can be very difficult to wear down. The basic strategy for fighting a monster most of the party can't hurt is to protect and support whichever characters *can* hurt the monster. Everybody else simply buys time for the effective character or characters to wear down the foe, and the party does its best to make sure the character doing the hard work stays healed up and in the thick of the fight.

High-AC foes

Enemies with superior Armor Class may be virtually impossible for your character to hit with melee or ranged attacks. Fortunately, your character can hit anything if you roll a natural 20 on your attack roll, so if nothing else, you can simply have your character flail away at the enemy until you get a lucky roll. Here are some different ideas:

- ✔ **Flank and aid another:** If your foe seems impossible to hit, surround it to get the +2 attack bonus for combat advantage through flanking . . . then have as many characters as possible use the Aid Another action in order to provide one character with the best chance of hitting extra attack bonuses.

- ✔ **Maximize one character:** Use powers that confer attack bonuses on your allies to power up the most effective character in the party. Powers such as *lance of faith, bless,* or *spiritual weapon* can grant significant attack bonuses. This is a leader-role thing, so clerics and warlords have the most powers of this sort.

Elusive foes

Some enemies are hard to hurt because they're simply not there for your character's attacks. Good examples are insubstantial creatures such as specters or shadows that can attack through the walls, or skirmishing monsters who use high movement rates and mobility powers to whack your character and then bound away before your character can reply.

Try the following strategy when your character is facing an elusive foe: Ready an attack to strike at your adversary whenever he or she comes within reach. Even if your foe's movements and attacks don't normally provoke opportunity attacks, a readied attack isn't an opportunity attack; your character can get a swing at the enemy when he or she moves in to attack. It works better than standing around waiting to get hit.

Chapter 20

Making the Most of Magic

In This Chapter

▶ Fine-tuning your wizard's spell selection

▶ Using magic powers in combat

▶ Getting the most out of magic rituals

▶ Maxing out your character's magic items

*F*lashing steel and deeds of agility are great, but the most spectacular and imaginative part of the D&D experience is magic — the supernatural powers and enchanted items many heroes use to break the rules of reality. A *fireball* drops the evil wizard's orc bodyguards; an *invisibility* spell on the party's rogue lets her get into position for a lethal sneak attack; the attacking mummy is set ablaze by the fighter's magical *flameburst* battleaxe. D&D has been summed up as simply as "the game where you fight monsters with magic," and that says it all.

In 4th Edition DUNGEONS & DRAGONS, there's much less difference between *casters* — characters who use spells or other supernatural powers to attack — and noncasters than there was in previous editions. All characters now choose special powers, and they "use up" at least some of the powers (powers with a daily usage) as they adventure. However, most players would agree that characters who use the arcane or divine power sources and primarily attack at range are casters because they're attacking with magic prayers and spells. Clerics, warlocks, and wizards are all casters.

In this chapter, we tell you about the fine arts of choosing a wizard's spell repertoire for the day, casting effectively in battle, and maximizing any character's power with the acquisition of the right magic items. We also show you some baseline magic item purchases to quickly equip higher-level characters.

Selecting Wizard Spells for the Adventure

Wizards are unique among magic-using characters because they have a limited ability to change their powers every day, thanks to the Spellbook class feature. This means that the wizard has the greatest flexibility of all the classes, casters or noncasters. If you're playing a wizard, you can reinvent your wizard as an entirely new character every time you decide which daily and utility spells you want your character to prepare. So how do you know which are the right spells to take?

Here's an easy process to follow when you're considered which spells you want your character to prepare for the day's adventuring:

1. **Consider the scenario.**

   What are you trying to do? Is the party going monster-hunting? Select spells to find and kill monsters. Is the party going to explore a trap-filled tomb? Take utility spells that will let the party get around or through traps. Is the party trying to infiltrate an evil thieves' guild? Take spells of disguise, enchantment, and subterfuge.

2. **Review what you know.**

   What do you know about the obstacles you expect to meet in the adventure? If the party has learned that the evil tyrant's castle is guarded by ogre berserkers, you can expect to run into lots of ogres. Change out spells that attack Fortitude defense for spells that attack Will defense; ogres are physically tough, but they're pushovers for mental effects. If you discover you don't have any information at all, can you use any of the rituals you know to gain more before you commit to your spell selection for the day? (If not, perhaps you should make gaining information your mission for the day and then go in with *magic missiles* blazing after you know a little bit more!)

3. **Choose your mission.**

   How do you want to accomplish your goals in the current adventure? What mix of player characters showed up for the game tonight? Is the party short a leader, and therefore in need of some extra magical protection? Here are some of your choices:

   - *Direct attack:* Your character's role for the day is to provide magical firepower for the party of adventurers. Select utility powers that will help you fight better, such as *shield.* Load up on daily attack spells that deal lots of damage, like *acid arrow* and *fireball.*

   - *Maneuver:* Your character is going to help the party get to where it can do the most good. Select utility powers that help other characters to move (for example, *jump* or *levitate*) and offensive powers that emphasize immobilizing enemies, such as *sleep* or *web.*

• *Reconnaissance:* Your character is going to gather information pertaining to the mission. Utility spells such as *disguise self* or *invisibility* may be useful in allowing your character to slip into places he or she is not supposed to be, or to scout out dangerous locales before the party walks into a deadly ambush.

• *Protection:* Your character is going to help the party stand up to damage and fight better. Prepare utility spells that can help your comrades and generally contribute versatility and extra options, such as *invisibility* or *resistance.* For your daily attack spells, choose powers that deny or hinder enemy action, such as *Bigby's icy grasp* or *wall of fire.*

Many wizard players get in the habit of leaving their favorite spells permanently "penciled in" on their character sheets, but you're missing out on a subtle and powerful class feature if you never use your wizard's spellbook!

Who uses magic?

In earlier editions of the DUNGEONS & DRAGONS game, characters used magic in two basic forms: spells some character classes could cast (primarily clerics and wizards), and magic items any character might carry. In the 4th Edition DUNGEONS & DRAGONS game, *every* character has powers that can be used only once per day each. In a sense, every character is a spellcaster (at least by the standards of earlier editions) even if their "spells" are actually exploits of pure martial skill.

In this context, the difference between powers that are overtly supernatural and powers that are based on physical skill and effort just isn't that important. But generally speaking, arcane and divine powers are "magic," and heroic powers aren't — unless, of course, you use a heroic power like *crushing blow* to smash the enemy with a *+4 giantslayer warhammer.* That hammer is surely magical, even if your power isn't!

The line between what's magic and what's not is further blurred by the fact that many powers based on the magic power sources (arcane and divine) aren't really much like spells used to be in earlier editions. For example, the paladin is a character who uses the divine power source. Few of his evil-smiting powers really look like what the game used to call "spells," and no one would mistake a plate-armored paladin for a character who is primarily a "spellcaster." He's a defender, one of the toughest and most physically resilient characters in the game.

For the purposes of our discussion in this chapter, *casters* are characters who are built to attack enemies at range with arcane or divine powers. Noncasters are everyone else. Using this definition, here are the casters in the D&D game:

✔ Devoted Clerics, warlocks, and wizards are casters.

✔ Fighters, paladins, rangers, rogues, and warlords are noncasters (although rangers using the Archer build are a lot like casters).

✔ Battle Clerics work like casters when they use ranged powers and non-casters when they use melee powers.

Casting in Combat

You can secure all the advantages you like with rituals and useful utility powers, but sooner or later, your caster is going to have to fight the monsters. If you're playing a Devoted Cleric, a warlock, or a wizard, your character has no weapons worth speaking of other than magic.

As a caster, the last place you want to be is right in front of the monsters or villains, where they can pound on your character with their melee attacks. Unfortunately, this decision isn't always up to you. Sometimes you get caught off-guard or trapped in tight quarters, and the monsters are in your face before you can get out of the way.

Getting caught in a melee is bad for two reasons. First of all, your character is exposed to the enemies' best and most dangerous attacks. No sane wizard wants to be anywhere near an angry ogre with a big spiked club. Second, area powers and ranged powers (the majority of powers your character uses in combat) provoke opportunity attacks. (See Chapter 19 of this book for more about opportunity attacks.) So, not only is your character exposed to direct attack, you're putting your character in a situation where he or she might not be able to safely use the best weapons at his or her disposal.

Fortunately, there are a few ways to slither out of this difficult position:

- ✔ **Shift:** Your character can step one square away from the foe threatening him or her without provoking an opportunity attack for moving. If your character is no longer adjacent to any enemies, he or she can then safely use area or ranged powers. Be careful about trying this on large opponents such as ogres or giants, though — some of them have a special ability called Threatening Reach, which means you're still in danger even if you are no longer adjacent to them.

- ✔ **Close powers:** A fair number of powers have a range of "Close." Unlike area powers or ranged powers, Close powers don't provoke opportunity attacks. If you can't shift out of trouble, use a Close power instead of your longer-ranged powers.

- ✔ **Teleport:** If you have a teleport power (for example, the eladrin's *fey step* or the wizard's *dimension door*) you can safely move away by teleporting before using your area or ranged attack.

- ✔ **Delay:** Consider delaying your action until one of the other player characters is able to push, pull, or slide the enemy away from you, or otherwise create an opportunity for you to use your area or ranged powers safely.

Rituals: The Magic You Didn't Know You Had

One of the interesting innovations in the 4th Edition D&D game is the ritual magic system. In earlier editions, your cleric or wizard had to decide whether to prepare combat-useful magic such as *invisibility* and *searing light* spells, or spells that might help the party navigate through the dungeon (for example, *knock* or *endure elements*). If you had too many of your spell slots tied up in spells that weren't useful in combat, you risked running out of things to do during fights. If you didn't have enough of those utility spells, the party's day of adventuring might come to an abrupt end when you hit an obstacle you didn't have the right spell for.

Fortunately, the 4th Edition D&D game is much friendlier. First of all, every character gains utility powers that are segregated from attack powers, so you never have to worry about whether you've devoted too many resources to spells that aren't useful in combat. Second, your character now has access to magic rituals that replace many of those marginal spells from earlier editions. Rituals don't use up *any* of your power slots, and they have no limitation on how often you can use them. All they cost you is time and money.

Basically, a *ritual* is a set of written instructions for creating a magical effect. Each time your character follows the instructions, he or she gets the ritual's result. You can cast the same ritual ten times in a day if you want to, as long as you have the ritual book, the necessary components, and the time to do so. The instructions have to be written down in a ritual book or on a ritual scroll because even the simplest rituals are complicated enough that characters can't just memorize them. However, there's no limit to the number of rituals your character might eventually master.

Rituals are covered in Chapter 10 of the *Player's Handbook*.

We call rituals "the magic you didn't know you had" because *any* character could conceivably learn to perform rituals. All your character needs is the Ritual Caster feat (which clerics and wizards get for free). Your character does have to be trained in either Arcana or Religion to select that feat, so if his or her class doesn't provide those skills, you'll need to use a Skill Training feat first. But the point remains that, for the relatively low cost of one or two feats, any character in the game can make himself or herself capable of doing things like teleporting the party thousands of miles, raising the dead, or enchanting magic items.

Learning rituals

The trick with rituals is that your character knows only the rituals that he or she has recorded in ritual books. To get a ritual book, your character must find it as treasure, spend money to buy a copy (the ritual's market price), or master a ritual as part of a class feature. Clerics and wizards begin at 1st level with a small number of rituals they've already mastered, and wizards get to learn new rituals for free at 5th, 11th, 15th, 21st, and 25th level. (See the wizard class description in the *Player's Handbook*.) Early in his or her career, your character might have only a couple of rituals. You'll need to slowly build up that library to include all the rituals that you think are worthwhile for your character.

Before you start on your tour of the ritual chapter, there's one important thing you should know: Your character can only learn rituals of equal or lower level. For example, if your character is a 7th-level wizard, he or she can only perform rituals of 7th level or lower.

You don't have to be trained in the key skill for the ritual. For example, Raise Dead uses Heal as its key skill, but any character who can perform rituals can perform the Raise Dead ritual. Sometimes it's helpful to be trained in the ritual's key skill, but it's not a requirement. In previous editions of the D&D

game, Raise Dead was exclusively the province of the cleric class, but any character with the Ritual Caster feat can give it a shot — as long as they're 8th level or higher and have a ritual book of Raise Dead handy.

Using rituals

To use a ritual, your character must have a copy of the ritual handy in either a book or a scroll. If it's in a book, your character must have mastered the ritual — which means your character's level must be equal to or greater than the ritual's level. If it's in a scroll, you don't have to have it mastered. Scrolls are "ritual cheat sheets," already pre-cast up until the last few steps so that any character, whether or not they have the Ritual Caster feat, can follow the directions and perform the ritual on the scroll.

As we mention earlier, rituals cost time and money. Time is the ritual's casting time. For example, the Raise Dead ritual takes 8 hours to perform. Money is simply the ritual's cost — each time your character performs that ritual, he or she has to spend the appropriate sum in various arcane reagents, rare herbs and salves, or what-have-you. For example, Raise Dead costs 500 gp to perform. Fortunately, you don't have to specify the exact components for any given ritual; you can just write "700 gp of mystic salves" on your character sheet, and when your character performs Raise Dead, scratch that off and write in 200 gp instead.

Some rituals have another cost — they may cost your character some number of healing surges. These are extremely taxing rituals that you just can't perform easily. The Forbiddance ritual is a good example; it costs you 5 healing surges. Usually, rituals that cost you in this way are intended to be used outside of adventuring; they're more for background and story than tactical play.

Rituals usually succeed, if success is possible (you can't raise someone who's been dead more than 30 days, for instance), but sometimes the results improve dramatically depending on the result of a key skill check. For instance, when your character casts Cure Disease, a skill check result of 0 or less actually kills the poor sod you're trying to heal. (Although if you kill him, the disease is gone!) If you achieve a skill check result of 30 or better, he takes no damage at all.

Powering Up with Magic Items

The arcane and divine powers your character commands represent only a portion of the magical power available to the typical adventuring party. The other half of the equation is the party's collection of magic items. For example, the fighter carries a magic sword and wears magic armor; the rogue has a

Rituals every party should have

Some rituals are a lot more important than others. As your character gains levels, he or she should make sure to find, buy, or select these rituals for the good of the whole adventuring party:

✔ **Knock (level 4):** Got a door your party can't open or destroy? The Knock ritual can overcome that obstacle.

✔ **Cure Disease (level 6):** Few monsters have disease attacks, but when your character gets hit with one, you want to get better — fast.

✔ **Sending (level 6):** The closest you can come to a cell phone in the D&D world. Sending allows you to report to a distant patron, contact a lost player character, ask a friendly sage a question . . . anything you can think of in 25 words or less.

✔ **Linked Portal (level 8):** This extraordinarily useful ritual is basically a whole-party teleport with a range in hundreds or thousands of miles. Need to get to Waterdeep before lunchtime? This is the ritual for you. The casting time is only 10 minutes, so it's also a good way to bug out of a dungeon if you can just drop out of sight for a short time.

✔ **Raise Dead (level 8):** Nothing ruins your whole day like getting killed. Raise Dead can fix that and get your hero back in the fight (with an 8-hour delay, anyway). What more needs to be said?

✔ **Remove Affliction (level 8):** Like Cure Disease, you need to have this ritual in your back pocket in case one of the party members gets hit with something nasty and permanent — for example, being petrified by a medusa.

magic crossbow and an *elven cloak;* the wizard has a wand of *fiery bolts;* and the cleric wears a *helm of battle.* Spells are just for arcane casters and prayers are for divine casters, but any character can carry a powerful magic item.

When you create a 1st-level character, that character begins with low-grade, nonmagical gear and a handful of pocket change. But as your character has successful adventures, he or she recovers staggering amounts of wealth and magic items of great and terrible power. Your character's collection of magic items is just as much a part of him or her as the choice of class, powers, skills, and feats. A fighter who owns *winged boots* is a very different character from a fighter who owns *dwarven greaves.*

Most magic items have an enhancement value — a "plus" — associated with one of your character's basic stats. For example, magic armor enhances your character's Armor Class, magic weapons enhance attack and damage rolls, and magic cloaks enhance Fortitude, Reflex, and Will defenses. If your character wears a *+2 elven cloak,* you get to add 2 to each of those defenses as long as your character wears that cloak. In addition, items may have properties and powers. Properties are persistent, always-on abilities; for example, the *helm of battle* grants your character a +1 item bonus to initiative checks. Items' powers are much like your character powers; they're specific abilities your character can trigger at will, once per encounter, or once per day.

Types of magic items

Magic items come in a variety of different forms, ranging from mighty magic swords, to life-saving potions, to artifacts of godlike power. By the time your character gets a few experience levels under his or her belt, you'll probably have a good array of magic items to choose from.

Here's a quick tour of the types of magic items you're likely to find or purchase:

✔ **Armor:** Magic armor works much like normal armor, except better. The enhancement bonus of magic armor is added to the AC bonus provided by the armor. So, for example, normal scale mail gives a +7 armor bonus to AC, but *+2 scale mail* adds 9 points to AC.

✔ **Weapons:** Magic weapons add their enhancement bonus to each attack and damage roll your character makes with the weapon. For example, a 4th-level character with a Strength of 16 and a longsword has an attack bonus of +8 (+2 for the character's level modifier, +3 for Strength modifier, and +3 for the longsword's proficiency bonus) and deals 1d8+3 points of damage. If the same character fights with a *+2 longsword,* the attack bonus becomes +10, and the character deals 1d8+5 points of damage per hit.

✔ **Implements:** Just as melee characters or archers use magic swords or bows, casters use magic implements. Implements include holy symbols, orbs, rods, staffs, and wands; different characters use different implements. For example, clerics and paladins use holy symbols, whereas warlocks and wizards use wands, orbs, rods, or staffs. Implements work exactly like magic weapons — if your wizard has a *+2 wand,* you add +2 to your attack and damage rolls with spells your character casts with it.

✔ **Slot items:** Unlike an entire suit of magical armor, slot items are worn just on a specific part of the body. Your character can wear only one magical item per slot — a character can't use two arm slot items (say, *bracers of defense* and a *shield of protection*) at the same time. The body slots are neck, arms, feet, hands, head, and waist, and each body slot is associated with a particular type of bonus or advantage. For example, neck slot items always confer bonuses to your character's defenses; you'll never find a defense-boosting item that isn't a neck slot item.

  • *Neck slot items:* Amulets, cloaks, and scarabs are worn around the neck. Neck slot items are very important, because they add their enhancement bonus to all three of your non-AC defenses: Fortitude, Reflex, and Will defense. For example, if your rogue wears an *amulet of cleansing +3,* you add +3 to each of your character's defenses.

  • *Arm slot items:* Items that are worn or carried on the arm, such as bracers and shields. These items don't have any enhancement bonus (so there's no such thing as a *+2 shield* in the 4th Edition Dungeons & Dragons game), but they usually have powers or properties that help your character's defenses in other ways.

- *Feet slot items:* Items your character wears on his or her feet (and/or lower legs), such as boots and greaves. Most are magic boots of one kind or another. Like your arms slot items, they don't have enhancement bonuses. Most feet slot items add to your character's mobility or bestow movement powers of one kind or another.

- *Hand slot items:* Items your character wears on his or her hands, such as gloves and gauntlets. Again, they don't have any enhancement bonus, but they instead contribute to offense or skill use with various properties and powers.

- *Head slot items:* Items worn on the head, such as helmets, circlets, and crowns. Usually they bestow powers of perception, defense, or authority. They don't have enhancement bonuses and don't figure into any of your character's stats otherwise.

- *Waist slot items:* Items worn around the waist, such as belts. They don't have enhancement bonuses to add to any of your stats. Instead, they generally have properties or powers that add to your defenses and resistances.

✔ **Rings:** Well, we all know about magic rings now, don't we? Don't worry; not every ring is The One Ring to Rule Them All. A character can wear and gain the benefits of up to two magic rings (one on each hand). Wearing more than that means that none of the rings function. Magic rings usually come with a useful property and a good power, usually usable once per day (or recharged when your character reaches an adventuring milestone).

✔ **Wondrous item:** This is a catch-all category of weird things your character usually doesn't wear, so they're not tied to any particular item slots. They also don't provide enhancement bonuses. However, this category includes a variety of powerful and useful items, such as *bag of holding, sending stones,* and *flying carpet.* We just can't offer much in the way of generalizations about wondrous items, because they're all diverse and unique.

✔ **Potion:** A potion is a one-use restorative beverage. When your character drinks it, the potion's magic provides some amount of healing or recovery, and the potion is used up. The most powerful potions can even restore life to the dead, but most potions you find are simple *potions of healing* — 10 hit points in a little glass vial that costs you 1 healing surge. Usually, potions don't restore as many hit points as one of your character's own healing surges, but at least you can control when your character drinks a potion. If the party's cleric is incapacitated and you've already used your second wind, it might be the only healing your character can get.

Magic item descriptions begin on page 227 of the *Player's Handbook.*

Acquiring magic items

Magic items sound great, don't they? You might think that every character should have some, and in the vast majority of D&D games, they do. Your character can find magic items in monster-guarded dungeon vaults, use his or her share of recovered treasure hoards to purchase magic items, or even build new items by using magic rituals. But here's the downside: Your character's acquisition of magic items is entirely in the hands of your Dungeon Master. If your DM doesn't include magic items in the treasure stashes of the monsters the party defeats, well, your character won't find many. And if your DM decides that magic items just aren't bought and sold in his or her campaign, you won't be able to turn big piles of gold into a *wand of fireball* and a *dragon-slayer* sword. You have to live with what your DM lets your character have.

Finding items

Monsters often guard hoards of staggering wealth, including long-lost devices with mighty enchantments. Champions of evil are sometimes armed and armored with powerful magic items, which are there for the taking after the party has defeated the previous owner.

The difficulty with items your character finds in monster hoards or on the persons of defeated villains is that they don't come with name tags and instruction manuals. Many DMs don't waste much time on making you guess what magic items your character is carrying, because nothing is more annoying than listening to a player constantly say things like, "Okay, I rolled an 18 for my attack roll . . . plus whatever the bonus on this sword is, so maybe it's a 19 or a 20. So did I hit or what?" But some DMs like to throw curveballs at you such as items that your character doesn't understand right away, so be prepared.

If you find yourself in possession of an item your character can't identify, you may be able to figure it out with a successful Arcana, History, or Religion skill check. Failing that, there are a few rituals that might help you out — for example, Consult Mystic Sages or Consult Oracle. These are costly, so don't resort to using a ritual for every item your character finds.

Buying and selling items

The second most common way to acquire magic items is to simply buy them. If your character loots a dragon's hoard and finds 20,000 pieces of gold, you have 20 grand to spend. In D&D, the point of gaining wealth is so that you can spend it on the biggest, most impressive magic items you can find for your character, and then go get even *more* treasure so you can buy even *better* magic items.

Buying magic items works in both directions, of course. When your character finds a *+3 flaming adamantine longsword,* that old *+2 longsword* doesn't look so useful anymore. You can sell items, too — but you usually only get 20 percent of the purchase price. Don't sell old items unless you're really and truly done with them.

In general, your character needs to find a good-sized city in order to buy or sell an expensive magic item. The reasoning is that no one in a flea-speck-sized village way off in the middle of nowhere has a *+3 sword* to sell. The bigger the town, the better the odds of finding good magic items to buy. To get your hands on a really impressive item, you might have to go to someplace fantastic like the bazaar in the efreeti City of Brass.

Enchanting items

A lot of DMs are old-school on the topic of buying magic items, and may not allow you to just buy a wondrous enchanted device crafted by mighty dwarven armorers many centuries ago with the tawdry loot you dragged out of the nearest monster-infested hole in the ground. Fortunately, you have a way around this: The *Enchant Magic Item* ritual. If your DM won't let you buy *gauntlets of ogre power,* maybe you can convince the party's wizard to make you a pair.

As it turns out, the cost of *Enchant Magic Item* is exactly equal to the market price of the magic item you want to buy. So, really, when you enchant your sword, you're just buying a magic sword out of thin air (although you need a plain old sword to work with, so it's not really conjured out of nothing at all). It takes an hour, and the ritual caster can't create items that are higher than his or her level. But if your party has a couple of days of down time and a lot of money to spend, there's no reason you can't create any item in the *Player's Handbook* that's your character's level or lower. Some people think it just "feels" better in the game to imagine that a skilled wizard or devout cleric is crafting a magic item with muttered invocations and mystic reagents, as opposed to stepping out to the Magic-Mart and throwing around the gold.

Defining the Magic Item Baseline

Heads up! The D&D game *assumes* that your character has a selection of magic items appropriate to his or her class and level. The level of monsters your character encounters is based on this assumption. You may think it's absolutely snazzy for your 10th-level fighter to walk around with a *carpet of flying,* but if your fighter doesn't have a magic weapon by 10th level, you're going to find that it's hard to hold up your end in a fight.

In many D&D games, you don't start with 1st-level characters; you start with higher-level characters, who really need to have a small collection of magic items to actually live up to their level. This often happens when a new player is joining an existing game, or if the DM is beginning a new game and wants to start with a particular higher-level adventure. Your DM might tell you something like, "Make up a 5th-level character and equip him or her appropriately." So how do you know what's appropriate?

Here's the Golden Rule for equipping higher-level characters from scratch. First, determine your character's starting level (in our example, 5th level). Your character begins with:

- One magic item of his or her level +1

- One magic item of his or her level

- One magic item of his or her level –1

- Cash (in gold pieces) equal to the value of a magic item of his or her level –1, which you can use to buy another item, purchase rituals and ritual components, buy potions, or just save for later.

So, for a 5th-level character, you get: one 6th-level item, one 5th-level item, one 4th-level item, and 840 gp (the normal value of a 4th-level item) to buy other stuff with.

The Golden Rule of equipping characters with magic items creates some basic implications: First, you can have a total of four magic items (not counting potions and such); second, your lowest-level item is either equal to your level –1 (in which case you have no gold left over) or your level –2 (in which case you have gold left over to pick up some potions and have some pocket change). In general, we think it's wise to have a potion or two in your belt and a few gold pieces to spend, so that's the way our recommendations play out in the rest of this chapter.

With the four magic items, you should make sure you cover three things without fail: Your character's weapon or implement, armor, and neck slot item. Those are the three categories of items that carry enhancement bonuses, and therefore add directly to your character's combat effectiveness by improving his or her attack bonus, damage bonus, Armor Class, and the three defenses (Fortitude, Reflex, and Will). For most players, it's always best to carry the highest enhancement bonuses in these three slots that the Golden Rule allows — it's the simplest way to keep your character's combat stats as high as you can. That means your fourth item doesn't have to support a vital stat, so you can pick up whatever item strikes your fancy. Players who know their way around the magic item system can find items that offer better powers or properties than a straightforward +1 enhancement, but we're not talking to those guys — we're creating these tables for you.

In following sections, we provide recommended "gear buys" for characters up to 15th level in each of the four base classes (fighter, rogue, cleric, and wizard). These are summed up in this chapter in Tables 20-1 through 20-4. If you need to equip a character fast, these are handy shortcuts . . . and if you're slowly acquiring items as your character levels up over time, they illustrate the sort of magic items your character should aspire to have.

Your character is not *entitled* to treasure and magic items of the stated amount. Your character's acquisition of treasure is entirely in the hands of your Dungeon Master. You may lag behind drastically for a long time, only to score an epic hoard by slaying a mighty dragon. Or your character might get lucky and find particular items that are significantly more than he or she might normally be able to afford based on the Golden Rule.

Fighter magic items

If you're playing a fighter, your primarily concern is finding good weapons and armor. The better your character's armament, the better he or she fights. Table 20-1 lists our recommendations for the fighter's starting magic items by level.

Table 20-1	Typical Fighter Magic Items by Level
Level	**Recommended Magic Items and Gear**
1st	By starting package (see Chapter 17)
2nd	*+1 frost* weapon (3rd); *+1 dwarven* armor (2nd); *+1 amulet of protection* (1st); 3 *potions of healing;* 210 gp
3rd	*+1 frost* weapon (3rd); *+1 blackiron* armor (4th); *+1 amulet of protection* (1st); *bracers of mighty striking* (2nd); 2 *potions of healing;* 60 gp
4th	*+1 frost* weapon (3rd); *+1 blackiron* armor (4th); *+1 amulet of cleansing* (5th); *bracers of mighty striking* (2nd); 2 *potions of healing;* 60 gp
5th	*+2* weapon (6th); *+1 blackiron* armor (4th); *+1 amulet of cleansing* (5th); *shield of protection* (3rd) or *gloves of piercing* (3rd); 2 *potions of healing;* 60 gp
6th	*+2* weapon (6th); *+2 dwarven* armor (7th); *+1 amulet of cleansing* (5th); *shield of protection* (3rd) or *gloves of piercing* (3rd); 2 *potions of healing;* 220 gp
7th	*+2 thundering* weapon (8th); *+2 dwarven* armor (7th); *+2 amulet of protection* (6th); *horned helm* (5th) or *ironskin belt* (5th); 3 *potions of healing;* 650 gp
8th	*+2 thundering* weapon (8th); *+2 blackiron* armor (9th); *+2 amulet of protection* (6th); *bracers of defense* (7th); 3 *potions of healing;* 650 gp
9th	*+2 thundering* weapon (8th); *+2 blackiron* armor (9th); *+2 amulet of cleansing* (10th); *bracers of defense* (7th); 3 *potions of healing;* 650 gp
10th	*+3* weapon (11th); *+2 blackiron* armor (9th); *+2 amulet of cleansing* (10th); *shield of defiance* (8th) or *gauntlets of the ram* (8th); 3 *potions of healing;* 650 gp
11th	*+3* weapon (11th); *+3 dwarven* armor (12th); *+2 amulet of cleansing* (10th); *shield of defiance* (8th) or *gauntlets of the ram* (8th); *potion of vitality;* 600 gp
12th	*+3 frost* weapon (13th); *+3 dwarven* armor (12th); *+2 amulet of cleansing* (10th); *ring of protection* (11th); 3 *potions of vitality;* 1,000 gp
13th	*+3 frost* weapon (13th); *+3 dwarven* armor (12th); *+3 cloak of survival* (14th); *ring of protection* (11th); 3 *potions of vitality;* 1,000 gp
14th	*+3 flaming* weapon (15th); *+3 dwarven* armor (12th); *+3 cloak of survival* (14th); *winged boots* (13th) or *shield of protection* (13th); 3 *potions of vitality;* 1,000 gp
15th	*+3 flaming* weapon (15th); *+4 masterwork* armor (16th); *+3 cloak of survival* (14th); *winged boots* (13th) or *shield of protection* (13th); 3 *potions of vitality;* 1,000 gp

---

Magic items with daily powers

Some magic items contain daily powers, powers that can be used once per day. Just as you have a limit to the number of daily powers your class provides, you have a similar limit in regards to magic items. This limit depends on your level. At the heroic tier of play (levels 1–10), you can use one magic item daily power per day. This limit increases to two at paragon tier (levels 11–20) and three at epic tier (levels 21–30). Each use of a magic item daily power must come from a different magic item. In addition, each time you reach a milestone (or defeat encounters worth a specific total of XP based on your character level) during a day of adventuring, you gain one additional use of a magic item daily power. This additional use must be for a power you haven't yet activated for that day.

Weapon and *armor* on Table 20-1 refer to whichever weapon your fighter favors and the armor he or she prefers to wear. If your fighter is built for using heavy blades, you should be picking up magic longswords, greatswords, or bastard swords. If you spent a feat on armor training to upgrade from scale armor to plate armor, use these gear recommendations to choose magic plate armor instead of magic scale armor. In other words, fill in the blanks as appropriate for your own fighter.

For the fighter, we like weapons that come with encounter powers that boost damage and add some control, especially after you've already scored a hit. These are easy for you, the player, to use — you don't have to worry about difficult daily resource management with your weapon, and you don't have to worry about triggering the power and then missing. *Frost* weapons slow the target you trigger the power against, which is a great way of making sure your enemy doesn't get away.

We also recommended easy-to-play armors where possible. *Blackiron* armor is simple because all it has is a very nice property — resistance 5 to fire and necrotic damage. You never have to think about when to activate it because it's always on. *Dwarven* armor does come with a daily power to manage, but it's an easy one that might save your bacon someday; it's effectively a free-action heal that doesn't cost you a healing surge.

At 15th level, you can reach 16th-level magic armor . . . which allows you to choose *+4* armor, the minimum enchantment necessary to choose master-work armor (see page 212 of the *Player's Handbook*). Going from *+3 scale armor* to *+4 dragonscale armor* boosts your Armor Class by 4 points with a single magic item selection. If you're a defender, you *have* to have master-work armor as soon as you can possibly acquire it.

Rogue magic items

A rogue wants to acquire good magic weapons as much as the fighter does, but a rogue also wants to pick up interesting and useful magic items for avoiding detection and getting around in the dungeon. Table 20-2 lists our recommendations for the rogue's magic items by level.

Table 20-2	Typical Rogue Magic Items by Level
Level	**Recommended Magic Items and Gear**
1st	By starting package (see Chapter 17)
2nd	*+1 keen* weapon (3rd); *+1* armor (1st); *+1 cloak of resistance* (2nd); 3 *potions of healing;* 210 gp
3rd	*+1 keen* weapon (3rd); *+1 darkleaf* armor (4th); *+1 cloak of resistance* (2nd); *bracers of mighty striking* (2nd)
4th	*+1 keen* weapon (3rd); *+1 darkleaf* armor (4th); *+1 amulet of cleansing* (5th); *bracers of mighty striking* (2nd); 2 *potions of healing;* 60 gp
5th	*+2* weapon (6th); *+1 darkleaf* armor (4th); *+1 amulet of cleansing* (5th); *catstep boots* (3rd) or *gloves of piercing* (3rd); 2 *potions of healing;* 60 gp
6th	*+2* weapon (6th); *+1 darkleaf* armor (4th); *+1 amulet of cleansing* (5th); *bracers of defense* (7th); 2 *potions of healing;* 60 gp
7th	*+2 keen* weapon (8th); *+2* armor (6th); *+1 amulet of cleansing* (5th); *bracers of defense* (7th); 3 *potions of healing;* 650 gp
8th	*+2 keen* weapon (8th); *+2 darkleaf* armor (9th); *+2 elven cloak* (7th); *bracers of defense* (7th)
9th	*+2 keen* weapon (8th); *+2 darkleaf* armor (9th); *+2 amulet of cleansing* (10th); *bracers of defense* (7th); 3 *potions of healing;* 650 gp
10th	*+3* weapon (11th); *+2 darkleaf* armor (9th); *+2 amulet of cleansing* (10th); *boots of striding* (9th)
11th	*+3* weapon (11th); *+3 sunleaf* armor (12th); *+2 amulet of cleansing* (10th); *boots of striding* (9th); 3 *potions of healing;* 650 gp
12th	*+3 frost* weapon (13th); *+3 sunleaf* armor (12th); *+2 amulet of cleansing* (10th); *ring of protection* (11th); 3 *potions of vitality;* 1,000 gp
13th	*+3 frost* weapon (13th); *+3 sunleaf* armor (12th); *+3 elven cloak* (12th); *goggles of night* (14th)
14th	*+3 flaming* weapon (15th); *+3 elven battle* armor (13th); *+3 elven cloak* (12th); *goggles of night* (14th); 3 *potions of vitality;* 1,000 gp
15th	*+4* weapon (16th); *+3 elven battle* armor (13th); *+3 amulet of cleansing* (15th); *goggles of night* (14th); 3 *potions of vitality;* 1,000 gp

For your rogue's weapon, you absolutely should choose a light blade of some kind — a dagger or short sword (or, if you use a Weapon Proficiency feat, a rapier). Our recommendations focus on magic weapons that are available as light blades. When playing a rogue, you face a tricky problem in that you might need a second magic weapon. The fighter is happy to stick with a melee weapon, but a fair number of rogue powers are designed for use with the crossbow or with thrown weapons such as daggers or shuriken. If your character build involves powers of this sort, you have two choices: You can carry a second magic weapon as your "fourth" item, or you can make sure your primary weapon is a dagger. Because the dagger can be thrown, your melee weapon will work for many of your ranged powers. Magic daggers (and other magic thrown weapons) return after you throw them, so you don't have to worry about disarming yourself.

We like the *keen* weapon property early in a rogue's career because it gives your character the chance to manufacture critical hits. It's a milestone power, which means once you use it, it's gone for the day . . . unless you hit an adventure milestone, and get the opportunity to recharge the power. In our experience, adventure milestones come about once every two encounters, so a milestone power is really an "every other encounter" power instead of an encounter power. In any event, rogues really like critical hits because most rogue powers offer a high potential damage anyway, and their bonus sneak attack damage dice get maxed in the critical hit, too. In other words, a fighter's critical hit might add 5 or 10 points of damage to his or her shot because of the maximum-damage rule, but a rogue's critical hit often adds 20 or more damage for maxing.

For your armor choice, there are several good options, but we like *darkleaf* armor as the most broadly useful. It offers a +2 AC bonus against the first attack you see in each encounter. With a bit of luck and skillful use of your rogue's powers, your character won't be subjected to more than a couple of attacks per encounter anyway.

Finally, one unusual item that deserves a bit of explanation is *goggles of night*. It confers the ability to see in the dark. Now, most of the time your character is going to be around other characters who *can't* see in the dark, so this may be of limited usefulness. But if your character ever does any scouting or slinking around away from the rest of the party, he or she certainly doesn't want to have to carry a torch. That sort of gives away the stealthy character's presence. We think you'll find opportunities to put your *goggles* to good use.

Cleric magic items

Clerics face a tough challenge with magic items — they need two "weapons" (a melee weapon plus a holy symbol) plus armor and that vital neck-slot item to cover their defenses. Because your cleric's melee attacks are generally conveyed through a melee weapon but ranged attacks need a holy symbol, it's important to carry two offensive items with high enhancement bonuses to score hits with your cleric's powers. In addition, clerics are expected to know at least a couple of the more important healing rituals in case their companions run into serious afflictions (such as death). Consequently, our recommendations in Table 20-3 don't include many of the ancillary items like bracers, helmets, or boots that other characters might choose.

Table 20-3	Typical Cleric Magic Items by Level
Level	**Recommended Magic Items and Gear**
1st	By starting package (see Chapter 17); rituals of Gentle Repose and Silence
2nd	*+1 resounding* weapon (2nd); *+1* armor (1st); *+1 amulet of protection* (1st); *+1 symbol of hope* (3rd); rituals of Gentle Repose and Silence
3rd	*+1 resounding* weapon (2nd); *+1 delver's* armor (3rd, chosen in place of a 4th-level item); *+1 cloak of resistance* (2nd); *+1 symbol of hope* (3rd); rituals of Gentle Repose and Silence
4th	*+1 resounding* weapon (2nd); *+1 exalted* armor (5th); *+1 safewing amulet* (3rd, chosen in place of a 4th-level item); *+1 symbol of hope* (3rd); *potion of healing;* 110 gp of ritual components; rituals of Gentle Repose and Silence
5th	*+1 resounding* weapon (2nd); *+1 exalted* armor (5th); *+1 safewing amulet* (3rd, chosen in place of a 4th-level item); *+2 holy symbol* (6th); 145 gp of ritual components; rituals of Gentle Repose, Hand of Fate, and Silence
6th	*+2 resounding* weapon (7th); *+1 exalted* armor (5th); *+1 safewing amulet* (3rd); *+2 holy symbol* (6th); 145 gp of ritual components; rituals of Gentle Repose, Hand of Fate, and Silence
7th	*+2 resounding* weapon (7th); *+1 exalted* armor (5th); *+2 amulet of protection* (6th); *+2 symbol of hope* (8th); 265 gp of ritual components; rituals of Cure Disease, Gentle Repose, Hand of Fate, and Silence
8th	*+2 resounding* weapon (7th); *+2* armor (6th); *+2 cloak of survival* (9th); *+2 symbol of hope* (8th); 265 gp of ritual components; rituals of Cure Disease, Gentle Repose, Hand of Fate, and Silence
9th	*+2 resounding* weapon (7th); *+2 exalted* armor (10th); *+2 cloak of survival* (9th); *+2 symbol of hope* (8th); 265 gp of ritual components; rituals of Cure Disease, Gentle Repose, Hand of Fate, and Silence

(continued)

Table 20-3 *(continued)*

Level	Recommended Magic Items and Gear
10th	*+2 resounding* weapon (7th); *+2 exalted* armor (10th); *+2 cloak of survival* (9th); *+3 holy symbol* (11th); 645 gp of ritual components; rituals of Endure Elements, Gentle Repose, Hand of Fate, Raise Dead, and Silence
11th	*+3 resounding* weapon (12th); *+2 exalted* armor (10th); *+2 cloak of survival* (9th); *+3 holy symbol* (11th); 120 gp of ritual components; rituals of Gentle Repose, Raise Dead, and Silence
12th	*+3 resounding* weapon (12th); *+2 exalted* armor (10th); *+3 periapt of wisdom* (13th); *+3 holy symbol* (11th); 1,425 gp of ritual components; rituals of Gentle Repose, Hand of Fate, Linked Portal, Raise Dead, Remove Affliction, Sending, and Silence
13th	*+3 resounding* weapon (12th); *+3 tombforged* armor (14th); *+3 periapt of wisdom* (13th); *+3 holy symbol* (11th); 1,425 gp of ritual components; rituals of Gentle Repose, Hand of Fate, Linked Portal, Raise Dead, Remove Affliction, Sending, and Silence
14th	*+3 resounding* weapon (12th); *+3 tombforged* armor (14th); *+3 periapt of wisdom* (13th); *+3 symbol of battle* (15th); 1,425 gp of ritual components; rituals of Gentle Repose, Hand of Fate, Linked Portal, Raise Dead, Remove Affliction, Sending, and Silence
15th	*+4* weapon (16th); *+3 tombforged* armor (14th); *+3 periapt of wisdom* (13th); *+3 symbol of battle* (15th); 1,425 gp of ritual components; rituals of Gentle Repose, Hand of Fate, Linked Portal, Raise Dead, Remove Affliction, Sending, and Silence

Your armor and weapon choices are somewhat limited, simply because the only type of heavy armor clerics are proficient in is chain armor, and the only weapons clerics begin with are simple weapons. If you want access to a much broader range of weapon and armor choices, choose the Armor Training (Scale) or Weapon Proficiency feats. With that said, we like the *resounding* weapon best for the cleric because dazing an enemy once per encounter is very useful — especially if you can use it in conjunction with a power that knocks the target prone or pushes him.

Your other weapon is your holy symbol. Fortunately, there aren't many tough decisions here. Holy symbols are pretty much designed to do things clerics like, so any one you pick is going to be useful.

Although cleric armor choices are somewhat limited, *exalted* armor is right down your alley. It gives you extra healing as a milestone power. As a leader, it's important to be able to pour on the healing when the party is in trouble.

Milestone powers fall somewhere between daily powers and encounter powers; in play, you generally get to use one about once every two to three encounters, or a couple of times in a single day of adventuring.

The biggest difference you may have noticed between the cleric's recommended items and those of the fighter and rogue are all the rituals. Because clerics are skilled ritual casters, your character has the ability to use magic rituals. All clerics begin with two rituals "for free" — Gentle Repose and one other 1st-level ritual of your choice. As your cleric character gains levels, try to set aside some of your equipment budget for buying a small number of rituals and staying stocked up on ritual components. You hope you never have to use it, but once you hit 8th level, you should seriously consider buying the Raise Dead ritual.

Wizard magic items

You might think a wizard has no use for magic weapons or armor. After all, spells are the weapons of choice for a wizard, and a wizard can't wear much armor anyway. However, wizards do indeed invest in magic weapons of a sort — wands, orbs, or staffs, their magic implements. Just as fighters carry magic swords to fight better, wizards use magic implements to cast spells better. Like clerics, wizards also are ritual magic users, so you'll also need to keep up on your character's ritual selection. Table 20-4 shows our recommendations for equipping your wizard character with magic items and a good selection of important rituals.

Table 20-4	Typical Wizard Magic Items by Level
Level	*Recommended Magic Items and Gear*
1st	By starting package (see Chapter 17); rituals of Comprehend Languages and Tenser's Floating Disk
2nd	*+1 staff of the war mage* (3rd); *+1* armor (1st); *+1 cloak of resistance* (2nd); 2 *potions of healing;* 120 gp of ritual components; rituals of Comprehend Languages, Eye of Alarm, and Tenser's Floating Disk; 40 gp
3rd	*+1 staff of the war mage* (3rd); *+1 darkleaf* armor (4th); *+1 cloak of resistance* (2nd); 2 *potions of healing;* 120 gp of ritual components; rituals of Comprehend Languages, Detect Secret Doors, Eye of Alarm, and Tenser's Floating Disk; 75 gp
4th	*+1 staff of the war mage* (3rd); *+1 darkleaf* armor (4th); *+1 amulet of cleansing* (5th); 2 *potions of healing;* 130 gp of ritual components; rituals of Comprehend Languages, Detect Secret Doors, Eye of Alarm, Knock, and Tenser's Floating Disk; 50 gp

(continued)

Table 20-4 *(continued)*

Level	Recommended Magic Items and Gear
5th	*+2 staff* (6th); *+1 darkleaf* armor (4th); *+1 amulet of cleansing* (5th); *catstep boots* (3rd); 60 gp of ritual components; rituals of Comprehend Languages, Detect Secret Doors, Eye of Alarm, Knock, and Tenser's Floating Disk
6th	*+2 staff* (6th); *+1 bloodthread* armor (5th); *+2 cloak of resistance* (7th); *catstep boots* (3rd); 220 gp of ritual components; rituals of Comprehend Languages, Detect Secret Doors, Eye of Alarm, Knock, and Tenser's Floating Disk
7th	*+2 staff* (6th); *+2 delver's* armor (8th); *+2 cloak of resistance* (7th); *bag of holding* (5th); 340 gp of ritual components; rituals of Comprehend Languages, Detect Secret Doors, Eye of Alarm, Knock, Sending, and Tenser's Floating Disk
8th	*+2 staff of winter* (9th); *+2 delver's* armor (8th); *+2 amulet of protection* (6th); *bracers of defense* (7th); 340 gp of ritual components; rituals of Comprehend Languages, Detect Secret Doors, Eye of Alarm, Knock, Sending, and Tenser's Floating Disk
9th	*+2 staff of winter* (9th); *+2 bloodthread* armor (10th); *+2 safewing amulet* (8th); *bracers of defense* (7th); 340 gp of ritual components; rituals of *comprehend languages, detect secret doors, eye of alarm, knock, sending,* and *Tenser's floating disk*
10th	*+3 staff* (11th); *+2 bloodthread* armor (10th); *+2 cloak of survival* (9th); *bracers of defense* (7th); 460 gp of ritual components; rituals of Comprehend Languages, Detect Secret Doors, Eye of Alarm, Knock, Linked Portal, Sending, and Tenser's Floating Disk
11th	*+3 staff* (11th); *+2 bloodthread* armor (10th); *+3 cloak of resistance* (12th); *boots of striding* (9th); 340 gp of ritual components; rituals of Comprehend Languages, Detect Secret Doors, Eye of Alarm, Knock, Linked Portal, Sending, and Tenser's Floating Disk, and Wizard's Sight
12th	*+3 staff of the war mage* (13th); *+3* armor (11th); *+3 cloak of resistance* (12th); *ring of protection* (11th); rituals of Comprehend Languages, Detect Secret Doors, Knock, Linked Portal, Tenser's Floating Disk, and Wizard's Sight
13th	*+3 staff of the war mage* (13th); *+3 ghostphase* armor (14th); *+3 cloak of resistance* (12th); *ring of protection* (11th); 1,400 gp of ritual components; rituals of Comprehend Languages, Detect Secret Doors, Knock, Linked Portal, Shadow Walk, Tenser's Floating Disk, and Wizard's Sight

Level	Recommended Magic Items and Gear
14th	*+3 staff of the war mage* (13th); *+3 ghostphase* armor (14th); *+3 stormwalker's cloak* (15th); *Keoghtom's ointment* (12th); 1,400 gp of ritual components; rituals of Comprehend Languages, Detect Secret Doors, Knock, Linked Portal, Shadow Walk, Tenser's Floating Disk, and Wizard's Sight
15th	*+4 staff* (16th); *+3 ghostphase* armor (14th); *+3 stormwalker's cloak* (15th); *belt of battle* (14th); rituals of Comprehend Languages, Detect Secret Doors, Knock, Linked Portal, Shadow Walk, Tenser's Floating Disk, View Location, and Wizard's Sight

We've selected staffs as your implement of choice for the purpose of this table. Staffs have the benefit of serving both as melee weapons and magic implements, so if you find yourself stuck in melee without any close-range powers, you can swing away. However, you should pick the implement that matches your Arcane Implement Mastery class feature — take a magic orb or wand instead of the staff, if that's the implement your character favors. Of the magic staffs, we like the *staff of the war mage* best, because the ability to expand a blast or burst by 1 square means you might catch a couple of extra monsters in the area of a big-damage spell.

You might be a little surprised to see armor on this table, but don't get too excited; it's only cloth armor. However, even though the armor itself doesn't contribute all that much to your wizard's Armor Class, the enhancement bonus still counts — and several magical armors available in cloth are quite useful for the wizard. For example, *bloodthread* armor grants an additional bonus to AC and saving throws if you're bloodied. As a wizard, you try hard to not get hit at all, but if the monsters do get to you, armor that improves as your condition deteriorates makes for a good life insurance policy. If you spend a feat to train in leather armor, you can find plenty of good choices there, too.

Like the cleric, you're automatically invested in the ritual magic system because of your class features. In fact, wizards gain additional "free" rituals as they gain levels, learning two new ones at 5th, 11th, 15th, 21st, and 25th level. You can build up a pretty good selection without ever buying a ritual. If you don't have a lot of gold to spend on expensive ritual components, you should take up a collection from the other party members — most rituals you cast are clearly for the benefit of the whole party, and it's not fair for your wizard to pay those expensive ritual costs with his or her cut of the treasure. Most experienced players are pretty reasonable about this, and they'll agree to set aside a modest portion of the party treasure in order to make sure the wizard is capable of casting that teleportation ritual that might save everybody's bacon when things go bad.

Chapter 21

Roleplaying and Working Together

. . . .

In This Chapter

▶ Choosing an alignment

▶ Bringing your character to life

▶ Being a team player

▶ Winning friends at the table

▶ Understanding things to do and things not to do

. . . .

*W*e spend most of this book immersed in the nuts and bolts of character creation and the mechanics of game play. But the DUNGEONS & DRAGONS game isn't just a game of statistics and rules. It's also a game of *imagination*. When you take control of your D&D character, you can pretend for a short time that you're someone else entirely — a mighty swordsman, a dangerous wizard, a sly and cunning rogue — and that all the evil in the world can be beaten senseless with a broadsword or a *wand of fiery bolt.* In fact, for a lot of people, roleplaying (the process of pretending you're someone else) is the whole reason they play the game. Character statistics and game rules just help you figure out what happens next.

In this chapter, we tell you about the art of roleplaying and show you how to breathe personality, life, and purpose into your character. We also take a look at ways you can make yourself appreciated by everyone else at the table, both as a character and a player.

Roleplaying with Style

D&D is very entertaining as a pure tactical exercise; many players are perfectly content to view the game as consisting of puzzles to be solved, many of which involve fantastic combat scenarios. But the game really shines when you make an effort to get out of your own skin and put yourself in the place of the character you've brought to the table. After all, in real life, you'd run screaming from a howling, blood-maddened werewolf intent on ripping your throat out and tearing you limb from limb. But your dashing rogue Saros can stand his ground calmly, rapier in hand, and even make a quip about his fearsome foe. It's not that much more of a leap to think about how Saros might respond to other sorts of challenges and situations.

Choosing your character's alignment

One of the fundamental guides for playing your character is *alignment.* Alignment is a quick summary of what your character stands for and how he or she tries to live life. Your choice marks your character as a good guy or a bad guy, and alignment allows you to quickly determine how other folks in the world see your character — and how you should see others. For example, you can see at a glance that a lawful good dwarf probably has nothing kind to say to a chaotic evil orc, and vice versa.

Alignment consists of a straightforward good-unaligned-evil scale, with an important detail added: Some good creatures are also lawful, and some evil creatures are also chaotic. In other words, there are really two good alignments — good and lawful good. Likewise, there are two evil alignments — evil and chaotic evil. In addition, many creatures are simply unaligned.

Here's a quick primer on these five choices:

- ✔ **Good:** You believe it is right to aid and protect those in need. You don't have to be completely altruistic, but you're willing to make personal sacrifices to help others if that's what it takes. Good characters accept authority and order, but if they have to break rules to help people, they don't hesitate to do so.

- ✔ **Lawful good:** You also believe in aiding those who need your help, but you think the best way to do that is by establishing and defending just laws and benevolent order. Lawful good characters would rather work "within the system" when laws fail to protect those who need help, but they don't mindlessly acquiesce to misused authority; they feel morally obligated to challenge injustice in any guise.

- ✔ **Evil:** You're willing to hurt or oppress other people to get ahead. Maybe you lack compassion or maybe you think moral conventions shackle you and keep you from taking what's yours. Or maybe you wallow in the vile, the despicable, and the depraved, celebrating evil gods and hurting others for the sheer pleasure of it. Evil characters often build social orders that are cruel or tyrannical, and they can be zealous supporters of such systems.

- ✔ **Chaotic evil:** You share the evil character's willingness to hurt or oppress others to get what you want, but you simply don't respect any social order or convention other than *might makes right.* In the absence of any strong authority that can compel your grudging obedience, you seek to gratify your every impulse, no matter how cruel or debased. Chaotic evil characters generally lead lives of plunder, cruelty, and avarice; the only question is whether they do so openly or hide their wickedness.

✔ **Unaligned:** You haven't taken a stand for good or evil yet. Many people and creatures in the D&D world are unaligned. Animals, for example, aren't good or evil; they just are. People can be kind and benevolent without having the good alignment, and likewise they can be violent and dangerous without having the evil alignment (a barbarian tribe or guild of thieves, for example).

Your character's code of behavior and personal standards should reflect his or her alignment. For example, if your character is good, he or she acts as his or her conscience dictates to help people, without caring about what other people expect of him or her. The character especially hates it when people try to intimidate others and tell them what to do. On the other hand, an evil character might play by the rules but has no mercy or compassion. He or she seeks power and wealth, and doesn't care who gets hurt on his or her way up — but he or she generally adheres to the codes, laws, or standards of his or her race or society, using these as tools to further his or her own ends.

You can read more about how your character's alignment influences his or her approach to life on page 19 of the *Player's Handbook*.

What alignment you choose is generally up to you, but the vast majority of D&D player characters are good, lawful good, or unaligned. Your Dungeon Master may warn you that your character's actions are not conforming to his or her chosen alignment. If you have your character act in an evil manner, your DM may rule that your alignment is, in fact, evil — evil is as evil does, after all.

Be careful about playing an evil character. Many DMs prefer that all the characters in the party be good or unaligned. It makes a lot more sense for heroic characters to take up adventures about protecting the innocent or stopping the depredations of evil monsters. It's also easier for non-evil characters to cooperate within the party. The game works fine no matter what alignment you choose, but you should check with the DM before you decide on an evil alignment for your character.

Building a persona

Alignment is a pretty broad brush to paint with. It tells you something about what your character stands for and how he or she thinks the universe ought to run, but it doesn't tell you much about his or her personality. Consider the lawful good paladin: You're just a goody two-shoes, right? Well, you might play that paladin as a saintly martyr, a beatific and blameless agent of good who goes willingly to face nigh-certain death in the service of his or her deity. Or the character might be a grim crusader, tireless and unswerving in his or her determination to bring justice to evil wherever it lurks. Or you might even play that paladin as a great captain, a bold and courageous knight who urges on his or her companions with never-say-die cheerfulness and confidence. How you play that character is up to you.

Personas tend to evolve in play; your character ought to learn from his or her adventures and experiences, just like a real person does. Chapter 2 of the *Player's Handbook* offers some advice for crafting your imaginary persona: Consider situations when roleplaying opportunities abound and think of one or two salient traits that your character shows in such situations. For example:

- ✔ **Social interactions:** When your character speaks with a nonplayer character outside of combat, you're engaged in a social interaction. How do other characters perceive you in such situations? Are you charming or dour? Talkative or laconic? How trusting are you? Naïve or skeptical?

- ✔ **Decision points:** When your character has to choose between several different courses of action — for example, whether to launch a frontal assault on a villain's lair or find some way to insinuate himself or herself into the ranks of the villain's minions — you face a decision point. Usually decision points are debates among the players about what their characters ought to try next in the adventure. Not only do you want to make a sound decision, but you'd like that decision to be something your character would logically argue for. In such decisions, are you assertive or easygoing? Pragmatic or unflinchingly honest? Hard-hearted or compassionate?

- ✔ **Dire straits:** When things take a dangerous or unpleasant turn, you're in dire straits. There's nothing like it for revealing character. When the chips are down, how do you respond? Are you brave, reckless, or cautious? Do setbacks fill you with the desire to seek vengeance or do you shrug them off? How are your nerves under stress? Are you impulsive or patient?

In conjunction with your character's alignment, race, and class, you should have enough to craft a reasonably unique character. Some traits may be a little hard to reconcile with your alignment, but maybe those traits are weaknesses or failings — places where your character doesn't quite measure up to his or her self-imposed standards.

Creating mannerisms

After you figure out what your character stands for and what sort of personality he or she has, think of ways that you can portray that easily and consistently at the gaming table. You don't have to view each D&D session as a trip to the Renaissance Faire in full costume, but if you can think of a couple of memorable "hooks" to use at the table, you'll find that the other players have an easier time envisioning who your character is and what he or she stands for.

Habitual sayings

Does your character have any distinctive trademark phrases or battle cries? If you can't think of any, look to your character's choice of deity. Dwarves often worship Moradin, the god of the forge. If you're playing a dwarf, you could do worse than to swear, "By Moradin's beard!" or "Moradin's hammer, what a bad idea that was!"

Voice or speech pattern

Take on a unique character voice or way of speaking that you can manage so easily you forget you're doing it. If you're playing a dwarf, growl and splutter and talk as if you're angry. If you're playing a fighter with a low Intelligence score, frown seriously and speak slowly, as if you're working hard to sort out what you're trying to say. If you're playing a pretentious tiefling or imperious wizard, refer to yourself in the third person, or even use the "royal we." Maybe your chivalrous paladin even uses a few "thees" and "thous." If Thor can shout, "I SAY THEE NAY!" in Marvel Comics, it'll work for you at the gaming table.

Gestures

Gestures are a little harder because there's only so much you can do while seated at a table. But maybe your pious cleric Jorhune steeples his fingers in front of his chest when he speaks, whereas your devious rogue Shadow rubs her hands together avariciously, or your intellectual wizard Evard strokes his beard (or chin, if you lack the necessary facial hair) and casts his eyes up toward the ceiling while he contemplates a decision. Facial expressions are good ground for role playing, too. You can scowl or glower, stare stupidly with a slack-jawed expression, or squint crookedly and mutter to yourself. (We just sort of hope you don't do those things normally, so that your friends can actually detect that your efforts are roleplaying.)

Favored tactics

Here's an easy one that doesn't require any out-of-your-skin acting at all: Pick a couple of battle techniques your character likes to use and make those your favored tactics. If your fighter recklessly charges into battle and always uses his Power Attack feat on the first round of combat, that's a distinctive hook — everybody at the table will start looking for you to try it in every fight. Maybe your wizard loves lightning spells, and so uses *lightning bolt* in preference to any other spell. Look for trademark maneuvers and try to put your own distinctive stamp on them.

Knowing when to stop

Believe it or not, it's possible to have too much of a good thing. Different D&D groups have different standards for how much roleplaying is the right amount; we've played in very entertaining game sessions in which no dice were rolled at all because the nights were taken up with tense negotiations or tricky sets of investigations and interviews, all resolved purely in "character voice." But sometimes you need to stop talking and start rolling the dice. If D&D had referees who kept an eye on your roleplaying, here are three things that would draw penalty flags:

- ✔ **Delay of game:** Sometimes a dungsweeper is just a dungsweeper. Don't expect that you have to engage in meaningful conversation with every nonplayer character (NPC) your character happens upon. We've seen people spend 30 minutes of real-time haggling with a shopkeeper over the price of a pick and shovel. For goodness' sake, just have your character throw a couple of gold pieces on the counter and get on with the real adventure! You might not have noticed the other players at the table gnawing off their own ears because you won't give it a rest.

- ✔ **Excessive roleplaying:** A little bit of real-world acting goes a long way. Talk in a funny accent, scowl and glare a lot, use acidic sarcasm (hopefully not directed at other players), but don't take it too far. We've seen a player who insisted on perching on her chair and screeching unintelligibly because her druid character was wildshaped into an eagle. When you freak out or annoy the other players, you're roleplaying excessively.

- ✔ **Intentional grounding:** Try not to have your character take stupid or counterproductive actions because you think that's what your character *should* do. For example: "Well, Kerro is scared of undead, so I guess I'll spend this round yammering in terror. Oh, I know I made my saving throw. But I think it's what Kerro would do." Be a little helpful to the rest of the party and roleplay Kerro overcoming his fright enough to swing a sword or cast a spell, even though he's shaking in his boots. Your friends will like Kerro much better that way.

Working Together

Every character in the D&D game is the best at something, but no character can be the best at everything. What that means is simple: Good teamwork is a skill of vital importance to a D&D party. Learning how to cooperate with the other players at the table and work together effectively is important.

- ✔ **The first rule of working together is building a balanced adventuring party.** Try to cover the four character roles: defender, striker, controller, and leader. Every character class has strengths and weaknesses; for example, if everyone in the group plays wizards, all the characters will be terribly vulnerable to monsters fast enough to reach them before they can drop the monsters with their spells. A party of nothing but fighters has no way to sneak past the iron golem guardian, but a rogue might be able to slip through the room with good Stealth checks, or a wizard might be able to overcome the obstacle with a well-timed *invisibility* spell.

✔ **The second rule of working together is making sure that everybody has the opportunity to do what he or she does best.** For example, don't put the party's rogue in the position of being a front-line defender; make sure the fighter in the party is standing in front of the bad guys so that the rogue has the opportunity to maneuver for a flank attack.

✔ **The third rule of working together is staying on top of what your allies are trying to do.** If your party's wizard is about to unleash a *fireball* spell, don't have your fighter run right into the middle of the orc warriors to launch an attack — the wizard won't be able to throw his or her spell without endangering your character. Don't be afraid to engage in a little "table-talk" and ask other players what they're planning. Most DMs don't mind a reasonable amount of table-talk, as long as you don't start designing ten-step battle plans in the middle of combat.

Cooperating in a fight

As you might expect, the most important place to use good teamwork and cooperative tactics is in a fight. When you fail to cooperate outside of combat, the result is usually not too much more serious than a delay of some kind. When you fail to cooperate in a fight, you're likely to get somebody's character killed. Death is not a permanent career-ender in D&D, but it's no fun, either. It costs a lot of gold pieces to bring a character back from the dead, so it behooves everybody at the table to work hard to make sure that nobody's character gets killed.

Cooperative tactic #1: Flanking

The first tactic everybody should use is flanking. *Flanking* involves catching monsters directly between two allies. If you and your buddy can work together to flank a monster, you each gain combat advantage over that monster, which means a +2 bonus on your attack rolls. Moreover, if one or the other of you happens to be playing a rogue, that player will also get bonus sneak attack damage against the flanked foe.

If you don't have enough friends available to flank a monster (or it's just too dangerous to move to a flanking position), there are other ways to gain combat advantage. For example, the cleric power *spiritual weapon* grants combat advantage to all the cleric's allies against the target of the prayer. Similarly, powers that stun or knock prone can also generate combat advantage for the rest of the party.

Cooperative tactic #2: Aiding another

When you're fighting an enemy who is very hard to hit, or you need to give a character in trouble the best defense possible against an attack, consider using the aid another action. (You can find a description of this action on page 287 of the *Player's Handbook*.) Instead of making an attack against your foe, you can make a melee attack against an AC of 10. If you succeed, one ally of your choice gains either a +2 attack bonus or a +2 Armor Class bonus.

Here's an example: Say two characters are fighting an opponent with an Armor Class of 24. One character has an attack bonus of +5 and deals an average of 5.5 points of damage per hit, and the other has an attack bonus of +8 and deals an average of 11 points of damage per hit. If they both just attack, the expected damage is 2.75 plus 0.55, or 3.3 points of damage per round. If the weaker character aids the better, there's an 80 percent chance the average damage output jumps to 3.85, because the weaker character successfully aids another on a roll of 5 or higher. (There's a 20 percent chance the damage output drops to 2.75, too.) That averages out to an expected damage output of 3.63 instead of 3.3 for attacking separately.

Cooperative tactic #3: Delaying

It's only natural to jump up the instant your turn comes around and whack the bad guys. But sometimes the smartest way to play is to be a little patient. If you think that you have an ally who will move before the monster does, you can delay your action and wait for your ally to get into position. By waiting, you might give yourself and your friend the benefit of making a flanking attack when that opportunity didn't exist before.

Delaying is also a good tactic when you have allies on your side who have powers that might help everyone attack. If the cleric in your party is about to cast a *bless* prayer, you can simply wait to make your attack until *after* the cleric casts his or her prayer. Now you have a free +1 bonus on your attack roll that didn't exist before the cleric took his or her turn. Obviously, if the cleric's turn comes up *after* the monster(s) take their turn, you might not want to wait. But keep an eye on the initiative order in the fight and look for opportunities to coordinate your actions for the greatest effect.

Buffing your teammates

The term *buffing* means improving a character with magic or special abilities so that he or she can fight better. A power such as the wizard spell *resistance* is a perfect example of a buffing effect — the character on the receiving end of this spell temporarily gains resistance to a single damage type, such as fire or psychic. As you can imagine, this would be a great spell to help the fighter deal with an angry magma beast. Clerics are especially good at buffing their teammates because most of their powers buff their teammates in some way.

Table 21-1 lists some great buffing powers.

Table 21-1	Top Buffing Powers	
Power	**Level and Class**	**Effect**
Bless	2nd-level cleric	All allies get +1 attack bonus.
Divine glow	1st-level cleric	Affected allies gain a +2 bonus to attack rolls until the end of your next turn.
Guide the charge	6th-level warlord	An ally who charges adds your Intelligence modifier to the damage he deals and pushes the target 2 squares.
Invisibility	6th-level wizard	One ally turns invisible until he or she attacks, but gains combat advantage.
Resistance	10th-level wizard	One ally gains resistance to a single damage type equal to your level + your Intelligence modifier.
Righteous brand	1st-level cleric	If you hit, one ally gains an attack bonus equal to your Strength modifier on melee attacks against the target until the end of your next turn.
Shield of faith	2nd-level cleric	All allies nearby gain +2 AC bonus.
Stoneskin	16th-level wizard	One ally gains resist 10 to weapon damage.
Warlord's favor	1st-level warlord	If you hit, one ally gains an attack bonus equal to 1 + your Intelligence modifier against the target until the end of your next turn.
Wrath of the gods	6th-level paladin	All nearby allies add your Charisma modifier to damage rolls.

You can also buff your teammates by choosing powers that blind, daze, stun, or knock prone enemies. All these conditions mean that the affected creature gives up combat advantage to attackers, so your allies gain a +2 bonus to attack the creature you've affected. (However, you need to time your attack when you knock enemies prone — they can just stand up again on their turn, so it works better if you knock them prone right *after* their turn instead of right *before* their turn.)

Saving downed characters

Sooner or later, it's going to happen: Some character in the party is knocked to 0 or negative hit points by a monster's attack. (A character is dying and unconscious at 0 hit points or less and dies when his or her hit points reach a negative number equal to his or her bloodied number. For more details, see the "Death and Dying" section in Chapter 9 of the *Player's Handbook*.) Getting that character back into the fight requires some real cooperation and clever play, especially if the fight's still going on. So what do you do when one of the other characters drops?

You have two ways to fix a character sitting at 0 or less hit points: Stabilize him or her with the Heal skill or use a power or magic item that heals the dying character. When a dying character gets a healing effect, he automatically goes to 0 hit points, and *then* you apply the healing amount — so you never have to worry about a healing effect not restoring enough hit points to get a character out of the negatives. The Heal skill is by far the inferior approach because all it does is keep the character from dying; use healing magic if you have any at all.

Try this short checklist the next time a character goes down in your game:

- **Is the character beyond help?** If your companion's been reduced to negative hit points equal or exceeding his or her bloodied value, there's no hurry. The character is dead, and he or she won't get any deader.

- **Is the character in immediate danger of dying?** A character reduced to negative hit points won't die right away; he or she makes a death saving throw each round and must fail three times before he or she dies. You don't have to panic until the character misses that second death save, so you might be able to wait for the right chance to aid him or her. However, watch out if there are monsters standing around with nothing better to do than finish off a helpless character.

- **Can you help the character?** If you have no healing potions or spells and can't use the Heal skill worth a darn, you might not be able to do much good anyway. You can stand over your fallen friend and keep a monster from finishing him or her off, but that's about it.

- **Can you reach the character?** You might have no way to actually get to a dying comrade. If you're threatened by dangerous enemies and might cause your own character's death by trying to reach your buddy, you might only complicate the situation by trying to help.

- **Can you afford the action to help this round?** Usually, it's good play to try to get your friends back into a fight. But if spending your turn going to your fallen friend's aid will give the monster or villain the opportunity to wreak even more damage, you might not be able to afford the luxury of ignoring the bad guys to aid your friend. For example, if you have the dragon down to just a couple of hit points, you might be smarter to try to finish it off than to let it take another turn.

✔ **Will you make the character a target by healing him or her?** Generally, intelligent monsters don't waste actions pounding on adventurers who are already down as long as there are others still on their feet and fighting. If you're battling a berserk hill giant who lays out 30 points of damage with each swing of his or her axe, the safest place for your wounded friend might be lying helpless in negative hit points. When you heal up your friend, usually you bestow a single healing surge starting from 0 hp. Your healed comrade therefore wakes up prone and at ¼ his or her normal hit points. It's almost always better to have your comrades conscious and on their feet, but make sure the hill giant has something better to do than cut your friend in half when he or she stands up.

Minding Your Table Manners

So far in this chapter, we talk about a lot of things you do to breathe life into your character and to play your character constructively with the other players at the table. Now we broach a somewhat awkward topic: Your behavior as a *player,* not just a person controlling a character in the game.

Most D&D games are regularly occurring social gatherings of a group of friends who share a common interest. Just like weekly poker games, or PlayStation slugfests, or bar crawls, or whatever it is you do for fun with your friends, it's just good manners to be a considerate guest or a pleasant host. You want to have fun and help everyone else have fun; you don't want to be the guy or gal who's making everyone else miserable.

The following sections take a quick look at five things you can do to contribute to everyone's gaming experience, and five things you ought to avoid if you want everyone to have fun.

Five do's

It would be easy to give you a long list of things to avoid, but we don't think that's as helpful as pointing out some positive steps you can take right from the get-go to make game night more fun for everyone:

✔ **Think about what you want to do on your turn while other people are taking their turns.** Time is the single most precious commodity at the gaming table. Most D&D sessions run about three or four hours. If you take ten minutes to figure out what your perfect move is during each round of every combat you get into, you're taking more than your share. Instead of everybody getting a chance to bash through five or six exciting encounters in the course of that session, you might limit them to half that many. Plan ahead so that your turns don't take forever, and everyone gets to play more D&D.

While your friends hack at the monsters and the monsters hack back, figure out which of your powers you're likely to use when your turn comes up again. Think about which foe you're going to attack and whether you need to maneuver or use any magic item powers to make it all work. Sometimes your plans will get spoiled by things that happen when it's not your turn — but sometimes they won't, and you'll give everybody at the table a little more D&D for their time.

✔ **Do the math ahead of time.** By the third or fourth time you've attacked with your longsword, you ought to know what your attack bonus is. Ditto for the damage dice on that *fireball* spell you cast a couple of times a night. Don't figure these things out from scratch each time you pick up the dice — be proactive and organized. Look at the actions you undertake all the time and add up your bonuses and modifiers before you come to the table. No one minds too much if you don't know your character's carrying capacity off the top of your head, but you shouldn't have to figure out your Armor Class each and every time some monster takes a swing at you.

Part of this tip involves figuring some numbers before you come to the game, but the other part of this tip is hard for some folks: Write things down in places where you can find them easily. We suggest using a standard character sheet for this sort of thing; you can find one in the back of the *Player's Handbook* or check out a thousand variations by poking around the Internet. Wizards of the Coast provides free character sheets in PDF format, which you can download and print out, at www.dndinsider.com.

✔ **Exercise some common courtesy.** If you told your buddies you were going to meet them at 7 o'clock to go out to the movies, you wouldn't expect them to be happy with you if you wandered in at quarter past eight. The same thing applies for a D&D game. Show up on time so your buddies don't have to wait for you before they start playing. If you find you can't be on time, call somebody to let 'em know you'll be late. At least that way your friends can decide whether to wait for you or to start the game without you.

Miss Manners is right more often than she's wrong at the gaming table. Throw in some cash for the pizza. Bring the chips and soda (at least some of the time). Be a good guest. Heck, you know this stuff. Just be considerate.

✔ **Stay on target, stay focused, stay in the game.** Every D&D game we've ever attended featured at least some amount of senseless cutting up and Monty Python movie quotes for no particular reason. Gaming is fun; it's a social activity. Part of the reason you're at the table is because you enjoy the company of the people you're gaming with, and you want to socialize. But try to recognize when people are trying to move the game along and get somewhere, and when people are kicking back and shooting the breeze.

When the game's on, pay attention to what's going down. If the Dungeon Master is talking, pay attention! Nothing is more annoying than a DM giving a crucial encounter setup, adventure background, or key bit of NPC conversation, only to have one of the players pipe up and say, "Huh? I was looking at my spells."

✔ **Help your friends to shine.** This one's a little tough. When you have the chance to grab the spotlight, it's natural to want to do exactly that. But sometimes it's actually more rewarding to let another player at the table have that moment in the sun.

Try to look out for situations that a particular character is suited for and defer to that other character if you can. For example, if you're playing an armor-plated fighter and the party needs to scout out a side passage that might lead into a monster's lair, you might say, "I'm the toughest guy, I'll go look." Or you might look over to your friend who's playing the stealthy rogue and say, "Steve, Kerdigard's no good at scouting. I'll follow your lead on this." Every character at the table is the best at something, so let your friends show off at the things their characters do best.

Five don'ts

Now for the flip side — here are some things you should try to avoid doing at the table:

✔ **Don't hog the spotlight.** If there are four players and a DM at the table, you should assume that you're entitled to about one-quarter of the DM's time. If you insist on being the character who scouts every tunnel, tackles every puzzle, talks to every NPC, and dictates the strategy for every fight, you're being a bore. You're not the star of the show; D&D is a movie with an ensemble cast, so you have to expect that sometimes other players will get good lines, too.

It's usually okay to take point on something that your character is the best at or to roleplay a long conversation that's of vital interest to your character, but remember that you've got the spotlight, and it's good to share it.

✔ **Don't disrespect the other characters.** Back in the Dark Old Days of gaming, many players thought of D&D as a fiercely competitive game. Squabbling over the best magic items in treasure hoards, stealing from inattentive allies, or even bullying lower-level characters were accepted behaviors in some games. None of that old-school garbage flies these days. Who wants to use their leisure time to play in a game where their characters get picked on, shoved around, or stolen from? We'd rather go back to grade school.

So don't slip the DM notes saying that your 10th-level rogue is going to pick the fighter's pockets when he isn't looking. Don't threaten to vaporize your allies with a powerful spell if they don't let you have the *ring of protection* the evil wizard was wearing. Don't sneer at people, run down their characters, or generally go out of your way to let them know how stupid you think they are for being in the same game with you. It doesn't play well in real life, and it's just as unwelcome at the gaming table.

✔ **Don't be a poor loser**. It's natural to want to be successful in the game. When things don't go your way, try not to take it personally. Sometimes your character's going to get killed in horrific and spectacular ways. It happens.

We've seen more than a few players absolutely enraged, embittered, or brought to the point of tears by the death of a beloved character. If you play a long-running campaign and get attached to your alter ego in the DM's world, it's only natural to feel disappointed when the game doesn't go your way. Try to remember, if your character's never in any real danger, there isn't all that much excitement to any game. On occasion, you're going to have a character get mauled because the other 90 percent of the time, it's way more exciting to be worried about what's going to happen next.

Usually, characters get killed in one of two ways: You did something stupid and it didn't work out, or a monster just got lucky. When an ogre rolls a critical hit against your 2nd-level wizard and deals out 33 points of damage, well, the ogre got lucky. Why get mad about it? The vast majority of DMs don't start an encounter with the intent of killing a specific character, so don't blame the Dungeon Master! That's just the way the dice fell. Besides, truly horrific character deaths make for great "war stories."

✔ **Don't disrespect the supporting cast.** Most D&D adventures are populated with a whole host of "supporting cast" — nonplayer characters the DM uses to populate the places your character visits. Sometimes these NPCs are patrons or employers who give your character directions to the adventure. Sometimes they're sources of information, folks who might know interesting rumors or who can point you toward useful resources. And sometimes they're nothing more than window dressing, a little bit of color the DM uses to give you a chance to roleplay your character. It's bad form to make the DM feel stupid for putting a "talky" encounter in front of you instead of something your character can just kill.

So how do players abuse NPCs? One classic bit is acting like a thug or putting on a show of sneering superiority because you're pretty sure your character is a few levels higher than the poor schmuck he or she is talking to. We don't know why some players enjoy the pretend-bullying of imaginary people, but they do. Another common tactic is the "outrageous insult and take-back." It runs like this: "I shove my wand of *fiery bolts* up the baron's nose and tell him his brains are gonna be all over the ceiling if he doesn't give us what we want. Ha, ha! No, I don't really do that."

The point of all this is that there's *constructive* roleplaying, and there's *destructive* roleplaying. While you're slapping around the town guards because you're playing a 10th-level character and they're 1st-level NPCs, the clock's running on the real adventure, and the DM isn't having any fun. You want to keep the DM happy and show his or her game world some respect.

✔ **Don't argue with the DM**. The Dungeon Master isn't infallible. Sometimes he or she will remember a rule wrong, forget that you're holding your action, or overlook an obvious plot hole in the adventure. But it's accepted gaming etiquette to let the DM run the game as he or she sees fit. The DM is the guy or gal who's putting in a lot of extra work to make the game fun for everybody else. Cut him or her some slack.

That said, you're within your rights to ask a DM to check a rule that you think he or she got wrong. If the DM says, "Joe, the evil cleric used *command* on Kerdigard to make you attack your friends," you can point out that you're not sure if the *command* prayer can actually make your character swing at his friends. If the DM insists he or she is right, the best thing to do is let it slide and go along with the way the DM wants to play it. That way you don't stop the game altogether and leave the other players sitting around waiting for the argument to resolve. You can always take up your point later on, after the game session is over.

If the DM is spectacularly wrong, spitefully inconsistent, uses NPCs to bully your characters (see the previous bullet), or refuses to be questioned, you might be dealing with a pocket tyrant. You'll have to decide whether you can live with playing the game by the, ah, unique rules the DM uses for his or her game, or whether you'd rather not let this person tyrannize your gaming time. If the DM is a great storyteller, maybe you can put up with his or her butchery of the rules. But if he or she runs a bad game all around, maybe someone else at the table would be a better DM.

Chapter 22

Character Building for Experts

In This Chapter

▶ Creating competitive characters

▶ Finding the best character combos

▶ Getting ahead with paragon paths

▶ Cherry picking good powers with multiclassing

Many players are perfectly happy choosing a character class and sticking to it, spending their character's whole career getting better at the path laid out in the *Player's Handbook*. However, some players are fanatics about building the toughest, most capable, most specialized character they can come up with. In fact, thousands of D&D players constantly debate the virtues of various character builds and share their efforts with each other in hundreds of message boards and mailing lists. When you factor in the additional options for classes, new feats, new items, new powers, and similar incremental improvements available in other D&D supplements, your character-building options are effectively infinite.

In this chapter, we discuss the art of extreme character building and show you how to use some advanced tactics to maximize your character's strengths while minimizing weaknesses.

Min-Maxing Your Character

D&D is a tough game on your character. Fierce orc berserkers try to hack characters into quivering chunks of meat with huge axes. Giants try to stomp characters into bloody paste. Dragons want to incinerate characters with fiery breath weapons. And, as if that weren't enough, characters spend most of their time stumbling through dismal dungeons with fun features like pit traps full of rusty spikes and the occasional yawning gate leading directly to an infernal plane of existence. To survive and thrive in this admittedly hostile environment, you need to build the strongest character you can put together.

Character optimization resources

You can build a bewildering variety of competent, min-maxed characters using just the *Player's Handbook.* But wait, there's more! If you like exploring various character builds and assembling the best characters you can imagine from the material at hand, you'll find that other D&D supplements offer tons of additional options. Check out the FORGOTTEN REALMS *Player's Guide,* the *Adventurer's Vault,* and *Martial Power* just for starters. (These three books are due out in September and October of 2008.)

In addition to looking for new options in other D&D supplements, you'll find that thousands of D&D fans discuss their favorite character-building tricks with each other every day. If you want to find good character builds fast, we recommend a visit to the official D&D message boards, hosted by Wizards of the Coast, the folks who publish the DUNGEONS & DRAGONS game. You can find the message boards at `www.wizards.com/dnd`.

The art of optimizing your character is known as *min-maxing* because you're maximizing your character's effectiveness and minimizing his or her weaknesses. When you min-max, you're looking for corners you can cut in the game rules. You're trying to make sure that you're getting the most you possibly can out of your character design. Some players look down on this sort of character building, but we think it's just good smart play.

Here's a simple example: Say you're trying to build a rogue character around the special effects of critical hits. You should choose the feats Press the Advantage or Surprise Knockdown because they offer good benefits on critical hits. For your preferred weapon, try to get your hands on a *keen* blade — you can use a minor action to shoot for a critical hit. If you score any hit at all with that blade, it's a critical hit and triggers your feat. Because accuracy is everything in pulling off that combination, choose an attack power that has a high innate accuracy; anything that attacks Reflex or Will defense instead of AC is generally going to be about 10 to 15 percent more likely to hit. That means an encounter power such as *king's castle* or *bait and switch* is the best way to start this combo. Better yet, you want to have combat advantage before you strike to make sure you have the highest possible attack bonus and the biggest possible payoff on a critical hit — take the utility power *tumble* so that you can get into a flanking position easily. Got all that?

Now, for *real* min-maxing, make sure your character carries a couple of *keen* weapons. After all, your *keen* blade gets that "manufacture a critical" power only once per day (well, it's a milestone power, so it's more like two or maybe three times per day) . . . but if you have more than one *keen* blade, you can pull this trick off more often. You probably can't afford to have multiple copies of your character's best weapon, but if your character is a 10th-level rogue, you can probably afford a couple of extra 3rd-level magic items; some spare *+1 keen daggers* would be a great investment for you. Don't tell your Dungeon Master we told you!

Min-maxing strategies

There are three basic courses you can follow when optimizing your character:

- ✔ **Maximizing strengths:** Pick something your character does well and throw every resource available into getting even better at it. A highly specialized character is generally far more dangerous in a fight than a character whose abilities aren't as tightly focused. So, if your character is already a good archer, maximize him or her by choosing archery-friendly powers and feats at every opportunity. Arm your character with the best magical bow you can afford. Improve your character's Dexterity score as much as possible. Yes, your character will be a bit one-dimensional, but if he or she is part of a balanced adventuring party, you're smart to specialize; your versatility lies in the fact that you're part of a team.

- ✔ **Covering weaknesses:** Make choices that patch holes in your character. For example, fighters usually have poor Will defense. Choose the Iron Will feat or buy a set of *coldiron armor* to cover that weakness. Wizards are fragile in melee; choose Armor Training feats to improve your Armor Class so that your wizard can stand up to more punishment than normal.

- ✔ **Increasing versatility:** Broaden your horizons by making choices that provide access to a variety of class features. For example, take advantage of multiclassing (discussed in the "Multiclassing: Maxing Out Your Choices" section, later in this chapter) to get access to a whole new list of class features. If you're playing a spellcaster, choose powers that have multiple uses. If you're playing a defender or striker character, choose attack powers that offer a variety of effects other than pure damage.

Although all these are decent strategies for optimizing a character, many experienced players believe that maximizing strengths is the way to go. Here's the reason: When you maximize your character's strengths, you generally get to decide when to use them. If you're playing a fantastic archer, you're in control of whether you shoot or don't shoot in any given combat round. On the other hand, when you cover a weakness, you aren't able to control whether or not your efforts will matter. If you build a fighter with a great Will defense, you don't get much benefit out of an encounter in which your fighter isn't threatened by attacks targeting Will defense.

Exploiting good interactions

The real art of character optimization lies in finding good interactions between your character's mechanical elements — pieces of your character such as race, selection of powers, or selection of feats. Anybody can make good choices about which feats to learn, what equipment to carry, or which spells to keep handy. We're going to look at making choices that synergize with each other.

That may sound like a lot of gobbledygook, so check out this example. Say that your character is a cleric, and you like thumping bad guys with your mace. Here's a good combination: First, choose a theme like thunder. Select attack powers such as *wrathful thunder* and *split the sky.* Choose the Raging Storm feat to gain bonus damage with thunder powers or the Solid Sound feat to gain a defense boost. Make sure you arm your character with a *resounding* or *thundering* weapon because those let you pull off additional thunder effects once per encounter. As you can see, your choices in three distinct game areas — feats, equipment, and powers — all work together to make this character far more effective than he or she would be if you made any of those choices in isolation and didn't follow up with complementary choices in the other game systems.

Here's a quick checklist of game elements that you can mesh together to make your character a true Frankenstein monster of min-maxing:

- **Ability scores:** Can you find a way to exploit your character's highest ability score(s)?

- **Character class:** Do your character's ability scores make sense for his or her class? Is there another class your character's ability scores make him or her well suited for? If so, that might be a good class to multiclass into.

- **Powers known:** Does your character know powers that make the best use of his or her key ability score?

- **Feat selections:** Do your feat selections make use of your character's best ability score and your character's power choices?

- **Equipment choices:** Do you have the right armor and weapons for your character's ability scores and his or her powers?

- **Magic items:** Are there magic items that can help your min-maxing strategy? Would a more powerful weapon allow your min-maxing plan to work better?

Choosing a Paragon Path

When your character reaches 11th level, you get to select a paragon path — basically, a second set of class features and some unique powers that describe some sort of impressive and unique specialization in your character class. For example, the cleric paragon paths in the *Player's Handbook* include angelic avenger, divine oracle, radiant servant, and warpriest.

Want more choices?

If you want more paragon path choices, here's a sneaky way to do it: Choose a multiclass feat at some point when your character is still in the heroic tier. You now qualify to select a paragon path from either your character class or the character class you've chosen to multiclass into. For example, if your character is a cleric and you choose the Student of the Sword feat, you can select any cleric or fighter paragon path instead of just cleric paragon paths.

You can find paragon paths in Chapter 4 of the *Player's Handbook*, right after the power descriptions for each class. Paragon paths are often featured in many other D&D supplements.

All paragon paths share the same basic structure and offer your character these benefits:

✔ **Path features (11th level):** Each paragon path offers several abilities analogous to class features. For example, the Radiant Servant cleric paragon path grants the features Illuminating Attacks (your radiant powers score critical hits on 19 or 20) and Radiant Action (when you use an action point, choose an enemy to take radiant damage). One of these features is always keyed to the use of action points.

✔ **Encounter attack (11th level):** You gain a new encounter power when you select your paragon path. In the case of the Radiant Servant, it's *solar wrath* — a huge burst power that deals good damage to your enemies and also stuns undead and demons.

✔ **Utility power (12th level):** When your character reaches 12th level, you gain a utility power determined by your paragon path. The Radiant Servant gains a power called *healing sun,* which heals nearby allies and does minor damage to undead or demons.

✔ **Path feature (16th level):** You gain another path feature at 16th level. For example, the Radiant Servant gains the feature Lasting Light — any saving throws made by demons or undead to remove conditions you caused receive a penalty.

✔ **Daily attack (20th level):** The capstone power for each paragon path is a daily attack power gained at 20th level. These are some of the most spectacular and devastating attacks in the game. For example, the Radiant Servant's 20th level power is *radiant brilliance,* which deals decent radiant damage to a single target and then causes it to explode on the following turn, damaging all enemies standing nearby it.

Your paragon path is purely additive; it's all stuff that your character gets in addition to selecting powers for his or her base class. In other words, choosing a paragon path never detracts from your character's ability to keep advancing in his or her original class.

Epic Destiny for the Win!

When you reach 20th level, you complete your character's paragon path, but at 21st level, you embark on the final phase in your character's legendary career: your epic destiny.

You can think of epic destiny as your character's road to immortality. Will he or she become a god and ascend from the mortal realms? A mythic king or hero, about whom stories will be told for thousands of generations? Or a mighty champion fated to be reborn again and again, fighting evil over countless lifetimes? Whatever your epic destiny is, it's the stuff that legends are made of.

In terms of game mechanics, epic destinies work much like paragon paths. Your character still continues to advance in his or her class, so you keep on picking new wizard attack powers (for example) when your wizard reaches 23rd, 25th, 27th, and 29th level. In addition to continuing your existing progression, you also gain specific powers tied to your epic destiny choice:

- ✔ **Destiny feature (21st level):** Each epic destiny offers at least one feature at 21st level. For example, the Archmage's feature is Spell Recall — each day you can choose one daily spell to use twice that day instead of once.

- ✔ **Destiny feature (24th level):** You gain a new destiny feature when you reach 24th level. For example, Archmages gain Arcane Spirit — when Archmages are killed, they can detach their spirits from their bodies and continue the adventure in a ghostly form (although if that form is killed too, that's it for the Archmage).

- ✔ **Utility power (26th level):** When your character reaches 26th level, you gain a utility power determined by your epic destiny. The Archmage gains a power called *shape magic,* which simply allows you to regain any arcane power you've already used. (Considering this may be your 25th-level daily attack spell, that can be pretty impressive!)

- ✔ **Destiny feature (30th level):** You gain your final path feature at 30th level. For example, the Archmage's last feature is Archspell, which lets you select one daily spell and cast it as an encounter power instead of a daily power.

Although epic destinies are pretty impressive, there are other good perks for epic characters. First of all, the feats available to epic characters are extremely strong. Secondly, the magic items characters tend to collect at epic levels include some truly awesome powers. A high-level paladin wearing *+6 soulforged godplate armor* has an armor bonus of +20, just from armor alone! Add half the character's level, a heavy shield, and a feat or two, and that paladin might be walking around at close to Armor Class 50.

Multiclassing: Maxing Out Your Choices

Perhaps the single best tool at your disposal for optimizing your character is *multiclassing:* spending a feat or two to pick up class features or powers from a second class of your choice. For example, your character might start out as a 1st-level fighter, which gives you everything you'd expect. But after your character gains a level or two, you might decide you want to gain some tactical command ability, so when you reach a level where you can select a feat, you take the multiclass feat Student of Battle — warlord training. Eventually you might spend additional feats (Novice Power, Acolyte Power, and Adept Power) to actually substitute some warlord powers for the fighter powers you otherwise would have learned.

You can find the rules on multiclassing in Chapter 6 of the *Player's Handbook*.

There are some downsides to spending multiple feats on multiclassing:

- **Feats you spend on multiclassing aren't getting spent on other, more direct ways to power up your character.** For example, you could instead use the feats to directly increase your character's Armor Class or effectiveness with a chosen weapon by taking the Armor Training or Weapon Focus feat, respectively.

- **Multiclassing is power-neutral.** For the fighter in the preceding example to gain a warlord encounter power, he or she has to scrap an appropriate fighter power. That character is worse at being a fighter than he or she would be without multiclassing.

That said, multiclassing is the min-maxer's dream. Multiclass feats are usually pretty good deals; for the cost of a single feat, you can usually find a decent daily power and some useful skill training from the class you chose to multi-class into. A single feat invested in cleric or warlord training (Initiate of the Faith, or Student of Battle) gives your character the ability to use *healing word* or *inspiring word* once per day. Sure, it's normally an encounter power for a single-class cleric or warlord, but being able to hand out a healing surge even just once per day is a very useful capability to keep in your back pocket.

The advantages to taking multiclass feats are

- ✔ **Powers you gain through multiclassing let you break out of your character's role.** For example, leaders usually don't have much in the way of high-damage encounter powers, but if you multiclass into a defender or striker class (say, fighter or rogue) you can pick up an encounter attack power that deals more damage than any cleric or warlord power you can find at the same level. Likewise, fighters don't have much in the way of ranged attack powers, but a fighter who multiclasses into ranger or warlock can pick up some impressive powers that deal damage at range.

- ✔ **Multiclassing qualifies you to choose your paragon path from those available to your class *and* the class you multiclassed into.** If nothing else, you can find lots of room for imaginative character-building with this trick. For example, the Warpriest is a cleric paragon path, but it's quite attractive to a fighter as well. If you can imagine your fighter "catching religion" a few levels into his or her career, you might find Warpriest to be the paragon path you want for your character.

You can find the best multiclass opportunities when your character has a very high ability score that's useful for another class too. For example, Battle Clerics, fighters, paladins, and warlords all care about Strength for melee attacks; they're natural multiclass opportunities for each other. With one good score (Strength) your character can use powers from two different classes. Table 22-1 sums up these natural multiclass affinities for you.

Table 22-1	Multiclass Affinities
If You Have a High . . .	*. . . You Should Think about Choosing One of These Multiclass Feats*
Strength	Student of the Sword (fighter), Soldier of the Faith (paladin), Warrior of the Wild (ranger), Student of Battle (warlord). If your Wisdom is at least 13, Initiate of the Faith (Cleric) is good too; just choose Strength-based cleric powers.
Constitution	Pact Initiate (warlock). You need a Charisma of 13 or better, but you should choose Constitution-based warlock powers.

(continued)

Table 22-1 *(continued)*

If You Have a High . . .	. . . You Should Think about Choosing One of These Multiclass Feats
Dexterity	Sneak of Shadows (rogue), Warrior of the Wild (ranger).
Intelligence	Arcane Initiate (wizard)
Wisdom	Initiate of the Faith (cleric). If your Strength and Charisma are both 13 or better, Soldier of the Faith (paladin) is also a good choice; just choose Wisdom-based paladin powers.
Charisma	Pact Initiate (warlock)

Part IV

The Art of Dungeon Mastering

The 5th Wave   By Rich Tennant

Hank orders ideas for his dungeon of the week.

Well, shoot! This isn't a case of the willys. This is a case of the heebee jeebees!

CREATIVE IDEAS INC

In this part . . .

The single most important factor in a successful D&D game is the Dungeon Master. Every player gets to concentrate on playing one character at a time and exploring the fantastic world around his or her character, but the DM plays a cast of thousands and, in fact, creates the world that the other players explore. Being a DM is like being a novelist whose characters are completely out of his control — because you don't know what the heroes of the story are going to do and how they're going to interact with the adventure and the game world, you're just as surprised by the shape of unfolding events as the players are. With a good DM, the D&D game is filled with excitement, wonder, intrigue, humor, suspense, and unforgettable moments players will talk about for years afterwards.

Chapter 23

Running the Game

In This Chapter

▶ Understanding the Dungeon Master's job

▶ Setting up the adventure

▶ Dividing the game into easy-to-run segments

▶ DMing social encounters, exploration and travel, and combat

▶ Running monsters in combat

*T*he first and most important ingredient of a DUNGEON & DRAGONS game is a good Dungeon Master. The DM serves as referee, judge, storyteller, supporting cast, scenery builder, villain creator, monster player, and dungeon crafter. Without the DM's efforts, all the other players are left with interesting characters but nothing to do with them. We can't stress this one enough: You need a DM to run the D&D game, and the better your Dungeon Master, the better the game is going to be.

Ideally, you should learn how to be a DM by observing an experienced and talented Dungeon Master work his or her magic — preferably by playing in that DM's game. However, we can't promise that you'll be able to start your D&D gaming experience by landing in the hands of a talented DM. If you and your friends are all pretty new at the game, someone at the table will have to step up and do the DM's job, and it might as well be you. Although it's challenging to be the DM, and it takes a little extra time and preparation, you'll also find that it can be very rewarding. When you realize that everyone else at the table is going to remember *your* dungeon for years afterwards, reliving their characters' triumphs (and failures) over and over again, you'll understand what we're talking about.

In this chapter, we discuss the basics of being a Dungeon Master. We tell you all about the role of the Dungeon Master in running the D&D game, and we show you how to administer the game with fairness, consistency, and an eye for dramatic tension. Before you know it, you'll be one of those great DMs that other players hope to learn from.

We help you get started DMing in this book, but if you're really interested in being the DM for your group and you're craving more hints, tips, tricks, and advice, be sure to check out *Dungeon Master 4th Edition For Dummies* (due out in fall 2008).

DMing: The Best Role in the Game

If you're new to the game, you're probably wondering what in the world a Dungeon Master *does*. There isn't really a short answer to that question. As DM, you run the game. You narrate the story of the player characters. You play the monsters. You build the world. You design the dungeons. You hand out the treasure. You play the villains, and you give the other players in the game the opportunity to feel great about beating evil into paste with a greatsword or a *lightning bolt*. You're the director of this movie, and you're the person who's going to put people on the edge of their seats time and time again.

Because "you do everything," isn't a particularly helpful answer, in the following sections, we break down the big parts of the DM's role and discuss them at length.

Preparing an adventure

Are the heroes pillaging the long-lost Crypt of Azar-Malzz? Defending the town of Pommeville from a plague of werewolves? Stomping out the cult of Elemental Evil? Searching the depths of an old dwarven stronghold? When you're the DM, you decide what challenge the adventurers are facing. You pick the monsters they fight, and you decide the stakes.

Preparing an adventure takes some extra work, usually between game sessions. You need to design your own adventure or pick up a published adventure from your hobby store or at www.dndinsider.com. (See the section, "Choosing an Adventure to Run," later in this chapter.) You should read ahead so that you know what four or five encounters or situations the heroes are most likely going to encounter in each game session, and be ready to run those encounters on game night.

Building the world

So what's outside of the dungeon? Is there a spider-infested forest surrounding the place? Is there a town nearby? Who lives there? What sort of adventures can the inhabitants point the player characters toward? What lies over the next range of hills? Who built that ruined castle, and who or what lives there now?

Running a D&D game gives you a perfect excuse to indulge yourself in the fine art of world building. You get to craft an entire kingdom for the players to explore when they decide to take a break from plundering whatever dungeon you put in front of them to start with. Sometimes you simply use your world-building to provide your dungeons and monsters with a place to live. Other times, you're weaving an intricate and living setting to serve as the backdrop for the heroes' story. Whatever the case may be, your players expect you to know (or expertly make up on the fly) countless answers about what their characters see around them as they travel through the world.

You don't need to start by building a whole world at once; some of the best campaigns begin as tiny kernels, nothing more than a dungeon and a nearby town that the players shuttle back and forth between. Start small and answer the questions one at a time as they come up.

Playing NPCs

As a DM, anytime the player characters interact with another person or intelligent monster (also known as an NPC, or nonplayer character), you speak for that being. Many DMs feel that this is the most fun part of the job; you get to try out all kinds of parts, including power-mad dark overlords delivering villainous monologues, stammering stable boys, gruff innkeepers, shifty informants, imperious wizards, absent-minded sages, sinister dragons chatting with the adventurers they expect to serve as their next meal, regal eladrin lords too proud to ask for help, or slow-witted ettins who take turns speaking with each head. The world is full of people and monsters for the heroes to talk to, and it's your job to figure out what they're going to say and deliver their lines.

Sometimes, this is pretty easy. When you're starting an adventure by having a mysterious wizard hire the party to accomplish a specific task, you have a fair idea of what the wizard wants, how she's going to pay the party, and what

Using a published campaign setting

A number of professionally designed campaign settings are available in your friendly local gaming store. A published campaign setting is a ready-to-use world for your D&D game, usually filled with countless ideas for adventures just waiting for you to bring to life. Two good options you'll find out there right now are the FORGOTTEN REALMS *Campaign Guide* and the EBERRON *Campaign Setting*, both published by Wizards of the Coast, Inc. Whether you prefer to build your own world or use someone else's is up to you, of course. But even if you decide to create your own campaign, you can find lots of cool and interesting elements to borrow from in a published setting.

she's willing to tell them about the perils they'll face on their mission. On the other hand, players (as their characters) sometimes strike up random conversations with people you never expected to have to know anything about. When the players ask the captain of the lord's guard if he likes working for Baron Duncastle, well, you have to decide what the answer to that question is, whether or not the guard captain feels like sharing it, and how he'll do so.

If you don't know already, take a moment and consider what the NPC wants to get from the player characters in the conversation that's coming up. It might be as simple as, "I want these people to go away and leave me alone." It might be more complicated: "I don't want anything in particular, but if they drop a bag of gold in my lap, I'd try hard to be helpful." It might be downright devious: "I want these people to go off to Grimdeath Keep and tell me when they're going so that I can tell my evil master when to ambush them."

Don't be afraid to ham it up. Chances are good that you're not a professional actor, but who cares? Let it all out when you're speaking for your monsters and NPCs. You want the players to *remember* this person or monster and this conversation later, or you wouldn't be having a social encounter now, would you?

Running monsters

Playing monsters is the other part of the job most DMs love. When the player characters get into a scrap with a ferocious monster or an evil villain, you run the bad guys in the fight. You decide what they're going to do — which of the heroes they attack, what tactics they use, and when they give up and surrender or run away. You roll their attack and damage rolls, make their saving throws, and keep track of their hit points. We go into more depth about how to run monsters in combat in the later section, "Getting the Most out of Your Monsters."

Your goal when you run the bad guys in the fight is not necessarily to find the most efficient way to slaughter the player characters. You're trying to challenge the players and help to build a riveting and suspenseful story. You want each fight to feel distinctive and memorable, and you want to run the monsters and villains as intelligently (or unintelligently) as they really would fight.

The key ideas are *excitement, suspense,* and *believability* — not just running up the body count.

✔ *Excitement* is all a matter of presentation. If you approach your material with a sense of excitement, using active words and using a high level of energy, then the players will pick up on your cues and the excitement will carry through.

✔ *Suspense* relies on making sure that you build toward a climax with powerful and vibrant narration. For example, "Water drips from the ceiling of the dungeon corridor ahead. As you make your way, roll a Perception check. Great roll! You hear a strange scraping sound in the distance, as though something heavy and sharp were being dragged across the stone floor. The sound is growing louder, as though the source is closing in on your location." Using a build up like this before you reveal the monsters and start the encounter is one way to build suspense and anticipation in the minds of the players.

✔ *Believability* is simply a matter of staying true to your material and to the fiction of D&D. Everyone has already bought off on the suspension of disbelief needed to imagine a world of medieval weapons and armor, magic, and monsters. You just need to help sell it by making the fiction real. Use evocative descriptions that key off all the senses of the players—how something sounds, what it looks like, what it smells like, what it feels like. Use names that sound real and fit the fiction of your world. Bob the Slayer is kind of goofy and will lead to goofy play, but Rundarr the Vile sounds like a believable person in a D&D world. Keep it believable, and the action of the game will reach a whole other level.

Adjudicating results

Most of the time, the game rules are clear. This is especially true with attacks, power use, and physical skills such as Acrobatics, Athletics, and Endurance. But part of the fun of a roleplaying game such as D&D is that a player can have his or her character try anything he or she can think of — and a fair number of those spontaneous actions are things that the rules don't cover. The DM has to make a call on the fly to decide whether these fun and unusual actions succeed or fail.

For example, the heroes are fighting in an evil temple when one of the players tells you that his character Baredd is going to kick over a brazier full of glowing red coals so that it'll singe the skeleton he's fighting and kick up hot embers in its face. Sorry to say it, but there aren't any rules in the game for exactly what it takes to kick over a heavy, solid metal brazier and make the coals fly in the right direction. But it's a heroic move that sure sounds cool, so you want to reward your player for thinking outside the box. You have to decide what kind of roll Baredd ought to make, how much damage hot coals do, and whether the skeleton is even bothered by a face full of embers. (Off the cuff, we'd say have Baredd make a DC 20 Strength check, the skeleton takes 1d6 fire damage from the coals, and no, it doesn't care about embers in its face since it doesn't have any skin to worry about crisping. But we're ruling on the fly, too.)

The best way to be fair as a DM is to be consistent. If you decide that a rule works in a specific way, make sure you always use it in that way. Don't play favorites. Treat all player characters the same way, and treat your NPCs and monsters the same way, too.

If you come off as a DM who doesn't play fair, who treats some characters differently from others, or who obviously cheats without reason, then you'll lose the trust of the players and your game will suffer.

Keeping up with the characters

Last, but not least, a good DM stays involved with each one of the players' characters. In a perfect world, you'll eventually get around to showcasing every character in an adventure that's tailored to that character's strengths, personality, and backstory. If your buddy Joe is playing Torvald, the paladin who's secretly an exiled prince of the kingdom of Erewhon, sooner or later it would be great to create an adventure that pits Torvald against the evil baron who arranged for his exile — and who now has his eyes on Erewhon's throne. You can't do that with every adventure, but it's a fine idea to run something personalized for your players once in every two to three adventures, spotlighting a different character each time you do so.

On the nuts-and-bolts side, you also want to keep up with the player characters' abilities and gear. It's important for you to know just how tough the player characters really are, whether they're ahead of the curve or behind the curve on arming themselves with great magic items, and what sorts of feats and powers they have at their disposal. Specifically, you should be aware of which paragon paths your players are angling for and what feats their characters are trying to qualify for as they advance in level. Helping your players to realize characters that are cool, powerful, and distinctive is one of the real pleasures of DMing.

Choosing an Adventure to Run

Your first challenge as a new Dungeon Master is to figure out what kind of adventure you're going to serve up to the players. You have two basic options:

- ✔ **Designing your own adventure:** We cover this extensively in Chapter 24 of this book. Basically, you collect a suitable array of monsters and challenges and create a good plot or story to involve the players. When you design your own adventure, you have the advantage of knowing exactly what your players are like and what characters they're going to bring to the game.

✔ **Using a published adventure:** With a little looking around, you can find literally hundreds of adventures published by various game companies. Check out your local hobby store or bookstore for starters. A good place to start is with the H-Series of low-level adventures for the D&D game. (*H1: The Keep on the Shadowfell, H2: Thunderspire Labyrinth,* and *H3: The Pyramid of Shadows* present enough adventuring material to take your player characters from 1st level to 10th level.) *Dungeon Magazine* is an outstanding resource that publishes adventures and adventure hooks every week as part of the online D&D Insider Web site. Check it out at www.dndinsider.com.

A published adventure definitely saves you time and effort, but no game designer can know exactly how your gaming group works or what sorts of things your players are interested in doing, so you'll need to customize the material to meet your specific needs. And make sure you get an adventure specifically designed for use with 4th Edition D&D so that you can hit the ground running without the need for lot of additional work on your part.

When writing your own adventure or choosing a published adventure to run for your friends, keep your adventuring party's character level and class mix in mind. Ideally, most of the combat encounters in the adventure should have an encounter level that ranges from one or two levels below the party's level (for an easy encounter) to two to four levels higher than the party's level (for a hard encounter). Check out Chapter 4 of the *Dungeon Master's Guide* for more information.

Task-Oriented DMing

As with many things, the best way to learn how to be a Dungeon Master is to just try it. Through trial and error, you'll eventually get the hang of what a Dungeon Master needs to do to make a game run. There's nothing like jumping in at the deep end, after all . . . but if you find this prospect a little intimidating, then read on. As best we can, we try to reduce the DM's job to a set of processes that we call *task-oriented DMing*.

Here's the theory: Most game play takes place in one of five basic tasks — talking, exploring, fighting, setting up, or free time. What you need to do as a novice DM is identify what kind of task you're currently engaged in and follow the appropriate process. Table 23-1 describes each of the basic tasks.

Table 23-1	Guidelines for Identifying Your Task	
Task Type	*Sample Situations*	*Things You Might Hear or Say*
Setting up	Telling the players what their characters know about the adventure or the mission at hand. The PCs prepare to go into dungeon.	DM: "You are summoned to the baron's secret council chamber. He studies you for a long moment and then says, 'Friends, we've got a troll problem.'" DM: "You're looking at the the the cave mouth. Any special preparations?" PC: "Before we leave town, I want to buy some magic arrows."
Talking	The PCs are questioning a patron or an employer about the mission. The PCs are convincing someone to give them information or do something for them.	PC: "How many trolls are we talking about, Your Lordship?" PC: "So what'll you pay us to fix this troll problem for you?" PC: "If we agree to track down the orcs that have been killing animals in the forest, will the centaurs let us pass?"
Exploring	The PCs are deciding which way to go in a dungeon corridor. The PCs are searching a room or investigating a scene.	DM: "You come to a T in the passage. You can go left down a set of slick, wet stairs, or you can turn right, where there's a door of oak bound with iron. Which way now?" PC: "I'll take a careful look down the well, shining my lantern that way." PC: "I search the big green face on the wall and see if there are any hidden buttons or compartments or anything around it."
Fighting	The PCs kick in a dungeon door and attack whatever monster they see in the room. The PCs walk into an ambush.	PC: "A troll? I charge!" DM: "Something *big* in that pile of garbage just moved. Roll initiative, everybody!" DM: "Suddenly a centipede as big around as a barrel drops down from a crevice overhead and darts at Torvald! It's got surprise . . . Torvald, what's your AC?"

Task Type	Sample Situations	Things You Might Hear or Say
Free time	The PCs kill time in the game.	DM: "Nothing comes sniffing around your camp while you rest, and the night passes without event. It's morning, you're all rested, and your powers have refreshed."
	The players are talking about which path of an adventure to follow next.	PC: "We can follow the map to the Caves of Doom, or we can follow these troll tracks we just found. What do the rest of you think?"

It's not always going to be clear what task you're in at the moment. In fact, it's possible for one group to be engaged in multiple tasks at the same time. For example, if the heroes just won a fierce fight against a band of savage lizard-folk warriors, you might have the rogue searching the chamber for hidden treasure, the cleric busily fixing up the fighter with healing prayers, and the wizard quietly questioning the two villagers the heroes just rescued from the clutches of the cruel lizardfolk.

Here's a quick primer on prioritizing tasks:

- **Setup.** This is when you tell the players what their characters know about the upcoming situation and when you let the players prepare their characters for the adventure. Set-up ends as soon as you have something else to do. Usually, you go from setup into exploration or combat.

- **Exploration is the default condition.** If you're done with setting up but the PCs haven't yet hit an obstacle or encounter of some kind, you're in exploration. Usually, PCs explore until they hit an obstacle to deal with (see the following section, "The exploration tasks"), a character to talk to, or a monster to fight.

- **Talking trumps exploration.** When you meet someone or something in the game, it's called an *encounter.* Many encounters take you straight to a fight, but some offer the possibility of talking in place of fighting. If there's a conversation going on, resolve that first before you move on to any other tasks. Of course, fights sometimes break out in the middle of conversations. When you finish your conversation, you go back to exploration mode.

- **Combat trumps everything else.** If there's a fight going on, everything else can wait. The fight continues until one side or the other runs away, surrenders, or is defeated. When the fight is finished, you usually default back to exploration again.

✔ **Free time ends as soon as you have something else to do.** Free time is usually "time out" from one of the other tasks. For example, if the party is exploring a cave system and winds up having a discussion about which way to go and how to use their magic to move safely and stealthily, you've put the exploration job on hold for a few minutes. There's nothing wrong with that; as soon as the players reach a decision, just pick up with the exploring again.

The exploration task

Exploration is the default state of the game. When you're exploring, you're soliciting from the players some decision or direction about which way their characters are going and what they're looking for. Then you resolve that decision and continue until the heroes come to an obstacle, meet with an encounter of some kind, or reach another decision point. As a general rule, when running the activity of exploring, a DM follows these steps:

1. **Describe the options.**

   Tell the players what paths are available for their characters. For example: "The rubble-choked stairwell descends into a dusty old vault beneath the ruined monastery. There's a large, dark well shaft in one corner of the room with a low stone wall around it, a passage leading off toward the east, and an old wooden door in the north wall. What do you do?"

2. **Get the players to tell you what their characters are doing.**

   Sometimes this might be a group action — "We'll take the passage to the east," — or sometimes this may be an individual action, such as, "I'm going to search the door for traps."

3. **Identify player responses.**

   Identify the action the player character is attempting to perform. Don't be afraid to ask a player to be more specific or helpful. If she tells you something like, "I'll go search the old well," you can ask, "Are you just leaning over the well to look down? Are you searching around the stone rim? Or are you going to climb down in there?"

   If you're not sure how to resolve what the player character is attempting, try the following:

   • Is she trying to use a specific skill such as Perception or Thievery?

   • Is he trying to shove or move something? (A Strength check may be in order.)

   • Is she just looking around? (A Perception check may be in order if there's anything to see or hear.)

- Is he trying to move on, in, or through something? (Athletics or Acrobatics skill checks may be in order.)

4. **Interrupt with obstacles or encounters.**

   If the player characters meet up with an obstacle, a trap, or a creature of some kind, interrupt the exploration and either tell the players what obstacle the characters have met with, resolve the trap, or move to a social encounter or combat encounter, as appropriate.

   Some examples of this sort of interruption include

   - "The door's stuck. It won't open. If you want to try to force it open, you'll have to make a Strength check."

   - "The inside of that well is smooth and slippery. You have to make a DC 20 Athletics check to descend safely."

   - "When you step into the east passage, you hear a click and feel a pressure plate depress slightly under your foot, and then a hidden device shoots a steel dart at you! What's your Reflex defense?" (You then roll to see whether the trap hits and, if so, how much damage it does.)

   - "You hear a grinding, rumbling sound from the wall behind you, and suddenly a hulking bug-eyed monster the size of an ogre bursts through the wall and attacks! Roll initiative everybody!"

5. **Advance to the next decision point.**

   Assuming that nothing jumps out and tries to kill the heroes, you can move to the next place where they need to make a decision. If the heroes follow a ten-mile long trail through the forest to the old ruins, and nothing in particular happens during that hike, you can just say, "You hike for about five hours, and then you reach a dark and dismal hollow in the middle of the forest where an old broken tower stands in the gloom."

The conversation task

Many of the most important challenges in the D&D game don't involve any combat at all. Player characters can talk to almost anything they meet. Sometimes conversation is clearly not going to help; dungeons are full of big, hungry, stupid monsters who want nothing more than to eat anybody they meet and can't or won't introduce themselves properly first. And other times, conversation is possible, but it just won't go anywhere; not every castle guard or innkeeper knows something that the players can use in their current adventure (or any adventure at all, for that matter).

Conversations in the game tend to fall into three categories: avoiding fights, gathering information, and asking for help. As a general rule, when running conversation scenarios, a DM follows these steps:

1. **Describe the scene and the NPC.**

   Tell the players who or what their characters have met, what that person or monster looks like, and what he or she is doing.

2. **Decide what the NPC wants.**

   See the earlier section "Playing NPCs" for more on this.

3. **Give an opening line.**

   A good way to signal that this is going to be a talking encounter is to have the NPC or monster speak first. Figure out what this NPC will say, how he, she, or it will say it, and then deliver your opening line. For example: "The ogre standing in the middle of the road squints at you and scratches his chin. 'This is Og's road!' He growls. 'But you give Og some gold, and Og be happy to let you use it.'" Feel free to have fun with it and really play the part!

4. **Pursue the conversation.**

   Let the players respond to your opening line (or have your monster or NPC respond to theirs), and then continue the conversation as long as necessary. If you need to, take a minute or two to think it over, and let the players know that you're trying to figure out what the NPC or monster says next.

5. **Say goodbye and hang up.**

   When the conversation's over, make sure you let the players know that this monster or NPC is done talking and that you consider the conversation to be at an end. For example, say something like, "Og counts the coins you gave him, which seems sort of hard for him. Then the ogre grins with a mouth full of crooked fangs and says, 'Have good trip on Og's road!'"

The combat task

Running a fight can be pretty complex, but here's the good news — there's little doubt about whether or not you're in a combat encounter. If the player characters are trying to kill someone or something, or vice versa, your job is clear: You have to get the battle resolved before anything else happens. See Chapter 8 for full details on combat.

Here's the basic process for running the combat task:

1. **Fix everyone's position.**

   Figure out where the heroes and monsters are standing at the beginning of the combat encounter. In a dungeon, this is pretty clear: If the heroes bust open the door to Room 7, the Armory, any monsters that your adventure notes as occupying Room 7 will be inside the room. If you don't know exactly where the monsters are in the room, assign them as you see fit.

If the battle is not in a dungeon, you may have to be more creative. In a wilderness setting, you'll want to determine the encounter distance based on how far apart the heroes and the monsters are likely to be when they to spot each other.

2. Is this an ambush?

If there's a chance that one side isn't aware of the other side when the encounter begins, figure out who sees whom first by making Perception checks for the monsters and using the passive Perception scores of the characters. See Chapter 3 of the *Dungeon Master's Guide*.

There are four basic scenarios that you want to consider when deciding who might be ambushing whom:

- *Heroes storm the room.* The PCs kick open a dungeon door and leap in, swords bared. Usually, no one should be surprised; the bad guys might be startled by the sudden appearance of the heroes, but the heroes don't know for sure that there's someone to fight in the room. Skip the surprise round and go to initiative.

- *Monster jumps out.* A monster is watching the place a hero might walk into or through, and it leaps out to attack as soon as the hero appears. The monster is aware of the hero, but the hero might not see the monster before it attacks. Usually, it's fair to have the monster make a Stealth check (maybe with a big bonus, if it has a great place to lurk) and then allow the character under attack to make a Perception check to see the monster before it springs. If the character spots the monster, there is no surprise. If the character doesn't spot the monster, the monster surprises him or her.

Using a skill challenge

Sometimes you want a social encounter or a challenge encounter to require skill checks. Now, a single skill check works in many situations, but sometimes you want a social encounter to have tension and drama. You can accomplish this with a skill challenge. In a skill challenge, all of the player characters participate (just as they do in a combat encounter). The party needs to attain a certain number of skill check successes before a certain number of failures to win the challenge. For example, you might decide that the conversation with Og requires four successes before two failures for the PCs to win the encounter and get to use the road without a fight. PCs can use any of these skills: Bluff, Diplomacy, Insight, or Intimidate to influence Og. Check out Chapter 5 in the *Dungeon Master's Guide* for more information on building and running skill challenges.

- *Heroes sneak up on the monster.* The heroes have a good idea that there's a monster someplace up ahead, and they try to take it by surprise. The heroes are aware of the monster, but the monster may not be aware of the heroes. Usually, you'll have the heroes doing the sneaking try their Stealth skill or use stealthy magic (like the *invisibility* spell) to get close. The bad guys get the opportunity to make Perception checks to detect the heroes; if they fail, they're surprised. Otherwise, roll initiative normally.

- *Chance meeting.* The heroes and monsters blunder into each other. Maybe the heroes are walking along a forest trail when they meet a dire wolf out hunting, or maybe they're confronting a gang of ruffians in a bad part of town when someone draws a blade. Whatever the case, neither side has any special advantage over the other; the best thing to do is to just roll initiative and start the fight.

3. **Set out the battle grid.**

   Draw out the terrain or room outline on a battle mat, or lay out your *D&D Dungeon Tiles* to create the encounter area. Then place the miniatures or markers for the characters and the monsters in their appropriate positions. This will help players figure out where they can and can't move.

4. **Roll initiative.**

   Everybody on both sides of the fight rolls initiative to determine the initiative order for the fight.

5. **Surprise round.**

   If one side surprises the other, those characters or monsters can perform a standard action before the other side gets to act. See Chapter 3 of the *Dungeon Master's Guide.*

6. **First round.**

   Now start resolving combat rounds by letting each participant (player characters and monsters) take a turn.

   A. **Count down the initiative order.** Beginning with the highest initiative roll, resolve each character or monster's actions for the round.

   B. **Monsters and villains act.** When it's a monster's or a villain's turn to act (some bad guy you're running, because you're the DM), decide what that bad guy is going to do this round. Resolve the action. See the section "Getting the Most out of Your Monsters," later in this chapter, for advice on running monsters in combat.

   C. **The heroes act.** When it's a player-controlled character's turn to act, tell the player that it's his or her turn and ask him or her what the character is going to do. Resolve whatever actions the player character attempts.

> **D. Finish the round.** When everyone has acted, you've finished the round. This is a good place to pause and take stock of what's going on. Are there other monsters nearby that might hear the fight and come to investigate? Do the monsters decide to break off the battle and run for it? (They'll have to wait for their next action to begin running, of course.)

7. Go to the next round.

> After you reach the end of the initiative order in the first round, the round's over. Go back up to Step 6 and begin the next round.

A combat encounter lasts until one side or the other is defeated, runs away, surrenders, or manages to call a truce.

The free time task

You'll begin most adventure sessions and most new adventures with some DMing that isn't really "on the clock." For example, if you know that the players are about to go explore the Caves of Doom, you'll usually provide a little information about why their heroes are interested and how they got there. At a bare minimum, you ought to say something like, "You've heard of a great treasure hidden somewhere in the monster-haunted Caves of Doom, so you've hiked into the Dragonbone Hills. You're now standing in front of a gaping cave mouth in the side of a hill. Any special preparations before you go in?" (That's an extremely minimal set up, but most players will cut a new DM some slack and go along for now.)

Free time is also good for evaluating options and attending to tasks that take time, but don't need DMing. For example, if the heroes are going to rest up for a week in town, the player running the wizard might look at you and say, "While we're waiting, I'm going to enchant a couple of magic items." You don't need to run through any real process for this. Just assess the cost and have the player pay up the gold pieces required. Similarly, debating the question of which way to turn next in an adventure, or what adventure to set off on, is also a good free time task.

Finally, even in the tightest-run games, there's a lot of screwing around. People sitting around the table will drop out of game mode and chat about movies they've seen, how things are going at work, or memorable scenes from old games. As DM, you're not in charge of all this. We only mention it because it's important for you to recognize free time when the players happen to stumble into it. Clam up for a few minutes, let the players gab or joke, make a trip to the bathroom or whatever, and then get back into the game when you think the players are ready.

Getting the Most out of Your Monsters

One of your most important jobs as DM is to run the monsters and bad guys in a fight. The first thing you need to do to run a monster in a fight is to learn where to find key information about the monster — getting a handle on the format in which monsters and villains are normally presented. When you know how to navigate a monster description or stat block, you'll want to learn how to make decisions for the monsters that make sense and suit the situation, without cutting the players too much of a break or being too tough on them.

Figuring out monster stats

Monsters have many of the same critical numbers that characters do. They have hit points, Armor Class and other defenses, attack bonuses, skills and feats, and even ability scores.

In most D&D supplements or adventures, monsters are presented in a *stat block.* To run a monster in combat, you need to have an idea of how the format reveals crucial information about the monster or villain in question.

Take a look at the nearby sidebar, "Harpy," which shows the stat block for the harpy monster.

You can find the key for reading the *Monster Manual* entry on pages 4–7 of the *Monster Manual.* But just to help you out, here's a quick look at some of the more important pieces of information hidden in this format:

- **Level and role:** The monster's level and role in a combat encounter. The harpy is a level 6 controller.
- **Size:** Most monsters range from Tiny to Huge. A monster's size influences several other stats. The harpy is Medium size.
- **Origin type and keyword:** The harpy is a fey humanoid.
- **XP:** How much experience the monster is worth.
- **Initiative:** The modifier for initiative rolls.
- **Senses:** The special senses a monster has, if any, as well as its Perception check modifier.
- **HP and Bloodied:** The number of hit points this monster has and its bloodied value.
- **Defenses:** The monster's AC, Fortitude, Reflex, and Will defense scores.
- **Immune or Resist:** If a monster has any special immunities or resistances, they are listed here. In the harpy's case, it ignores 10 points of thunder damage when attacked.

Harpy

Harpy	**Level 6 Controller**
Medium fey humanoid	XP: 250
Initiative: +5	**Senses:** Perception +5

HP: 71; **Bloodied:** 35

AC: 20; **Fortitude:** 17; **Reflex:** 17; **Will:** 19

Resist: 10 thunder

Speed: 6, fly 8 (clumsy)

Claw (standard; at-will)

+11 versus AC; 1d8 + 2 damage

Alluring Song (standard; sustain minor; at-will)

◆ **Charm**

Close burst 10; deafened creatures are immune; +12 versus Will; the target is pulled 3 squares and immobilized (save ends). When the harpy sustains the power, any target that has not yet saved against the effect is pulled 3 squares and immobilized (save ends).

Deadly Screech (standard; recharge 5 6)

◆ **Thunder**

Close burst 4; +12 versus Fortitude; 1d6 + 4 thunder damage, and the target is dazed (save ends).

Alignment: Evil	**Languages:** Common

Skills: Stealth +10

Str: 15 (+5)	**Dex:** 15 (+5)	**Wis:** 14 (+5)
Con: 15 (+5)	**Int:** 10 (+3)	**Cha:** 19 (+7)

✔ **Speed:** The monster's speed in one move action, counted in squares on the battle grid. This section also discusses special movement forms a monster may have, such as the harpy's ability to fly.

✔ **Attacks/Powers:** The monster's attacks and powers are listed next, including attack bonus, what defense the attack targets, and damage. Some powers can be used every round (at-will), some only once per battle (encounter), and others can be recharged during the battle. At the start of the harpy's turn, check to see if its *deadly screech* power recharges. Roll 1d6. If you roll a 5 or a 6, the power recharges and can be used again.

For each attack and power listed, you have info about modifiers and what defense the attack or power targets. When the harpy attacks, roll 1d20 and add the modifier for the power used (+11 versus AC for the claw attack, for example, or +12 versus Will for the *alluring song*).

✔ **Alignment and Languages:** What alignment is typical of the monster type in question, and what languages it usually speaks.

✔ **Skills:** If a monster has training in any skills, they are listed here.

✔ **Ability Scores:** The monster's ability scores are shown. The number in parentheses is the modifier used when the monster makes an untrained skill check or ability check.

✔ **Equipment:** Finally, if a monster carries any equipment, it's listed here.

Deciding what the bad guys do

After you've looked up a monster in the *Monster Manual* or created an evil NPC and you know what that monster or villain *can* do, it's natural to ask what it *will* do. The stat block helps in this regard. In the case of the harpy, it switches from claw attacks and its *alluring song* power round after round, occasionally breaking out its *deadly screech* power. Monsters with a few more powers have more choices, but not so many that you can't handle the decision making.

Any monster or villain should consider taking one of three actions each round. Not all monsters will be able to use all three choices; for example, an ogre doesn't command any magic or have any special attacks. Just ignore the choices that don't apply. The three choices for a monster's or villain's action in a given round are as follows:

✔ **Hit something:** If the monster or villain is standing next to one of the heroes, it can make a basic melee attack. Use the monster's basic melee attack, whatever that may be; you roll a d20, add the attack bonus, and see whether the score equaled or beat the player's AC. (If the monster has a basic ranged attack — for example, a goblin with a crossbow — it can attack at range, of course.)

✔ **Move:** If the monster isn't standing next to one of the heroes but needs to get next to a hero in order to use its basic melee attack, it will need to move and get into fighting range. A monster can move up to its speed and make a single attack in the same round. Or the monster can move up to twice its speed and make a single attack by taking a charge action. (See page 287 in the *Player's Handbook.*)

✔ **Use a power:** If the monster or villain can cast spells or has some other kind of power, it can use a power instead of making a basic melee or ranged attack. Use your discretion — some powers can be used only once, and others can be used again only after they recharge (see the Attack/Powers bullet in the previous section).

Fighting smart, fighting dumb

Say you've got a half-fiend red dragon attacking the players. It's got a fiery breath weapon, awesome melee attacks, nasty evil spell-like abilities, and — oh yeah — it can fly, too. Which of its attacks will it use on its next round, and which character will be ground zero for all this dragon beat-down?

The first thing you want to do is take a look at your monster's Intelligence score. Is it a voracious, mindless creature like a huge monstrous centipede? If so, the most realistic thing for that monster to do is simply move toward the nearest character and try to eat him or her. That's what big, dumb bugs would do. Is it a clever and malicious opponent like a demon or devil? If that's the case, it fights with cunning and cruelty, switching easily from attack to defense and using patience and guile if necessary.

Here's some guidance on making your tactical decisions when you're running a monster or villain:

- **Intelligent foes *plan*, but dumb foes *react:*** A bugbear warrior knows that the heroes' cleric can heal up the good guys as fast as the warrior can carve them up, so he goes after the cleric with a vengeance. A dire wolf is much more likely to whirl and snap at the last character who hurt it.

- **Lead with your best:** Most monsters don't save their best attack for last. An evil wizard doesn't go through a battle throwing minor powers around when he has major powers to use. The game assumes that monsters use their best attacks.

- **Rolling to pick a target:** If you honestly don't know which character a monster is more likely to attack, there's nothing wrong with deciding the monster will randomly pick which PC to attack — for example, if four characters are within range, assign each a number and roll a d4; if two characters are close, simply roll a d6 and call evens for one PC and odds for the other.

Chapter 24

Building a Dungeon

In This Chapter

▶ Exploring adventure creation

▶ Using a sample dungeon

*I*n the previous chapter, we examine the Dungeon Master's role in running a DUNGEONS & DRAGONS game. In this chapter, we examine the basics of adventure creation. Adventure is the framework through which players work together to create memorable tales of fantasy and adventure. An adventure can be an epic tale that spans multiple locations, but at its heart, an adventure focuses on the dungeon.

In this chapter, we look at creating encounters, which are the building blocks of adventures. In the end, we get to the roots of D&D and provide you with a classic dungeon crawl to get you started.

Chapter 4 of the *Dungeon Master's Guide* goes into greater depth on creating D&D encounters, and Chapter 6 of that book discusses the art and science of creating adventures. Use the material here as a guide and to see one way to construct an adventure, and then go to the core rulebooks for more details and advice.

Creating a D&D Adventure

The player who takes on the role of the Dungeon Master has a wealth of cool and intriguing ideas to share with others. Not everyone has the discipline to write epic novels or the talent to paint vast vistas from his or her imagination, but anyone can find an outlet for creative expression and great fun as a Dungeon Master for a D&D game.

Bear in mind that when you create a D&D adventure, you don't have to fill in all the holes or connect all the dots. Unlike writing a story, where the writer determines not only the beginning of the tale but the middle and the end as well, the DM just sets the scene. What happens is determined by how the player characters react and how the dice fall. The DM sets up the basic plot and structure of the adventure, but he or she doesn't come up with any of the conclusions.

This leads to one of the great enjoyments of the game: surprise. The DM might know what monsters and scenes the adventure includes, but he or she doesn't know how things will turn out. The twists and turns of adventures are often as surprising to the DM as they are to the players.

Parts of an adventure

Adventure creation may seem like a daunting task. The best way to approach it is by examining the individual parts of an adventure. An *adventure* is a collection of related encounters that offer a rudimentary storyline. (An adventure is also sometimes called a *quest* or a *module,* which goes back to the days when the industry referred to published adventures as modules.) An adventure promises a story, offers challenges that allow each player character to shine, and provides opportunities for action and roleplaying.

The DM needs to think in terms of beginnings, scenes, and situations that kick off action and offer players choices of behavior. "What does your character do now?" is a question DMs often ask players. Don't think in terms of endings, because you want your adventure to reach a conclusion through the actions and ideas of the players and their characters.

The premise and motivation

An adventure starts with a premise, a hook that catches the players' interests and involves their characters in some motivating manner. Think in terms of setup and build from there. The player characters can get involved in the premise, but they need a motivation to carry on. More than one motivation might suggest itself, and different PCs can have different motivations that drive them to take on an adventure. *Character* motivations include greed, fear, revenge, morality, curiosity, and need. *Player* motivation boils down to seeking to gain experience to improve a character and to having fun playing the game.

Here are some examples of adventure premises and motivations:

- **Adventure premise:** A hostile kobold tribe has claimed the abandoned manor and is using it as a staging area for raids on defenseless travelers using the nearby trade road.

  Motivation: The adventurers are offered a large reward to stop the kobold raids.

✔ **Adventure premise:** A scholar of ancient lore needs a group of brave adventurers to explore the haunted graveyard and find the tomb of Eldrup the Insane.

Motivation: The scholar offers the adventurers a valuable magic item and ritual if they agree to find the tomb.

✔ **Adventure premise:** A gang of orcs has taken Oleem, the beloved pet cat of the village elder's daughter.

Motivation: One of the adventurers is extremely fond of the elder's daughter and hopes to impress her by rescuing Oleem.

You can imagine how any of these premises and motivations can create adventures. You just need to sketch out a number of related encounters, populate them with monsters and other obstacles, and draw a map.

Encounters

Encounters are where the action and drama of every adventure take place. Every encounter is kind of like a miniature, concentrated version of the entire adventure. An encounter has a hook and a setup. It has a location. It has a goal that, when attained, ends the encounter and pushes the characters deeper into the adventure.

Encounter goals usually can be summed up by the verb that best describes the required action — *capture, defeat, discover, destroy, escape, find, negotiate, obtain, protect, rescue,* and *survive* are a few examples. In an encounter, characters might have to *capture* the master thief, *discover* the secret door, *negotiate* with the ogre mage, or *rescue* the merchant from the mind flayer's slave pen.

There are three types of encounters:

✔ **Challenge encounters** provide some kind of hazard, trap, or obstacle that the characters must overcome to attain the goal. Skills, powers, and ability checks are the tools that characters usually employ to overcome challenge encounters.

✔ **Combat encounters** feature creatures or opponents that the characters might have to battle in order to win the encounter. Combat abilities and powers see the most use in these kinds of encounters.

✔ **Social encounters** involve a DM-controlled character (a nonplayer character, or NPC) whom the player characters must interact with to attain the goal of the encounter. They might have to talk to, convince, bluff, bribe, trade insults with, seduce, negotiate, intimidate, beg, or otherwise interact with the NPC in order to advance the plot. A social encounter can lead to or become a challenge or combat encounter, depending on how things work out. Such encounters rely on roleplaying talents, and skill checks are used to augment the roleplaying and to determine the reactions of the NPCs.

Encounters are typically keyed to areas on a map. Only when the player characters arrive at the specific map area can the encounter take place. When all the encounters in an adventure take place within the confines of a specific location (such as a dungeon), the adventure is called a *site-based adventure*. This is the easiest type of adventure to create and run because the whole story works off the map you draw and the encounters you key to it.

Adventure structure

Good adventures provide choices, points at which the players can make important decisions that have significant impact on what happens next. Choices can be as simple as providing the option to go right or left at an intersection in a dungeon corridor, or as complex as giving the characters the option to retrieve the *crimson wand of doom* or destroy it in the dwarven furnace of the undercity.

Good adventures combine the different kinds of encounters and vary the experiences they provide. Attack, defense, problem-solving, roleplaying, and investigation should all come into play in varying degrees. Good adventures are exciting. They provide rising and falling tension, building action, increasing stakes, and fantastic locations that add to the ambience. Finally, good adventures provide encounters that make use of the abilities of the player characters. If one of the players in your group has a rogue character, but you never provide that character with the opportunity to be stealthy and use his or her rogue skills, that player will have less fun and few opportunities to shine.

Site-based versus event-based adventures

The adventures discussed in this book are site-based adventures, meaning that they're set in a single location that is driven by exploration more than story or a complex plotline. Easy to create and easy to run, site-based adventures such as *The Tomb of Horrors* and *The Temple of Elemental Evil* are infamous among long-time D&D players for their simplicity and sheer genius.

A more challenging adventure to create is an *event-based adventure,* an adventure built around a series of events that the characters can influence through their actions. The characters have a complex goal or mission that they must accomplish, and the encounters that take place are a direct result of that effort. There may be maps for many of the encounters, but the events take place over a course of time or as triggered by previous events and keyed to a flowchart, timeline, or some combination of the two. Chapter 6 of the *Dungeon Master's Guide* provides more details on these sorts of adventures.

Conversely, don't restrict character actions or lead the characters around by their noses just to make sure they get to see every detail of your adventure. Don't create situations where the PCs are spectators, watching NPCs accomplish all the important tasks. Beware of putting your PCs in situations where they must be saved by the intervention of others — that's just not heroic. And don't look for ways to countermand or foil what the characters are capable of. Design interesting encounters where they can employ their abilities to the best advantage or use them in new and clever ways.

The end

Each adventure eventually comes to an end. As an adventure designer, you should provide a setup for a climactic encounter, but how the adventure ends depends on the players' actions. The climactic encounter should take place in a suitably impressive location. It should feature the boss villain of the adventure, perhaps someone the characters met early on or someone they heard rumors of but don't meet until the final scene.

Sometimes an adventure finishes with a satisfying conclusion that wraps up all the loose ends. Sometimes the boss villain gets away to challenge the characters another day. And, once in awhile, the characters discover that the boss villain takes his orders from a secret, more powerful nemesis they will meet in the future.

An adventure-builder checklist

As a beginning Dungeon Master, stick to the site-based adventures until you feel you have the hang of the basics of adventure design. Here's a checklist to help you get started as an adventure designer:

- ✔ **Brainstorm** the premise of the adventure and the motivations of your player characters.

- ✔ **Sketch a map** of the adventure location(s) on a sheet of graph paper. Number each encounter site on the map.

- ✔ **Choose the opponents** that will populate the adventure, from the weakest minions to the most powerful boss villains.

- ✔ **Flesh out and key each encounter** with notes, tactics, and statistics.

- ✔ **Check everything over** and try to think like your players. Look for clever ways to overcome certain encounters that don't necessarily rely on combat.

To choose monsters that are appropriate for the party's level, use the encounter level rules, monster roles (refer to Chapter 4 of the *Dungeon Master's Guide*), and the *Monster Manual* to select opponents that create an appropriate challenge for your party. In general, most of the encounters you create for a particular adventure should have encounter levels equal to or one level higher than the party's level. A few challenging encounters can have an encounter level that's two or three levels higher than the party's level, while a couple of easy encounters can be one or two levels lower than the party. The climax of the adventure can have an encounter level that's three or four levels higher than the party's. The levels of all the opponents in the encounter determine the encounter's level. Just add up each monster's experience points (XP). The total tells you the encounter level based on how many PCs are in the party. (The sample dungeon later in this chapter provides examples of this in play.)

Here's one final nugget of advice — you don't have to follow any set order when you create an adventure. You can start with a single cool encounter idea and build an adventure around it. You can sketch out a map and then fill in the details. Be creative, have fun, and don't sweat the details.

Sample Dungeon: Hall of the Spider God

This section explores adventure creation by providing you with a finished sample that you can play and use as a model for your own adventures. It's designed for a party of four 1st-level adventurers — a fighter, a rogue, a wizard, and a cleric. Use the ready-to-play characters presented in Chapters 3 through 6. It will be somewhat tougher if your party has fewer than four characters, and a bit easier if the party contains more than four characters.

Adventure premise

The long-abandoned dungeon of the evil wizard Volnudar is rumored to lie in the hills overlooking the town of Briston. In recent days, seven townsfolk have disappeared and strange creatures have been seen lurking in the shadows of the hills. The town elders have come to the reluctant conclusion that something stirs in the hidden corridors that once reverberated with the arcane evil of Volnudar. Now the call goes out: The town elders will reward the party of adventurers who investigate the hills and learn the fate of the missing townsfolk. The wizard is long gone, but something evil still resides in the vile dungeon.

What threatens the town and lurks in the dungeon? A band of monsters, led by the bugbear Broot, have made the dungeon their home and have been launching small raids into the town. They worship an even worse monster that they discovered in the dungeon — a giant spider that Broot has named Sperrin!

Using the battle grid

One side of the battle grid available at `www.dummies.com/cheatsheet/ dungeonsdragons4thedition` features a map of dungeon rooms and corridors. Use that map as Volnudar's hidden dungeon. The battle grid should be placed on the table within reach of all the players and the Dungeon Master.

If you have a vinyl battle mat or *D&D Dungeon Tiles* and some miniatures, you can use those instead. Just use Figure 24-1 as the basis for the dungeon you draw on the vinyl battle mat or the *D&D Dungeon Tiles* you lay out.

Using the character and monster markers

This sample adventure makes use of all the monsters provided as markers along the edge of the battle grid. The statistics for the monsters are provided later in this chapter. There are also markers that you can use to represent the adventurers, one for each of the four classes presented in this book.

Place the markers representing the adventurers in the corridor near the space marked A on the map. Let the players arrange the markers as they see fit, as long as all characters start out in the corridor squares to the far left side of the map. Remember that each character must occupy a space, and only one character can be in a square at any time.

Put the monster markers to the side. Don't place them on the battle grid until the adventure tells you to.

Adventure key

The Hall of the Spider God features five encounters. The key is numbered, but the encounters can occur in any order, depending on where the characters explore and when. Refer to the keyed locations when the characters approach or enter the numbered areas on the map (see Figure 24-1).

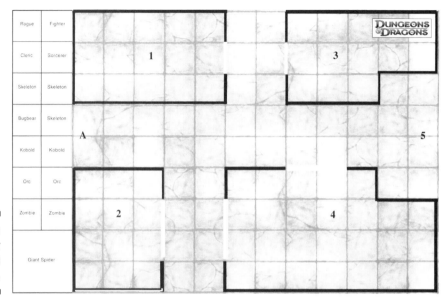

Figure 24-1:
The key for
the
dungeon.

Starting the adventure

After the players place the markers representing their characters, as described previously, the DM reads the following out loud:

> "You entered the hills above the town of Briston at the request of the town elders. Six members of the town have mysteriously disappeared over the past few days, and the elders have offered a reward for their safe return or an explanation as to their fate. You have heard rumors that an evil wizard once called these hills his home and that his dungeon remains somewhere beneath the hills. You also learned that mysterious creatures have been seen lurking in the hills, and the elders believe that these creatures might be the source of the trouble that has descended upon Briston.

> "After much searching, you discovered an opening in the hillside. Now you find yourselves in a dark corridor of shaped stone that must be part of the evil wizard's lost dungeon."

Encounter Area A
Encounter Level — None

Not every encounter provides a challenge or an obstacle. This one simply sets the stage for the rest of the adventure, and so it doesn't have a listed level.

The dungeon corridor where the PCs enter has a dank smell of stale air and age. Lichen streaks the corridor walls, glowing with an eldritch light that provides shadowy illumination.

Ask the players to make Perception checks for their characters. To make a Perception check, each player rolls a d20 and adds his or her character's Perception skill modifier. The DC for the check is 20.

Failed Perception Check (result is less than 20): The character doesn't hear or notice anything out of the ordinary in the dark corridor.

Successful Perception Check (result is 20 or better): The character hears the distant sound of snorts and guttural laughter. (This is coming from Encounter Area 5.)

Next: When the characters have looked around and made whatever preparations they want to, it's time to move deeper into the dungeon. If the characters stick to the corridor and head toward the sound, go on to Encounter Area 5. If they move toward one of the closed doors, go on to that encounter.

Encounter Area 1
Encounter Level 1 (400 XP)

When the characters approach the door to this room, read the following out loud:

> "The door ahead hangs open the smallest amount, revealing a narrow crack of torchlight in the room beyond. What do you want to do?"

This is a combat encounter. Ask the players what their characters are doing, based on the description of the scene you just read to them.

Inside the Room: The characters might swing open the door with wild abandon or send a rogue to sneak up and check things out first. Reveal the information about the room as you see fit, depending on how the PCs approach the area.

The room is lit by four torches spaced evenly on the walls of the chamber. A solid table and chair are near the door, and a tall, muscular, fur-covered, bear-like humanoid sits there, drinking from a large stone mug and picking at the charred remains of an animal carcass. This is Broot, a bugbear who leads the band of marauders that have claimed this dungeon as their base. He has a morningstar (a spiked mace) close at hand, and he can make a Perception check if the characters try to approach the room quietly. Also in the room are two kobolds, rushing around to make sure that Broot's plate is full of meat and his mug is full of ale.

Broot's followers believe that the giant spider that resides in Encounter Area 4 is a god. Broot thinks his followers are fools, but he goes along with them because, at the very least, Broot's luck has changed for the better since meeting the spider. He has named the spider Sperrin, and he plans to feed townsfolk to it in order to keep his band happy and his luck running strong.

The far end of the room serves as a prison for the townsfolk that Broot and his band have captured. Currently, three townsfolk (two men and a woman) are tied up against the far wall opposite the door.

There is also a locked chest (DC 16 Thievery check to open) near the table. It contains some of the loot that Broot and his band have recently collected. If the PCs open the chest, they find gems and gold pieces worth 200 gp among bloody clothes and dirty rags.

Initiative Check: As soon as the PCs notice Broot and the kobolds, or Broot or the kobolds spot the PCs, call for initiative checks. Everyone rolls a d20 and adds their initiative modifier to the result. The DM rolls for Broot and for the kobolds. The rest of the encounter plays out in rounds, with characters and monster acting in initiative order.

Markers: Place the bugbear marker along the top wall of the room, two spaces from the wall with the door. Place the two kobold markers anywhere else in the room that you want. The PC markers start in the corridor. There are no markers for the prisoners; feel free to use coins or some other items to mark the positions of the prisoners along the wall farthest from the door.

Broot: The bugbear is a violent, savage foe. He's extremely confident of his own abilities and will attempt to defeat the intruding adventurers with just the help of his two kobold servants. Use the statistics in the "Bugbear" sidebar for Broot.

Kobolds: The two kobolds are cowardly, letting Broot lead the attack while they help from behind. If Broot is defeated, the kobolds try to flee the room and get help.

The Prisoners: The characters must defeat Broot and the two kobolds before they can deal with the prisoners or the locked chest they find in the room. They can easily free the townsfolk and point them to the way out after the bugbear and his helpers fall.

The townsfolk seem grateful for being rescued but nervous and weary from their ordeal. If the PCs ask the townsfolk about how they got here or what else is in the dungeon, the townsfolk explain:

Bugbear

Bugbears are savage creatures that stand 7 feet tall and are covered in coarse hair. They have long sharp fangs and flat noses, and they possess a keen love of both food and treasure.

Bugbear Warrior   **Level 5 Brute**

Medium natural humanoid   XP: 200

Initiative: +5   **Senses:** Perception +4; low-light vision

HP: 76; **Bloodied:** 38

AC: 18; **Fortitude:** 17; **Reflex:** 15; **Will:** 14

Speed: 6

      Morningstar (standard; at-will) ◆ **Weapon**
      +7 versus AC; 1d12 + 6 damage

Alignment: Evil   **Languages:** Common, Goblin

Skills: Intimidate +9; Stealth +11

Str: 20 (+7)   **Dex:** 16 (+5)   **Wis:** 14 (+4)

Con: 16 (+5)   **Int:** 10 (+2)   **Cha:** 10 (+2)

Equipment: hide armor, morningstar

"Each of us was captured by that bugbear's marauders — orcs and kobolds of the fiercest kind. One of the orcs came in and took Elar and Tob away about an hour ago. The bugbear laughed and told the orc something about making sure that Sperrin knew where her meal was coming from. When we were first brought here, there was a seventh captive, little Jammy the tailor's son. He slipped free of his ropes and ran off into the darkness. We haven't seen him since, but we've heard the bugbear asking about him every time some of his marauders entered this room."

The townsfolk don't know anything else that will help the PCs. One of them has been hiding a handful of *goodberries* that he will give to the party as a reward for rescuing them. There are five *goodberries;* each one restores 1d4 hit points of damage when eaten.

Experience Points Award: The party divides 400 XP for defeating Broot and the kobolds, and for rescuing the townsfolk.

Next: The characters should attempt to find the rest of the missing townsfolk, little Jammy and the two prisoners taken to Sperrin.

Kobolds

Kobolds are small, lizard-like humanoids about the size of halflings, with a tail, scaly hide, and a horned, doglike head.

Kobold Skirmisher · **Level 1 Skirmisher**

Small natural humanoid · XP: 100

Initiative: +5 · **Senses** Perception +0; darkvision

HP: 27; **Bloodied:** 13

AC: 15; **Fortitude:** 11; **Reflex:** 14; **Will:** 13

Speed 6

> **Spear** (standard; at-will) ♦ **Weapon**
> +6 versus AC; 1d8 damage; see also *mob attack*.

Combat Advantage
> The kobold skirmisher deals an extra 1d6 damage on melee and ranged attacks against any target it has combat advantage against.

Mob Attack
> The kobold skirmisher gains a +1 bonus to attack rolls per kobold ally adjacent to the target.

Shifty (minor; at-will)
> The kobold shifts 1 square.

Alignment: Evil · **Languages:** Common, Draconic

Skills: Acrobatics +7, Stealth +9, Thievery +9

Str: 8 (–1) · **Dex:** 16 (+3) · **Wis:** 10 (+0)

Con: 11 (+0) · **Int** 6 (–2) · **Cha:** 15 (+2)

Equipment: hide armor, spear

Encounter Area 2
Encounter Level 1 (400 XP)

When the characters approach the door to this room, read the following out loud:

> "The door ahead is open wide. As you get closer, you can smell freshly turned dirt and hear a child crying. What do you want to do?"

This can be a combat encounter or a challenge encounter, depending on how the characters approach it. Ask the players what their characters are doing, based on the description of the scene you just read to them.

Inside the Room: The floor of this chamber, unlike the rest of this dungeon, consists of dirt instead of hewn stone. In the very center of the room stands a 5-foot wide circular stone platform. Atop the platform is a small, ruffled young boy — Jammy, the tailor's son. Jammy appears tired and frightened, sitting curled in a ball and trying not to look at the room's other inhabitants.

Two skeletons and two zombies surround the platform and Jammy. They stand almost completely still, swaying ever so slightly, the red lights smoldering in their otherwise empty eye sockets fixed menacingly on the small boy. Long ago, the evil wizard Volnudar used this chamber to experiment with spells designed to raise and control the undead. If any character makes a DC 16 Arcana check, he or she realizes that the stone platform glows with an ancient magic that protects whoever stands upon it from the anger and hatred of undead creatures. That's all that keeps little Jammy safe from the animated skeletons and zombies.

The room is completely dark except for the tiny lights glowing in the skeletons' eye sockets. The skeletons ignore the characters unless they step into the room. So, if the PCs can figure out some way to get Jammy safely out of the room without stepping onto the dirt floor, their characters won't have to battle the undead creatures. If the characters do enter the room, however, call for initiative checks. The skeletons and zombies move to attack and destroy any living creatures that enter the chamber. The only space in the room that is safe is atop the stone platform in the center.

Initiative Check: As soon as the PCs enter the room, call for initiative checks. Everyone rolls a d20 and adds their initiative modifier to the result. The DM rolls for the skeletons and zombies (one check covers both skeletons, and one check covers both zombies). The rest of the encounter plays out in rounds, with characters and monster acting in initiative order. Use the statistics in the "Skeleton" and "Zombie" sidebars for the monsters.

Markers: Place the two skeleton markers and two zombie markers around the square with the 2 in it (that's where Jammy sits atop the platform). The PC markers start in the corridor. Use a coin or some other item to mark the location of Jammy atop the platform in the center of the room.

Jammy: The characters must defeat the skeletons or otherwise get Jammy out of this chamber before they can have a meaningful conversation with the boy. Then they need to make a DC 16 Diplomacy check to calm him down enough for him to explain what happened. Once calm, he tells the PCs that the small lizard people chased him into the room, and he felt safe when they didn't follow him in. Then the skeletons and zombies rose up out of the dirt and surrounded him. He tells the PCs the following after they point him toward the exit:

> "There's something really bad in that room across the hall. Really, really bad." Then, after a pause and in a whisper, "It eats people."

Experience Points Award: The party divides 400 XP for defeating the undead creatures and/or rescuing little Jammy from the room.

Encounter Area 3 (Part 1)
Encounter Level 2 (500 XP)

This is a challenge encounter that has a trap and a locked door.

When the characters approach the door to this room, read the following out loud:

> "The door ahead is closed. The heavy wood of the door features ornate carvings of strange symbols that seem to glow with a faint light. What do you want to do?"

This starts out as a challenge encounter because the characters must find a way to get past the locked door. If they enter the chamber beyond, they face a combat encounter and the possibility of a magical reward.

Skeleton

Skeletons are the animated bones of humans that wear the tattered remnants of clothes and carry scimitars and shields. The only sign of life, other than the fact that they move with purpose and menace, is the malevolent red fire that glows in their empty eye sockets.

Skeleton Fighter	**Level 1 Soldier**
Medium natural animate (undead)	XP: 100

Initiative: +3 　　　　**Senses:** Perception +2; darkvision

HP: 29; **Bloodied:** 14

AC: 16; **Fortitude:** 13; **Reflex:** 14; **Will:** 13

Immune: disease, poison

Speed: 6

　　　Scimitar (standard; at-will) ♦ **Weapon**
　　　+6 versus AC; 1d8 + 2 damage

Alignment: Unaligned 　　　　**Languages:** —

Str: 15 (+2) 　　**Dex:** 17 (+3) 　　**Wis:** 14 (+2)

Con: 13 (+1) 　　**Int:** 3 (–4) 　　**Cha:** 3 (–4)

Equipment: heavy shield, scimitar

Zombie

Zombies are the animated corpses of humans that shamble about as they follow the commands of their sinister creators. Half decayed and partially consumed by worms, zombies wear the tattered remains of their grave clothes and smell like putrid death.

Zombie   **Level 1 Brute**

Medium natural animate (undead)   XP: 100

Initiative: –2   **Senses:** Perception +0; darkvision

HP: 30; **Bloodied:** 15

AC: 13; **Fortitude:** 13; **Reflex:** 9; **Will:** 10

Immune: disease, poison; **Resist:** 10 necrotic; **Vulnerable:** 5 radiant

Speed: 4

Slam (standard; at-will)
        +5 versus AC; 2d6 damage

Zombie Weakness
        Any critical hit to the zombie reduces it to 0 hit points instantly.

Alignment: Unaligned   **Languages:** —

Str: 14 (+2)   **Dex:** 6 (–2)   **Wis:** 8 (–1)

Con: 10 (+0)   **Int:** 1 (–5)   **Cha:** 3 (–4)

The Locked Door: The PCs can check the door and determine that it's locked. The door also has a mechanical trap that, when triggered by a Thievery or Strength check used on the door, shocks anyone touching the door or the lock for 1d6 + 3 damage. The trap resets after one hour. Here are some options for dealing with the door:

Perception Checks: Call for DC 10 Perception checks when the PCs start to examine the door. Any character that succeeds notices some scratches around the ancient lock. It looks like the marauders tried to gain entry into this chamber and failed.

Searching: A rogue character can search the door for traps by making a DC 20 Perception check. If the check succeeds, the rogue finds indication of a resetting mechanical trap, which probably discouraged the marauders from further attempts to open the door. If the check fails, the door appears to be safe and trap-free as far as the rogue can determine.

Thievery Check: If a rogue notices the trap (by making a successful Perception check), he or she can try to disarm it. This requires a DC 20 Thievery check. If the check succeeds, the trap is disarmed. If the check fails by 4 or less, the rogue can try to disarm it again. If the check fails by 5 or more, the rogue springs the trap.

Unlock the Door: A rogue can attempt to unlock the door. This requires a DC 16 Thievery check. If the trap has been disarmed, there is no danger. If it hasn't been disarmed, any attempt to pick the lock (whether it succeeds or not) springs the trap. If the rogue successfully picks the lock, even if doing so sets off the trap, the door can be opened any time thereafter.

Bashing Down the Door: If the rogue's Thievery check fails, or the party doesn't have a rogue, the door can be bashed open. This requires one character to make a DC 18 Strength check. This is an ability check; roll a d20 and add the character's Strength modifier. Here's a situation where a special action, *aid another,* can be used. One other character can help the acting character to try to bash open the door. The helping character also makes a Strength check, but the DC is 10. If the helping character succeeds, the acting character receives a +2 bonus to his or her Strength checks. The characters can make as many attempts as they want to bash down the door. The first time a character tries to bash down the door, he or she sets off the trap (if it hasn't been disarmed). Each attempt to bash down the door, successful or not, makes a lot of noise. Make a Perception check (DC 15) for the orcs in Encounter Area 5 each time a character makes a Strength check to bash down the door. If the orcs successfully hear the racket, the creatures from Encounter Area 5 (see the later section, "Encounter Area 5") start to move toward Encounter Area 3.

Experience Points Award: The party divides 500 XP for disarming the trap and opening the door.

Encounter Area 3 (Part 2)
Encounter Level 1 (400 XP)

When the characters open the door to this room, read the following out loud:

> "The door opens into a thick darkness. What do you want to do?"

The PCs need some sort of light in order to explore this chamber effectively. After they light a torch or otherwise illuminate the scene, read the following out loud:

> "The chamber features rows of dusty shelves and strangely shaped crates. Cobwebs hang from the ceiling, and dust swirls in the air around you. Then you hear a disturbing sound from somewhere deep in the shadows: a moaning, threatening sound, and the shuffle of heavy feet slowly moving toward you. What do you do?"

Inside the Room: This was one of the ancient wizard's storerooms. Few of his most powerful items remain, but if the PCs can defeat the chamber's guardians, they can find some helpful items and treasure here.

One human zombie and three skeletons guard this chamber. They were placed here long ago by Volnudar and continue to follow the last orders they were given — let no living creature enter this area and survive. Use the statistics from Encounter Area 2.

Initiative Check: As soon as the PCs light up the room or enter the chamber, call for initiative checks. Everyone rolls a d20 and adds their initiative modifier to the result. The DM rolls for the zombie and skeletons. The rest of the encounter plays out in rounds, with characters and monster acting in initiative order.

Markers: Place the zombie marker and three skeleton markers in the chamber, two near the center and two near the far wall. The PC markers start in the corridor.

Treasure: After the PCs defeat the undead creatures, they can examine the room. Among the crumbling scrolls and dusty vials, they find two *potions of healing*. It requires a minor action to drink a potion. After drinking the potion, the character spends a healing surge and regains 10 hit points.

If anyone decides to search, the character that gets the highest result Perception check over 20 finds a magic weapon wrapped in cloth. The weapon matches the character's primary weapon, except that it is a +1 version of that weapon (meaning it has a magical +1 bonus on attack and damage rolls and deals +1d6 damage on a crit). For example, if Regdar rolls the highest Search result over 20, he finds a *+1 greatsword* that he can use instead of his mundane weapon.

Experience Points Award: The party divides 400 XP for defeating the undead monsters.

Encounter Area 4
Encounter Level 3 (600 XP)

When the characters approach either of the doors that lead to this room, read the following out loud:

> "The door ahead is closed. You can hear chanting coming from beyond the door, but you don't understand the words. What do you want to do?"

The doors into this room are not locked. The PCs can open them easily.

Inside the Room: The first thing the PCs notice upon opening the doors is that great pans of burning coals (called braziers) are situated to either side of both sets of doors, filling the room with firelight and smoke. The second thing they notice are the two creatures kneeling before a raised platform covering the left half of the long wall. The creatures are kobolds, but they appear better armed and armored than the kobolds from area 1. Atop the platform, tied up and obviously frightened, are the last two townsfolk — Elar and Tob. The third thing is that the entire right side of the room is covered in curtains of thick, clinging webs.

If the PCs enter quietly, they can surprise the kobolds. That means that each of the PCs can perform one action (either a move or an attack) before the regular rounds of initiative begin.

When the battle is fully joined, Sperrin emerges from the webs to attack the intruders. Sperrin is a giant spider that the kobolds worship as a god. The townsfolk are meant to be a meal and a sacrifice for it.

Initiative Check: Everyone rolls a d20 and adds their initiative modifier to the result. The DM rolls once for the kobolds and once for the giant spider. The rest of the encounter plays out in rounds, with characters and monsters acting in initiative order. Use the statistics in the "Kobold dragonshield" and "Giant spider" sidebars for the monsters.

Markers: Place two kobold markers near the left side of the long wall. The PC markers start at whichever door they opened. Use a coin or some other item to mark the location of Elar and Tob atop the platform. The first time the giant spider gets to act, place its marker on the right side of the room.

Experience Points Award: The party divides 600 XP for defeating the kobolds and giant spider and for rescuing Elar and Tob from the room.

Encounter Area 5
Encounter Level 1 (300 XP)

Two orcs start out in the part of the corridor marked "5" on the map. Place their markers there when one of the following takes place: The PCs step into a square more than halfway along the corridor, or the orcs make a successful Perception check when the PCs make noise trying to open the door to Encounter Area 3.

Kobold dragonshield

Kobolds are small, lizard-like humanoids about the size of halflings, with a tail, scaly hide, and a horned, doglike head. Dragonshields wear scale armor and carry short swords.

Kobold Dragonshield   **Level 3 Soldier**

Small natural humanoid   XP: 150

Initiative: +4   **Senses:** Perception +2; darkvision

HP: 44; **Bloodied:** 22

AC: 18; **Fortitude:** 14; **Reflex:** 13; **Will:** 13

Speed: 5

Short Sword (standard; at-will) ◆ **Weapon**
> +8 versus AC; 1d6 +3 damage, and the target is marked until the end of the kobold dragonshield's next turn.

Dragonshield Tactics (immediate reaction when an adjacent enemy shifts away or an enemy moves adjacent; at-will)
> The kobold dragonshield shifts 1 square.

Mob Attack
> The kobold dragonshield gains a +1 bonus to attack rolls per kobold ally adjacent to the target.

Shifty (minor; at-will)
> The kobold shifts 1 square.

Alignment: Evil

Languages: Common, Draconic

Skills: Acrobatics +5, Stealth +7, Thievery +7

Str 14 (+3)   **Dex:** 13 (+2)   **Wis:** 12 (+2)

Con: 12 (+2)   **Int:** 0 (+0)   **Cha:** 10 (+1)

Equipment: scale armor, heavy shield, short sword

Use the orc statistics in the "Orc" sidebar for this encounter. These two creatures can be encountered alone, or they can join the undead in Encounter Area 3 to make a more challenging encounter.

Initiative Check: Make initiative checks as you have been doing throughout this adventure.

Experience Points Award: The party divides 300 XP for defeating the orc patrol.

Giant spider

A giant spider is an aggressive predator that uses a poisonous bite to subdue and eventually consume prey.

Giant Spider	**Level 3 Elite Brute**
Large natural beast (spider)	XP: 300

Initiative: +2 **Senses:** Perception +2; tremorsense 5

HP: 108; **Bloodied:** 54

AC: 15; **Fortitude:** 16; **Reflex:** 15; **Will:** 14

Speed: 4, climb 4 (spider climb)

Bite (standard; at-will) ♦ **Poison**
> +6 versus AC; 1d10 +3 damage, and the target takes ongoing 5 poison damage and is slowed (save ends both).

Claw (standard; at-will)
> +6 versus AC; 1d6 +3 damage

Double Attack (standard; at-will)
> The giant spider makes two claw attacks.

Stinging Web (standard; recharge 5 6) **Poison**
> Close blast 3; +4 versus Reflex; 1d6 +3 poison damage, and the target is immobilized (save ends).

Alignment: Unaligned **Languages:** —

Skills: Acrobatics +10, Stealth +10

Str: 18 (+5)	**Dex:** 18 (+5)	**Wis:** 12 (+2)
Con: 14 (+3)	**Int:** 1 (–4)	**Cha:** 8 (+0)

Wrapping up the adventure

What happens after the PCs have successfully rescued the townsfolk? They should return to the town elders and claim their reward (1,000 gp to split among the party). They may want to return and fully explore the ancient dungeon. What lies in the corridors beyond what the PCs have already seen? That's up to you, as the DM, but you could use it as the basis of the first adventure you create from scratch. Try it and have fun!

Orc

Orcs are aggressive humanoids with gray skin, coarse hair, and boar-like faces. They hate adventurers and seek to destroy them on sight.

Orc Raider	**Level 3 Skirmisher**
Medium natural humanoid	XP: 150

Initiative: +5   **Senses:** Perception +1; low-light vision

HP: 46; **Bloodied:** 23

AC: 17; **Fortitude:** 15; **Reflex:** 14; **Will:** 12

Speed: 6

Greataxe (standard; at-will) ◆ **Weapon**

+8 versus AC; 1d12 + 3 damage (crit 1d12 + 15)

Handaxe (standard; at-will) ◆ **Weapon**
Ranged 5/10; +7 versus AC; 1d6 + 3 damage

Alignment: Chaotic evil   **Languages:** Common, Giant

Skills: Endurance +8, Intimidate +5

Str: 17 (+4)	**Dex:** 15 (+3)	**Wis:** 10 (+1)
Con: 14 (+3)	**Int:** 8 (+0)	**Cha:** 9 (+0)

Equipment: leather armor, greataxe, four handaxes

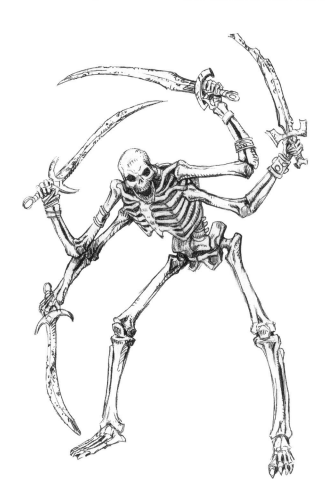

Chapter 25

Keeping Your Players Happy

. . . .

In This Chapter

▶ Knowing the player types

▶ Providing challenges for all players

▶ Making sure that everybody has fun

▶ Deciding what kind of game you want to run

. . . .

A great Dungeon Master doesn't merely run a good Dungeons & Dragons game; he or she also tells a riveting story. The D&D game works fine as a series of tactical exercises and problem-solving puzzles, but a great story-teller in the DM's seat can elevate the game to a whole other level. Building interesting story lines and villains for your adventures and presenting your players with the sort of challenges they want to face goes a long way toward making your game memorable and long-lasting.

In this chapter, we tell you about story-building and storytelling in the D&D game, and we show you some narrative, game-pacing, and campaign-building tips good for any D&D game.

Figuring Out Your Players

The first rule of any enterprise is to figure out what your customers want and give it to them. A D&D game is no different. If your players just want to kill monsters and not think too hard, they're not going to be happy with a subtle murder mystery or combat-light court intrigue. Similarly, if your players love to immerse themselves in their characters and enjoy the play-acting more than anything else, they won't be happy if you present adventures that don't give them opportunities to talk to the creatures and characters around them.

Most players fall into one of four basic categories:

> ✔ **Actors:** These are players who enjoy roleplaying for its own sake. Extreme actors would be just as happy to play D&D if it had no rules at all. Players who like this style of play often choose the ranger and rogue classes. They

like adventures that have lots of opportunities to talk to NPCs (not just villains and monsters), and they tend to dislike adventures that offer nothing but combat encounters.

✔ **Puzzle-solvers:** This type of player loves figuring out riddles and challenges in the game, and not just by rolling dice as characters in the game. Extreme puzzle-solvers would be just as happy to play D&D without rules, just like the extreme actors. Puzzle-solvers often play clerics, rogues, and wizards. Puzzle-solvers don't mind combat encounters because beating tactically challenging encounters (such as archers on a castle wall) is solving puzzles of sorts.

✔ **Hack-and-slashers:** These are players who just love to fight and beat up monsters. The bigger the fight, the happier they are. Hack-and-slashers live for dishing out the damage, and they're inclined to like the rules because the game rules help them figure out how much damage they can deal out. Hack-and-slashers often play fighters and wizards. Obviously, they like adventures with plenty of monsters to fight, and they don't like adventures that involve too much talking.

✔ **Competitors:** These are those players who play for the thrill of winning in whatever form it might take. They're happy to fight big fights and win, but unlike the hack-and-slasher, they're just as happy to win by doing roleplaying or solving tough puzzles. Competitors tend to be heavily engaged with the rules, and they don't like to throw out the rulebooks. You can throw a variety of challenges at a competitor, and he or she is happy. Competitors often play clerics, fighters, and wizards.

Now, here's the tricky part: You probably have players of more than one type in your game. One player may be an actor, another may be a hack-and-slasher, and a third player may be a competitor. The best way to keep everybody happy is to simply alternate the types of encounters to cater to your players' various interests. Intersperse roleplaying encounters with combat encounters and challenge encounters, and you can make exciting adventures that feel varied and fresh where everybody gets the game he or she wants at least some of the time.

Table 25-1 summarizes some key adventure characteristics or features and which players are happiest with them.

Table 25-1		Player Preferences		
Adventure Characteristic	**Actor**	**Puzzle-Solver**	**Hack-and-Slasher**	**Competitor**
Big but tactically simple fights	So-so	Okay	Great	Good
Fights with difficult tactical challenges	So-so	Good	Okay	Great

Adventure Characteristic	Actor	Puzzle-Solver	Hack-and-Slasher	Competitor
Challenging traps that can be avoided with some thinking	Okay	Great	So-so	Good
Encounters that offer the chance to question NPCs or piece together different stories	Great	Good	So-so	Okay
Monsters who can be negotiated with, deceived, or bluffed	Great	Okay	So-so	Good
Simple choices; easy to determine the next move or course of action	Okay	So-so	Great	Good
Complex choices; many different ways to proceed	Good	Okay	So-so	Great
Rich background and story elements	Great	Good	Okay	So-so
Opportunities to act rashly, take ridiculous actions, show off, or declare yourself king or queen	Okay	So-so	Great	Good
Opportunities to get ahead by knowing the rules better than anyone else	So-so	Okay	Good	Great

If you're trying to keep everyone happy with the same adventure, try to include some "good" or "great" situations for each player at your table.

You'll find that hack-and-slashers are a little difficult to entertain; they tend to be impatient and anxious to get to the next fight, and more than a few hack-and-slashers like to look for ways to manufacture fights if none are at hand.

This table makes hack-and-slashers look like the worst players, but that's somewhat misleading. If most of the players at the table enjoy a lot of combat and view playing D&D as a way to let off steam by pretending to kill monsters, well, who's to say that's not the right way for them to play the game? Hack-and-slashers are often pretty knowledgeable about the rules and tend to run decisive and effective characters. Sure, they're impatient to get to the fun, but a hack-and-slasher at the table can go a long way toward keeping the other players moving and motivated.

Narrating the Adventure

Knowing what your players like and catering to them is nothing more than good marketing. But a crummy movie with great marketing is still a crummy movie. What you need is some great writing and directing to get an entertainment experience that will have the players on the edges of their seats. So what can you do to run a game that's fast-paced, exciting, emotionally charged, and makes the players feel like they can slay dragons and challenge gods?

Getting ready, getting organized

It's so simple we hesitate to mention it, but we will anyway: Be ready to run your game. Read ahead on the adventure you're running, visualize how you're going to set up the key encounters and decision points, and plan for what you're going to do when the players take a wrong turn. You shouldn't be seeing an encounter for the first time when the players kick open the door to Room 7 and storm inside.

The corollary to reading ahead is organizing your materials to run the game efficiently and effectively. Nothing brings a game to a crashing halt like the DM saying, "Uh, hang on guys, I gotta do some reading." Pausing for a moment to check your notes is one thing, but sticking your nose in the book to read for 10 minutes means that your players are sitting around doing nothing but watching you read. That ain't great entertainment.

Good ways to be prepared include the following:

- ✔ **Check the rules ahead of time:** If you see that you're likely to run an encounter involving a whole gang of basilisks, refresh your memory on how the gaze attacks work and read the monster description the night before the game.

- ✔ **Make notes in your adventure:** Plan some actions or special moves for your monsters and villains ahead of time. Think about things that NPCs might say if the players wind up talking instead of fighting.

- ✔ **Keep a folder:** Organize your adventure notes and any records you're keeping (treasure the heroes find, NPCs they meet, and so on) so that you can quickly find information when you need it during play.

Creating evocative scenes

Your players are immersed in an imaginary world of soaring beauty, awesome magic, and horror beyond human endurance. It's your job to get this across with each scene you describe and every action your monsters and villains take. You don't have to stick three adjectives in front of every character or object you describe in the game, but you don't want to fall into the rut of droning, "The minotaur swings. He misses. The minotaur swings again. Uh, he gets an 18. Does that hit you?" Put some zip into it!

> **Boring:** "The room is 30 feet by 30 feet. There's a door in the north wall, and a stairway leading down. There's an ogre in here."

Better: "The room smells dank and musty. It looks like an old cellar, with thick cobwebs in the blackened rafters. A towering creature with long arms and a crooked, fang-filled jaw glares at you, clutching a spiked club in its knotted fists. Behind it you think you see a battered old door in the north wall, and a set of stairs leading down into darkness."

Boring: "The ogre charges and attacks. It rolls a 23. It hits you for 17 points of damage."

Better: "The hulking monster throws back its head and howls in rage, and then it throws itself at you! It brings its spiked club whistling down in a deadly arc — that's a 23 to hit. Unnh! A mighty blow sends you reeling. You take 17 points of damage. 'Ha! I SMASH!' the creature bellows."

Boring: "The hell hound breathes fire. You take 8 fire damage."

Better: "The coal-black hound suddenly belches out a great blast of searing green flames. You take 8 points of fire damage."

Using the cut-scene

One handy trick for DMing multiple tasks at the same time is the cut-scene. Here's the idea: Give one player and whatever task he's involved in 5 to 10 minutes of your time, but then put that situation on hold and switch over to work with another player on whatever she's doing. It's like a movie that hops between a couple of different characters doing different things. It's a great tool for pacing because it lets you briefly "cliffhanger" a player in a challenging position (which builds suspense) while you involve another player who otherwise wouldn't be immediately involved in the scene (which keeps the players out of the key action from getting bored).

Cut-scenes work best when the party is split up. If some characters are fighting against assassins in a dark alleyway while other characters are trying to help the elven ambassador make her escape, you can easily switch back and forth between the two groups.

Cut-scenes also work on a smaller scale, when players are engaged in different tasks in the same area. For example, say that the PCs are searching through an evil wizard's laboratory. One might be searching for secret doors, another might be looking through the mysterious old tomes on the bookshelf for any interesting clues, and a third player might be talking to the wizard's captive, a human hero chained to the wall. You might start by DMing the player's conversation with the captive hero. Then when you reach a good break in the conversation, you switch over to tell another player what her rogue found when she searched the room. Then you switch over to the player whose character was looking at the books. As the DM, you're the director of the movie; you decide which player you're going to talk to, for how long, and where you're going to cut away to next.

Running a Fun Game

If you're creating interesting adventures for your players and you're doing a good job of narrating and pacing the game, you're ahead of the eight ball. However, the game isn't all about the adventures you write and your ability to describe the action — you want to run a fun and entertaining game as much as a well-crafted one.

Using props

One great way to take your players from *listening* to *experiencing* is to introduce some props in your game. If the players defeat the sly rogue who's been carrying coded messages for the thieves' guild, make up a set of cryptic coded messages ahead of time, write them on a piece of paper, and crumple it up for effect — and if you stain the paper with tea or coffee, you might even get it to look a little like parchment. (If you don't want to mess with staining paper, you can find colored paper and parchment paper at any office supply store.) Not only will the puzzle-solvers in your group have a great time unraveling your code, but everyone else will like passing around a tangible object they can peer at and study, just as their characters would.

Old maps and secret messages are easy props to come up with. If you want to go a step further, try handfuls of old coins (especially foreign currency), tarot cards, books in foreign languages, and sketches or artwork. Anything that lets your players visualize the scene or item you're describing verbally is great. Not every encounter or challenge deserves a prop or handout, but a few here and there go a long way toward keeping your players interested and alert.

One prop you might not have thought of is a soundtrack. A little music played softly in the background as you play the game can be very evocative. You want to consider your music choice carefully, of course; the ideal piece is something that's orchestral, doesn't have many words or singing for the DM to compete with, and frankly just feels like it fits with the D&D game. Movie soundtracks can be great for this, especially from fantasy or science fiction movies — you could do worse than to play the soundtracks for the three *The Lord of the Rings* movies, for example. Some companies actually produce soundtracks specifically to serve as roleplaying background music.

Table rules

Every group of D&D players gradually evolves a set of *table rules* — conventions for starting new characters, looking up rules on the fly, urging other players to take specific actions, or simply whether to reroll or read as it lies when a die is cocked or falls on the floor. These rules really don't have much to do with the D&D game, because your table rules might conceivably apply to any number of other games you play with the same group of players. But it's a good idea to lay out your expectations on this sort of thing before an argument comes up about what is or isn't allowed at the table.

Some things you ought to clarify ahead of time include the following:

- ✔ What to do when a player can't make the game. (Specifically, is his or her character present in the party or not, and who controls the character if he or she is?)

- ✔ Which rulebooks and supplements you allow players to refer to in play. (Many DMs prefer that players don't look up monsters in a *Monster Manual* while their characters are fighting the creature in question.)

- ✔ Whether or not you allow "take backs" if a player figures out that his or her attack roll was really a 24 instead of a 21 after his or her action is over.

If you're a new DM running the game for an experienced group, you might want to simply adopt the table rules of the previous DM until you feel comfortable with instituting your own. You can find a good discussion on table rules on page 14 of the *Dungeon Master's Guide*.

How honest should you be?

You're DMing a furious fight. James' paladin Baredd gets hit by the evil wizard's *lightning bolt* and gets knocked down to 2 hit points. Then the wizard's ogre henchman rolls a 20 against Baredd and scores a critical hit with his great-club. Baredd's going to eat a lot of damage with that attack. Do you let this lucky hit kill Baredd outright? Or do you fudge the result and tell James that Baredd got hit for 15 damage, keeping the critical to yourself so that you don't kill James' character? (Now, even so, Baredd's at −13 hit points, which means he's unconscious and dying.)

There isn't an easy answer to this one. Some DMs let the dice do their work, and they don't cut any breaks for the player characters or the bad guys. Other DMs feel that a character death is a pretty big occurrence, and it shouldn't happen "by mistake" — so, as long as the dice were rolled behind the *DM's screen* (an accessory that a DM uses to keep notes and maps hidden from the players) and no players observed the result, it's okay to fudge by announcing a miss or two when a monster really would have hit.

Our recommendation for a beginning DM is to avoid fudging and to let your players know you're going to let the dice fall where they may. If you do decide to fudge the dice behind the screen, don't announce it to the players and don't make it obvious. You shouldn't intercede to rescue every character on the threshold of death, because if your players realize that there's no chance for their characters to be killed, their enjoyment of the game will be diminished — no risk and no challenge means no suspense. And if the players attempted something that was obviously highly risky (or simply stupid), you shouldn't protect them from the consequences of their own poor decisions.

One more thing: Just because the DM may fudge the rolls every now and then, we strongly advise you not to try to do this as a player. When DMs "cheat," it's usually for the effort of improving the play experience of everyone at the table. If you cheat by pretending you didn't roll badly as a player, you're doing it to beat the game. It's only going to lead to a diminished experience for you and may, in fact, cause a lot of trouble around the table if you're caught doing it. Most players can't abide a cheater, even one who's on their side.

Game balance

Keeping a game fun and interesting requires that you keep an eye on the balance of your game. Game balance basically comes down to these two aspects:

✔ **Measure risk versus reward.** This basically measures how dangerous your dungeon is compared to the payoff in treasure, experience, and the fun your players get out of the game session. If your adventures just cream party after party of PCs or if you can't remember the last time you got a PC down to half his or her hit points, your game might be out of balance. It's not fun to lose all the time — and believe it or not, it's not really fun to win all the time, either. A healthy game features a sprinkling of setbacks and retreats that the players can learn from.

✔ **Watch out for magic treasure that is useful only for one character.**
If you put a *+4 flaming keen bastard sword* in your adventure, you have to figure that the fighter in the party will claim this item. If the only other choices in the monster hoard are a *+2 ring of protection* and a couple of *potions of healing,* somebody in the party just scored ten times better than everybody else. You can give unique and powerful treasures to characters, but you can't give those items to the same character every game session.

Part V
The Part of Tens

The 5th Wave   By Rich Tennant

"I don't want to be Kerwin the Rogue. I want to be Cliff the roofer, who was sent here to check for leaks in the ceiling."

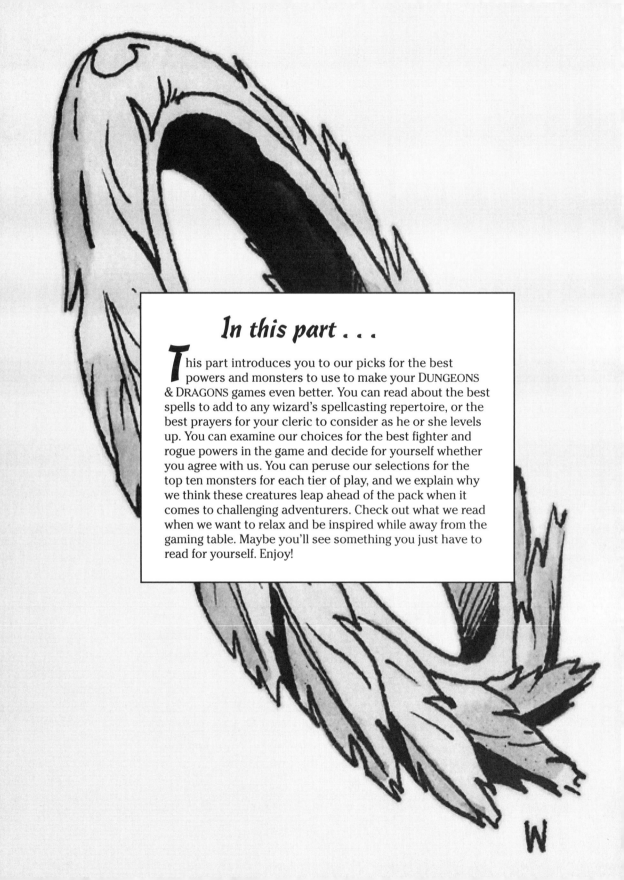

In this part . . .

This part introduces you to our picks for the best powers and monsters to use to make your DUNGEONS & DRAGONS games even better. You can read about the best spells to add to any wizard's spellcasting repertoire, or the best prayers for your cleric to consider as he or she levels up. You can examine our choices for the best fighter and rogue powers in the game and decide for yourself whether you agree with us. You can peruse our selections for the top ten monsters for each tier of play, and we explain why we think these creatures leap ahead of the pack when it comes to challenging adventurers. Check out what we read when we want to relax and be inspired while away from the gaming table. Maybe you'll see something you just have to read for yourself. Enjoy!

Chapter 26

The Ten Best Fighter Powers

*W*hat's so complicated about fighter powers? Fighters hit the bad guys with a big hunk of metal — usually sharp metal. When a fighter is higher level, he or she hits harder. How is that confusing?

Choosing the power offering the biggest damage potential at every level isn't a bad strategy. But we're going to help you mix up offense, defense, control, and versatility by pointing out powers that trade off damage for effects that are even more useful. Sometimes doing a pile of damage to one monster is exactly what you want, but other times you want to hit multiple foes or hit one foe and add a nasty side effect like stun or daze to your attack.

The very sneaky and confusing things you *do* need to look out for are the weapon keywords associated with fighter exploits. You can use any fighter power with any weapon . . . but many powers simply work better with a specific weapon, and you're missing out if you use the wrong weapon. We're not going to worry about weapon keywords in this list of ten best fighter powers, but you should when you build your character's list of favorite powers.

We excluded powers of 16th level or higher from this list on purpose. Naturally, high-level exploits are better than low-level exploits; if we compiled a list of fighter exploits strictly by power level, we'd use ten epic-level exploits. That's not so useful if you're playing a low-level fighter and you're trying to decide which power you need right now. This is a list of ten fighter powers that will help your character get off to a great start in his or her career, not the ten most awesome fighter powers.

For a full description of each power (its effects, amount of damage dealt, duration, and so on) listed here, see Chapter 4 of the *Player's Handbook*.

10. Anvil of Doom

13th-level encounter attack power

One of the most powerful rider effects you can dish out in an attack is stunning; when you stun a monster, you take away its next turn, and you also give all your allies combat advantage (a +2 bonus to hit) against that monster until it recovers. *Anvil of doom* is an encounter attack exploit that gives you decent damage (double weapon dice) and stuns the target, if you're using a hammer or a mace. If you're not, you just daze the target — but dazing is pretty good, too. Either way, you aren't going to be unhappy with dazing or stunning an opponent once every encounter.

Oh, and it's one of the two or three coolest power names in the game. Don't you want to say "I hit it with *anvil of doom*" every fight?

9. Reaping Strike

1st-level at-will attack power

At-will powers are relatively weak, but it's important to choose the right ones. In long battles, you can exhaust your encounter and daily powers, which means you're left with wearing down the enemy with powers that never run out. *Reaping strike* is good because you deal a little bit of damage on a miss — specifically, damage equal to your Strength modifier if you're using a two-handed weapon. Assuming your fighter has a Strength score of 18, that's 4 points of damage, guaranteed. It might not seem like much, but if you're fighting a monster that's extremely hard to hit, you might have to settle for "the death of a thousand cuts" to complete the battle.

8. Precise Strike

3rd-level encounter attack power

Every so often, you're going to come up against a monster or an enemy that you just can't hit. Its defenses are just too high. This might be because you've run into a difficult encounter with enemies that are three or more levels higher than you or because a boss monster might be wearing really good armor. Either way, the *precise strike* power allows you to trade damage for accuracy.

This power might deal only a single weapon die of damage plus your Strength modifier, but it comes with an automatic +4 attack bonus to help you hit when you really can't afford to miss the target.

7. Serpent Dance Strike

15th-level daily attack power

Okay, so if it's a 15th-level daily power, it had *better* be good. Fortunately, *serpent dance strike* measures up. You attack a target, and if you hit, you deal double weapon damage and knock the target prone. Then you can shift one square, and do the same thing to a second target. Then, you can shift again and do the *same attack* to a *third* target! Swing, step, swing, step, swing — three monsters take good damage and wind up on the ground. Knocking enemies prone is useful, because your allies gain combat advantage against them until they stand up. If you have a rogue friend, this power is especially good. (Granting combat advantage to a rogue really helps deal out the damage!) The only downside is that you can only knock down targets who are your size or smaller, so you can't put trolls or giants or big demons on the pavement with this power.

6. Unbreakable

6th-level encounter utility power

This is one of those defensive powers we mentioned at the beginning of this chapter. Once per encounter, reduce the damage you take from an attack by 5 + your Constitution modifier. If your Constitution is, say, 16, that means –8 damage from an attack that just hit you. That might not seem terribly impressive, but consider this: You're the front line, and you're going to get hit *in every single battle of your character's life.* We think the smart way to use a power like this is to fire it off the first time you get hit in an encounter; after all, you don't know how many times you're going to be hit in that fight, so you might as well make sure you use it each encounter.

5. Sweeping Blow

3rd-level encounter attack power

Sweeping blow is a great power because it's the first true area-effect attack you can get as a fighter. It affects every enemy in a Close burst 1 — in other words, every enemy adjacent to you. You can easily attack two or three enemies in one action with this power. Better yet, you get a nice accuracy bonus if you're wielding the right weapon, and the list of weapons is generous.

Sweeping blow is less useful in encounters where you're fighting a solo monster or monsters that are spread out over a good distance. However, we think you'll be able to use it to attack two enemies at once in 70 or 80 percent of your encounters. The only question is picking the right moment. For this power, you want to take advantage of its multiple-target effectiveness and wait until you can catch two or three bad guys with it . . . but it's better to use it early to less effect than to wait for the perfect moment and never use it at all.

4. Dizzying Blow

5th-level daily attack power

Early in your fighter's career, the damage differential between your powers is pretty simple: Is it a 1[W], 2[W], or 3[W] power? (That means normal weapon damage die, double weapon damage dice, or triple weapon damage dice.)

Usually it's better to accept a little less damage and deliver an attack with superior accuracy, multiple targets, or a good rider of some kind, but *dizzying blow* delivers on two of these counts at once: It's a 3[W] power that immobilizes the target. Immobilizing enemies makes your job as a defender easy; if the monsters can't reach your allies to attack them, you're doing a good job of defending them.

Dizzying blow is also interesting because it's an example of a type of a Reliable power. When you use a Reliable power, you don't expend it if you miss. There's nothing quite as disheartening as using your character's best daily attack and then just *missing* on the attack roll. The fighter's Reliable powers at least offer some insurance — sooner or later, you're going to hit *something* with that power, and you can keep on trying until you do.

3. Come and Get It

7th-level encounter attack power

This power allows you to pull all enemies within range 3 up to two squares (right next to you, in other words), and then you attack any enemies who end up adjacent to you. Although it's true that you get only 1[W] damage out of this, the tactical value of getting enemies adjacent to you so that you can control their movement with opportunity attacks is simply *huge* for a fighter. Remember, you're the guy that the monsters really don't want to be next to!

2. Comeback Strike

1st-level daily attack power

As a fighter, you occasionally take a pasting from the monsters. That's not a bad thing because you can take it better than any other character in the party, but it does mean that you're going to need healing on a frequent basis. Usually you can count on your cleric or warlord friend to look out for you, but sometimes that ally won't be there when you're in desperate need, and you'll have to look out for yourself. *Comeback strike* is a great insurance policy for this kind of situation because it combines a reasonable attack (double weapon damage dice) with the opportunity to spend a healing surge — it combines offense and defense in a single package. Plus, it's a Reliable power, so if you miss, you can try it again and again until you hit.

1. Tide of Iron

1st-level at-will attack power

And the winner is . . . *tide of iron!*

This is an excellent at-will attack that does normal weapon damage, pushes the target 1 square, and then gives you the opportunity to shift into the square you shoved your enemy out of. There's nothing like it for fighting your way through a door or maneuvering an enemy away from an ally you want to protect. It's especially good if you have the feat Heavy Blade Opportunity or a magic item that improves the effectiveness of pushes (for example, *gauntlets of the ram*).

Choosing a humble little at-will attack as the "best" fighter power may seem odd, but here's the deal: In most fights, you're going to use your at-will attacks more than any other attack. Your encounter attacks are better, of course, but they're good for only one swing each; an at-will attack might get used two, three, or four times in the same battle. Picking the right at-will attack is more important than you might think, and because of that, we recommend *tide of iron* as the best fighter power . . . unless of course you're a Great Weapon Fighter and don't carry a shield, in which case *reaping strike* is the way to go!

Chapter 27

The Ten Best Rogue Powers

on't tell anybody, but rogues just might have the most fun of any character in the game. Many rogue powers are built to hit an enemy hard and let you slip away without giving him the chance to counterattack, or they're built to just make the monsters look foolish. A rogue dishes out buckets of damage, and with a little luck, the bad guys will never lay a finger on your rogue.

The great majority of rogue powers require you to use a light blade, so that means you have only three weapons to choose from: the dagger, the short-sword, or (if you spend a Weapon Proficiency feat) the rapier. You should also keep an eye out for powers that have "kickers" for your Rogue Tactics class feature — you have to choose Artful Dodger or Brutal Scoundrel, and even if you otherwise like to mix and match powers from the different rogue builds, you get only one benefit or the other. We're not going to distinguish between these two options here, but more of the powers we list here are associated with the Artful Dodger tactics.

We left powers of 16th level or higher off this list, because we want to offer pointers on good powers you're likely to use earlier in your character's career. By the time you're playing 16th- or 17th-level characters, there isn't all that much more we can tell you about how to choose your powers!

For a full description of each power (its effects, amount of damage dealt, and so on) listed in this chapter, see Chapter 4 of the *Player's Handbook*.

10. Tornado Strike

13th-level encounter attack power

We start with an extremely versatile power, *tornado strike*. It works for both your melee attack or your ranged attack, and it gives you the chance to attack two different targets for double weapon damage dice against each one. It also gives you the ability to move 3 squares when you're all done attacking. With some clever play, you can pop out of cover, use *tornado strike,* and then duck back behind some useful obstacle (say, the party's fighter) all in one turn. Oh, and as an afterthought, you get to slide the target 2 or more squares. Even though this power features a slight power-up for the Artful Dodger, you really don't need to choose that tactic to enjoy *tornado strike;* you can shift your target at least 2 squares no matter what your Charisma score is. For best effect, make sure you slide the targets you attack away from you so that you're free to move without provoking opportunity attacks.

9. Sly Flourish

1st-level at-will attack power

This at-will power has the unusual distinction of being about the most damaging at-will power any character can have — if your Charisma score is respectable. Not only do you add your Dexterity modifier to your damage roll with this Dexterity attack, but you also add your Charisma modifier. If your rogue has a Charisma of 16, that's +3 damage above and beyond any other at-will attack power. That might not seem like much, but if you're a low-level rogue, two *sly flourish* attacks dish out about three attacks' worth of damage. Don't bother with *sly flourish* if your Charisma is less than a 14 or so; the other at-will powers offer good benefits too, and you should take this only if it will give you a +2 or better bonus on your damage.

8. Crimson Edge

9th-level daily attack power

Rogues have several daily powers that allow them to establish a significant advantage against a chosen foe and keep it for a long time. In the case of *crimson edge,* you get a highly accurate attack that deals moderate damage up front (double weapon damage dice), sets up good ongoing damage, and then grants you combat advantage against the target until he successfully saves against the ongoing damage. This sort of power is especially good when your party is fighting a solo monster or a single tough elite . . . although monsters like that normally succeed on their saving throws pretty quickly, so the ongoing damage and combat advantage won't last all that long.

Crimson edge is highly accurate because it's a weapon attack against Fortitude defense; normally, weapon attacks target Armor Class. Most monsters have Fortitude defenses about 2 to 3 points lower than their Armor Class, so in effect, this power grants you a nice bonus to hit. And, if you miss, it still deals half damage.

7. Leaping Dodge

16th-level encounter utility power

Okay, so we lied. We promised we'd keep this list to powers of 15th level or lower, but *leaping dodge* is just one level too high, and it's so spiffy we just couldn't help ourselves. Here's the deal: This is a power you can use once per encounter to interrupt an enemy's attack and jump out of the way. You have to be trained in the Athletics skill to use this power, but if some villain is about to clobber you with a vicious melee attack, it's easy as pie to just jump back 1 square and make his attack automatically miss. If your skill check totals 10 or better, you jump 1 square; 20 or better, 2 squares; 30 or better, 3 squares. As a 16th-level rogue, your Athletics skill check should be somewhere around +15 or so, so you're pretty much guaranteed of moving 1 square, and you'll get 2 squares most of the time. That will easily get you out of most melee or close attacks. Choose the Long Jumper feat if you select this power, and you'll jump twice as far!

6. Cloud of Steel

7th-level encounter attack power

This power lets you shoot a whole roomful of enemies with your crossbow, one bolt each. It doesn't do a lot of damage, but we like it because in the right encounter, you might pull off six or seven attacks with this one power. It's a Close attack, so it's safe to use in melee, and you don't even have to worry about hitting friends in the area — it targets enemies only. You can also use this power with thrown weapons such as shurikens or daggers, but you might have to carry a *lot* of them, and you'll need the Quick Draw feat to draw and throw 'em all. If you want to drop a whole crowd of low-grade minion monsters as easily as the party's wizard, this is the power for you.

5. Blinding Barrage

1st-level daily attack power

Blinding barrage is actually a lot like *cloud of steel.* You get to riddle several bad guys at once with your crossbow, thrown daggers, or sling. Better yet, you deal double damage dice to each target you hit and blind them for a round . . . and, if you miss, you still get half damage. So this power is more damaging than *cloud of steel,* carries a nice rider effect, and gives you half damage even on a miss. You might wonder why it's 6 levels lower, and here's why: This is a daily power, not an encounter power, and it affects a much smaller blast. You probably won't get more than two, maybe three, targets in this power's area, and you can use it only once per day.

4. Bait and Switch

3rd-level encounter attack power

Most of the 3rd-level rogue encounter powers give you solid damage (double weapon dice, or 2[W]), but *bait and switch* offers a significant advantage over the other powers of its level — it's an attack against Will defense instead of Armor Class. Your character is trying to deceive his or her foe and lure the target into leaving a deadly opening for a blade. In mechanical terms, you're attacking a defense that is probably 2 or 3 points worse than AC, so you're that much more likely to score a hit. It's a good idea to choose powers that allow you to attack a variety of defenses, just because you never know exactly what you're going to be fighting. *Bait and switch* also offers you the opportunity to move your enemy around the battlefield. It's a great way to get away from being surrounded by the bad guys or to get yourself next to a strong friend like the fighter before the monsters counterattack.

3. Tumble

2nd-level encounter utility power

This is a "money" power for the rogue. *Tumble* lets you shift up to half your speed as a move action; usually this will be 3 squares, as compared with the normal 1-square shift you can make without this power. You'll use it in every encounter of your character's career, either to move into position for a sneak attack or to get yourself out of trouble when the monsters surround you. No other 2nd-level power comes close to the battle-after-battle usefulness of *tumble*.

2. Slaying Strike

15th-level daily attack power

This power is fun because you get to dish out a truly staggering amount of damage. It's only a 3[W] (or triple weapon damage dice) power, with half damage on a miss . . . which isn't bad, really. But if you can wait until the target you intend to attack is bloodied (down to half hit points or less), the damage jumps up to 5[W], you score a critical hit on a roll of 17–20, and heck, you even get a couple of extra points of damage by adding in your Strength modifier. This is a power you want to make sure you hit with, so do anything in your power to make sure you have combat advantage against the hapless target before you pick up your d20. If you score a critical hit on a bloodied monster, you can easily ring up a 60- or 70-point hit with *slaying strike*, and that's going to put down whatever monster you were fighting more often than not.

1. Piercing Strike

1st-level at-will attack power

So, why does a lowly 1st-level at-will attack win the big money here? The answer is simple: *piercing strike* targets Reflex defense, not Armor Class. Most monsters have Reflex defense 2 or 3 points worse than their AC, so this is the most accurate rogue at-will power. If you have combat advantage against your enemy, you *need* to hit in order to make sure you deliver your sneak attack damage, so that means *piercing strike* is the attack of choice for the rogue's classic backstab. Over the course of your career, something close to half the attacks you make will be at-will attacks, so you might as well pick one that's going to hit.

Chapter 28

The Ten Best Wizard Powers

*Y*ou might think that wizards are pretty weak characters. They can't effectively wear armor. They have relatively low hit points and defense scores. What they do have is a great role — controller — designed to manipulate the environment and deal damage to a lot of enemies at the same time. Armed with arcane powers (called spells), wizards can dominate the battlefield. The trick is choosing the right spell for the job at hand. This chapter can help you with that.

Choosing the right spells at every level depends on the type of wizard you want to play. The Control Wizard, for example, concentrates on spells designed to restrict enemies in some way, whereas the War Wizard looks for spells that deal as much damage as possible.

We excluded powers of 16th level or higher from this list on purpose. Naturally, high-level spells are better than low-level spells; if we compiled a list of wizard spells strictly by power level, we'd pick ten epic-level powers and be done with it. That's not so useful if you're playing a low-level wizard and you're trying to decide which power you need right now. This is a list of ten wizard powers that will help your character get off to a great start in his or her career, not the ten most awesome wizard powers.

For a full description of each power (its effects, amount of damage dealt, duration, and so on) listed here, see Chapter 4 of the *Player's Handbook*.

10. Magic Missile

1st-level at-will attack power

In addition to being a great fallback power because you can use it every round, *magic missile* also counts as a ranged basic attack. That means that whenever a situation allows you to make a basic attack, you can use this arcane power instead of a dinky weapon.

9. Dispel Magic

6th-level daily utility power

Nothing says wizard like pulling out the exact right spell for the job and totally changing the nature of the situation. All the wizard's utility powers accomplish this in some fashion, but when the party is up against an enemy wizard, you want to be able to pull out *dispel magic.* This power allows you to eliminate the conjurations and zones cast by enemy wizards — and that means you get to adjust the battlefield to be more in your favor. And that's just cool.

8. Ice Storm

9th-level daily attack power

The wizard really shines when he or she can cast a spell that covers a large area of the battlefield, deals damage to the enemy, and also restricts the enemy in some way. *Ice storm* is an example where the wizard's role really comes together.

Now, as a daily power, you're going to want to save this spell for just the right occasion. It's a burst 3, which means it radiates out from its origin square to cover a whole lot of the battlefield — three squares in every direction! And you can place that origin square anywhere within 20 squares of your character. For most battles, that means you can put it anywhere you need to. Not only does it deal some damage to every enemy in the burst that you hit, it deals half damage to them if you miss!

And then, when the damage dealing is over, the *ice storm* just keeps on giving. Targets that were hit are immobilized until they save, and those you missed are slowed until they save. Plus, the spell creates a zone of difficult terrain that lasts until the end of the encounter. Use this power early in a fierce battle, and the rest of the party will be talking about it long after the experience points and treasure are divvied up.

7. Mirror Image

10th-level daily utility power

Sometimes the wizard just has to worry about himself. After all, wizards are fragile, and they won't do their party any good if they get chewed up and taken out of the fight early in an encounter. When it looks like the enemy is gunning for you, cast *mirror image* and most of your worries will go away (for a while, anyway). You create three duplicate images of yourself, which essentially means that the next three attacks that target you miss you, eliminating one of your duplicates each time.

6. Sleep

1st-level daily attack power

Here's another burst power that you can place anywhere within 20 squares of your character. ***Warning:*** *Sleep* targets all creatures in the burst, so be sure not to catch any of your allies with the spell! All targets, whether you hit or miss them, are slowed until they make a saving throw. Those targets that were hit, if they fail their first save, fall unconscious until they save against that effect. *Sleep* can be pretty swingy, but when the dice fall your way, it can put a whole lot of monsters out of action without killing them — and sometimes you want to leave a few monsters around to question when the battle comes to an end.

5. Lightning Bolt

7th-level encounter attack power

Lightning bolt is one of those iconic wizard spells that also lives up to its classic billing. Basically, it allows you to hit a primary target and two secondary targets with bolts of destructive lightning. The power has great range, deals damage to multiple targets, lets you roll a lot of dice, and looks cool when it is cast. What's not to love?

4. Fireball

5th-level daily attack power

Another classic, fireball is great because of its simplicity. Pick a square within 20 squares of your character, and watch a burst of fire spread out for three squares in all directions. Creatures in the burst are subject to an attack that deals solid damage, and even hits them for half damage if your attacks miss. ***Warning:*** Just be careful not to catch any of your allies in the burst, or they'll get crisped by this spell, too.

3. Shield

2nd-level encounter utility power

Here's another example of a power designed to save the wizard's skin when the monsters get past the fighter. When the wizard gets hit by an attack, he or she can cast *shield* to immediately raise his or her AC and Reflex defense by 4. Not only does the bonus last until the end of your next turn (so it can protect you from more than one attack), but if your new defense score is higher than the attack result, the original attack misses! Let's see the fighter do that!

2. Thunderlance

13th-level encounter attack power

Here's an example of a blast power that covers a 5 x 5 square area directly adjacent to the wizard and targets all creatures in that area. *Thunderlance* is an encounter power, so you can use it in every battle. Not only does it hit hard, but it also pushes the targets four squares away from you — this spell is great at clearing the area right around you from annoying monsters and other enemies.

1. Cloud of Daggers

1st-level at-will attack power

Cloud of daggers makes it to the top spot for wizard spells because it's an at-will power that deals damage at the front end, creates an area that lasts until the end of your next turn, and deals additional damage when a monster enters or starts its turn in the cloud. That means that, at least, the creature you originally target has the potential to take damage when you cast the spell, and it automatically takes damage at the start of its turn. Wicked, huh?

Chapter 29

The Ten Best Cleric Powers

lerics are leaders, which means they do things that help the rest of the party and make the party better. The powers you select always provide for these things, but you can lean a little more toward combat or a little more toward party optimization, depending on the specific powers you choose.

The things to watch for in selecting cleric powers are the keywords. Some cleric powers require the use of a weapon, whereas others require an implement — which is a holy symbol for clerics. Make sure to select powers that play to your use of either a weapon or an implement, and everything will work out fine.

We left powers of 16th level or higher off this list because we want to offer pointers on good powers you're likely to use earlier in your character's career. By the time you're playing 16th- or 17th-level characters, there isn't all that much more we can tell you about how to choose your powers!

For a full description of each power (its effects, amount of damage dealt, and so on) listed in this chapter, see Chapter 4 of the *Player's Handbook*.

10. Cure Light Wounds

2nd-level daily utility power

One of the main jobs the cleric accomplishes is keeping his or her party healthy and alive through the use of healing magic. One of the first chances you get to increase your healing portfolio is the *cure light wounds* utility power. The great thing about this power is that it heals without the need for your target to spend a healing surge — allowing the character to save the surge for later in the adventure.

9. Lance of Faith

1st-level at-will attack power

This at-will power provides decent damage for a power that you can call upon over and over, plus it provide one of your allies with a +2 bonus on the next attack the ally makes against your target. Good damage and the potential for even more hurt coming your enemy's way — just the thing to make you feel all leaderly like.

8. Flame Strike

9th-level daily attack power

This power is the newest version of a cleric classic, and it delivers even better now. With *flame strike,* you pick an origin square anywhere within 10 squares of your character, and a burst 2 explodes from that spot to attack all enemies within the burst. On a hit, each enemy takes a load of damage (especially if your cleric has a good Wisdom score), as well as ongoing fire damage until it succeeds at a saving throw. And even on a miss, the power deals half damage to the monsters in the burst. That's hot!

7. Cure Serious Wounds

6th-level daily utility power

An even better version of the *cure light wounds* prayer, this one lets your target regain two healing surges worth of hit points without spending any healing surges. This one is great to use when the fighter is still in the thick of a battle but his or her hit points are running low.

6. Awe Strike

7th-level encounter attack power

For the Battle Cleric with a good Strength score and a weapon, *awe strike* is a fun power to call upon in every battle. It doesn't deal a lot of damage, but it adds a bonus when it hits. It immobilizes your target until the end of your next turn. That means the target can't leave the square it's in, leaving it vulnerable to the attacks of the rest of your party.

5. Healing Strike

1st-level encounter attack power

Healing strike combines damaging a monster with healing for a unique mix of action and helping one of your allies. When you successfully hit a monster, roll solid damage while the ally you select spends a healing surge and regains some hit points. In addition, the monster is marked until the end of your next turn, meaning that it takes a penalty on any attacks it makes that don't include you as a target.

4. Daunting Light

3rd-level encounter attack power

This 3rd-level cleric encounter power provides the most damage of powers of this level, plus it allows you to give an ally combat advantage against your target. If you grant that benefit to a rogue, for example, then this monster is in for a world of hurt.

3. Mantle of Glory

13th-level encounter attack power

Here's another example of combining good damage against the enemy while helping your allies at the same time. *Mantle of glory* is a blast 5 attack that harms each enemy in the blast. But you also want to position this blast to catch your allies as well, because each ally in the blast gets to spend a healing surge and recover some lost hit points. It's really fun when the cleric can hurt the monsters and help his or her allies with the same action.

2. Mass Cure Light Wounds

10th-level daily utility power

Like the earlier cure spells, you want to add this one to your repertoire because it provides a free healing surge, which restores hit points equal to ¼ of the recipient's normal maximum. Even better, this power is a burst, allowing all your allies in the burst to take advantage of the healing — including yourself!

1. Sacred Flame

1st-level at-will attack power

You never run out of uses of your at-will powers, so make sure you take the ones you really want to use over and over again. We chose *sacred flame* as the top cleric power because it combines the cleric's two favorite activities — hurting monsters and helping allies. In this case, it provides an ally with temporary hit points. As a battle draws to a close but isn't quite over yet, this might be all the healing you have left to provide . . . but hit points are hit points, and they can keep your fighter going strong for another round. And that might make all the difference.

Chapter 30

The Ten Best Low-Level Monsters

*F*inish this sentence: "It isn't a great D&D game until we've fought a _____." What's your answer? A horde of orcs? A dragon? An evil wizard?

Although it's true that big red dragons, mind flayers, and mummies are great D&D monsters, you can't really throw powerful monsters like that at a party of 1st-level characters and expect them to survive. So, we split up this Top Monsters list by tiers of play — heroic tier (levels 1–10) are covered in this chapter, and paragon tier (levels 11–20) and epic tier (levels 21–30) monsters are covered in the following chapters.

We made an effort to spread out our picks among creatures of different types and different roles. (A creature's level tells you what level of characters a group of monsters of that type is a suitable challenge for; for example, four 2nd-level monsters are a good challenge for a party of four 2nd-level characters.) Every monster also includes its level and role so that a brand-new Dungeon Master can decide whether the players are ready for them.

10. Stirge (Level 1 Lurker)

Monster Manual page 248

What's creepier than a giant mosquito that can suck a person dry? A whole flock of giant mosquitoes, that's what. Stirges are fun because they introduce players to the power of some monsters to grab hold and deal ongoing damage until the target escapes. They also fly, and as lurkers, they love to leap out and surprise characters with their blood-sucking ways. Yes, they're individually weak, but there's nothing quite as horrifying for characters (and their players) as watching one of their comrades thrashing about with two or three stirges attached at the same time.

9. Hell Hound (Level 7 Brute)

Monster Manual page 160

Hell hounds make it onto the list because they're representatives of a class of monsters your players will be fighting against for their whole careers: elemental beasts. They're from other planes of existence (the Elemental Chaos, in the case of the hell hound) and are, therefore, from "outside" the normal world. Hell hounds are also interesting because they have an area-effect attack (their fiery breath) and the ability to deal extra fire damage with every bite. They also have a fiery aura that deals damage to any creatures that enter or begin their turns within its area of effect.

8. Young White Dragon (Level 3 Solo Brute)

Monster Manual page 84

We had to include a dragon, didn't we? It's in the name of the darned game, after all. This white dragon is a solo monster, meaning that it can take on a group of 3rd-level player characters all by itself. It has a load of hit points, the ability to attack multiple times in a round, and an icy breath weapon that can bring down a number of PCs at the same time. Add to that the fact that it can use action points to take extra actions on its turn, and you have a truly terrifying battle against a Large monster for low-level characters.

7. Deathjump Spider (Level 4 Skirmisher)

Monster Manual page 246

A surprising number of low-level D&D monsters are big bugs. Monstrous spiders are the scariest representatives of this crew, thanks to J.R.R. Tolkien. Who isn't creeped out by the notion of a spider the size of a person? The deathjump spider is good because it has a great power with a great name: *death from above*. It can leap as many as 10 squares and then shift up another 6 squares to deliver a potent bite that deals ongoing poison damage and knocks it target prone. Now that's creepy!

6. Werewolf (Level 8 Brute)

Monster Manual page 180

The werewolf is a classic monster. Everybody understands the fear of letting out the beast within, the feral killer deep inside. Not only is the werewolf an iconic legendary monster, it's also interesting in the context of the D&D rules. It's the best illustration of a monster with regeneration; unless characters have a silver weapon, they'll have a hard time keeping this creature from healing damage. Werewolves are shapechangers, which means players can never be entirely sure whether that surly villager might indeed be the great black wolf who attacked their characters out in the forest. And best of all, werewolves carry the dreaded disease of moon frenzy; those heroes bitten by werewolves are driven mad and become crazed killers (but don't actually change into werewolves themselves).

5. Ghoul (Level 5 Soldier)

Monster Manual page 118

Ghouls are undead creatures that haunt graveyards and crypts and feast on the dead . . . or, whenever they're handy, the living. Ghouls are terrifying to low-level heroes because one scratch of a ghoul's filthy claws may cause even the most resolute of heroes to freeze up in complete (but thankfully short-lived) immobilization. Fighting off a pack of ghouls requires the heroes to cooperate to defend friends who are temporarily unable to move. And just like the werewolf, the ghoul's bite carries with it a supernatural effect — in this case, an effect that stuns its target.

4. Dire Rat (Level 1 Brute)

Monster Manual page 219

Dire animals are unusually large, powerful, and foul-tempered versions of the normal creatures you're familiar with. Dire rats are the weakest and most common of these vicious animals. A dire rat can be six feet long and weigh more than 150 pounds. Dire rats are one of those classic bits of "dungeon dressing" that just seem to turn up any time you have a refuse pit, trash heap, or sewer to explore. And they can be pretty tough opponents for low-level heroes.

3. Ogre Skirmisher (Level 8 Skirmisher)

Monster Manual page 199

An ogre skirmisher can deliver quite a beating to a low-level party. An ogre skirmisher uses reach to pound a target up to 2 squares away for 1d8+4 damage each time it hits with that big club, and if it moves 4 squares before attacking it gains a skirmish bonus of +1d8 — an average of 14 points per hit! One swing is usually enough to bloody many 1st-level characters. An ogre skirmisher teaches players about fighting big, powerful, stupid, and mobile monsters, which is an iconic D&D experience. An ogre skirmisher encounter just screams out for clever player tactics such as stealth, bluffing, or the use of magic; if characters just go right at the ogre skirmisher and try to beat it at its own game of melee damage, they're going to get hurt.

2. Blazing Skeleton (Level 5 Artillery)

Monster Manual page 234

Thanks to Ray Harryhausen, everybody knows just what fighting skeletons ought to look like. What's scarier and more fantastic than battling against silent, remorseless things made from the fleshless bodies of the dead? Like the ghoul, the skeleton introduces players to the special advantages and weaknesses of undead monsters; they're resistant to fire and necrotic attacks, but they're vulnerable to radiant damage. Blazing skeletons are surrounded by a fiery aura that deals fire damage to creatures that start their turns in the aura, their claw attacks deal ongoing fire damage, and they have a ranged attack in the form of a *flame orb* that allows them to battle the player characters from a distance.

1. Orc Raider (Level 3 Skirmisher)

Monster Manual page 203

And the best low-level monster is . . . the orc! The iconic beast-man savage, the barbaric marauder, bloodthirsty warrior in the service of stronger and darker evils, the orc is simply the classic adversary for a low-level hero.

To be honest, orcs are actually the top pick because they're the perfect representatives of a broad group of creatures known as humanoids. Monsters like goblins, hobgoblins, kobolds, gnolls, and even lizardfolk all provide a very similar sort of encounter — the party fights a handful of savage warriors at a time. They use armor and weapons just like PCs do and may have champions or leaders who have character classes and use magic like PCs. Some are stronger, some are sneakier, some are halfling-sized, and some are human-sized, but essentially it's the same type of encounter regardless of the exact monster involved.

Although orcs are often thought of as low-level opponents, you should remember that orcs can have classes and levels, too. The run-of-the-mill orc raider is a 3rd-level skirmisher, but imagine running into an elite orc warband made up of 7th-level bloodragers, or an orc battle-priest who's a 5th-level eye of Gruumsh. A great orc chieftain and his chief bodyguards and advisors may be every bit as tough as the best party of heroic-tier adventurers.

Chapter 31

The Ten Best Mid-Level Monsters

*N*ow for the second part of our Top Monsters list, the ten best monsters for paragon-tier play (levels 11–20). A creature's level is roughly equal to character level; for example, four level 12 monsters are a good challenge for a party of four 12th-level characters.

These creatures are the most suitable for a paragon-tier game. As in Chapter 30, we've tried to spread out our picks among creatures of different types and different levels and roles. If you're a Dungeon Master, you can decide for yourself whether your players are ready to face these sinister creatures.

10. Cyclops Impaler (Level 14 Artillery)

Monster Manual page 46

Cyclopses are one-eyed giants from the Feywild that often serve more powerful masters. The impaler has all kinds of ranged powers that make it a great monster to put at the back of a band of other, more melee-oriented creatures. While the melee monsters pound on the adventurers, the cyclops impalers hurl spears and use their *evil eye* and *impaling volley* powers to harass the heroes from a distance.

9. Flesh Golem (Level 12 Elite Brute)

Monster Manual page 142

Golems are magical constructs, creatures of nonliving matter given animation through powerful spells and rites. The flesh golem is the most common example of this monster. It's made from bits and pieces of bodies, just like Frankenstein's monster, but the flesh golem is an unthinking machine. As a construct, a golem is powerful and unthinking, ready to fly into a *golem rampage* in an instant, moving across the battlefield and attacking every creature it encounters along the way. As an elite monster, one flesh golem is equal to two standard monsters of its level.

8. Wailing Ghost (Level 12 Controller)

Monster Manual page 117

The wailing ghost, or banshee, is the perfect example of an insubstantial monster — a creature that simply doesn't have real substance in the world, and thus can move through walls, doors, and other obstacles. Dealing with an insubstantial monster requires players to evolve special tactics and employ specific spells and weapons to deal full damage. Otherwise, every attack deals half damage to these terrifying undead creatures.

7. Umber Hulk (Level 12 Elite Soldier)

Monster Manual page 256

Here's one of our favorites. The umber hulk is an iconic DUNGEONS & DRAGONS monster — it's a creature invented specifically for the game, something that doesn't really stem from real-world myth or legend. Umber hulks are fun because they are Large monsters that use a *confusing gaze* attack. Just like the wailing ghost teaches players to deal with insubstantial monsters, the umber hulk teaches players a set of rules and tactics to overcome a monster that is dangerous even to look at.

6. Beholder Eye of Flame (Level 13 Elite Artillery)

Monster Manual page 32

Speaking of iconic creatures, here's the beholder! What could be more fantastic than a giant floating eyeball with little eye stalks sticking out, all of which shoot magic rays?

The eye of flame's eye rays can damage hapless PCs with fire, slide them up to 4 squares, or make them flee in terror. Oh, and with its big central eye the beholder can render its victims even more vulnerable to fire attacks. Its ability to inflict a devastating onslaught of attacks on the party of heroes is unparalleled . . . until they fight a beholder eye tyrant (Level 19 Solo Artillery) later in their adventuring careers, that is.

5. Mummy Lord (Level 13 Elite Controller)

Monster Manual page 192

The mummy lord is an undead cleric who's an elite monster complete with a fear aura, regeneration, melee attacks, ranged attacks, and a Close burst attack. This truly powerful creature can spread the dreaded disease of mummy rot to those it battles, leaving them with something to remember well after the combat encounter has ended.

4. Mind Flayer Mastermind (Level 18 Elite Controller)

Monster Manual page 188

Another unique creation of the D&D game, the mind flayer is the quintessential evil genius . . . with the ability to daze and immobilize PCs into helpless paste with its *mind blast* and *illusion of pain* powers and then pull out their brains and eat them while the PCs are standing around helplessly watching it happen. If there's a more horrible way to die in the D&D game than that, we frankly don't know what it is. Although a mind flayer is tremendously dangerous on its own, the real threat posed by the monster is its ability to mastermind and command other monsters. A mind flayer is the perfect evil overlord, and it's clever enough to use its servant monsters to wear down a group of paragon-tier adventurers before setting a lethal ambush to finish them off itself.

3. Vrock Demon (Level 13 Skirmisher)

Monster Manual page 58

Demons and devils of all sorts are some of the coolest and most powerful monsters in the D&D game. There are four or five that we could have picked to represent the evil-outsider-from-the-infernal-realms niche, but we settled on the vrock as the best example. The vrock is a dangerous melee combatant, but (like many demons or devils) it also possesses several dangerous special attacks. Many heroes find that they battle demons, devils, and such things over and over again as they rise to high-level play, and the vrock is a great representative of the type.

2. War Troll (Level 14 Soldier)

Monster Manual page 254

We simply couldn't exclude the troll from one of these lists. A war troll is a great paragon-tier monster that can challenge heroes for a number of levels. Just like the wailing ghost is a great example of an insubstantial monster, the war troll is a great example of a regenerating monster — a creature that's almost impossible to kill outright unless you have fire handy.

The war troll is quite common because it makes a great *meat shield* (a dull-witted but physically strong creature that can stand in between the heroes and the evil mastermind). Before the party can get at the evil wizard, mind flayer, or what-have-you, they adventurers have to cut their way through a gang of war trolls. A war troll fits well in almost any scenario or monster lair, and it's vile, repulsive, and loathsome. Every player loves to hate trolls, and you know what? The war troll deserves it.

1. Adult Red Dragon (Level 15 Solo Soldier)

Monster Manual page 83

The opportunity to fight a dragon (and pillage its hoard) is the reason you play the game.

A dragon's power varies depending on its color (species) and its age category. The older a dragon gets, the bigger and meaner it gets. An adult dragon is a handful for almost any paragon-tier party; we chose the red dragon because it's iconic and a good fit for the paragon-tier of play.

A dragon is armed with a number of dangerous and useful abilities — it flies, it has a great AC and a lot of hit points, it has tremendously good saving throws and the use of action points, it has a deadly breath weapon (fire, in the case of a red dragon), and it can tear you to shreds with its claws and teeth. What more could a group of brave adventurers want?

Chapter 32

The Ten Best High-Level Monsters

*N*ow for the third part of our Top Monsters list, the ten best monsters for epic-tier play (levels 21–30). A creature's level tells you what level of characters an equal number of monsters of that type is a suitable challenge for; for example, four level 24 monsters are a good challenge for a party of four 24th-level characters.

These creatures are the most suitable for a epic-tier game. As before, we've tried to spread out our picks among creatures of different types and different levels and roles. If you're a Dungeon Master, you can decide for yourself whether your players are ready to face these sinister creatures.

10. Yuan-ti Anathema (Level 21 Elite Skirmisher)

Monster Manual page 271

Yuan-ti are classic D&D monsters — half-snake, half-humanoids who constantly plot to rebuild their ancient empire. The anathema is a Huge-sized monster that is more snake than human; in fact, it appears to be made of dozens of giant snakes twisted together into an insane abomination that is often unleashed to wreck havoc on the world. Take a look at the picture we included in the color pages of this book!

9. War Devil (Level 22 Brute)

Monster Manual page 67

The war devil is a champion of the Nine Hells. They often lead lesser devils into battle or serve as generals for mortal tyrants of the most foul and powerful kind. The war devil has a mix of melee and devilish powers that make it a formidable opponent in the opening stages of epic play.

8. Voidsoul Specter (Level 23 Lurker)

Monster Manual page 244

This epic-tier threat appears as a ghostly, twisted apparition surrounded by an aura of *spectral cold* that deals damage and reduces defenses. In addition to a deadly melee attack, the voidsoul specter has a Close blast attack that pours on the damage while healing the monster. Nothing says danger like a pack of voidsoul specters emerging from the shadows to take on your epic-level adventurers.

7. Elder Purple Worm (Level 24 Solo Soldier)

Monster Manual page 214

Here's a classic D&D favorite. The elder purple worm is a real beater of a monster, just the thing to throw at a party of confident and fearless (maybe too fearless) adventurers in the low- to mid-epic tier. It's Gargantuan-sized. It has 1,145 hit points. It has the ability to swallow its prey whole. This is truly a monster to be reckoned with!

6. Death Knight (Level 25 Elite Soldier)

Monster Manual page 51

The death knight originally appeared in the early days of D&D as an evil answer to the heroic paladin, and it still fills that bill in the current version of the game. With a powerful soul weapon, the ability to issue divine challenges, and an aura that provides a benefit to undead allies, the death knight makes a great leader for a band of assorted undead creatures.

5. Pit Fiend (Level 26 Elite Soldier)

Monster Manual page 65

The pit fiend works best as the leader of a group of lesser devils actively seeking to end the adventuring career of the player characters. It has a deadly combination of melee attacks (including a *flametouched mace* and a *tail sting*) and ranged attacks (such as *point of terror* and *irresistible command*), as well as the ability to summon additional devilish allies whenever it needs them.

4. Storm Giant (Level 24 Elite Controller)

Monster Manual page 124

Giants begin to enter play during the paragon-tier, but they really come into their own at epic levels. The storm giant is at the top of the giant world, at least as far as the *Monster Manual* is concerned, hurling thunderbolts from afar, using howling winds to scatter enemies, and fighting with a lightning-edged greatsword when the battle gets up close and personal.

3. Ancient Blue Dragon (Level 28 Solo Artillery)

Monster Manual page 79

Ancient dragons are the most powerful versions of these majestic and deadly creatures, and the ancient blue dragon approaches the pinnacle of all dragon-kind. (Only the ancient red surpasses it.) As a solo monster, you can throw an ancient blue dragon at your player characters as early as level 26, and it still presents a challenge when they reach 30th level. Few single challengers can long stand against the fury of this terrible dragon as it unleashes lightning and thunder.

2. Tarrasque (Level 30 Solo Brute)

Monster Manual page 13

Few D&D monsters have inspired the stories of the dreaded tarrasque, a creature that embodies wanton destruction. Of a size that makes most other monsters look small, and with powers that will test the courage and abilities of even the toughest heroes, this abomination can easily serve as one of the final challenges for your adventurers as your long campaign comes to a brilliant and satisfying close.

1. Orcus (Level 33 Solo Brute)

Monster Manual page 206

The most powerful, most deadly, highest-level monster in the *Monster Manual* is Orcus, the demon prince of the undead. This demon lord is impressive, from its Gargantuan size to its twin auras, from its amazing Armor Class (48!) to its spectacular number of hit points (1,525!). Orcus has long been a player in the mythology of the D&D world, and in the 4th Edition of the game, the demon lord takes center stage. With a heavy mace known as the *Wand of Orcus* and all kinds of death-related powers and abilities, Orcus represents the most monstrous evil in the game — the perfect challenge for 30th-level epic heroes!

Chapter 33

The Ten Best D&D Novels

··

As much fun as the DUNGEONS & DRAGONS game is to play, you can't spend all of your time adventuring in the dungeons. That doesn't mean you still can't get your fill of D&D when you're away from the gaming table.

In this chapter, we look at one of the best out-of-game activities you can participate in while still staying in the spirit of D&D — reading D&D-based fantasy novels. Wizards of the Coast publishes a vast array of novels set in the various worlds of D&D, and we introduce you to some of the best out there in this chapter. In addition, we suggest some other fantasy novels that, while not specifically related to D&D, are definitely in the spirit of the game and can inspire players and Dungeon Masters alike in future game sessions.

Dragonlance Chronicles

By Margaret Weis and Tracy Hickman (published by Wizards of the Coast, Inc.)

This is the trilogy that launched the D&D novels lines, and it holds up today as an epic adventure revolving around a group of adventuring companions not unlike the characters you and your friends play in any D&D game. The epic struggle of the War of the Lance unfolds through *Dragons of Autumn Twilight*, *Dragons of Winter Night*, and *Dragons of Spring Dawning*. Many of the characters and situations introduced in these volumes spin off into new adventures throughout the line of DRAGONLANCE novels.

Dragonlance Legends

By Margaret Weis and Tracy Hickman (published by Wizards of the Coast, Inc.)

This sequel to *Chronicles*, *Legends* explores events in the lives of two popular characters — Raistlin and Caramon. Follow Caramon through time as he struggles to save his brother from a terrible darkness in *Time of the Twins*, *War of the Twins*, and *Test of the Twins*.

Icewind Dale Trilogy

By R.A. Salvatore (published by Wizards of the Coast, Inc.)

In this thrilling adventure set in the far northern reaches of the FORGOTTEN REALMS setting, you first meet the popular dark elf hero Drizzt Do'urden and his companions. With *The Crystal Shard*, *Streams of Silver*, and *The Halfling's Gem*, a powerful tale unfolds and sets the stage for the future adventures of the drow ranger and his friends.

R.A. Salvatore's War of the Spider Queen

By various authors (published by Wizards of the Coast, Inc.)

This epic story evolves across five books as civil war and chaos rocks the Underdark. As the most powerful dark elf houses clash in this tale set in the FORGOTTEN REALMS campaign's shadow regions, four heroes seek to save the underworld realm of Menzoberranzan from a terrible, approaching darkness. This series consists of these titles: *Dissolution*, *Insurrection*, *Condemnation*, *Extinction*, and *Annihilation*.

A Practical Guide to Dragons

By Lisa Trutkoff Trumbauer (published by Mirrorstone, Wizards of the Coast, Inc.)

This beautiful book about dragons is a great introduction to the world of D&D for new and younger readers. Extremely popular, the *Practical Guide* has led to a series of related titles, including *A Practical Guide to Monsters* and the *Dragon Codex* series of young adult novels set in a D&D world.

Storm Dragon

By James Wyatt (published by Wizards of the Coast, Inc.)

Set in the world of EBERRON, *Storm Dragon* brings together the ancient shards of the Prophecy of the Dragons to shake the foundation of the campaign. This novel is a great read and a good introduction to the world of EBERRON.

Swordmage

By Richard Baker (published by Wizards of the Coast, Inc.)

This is the first FORGOTTEN REALMS novel set in the new 4th Edition timeline. *Swordmage* follows the adventures of an exiled swordmage who confronts the sinister plots of a traitor, the fury of an orc warlord, and the ancient malice of an undead king.

The Orc King

By R.A. Salvatore (published by Wizards of the Coast, Inc.)

In the latest adventures of Drizzt Do'urden, hero of the far northern reaches of the FORGOTTEN REALMS world, the dark elf takes a stand to stop the orc tribes from marching to all-out war. This is the beginning of a bold new trilogy that will change the face of Faerûn forever.

Novels to inspire

A lot of great fantasy novels have been published. We talk about some of our favorite DUNGEONS & DRAGONS novels in this chapter, and we decided that we should also include a list of past and present non-D&D novels that continue to inspire us and broaden our imaginations. They might not be official D&D novels, but they certainly possess the same spirit, and many of these books inspired our earliest attempts at story and adventure creation. This list is by no means complete or exhaustive. Consider it as a starting point for your own discovery of novels to inspire you and fuel your imagination:

10. *Furies of Calderon* (first in the *Codex Alera* series) by Jim Butcher

9. *Conan the Barbarian* novels and short stories by Robert E. Howard

8. *The Elric Saga* series by Michael Moorcock

7. *The Adventures of Fafhrd and the Gray Mouser* series by Fritz Leiber

6. *Chronicles of the Deryni* series by Katherine Kurtz

5. *The Riftwar Saga* series by Raymond E. Feist

4. *The Mirror of Her Dreams* by Stephen R. Donaldson

3. *A Song of Fire and Ice* series by George R.R. Martin

2. *The Sword of Shannara* trilogy by Terry Brooks

1. *The Lord of the Rings* trilogy by J.R.R. Tolkein

The Sword Never Sleeps

By Ed Greenwood (published by Wizards of the Coast, Inc.)

This FORGOTTEN REALMS novel follows the adventures of the Knights of Myth Drannor, written by the creator of Faerûn! Can they step forth one last time to save Cormyr and forge their legend forever?

Glossary

aberrant: A monster origin, which includes creatures such as the aboleth or mind flayer.

ability: One of the six basic physical and mental attributes of a character or creature: Strength, Constitution, Dexterity, Intelligence, Wisdom, or Charisma. Each ability is given a numerical value — usually between 3 and 18 for an average human, although heroic humans have much better scores. Monsters have ability scores, too, and sometimes they can be high above (or way below) the human average.

ability check: A test or check in which you roll 1d20, add half your character's level, and then add the ability modifier for the appropriate ability to the resulting roll. Most things your character attempts in the game, including skill checks and attack rolls, are founded on the ability check mechanic.

ability modifier: The bonus or penalty your character gets for having a good or poor ability score. Modifiers are applied to ability checks, ability-based skill checks, and basic melee attack and damage rolls.

action: What characters can do on their turn in combat. A character can take one minor action, one move action, and one standard action on his or her turn. See also *action, minor; action, move;* and *action, standard.*

action, minor: A minor action is usually an action that isn't an attack or move but enables you to do something else, such as drawing a weapon or opening a door.

action, move: Moving up to your character's speed is a move action. Move actions also cover a number of movement-related activities, such as standing up after being knocked prone or shifting. See also *shift.*

action, standard: Most attacks your character can make require standard actions, such as attacking with a power, charging, or making a basic melee attack.

action point: A special resource that player characters (and some monsters) can spend to gain a bonus standard action for that turn. You begin each day of adventuring with one action point, but as you successfully overcome obstacles and defeat monsters, you may gain more.

aid another: A combat action that lets you grant another character a +2 attack or defense bonus instead of making an attack of your own.

alignment: A basic description of the morality of an intelligent creature. See also *good, lawful good, evil, chaotic evil,* and *unaligned.*

arcane: One of the power sources from which characters derive their abilities. Warlocks and wizards make use of the arcane power source. Arcane powers are commonly called spells.

area attack: A type of long-range attack in which the attacker blasts everything in the specified area. A *fireball* spell is an area attack.

Armor Class (AC): A number representing a creature's ability to avoid being hit in combat. An opponent's attack roll must equal or exceed the target's AC to hit it. Armor Class starts at 10 and is then modified for a character's level, Dexterity or Intelligence, armor worn, and magical protections.

astral diamond (ad): A unit of currency. Astral diamonds are fantastically valuable; each one is worth 10,000 gold pieces.

attack roll: A roll to determine whether an attack hits. To make an attack roll, roll 1d20 and add your character's level modifier, ability score modifier (depending on which ability score the attack is based on), plus any special modifiers that might apply, such as the enhancement bonus of a magic weapon or implement. If the result equals or beats the target's defense, your attack hits.

at-will power: A power that can be used every turn.

basic attack: A melee or ranged weapon attack you make without using a power. Usually, you use basic attacks for opportunity attacks or when another character grants you an attack on his or her turn.

beast: A monster type that includes non-intelligent creatures such as lions, tigers, and bears. Beasts also can come from more exotic origins.

bloodied: When a character or creature is reduced to half or less of the normal full hit point total. (Some abilities work better when used by or against bloodied characters or monsters.)

buff: To use a power that makes your character or allies stronger or better, such as a power that heals or gives a bonus to AC.

bull rush: A combat action in which your character tries to shove an opponent out of the way or into a specific position.

cast a spell: To use an arcane power. Using an arcane power isn't really different from using any other kind of power, but there's a long tradition in the game of spellcasters and casting spells.

caster: Table-talk for a character or creature that has the ability to use a supernatural power, especially if that power is arcane or divine in nature and isn't a melee attack. Devoted clerics, warlocks, and wizards are usually considered casters.

chaotic evil: An alignment. Chaotic evil creatures believe that it's okay to kill, rob, or plunder any creature weaker than themselves.

character: A fictional individual in the game setting, created and controlled by a player or DM. See also *player character (PC)* and *nonplayer character (NPC)*.

character class: One of the eight player character types or careers described in the *Player's Handbook*: cleric, fighter, paladin, ranger, rogue, warlock, warlord, and wizard. Class defines a character's talents and basic function in the game.

charge: A combat action in which a character moves up to his or her speed and makes a basic melee attack at the end with a +1 attack bonus. You usually can't use any powers when you charge.

check: A method of determining whether your character succeeds or fails when attempting an action. Most checks are ability checks. To make a check, roll 1d20 and add any relevant modifiers (usually, your level modifier and ability modifier). If this result equals or exceeds the Difficulty Class number assigned by the DM, the check succeeds.

class: See *character class*.

class feature: Any special ability, power, or characteristic derived from having levels in a character class.

class skill: A skill to which characters of a particular class have easier access than characters of other classes.

cleric: A player character class. Clerics are divine leaders. They are holy crusaders who combine potent healing abilities with powers that make enemies easier for other characters to hit or powers that protect other characters from harm.

Close attack: A type of short-range attack in which the attacker blasts everything in the specified area. For example, a Close burst 2 is an attack that affects every target within 2 squares of the attacker.

combat advantage: A situation in which the attacker can catch a defender off-guard. When you have combat advantage against a foe, you gain a +2 bonus on any attack you make. Conditions that cause combat advantage include being dazed, flanked, prone, or stunned.

concealment: An obscurity that prevents a character from clearly seeing a target. Concealment penalizes attacks against the concealed creature.

condition: A specific effect that's currently affecting a creature. Common conditions include blinded, dazed, dying, immobilized, marked, slowed, stunned, and weakened.

construct: A monster type which includes things that were built and animated through magic, such as flesh golems or shield guardians. Constructs are immune to some attacks and effects.

controller: A character role. Controllers are characters who favor offense over defense and have powers that can damage or hinder multiple enemies at once.

copper piece (cp): A unit of currency in the game. Copper pieces are worth 1/100 of a gold piece.

coup de grace: A combat action that allows your character to attempt a killing blow against a helpless opponent. (*Coup de grace* is French for "stroke of mercy.") If your attack hits, you automatically score a critical hit with whatever power you were using.

cover: Any solid barrier between an attacker and defender. Cover inflicts a penalty on the attacker's attack roll.

creature: A living or otherwise active being. The terms *creature, monster,* and *character* are sometimes used interchangeably.

crit: Table talk for a critical hit (or, as a verb, the act of clobbering someone or something with a critical hit). For example, "Did you just crit that orc?"

critical hit: A hit that strikes a vital area. To score a critical hit, you must roll a natural 20 on an attack roll. Crits usually deal maximum damage plus bonus dice based on the weapon or implement you're using.

daily power: A significant power that can be used once per day. You regain daily powers after an extended rest.

damage: A decrease in hit points. The exact type of damage is often specified (such as fire damage) so that you can determine whether the target has any special resistances or immunities that may decrease or negate the damage (such as resistance to fire).

darkvision: The ability to see in total darkness (handy if no light source is nearby!).

defender: A character role. Defenders have high hit points and good defenses (naturally), and they specialize in melee combat. They usually have abilities that discourage monsters from attacking softer targets in the party, such as controllers or leaders.

difficulty class (DC): The target number that you must meet or beat with a skill check or saving throw roll to succeed.

divine: One of the power sources from which characters derive their abilities. Clerics and paladins make use of the divine power source. Divine powers are commonly called prayers.

dragon: A reptile-like monster that usually has wings and a devastating breath weapon — a worthy challenge for any true hero!

dragonborn: A player character race. Dragonborn are big, strong reptilians who often wander the world as mercenaries. They have the ability to breathe fire (or other dangerous stuff) on their enemies, much like dragons. They make excellent fighters, paladins, and warlords.

Dungeon Master (DM): The player who runs the game for the other players. The DM creates the dungeons and lands the PCs explore, decides what sort of monsters or challenges the PCs must overcome, controls the monsters when they battle the adventurers, and referees the game.

dwarf: A player character race. Dwarves are mountain-folk who are the finest miners and metalworkers in the world. They are exceedingly tough and resilient and make excellent clerics and paladins.

eladrin: A player character race. Eladrins are an elf-like people who live in beautiful cities in the Feywild (the lands of faerie). They are agile and intelligent and make excellent rangers, rogues, and wizards.

elemental: A monster origin that describes creatures native to the Elemental Chaos, the plane of existence where the fundamental forces of the world are born. Demons, efreet, salamanders, and slaad are all elemental monsters.

elf: A player character race. Elves are a graceful woodland race who are the finest archers and hunters in the world. They do very well as clerics, rangers, and rogues.

encounter: Adventures consist of a series of encounters. Fights against monsters are called combat encounters. Noncombat encounters, in contrast, feature skill challenges or roleplaying situations such as negotiations.

encounter power: A power that you can use once per encounter. You regain encounter powers after a short rest.

epic destiny: A set of character abilities and powers you choose when your character reaches 21st level. You continue to advance in your original character class.

escape: A combat action in which you try to get away from an enemy who's grabbing you (see also *grab*), or you get out of a similar effect. An escape attempt is a move action.

evil: An alignment. Evil creatures don't care if they have to hurt others to get ahead, and they use power to enslave or tyrannize others.

experience points (XP): A measure of your character's personal achievement and advancement. Your character earns XP by defeating monsters and overcoming challenges. Characters continue to accumulate experience points throughout their careers, gaining new levels in their character class at certain experience point totals.

exploit: A martial power.

extended rest: A period of recuperation that lasts at least six hours of time in the game world. After an extended rest, a character's powers recharge.

feat: A special talent, knack, edge, or tactic your character possesses. For example, the Toughness feat increases the number of hit points a character has; the Weapon Focus feat increases the damage a character deals with weapons of a specific group; and the Linguist feat lets a character learn additional languages.

fey: A monster origin that describes creatures native to the Feywild, the realm of faerie. Fey monsters include various nature spirits or creatures with similar mystic origins, such as the dryad, hag, or satyr.

fighter: A player character class. Fighters have exceptional combat abilities and skills with weapons.

flank: To be directly on the other side of an opponent who is being threatened by another ally. A flanking attacker gains combat advantage against the flanked opponent.

Fortitude defense (Fort): One of the basic defense scores. Attacks affecting Fortitude defense generally include effects a character resists through sheer physical stamina or power, such as surviving the effects of poison or resisting movement.

gish: Table talk for a character who uses both martial and arcane powers. Usually, this character will be a fighter with wizard multiclass feats, so that he or she has a mix of fighter powers and wizard powers.

gold piece (gp): The standard unit of currency in the D&D game. One gold piece equals 10 silver pieces or 100 copper pieces; 100 gold pieces equal 1 platinum piece.

good: An alignment. Good creatures believe that aiding others is the right thing to do, and they're willing to stand up to evil in any form.

grab: A combat action in which a character tries to seize an opponent and keep him from moving away. When a character is grabbed, he or she can still act normally in most regards, except that he or she can't move unless you succeed in an escape attempt.

half-elf: A player character race. Half-elves are people descended from a mixture of human and elven ancestors, and combine many of the best features of both races. They excel as warlocks and do well as paladins or warlords.

halfling: A player character race. Halflings are clever, resourceful, and lucky. Despite their small statures, they are quite brave and adventurous. Halflings make very good rogues, rangers, and warlocks.

healing: A keyword describing a power or ability that restores lost hit points.

healing surge: A single "dose" of healing, normally equal to $\frac{1}{4}$ your character's normal full hit points. Most healing effects give you the ability to spend a healing surge; the number of healing surges you can use per day depends on your character's class and Constitution modifier.

hit: To make a successful attack roll, as in, "My attack's a 27, did I hit?"

hit points (hp): A measure of your character's health. Damage that characters take decreases their current hit points. Lost hit points are restored either by healing effects (drinking a *potion of healing,* for example), or by resting for a time.

holy symbol: An implement used by clerics and paladins.

human: A player character race. Humans are tough and adaptable, and can do very well in any character class.

humanoid: A monster type made up of creatures that are roughly humanlike, such as dwarves, elves, giants, goblins, and orcs.

immortal: A monster origin describing creatures native to the dominions of the Astral Sea. Angels and devils are immortals.

implement: A device that serves as a "weapon" for a cleric, warlock, or wizard. For example, a wizard might use a wand to deliver a spell attack instead of striking with a sword or bow like a martial character would. See also *holy symbol, orb, staff,* and *wand.*

initiative: A system for determining the sequence of actions during a battle. Before the first round of combat, each combatant makes a single initiative check. Each round, everyone acts in order from the highest initiative result to the lowest. Usually, you just use your first initiative roll for the whole fight.

initiative check: A check used to determine your place in the initiative order for a combat. An initiative check is 1d20 + Dexterity modifier + any special modifiers your character may have.

insubstantial: Not quite physically real. Some monsters such as ghosts and shadows are insubstantial. Insubstantial monsters take half damage from all attacks.

keyword: A descriptive word in a power or monster description that lets you know what groups that power or monster belongs to. For example, if a spell has the arcane and fire keywords, anything else that affects arcane powers or fire powers affects that spell.

lawful good: An alignment. Lawful good creatures believe in establishing order and enforcing just laws for the benefit of all creatures, and they're willing to fight evil in any form.

leader: A character role. Leaders are light on offense but have powerful healing and defensive abilities that help the other characters in the party fight better.

level: A measure of advancement or power applied to characters (for example, a 10th-level fighter), monsters (an 8th-level ogre), powers (a 4th-level divine prayer), and magic items (such as a 13th-level staff).

level modifier: A basic measure of skill derived from your character level. Your level modifier is equal to half your character level, rounded down. For example, a 5th-level character has a level modifier of +2, and an 18th-level character has a level modifier of +9.

low-light vision: The ability to see better than a human in conditions of dim illumination. Beings such as elves have low-light vision.

magic: Arcane and divine powers are generally considered to be "magic," as are effects or properties of magic items.

magic item: A piece of equipment that is enchanted to offer a bonus or special property of some kind. Magic items include armor; weapons; implements (holy symbols, orbs, rods, staffs, and wands); boots and greaves; shields and bracers; cloaks and amulets; belts; and wondrous items (a catch-all for everything else). Some magic items can be used or worn only on a specific part of the user's body (or body slot), and are therefore known as slotted items.

magical beast: A monster type made up of creatures with beast-like forms and supernatural powers or intelligence, such as displacer beasts, dragons, gorgons, and ropers.

mark: To challenge a creature with a power or effect that demands its attention. If a creature you mark makes an attack that doesn't include you, it takes a –2 penalty on its attack rolls. New marks wipe out old marks, so if the paladin challenges an enemy marked by a fighter, the paladin's mark applies and the fighter's mark is cleared.

martial: One of the power sources from which characters derive their abilities. Fighters, rangers, rogues, and warlords make use of the martial power source. Martial powers are commonly called exploits.

masterwork: Armor types constructed from such fantastic materials that the "weakest" version you might ever find possesses at least a +4 enhancement value.

min-max: The practice of trying to make your character as effective as possible by choosing the right powers, feats, and magic items.

melee: Combat at close range, in which combatants are trading jabs, thrusts, slams, or slashes with melee weapons or natural weapons.

melee attack: A type of attack in which the attacker targets a specific enemy (or enemies) he or she can reach with a melee weapon — although sometimes the melee "weapon" might simply be a touch that delivers the effect of a magical power.

milestone: A measure of your success in your current adventure. Usually, milestones are determined by the number of experience points you've earned so far. Reaching a milestone grants you an additional action point (see *action point*) and may provide other benefits as well.

monster origin: A keyword that describes what sort of creature a monster is: aberrant, elemental, fey, immortal, natural, or shadow. Most creatures native to the mortal world — humans, dragons, bears, goblins, and so on — are natural.

multiclass: A type of feat that allows your character to acquire a small number of class features, skills, or powers of another class.

nonplayer character (NPC): A character controlled by the DM. NPCs can be any of the people your character meets (such as innkeepers, merchants, and the rich noble that asked the party to retrieve a lost or stolen heirloom), as well as the villains or rivals your character encounters (such as evil clerics, wizards, rogues, and fighters).

opportunity attack: A single basic melee attack that a combatant may make when an opponent within reach takes an action that provokes an opportunity attack, such as moving without using the shift action or using a ranged attack.

orb: A type of magic implement. Implements function much like weapons for weapon-using characters; if you have a magic orb, it gives you an enhancement bonus of +1 or more that you can add to all attack and damage rolls you make when wielding that device.

paladin: A player character class. Paladins are divine defenders who are often champions of justice and good.

paragon path: A specific set of character abilities and powers you choose when your character reaches 11th level. You continue to advance in your original character class.

plane: A different realm or layer of existence, such as the Shadowfell, the Elemental Chaos, or the Astral Sea.

platinum piece (pp): A unit of currency equal to 100 gold pieces.

player character (PC): A character controlled by one of the players at the table, as opposed to the DM. Your character is your avatar in the game.

potion: A magic item that's basically a one-shot effect that any character can use.

power: A specific attack, defense, or utility effect a character or creature can use. Powers may be usable at-will, once per encounter, or once per day.

power source: The mechanism or origin of your character's heroic powers. The three power sources described in the *Player's Handbook* are martial, arcane, and divine, but other power sources exist too.

prayer: A divine power.

prerequisite: A condition or requirement that must be met before your character can get something. For example, the Hammer Rhythm feat has prerequisites of Strength 15 and Constitution 17.

pull: An effect that lets you drag another creature closer to you by the stated number of squares.

push: An effect that lets you move another creature away from you by the stated number of squares.

race: A character's species or kind. Race determines a character's general size and looks, and it also grants special bonuses to skills and ability scores. At the time of this writing, the races available for you to play are dragonborn, dwarf, eladrin, elf, half-elf, halfling, human, and tiefling.

range: The distance at which you can attack with a ranged weapon. For example, the shortbow has a range of 15/30 squares. If you shoot at 15 squares or less, the attack takes no penalty; if you shoot at 16 to 30 squares, it's a long-range attack, and takes a –2 penalty.

ranged attack: A type of attack in which the attacker targets a specific enemy (or enemies) he or she can fire at with a thrown weapon, missile weapon, or magical effect such as a spell or prayer.

ranger: A player character class. Rangers are martial strikers and have access to excellent ranged attacks (archery) and excellent melee attacks (two-weapon fighting). They are skilled warriors of the wilderness.

reach: The ability to make a melee attack against someone who isn't standing right next to you. Many big monsters have natural reach; human-sized characters can get reach by choosing long weapons such as polearms.

Reflex defense (Ref): One of a creature's basic defenses. It measures the ability to evade an attack through quickness or agility. Attacks that target Reflex defense are usually area blasts or rays that the target might dodge. In addition, attacks that bypass armor often target Reflex defense instead of Armor Class.

resistance: A special defense that allows a creature to ignore a set amount of damage from attacks of certain types. For example, wearing *+2 blackiron armor* gives you resist 5 fire and resist 5 necrotic. Any attacks with the fire or necrotic keywords deal –5 damage against you.

rogue: A player character class. Rogues are martial strikers. They are nimble characters who excel at using skills and making sneak attacks.

role: A term describing a character or monster's basic function in combat. Player character roles include defender, striker, controller, and leader. Monster roles include artillery, brute, lurker, skirmisher, and soldier.

round: A single unit of game time, especially in battles. A round represents about six seconds in the game world (but it takes longer than that in real time).

run: Run is a move action that lets you move up to your speed +2 squares. However, you take a penalty on your attack rolls and grant combat advantage until your next turn.

saving throw (save): A roll made to recover from the negative effects of a special attack, such as a spell or monster ability. For example, a powerful attack might leave the target weakened or incapacitated until he or she succeeds on a saving throw. Normally a creature can attempt a saving throw each round against each effect currently affecting it.

scroll: A magic item that's basically a one-shot use of a single specific ritual. For example, a scroll of *linked portal* lets your character perform the ritual *linked portal* one time, even if your character normally couldn't perform that ritual.

second wind: A combat action that lets you spend a standard action to use one of your healing surges. In addition, you gain a +2 bonus to all defenses until the start of your next turn. You can use second wind only once per encounter.

shadow: A monster origin describing creatures native to the Shadowfell, the plane of shadow that exists parallel to the mortal world. Shadar-kai, nightshades, and many undead are shadow monsters.

shift: A move action that lets you adjust your position 1 square in any direction. A shift doesn't provoke an opportunity attack.

short rest: Characters recuperate between encounters by taking a short rest that lasts at least five minutes in the game world. After a short rest, encounter powers are recharged.

silver piece (sp): A unit of currency equal to 1/10 of a gold piece.

slide: An effect that lets you move another creature a certain number of spaces in any direction you want.

spell: An arcane power.

stack: Combine multiple bonuses for a cumulative effect. Usually, you get only the best bonus of any given type that applies, but if you gain bonuses of different types, they all work together. For example, two effects granting a +2 power bonus to AC don't stack; they both grant power bonuses, so you get only the better of the two. If one effect granted a +2 feat bonus and the other granted a +2 power bonus, they would stack and grant a +4 bonus to AC.

staff: A type of magic implement. Implements function much like weapons for weapon-using characters; if you have a magic staff, it gives you an enhancement bonus of +1 or more that you can add to all attack and damage rolls you make when wielding that device. (The quarterstaff is a simple weapon that's pretty much a two-handed club.)

striker: A character role. Strikers are offense-oriented characters who excel in dealing a lot of damage to one target at a time.

sustain: Concentrating to maintain an active power's effect. Most powers don't require you to sustain them, but a few do; the details depend on each specific power. Sustaining a power can be a minor or standard action.

take 10: Instead of risking a bad roll on some skill checks, you can simply state that you want to "take 10." This gives you a result as if you'd rolled a 10 on your 1d20 roll, plus whatever modifiers apply. You can take 10 only when your character is not being threatened or distracted; the DM has the final say on whether you can take 10 in any given situation or check.

tiefling: A player character race. Tieflings are the descendants of humans who long ago bargained with infernal powers. They are a charismatic, self-reliant race. Tieflings make excellent warlocks, warlords, and wizards.

two-handed weapon: A weapon designed for use in two hands, such as a greatsword.

unaligned: An alignment (or more specifically, the lack of one). Unaligned creatures pursue their own interests. Unaligned heroes do help people, but usually because they expect some reward.

unarmed strike: An attack made by a character or creature without a weapon. (Most animals and monsters have natural weapons such as claws or teeth and, therefore, aren't considered "unarmed"; they don't make unarmed strikes.)

undead: A keyword that describes monsters that have died but won't stay buried, including ghosts, ghouls, vampires, skeletons, and wraiths. Undead are immune to some attacks and vulnerable to others.

wand: A type of magic implement. Implements function much like weapons for weapon-using characters; if you have a magic wand, it gives you an enhancement bonus of +1 or more that you can add to all attack and damage rolls you make when wielding that device.

warlock: A player character class. Warlocks are highly elusive arcane strikers. They use fearsome curses and deadly spells to defeat their enemies.

warlord: A player character class. Warlords are martial leaders. They specialize in melee combat, often standing side by side with the party's defenders.

weapon group: The family a particular weapon belongs to. For example, the light blades group includes daggers, short swords, and rapiers. Any power you can use with a light blade, you can use with any of these weapons.

Will defense (Will): One of the basic defenses. Will defense measures your character's ability to withstand ill effects through mental strength and willpower.

wizard: A player character class. Wizards are arcane controllers. They have low hit points and Armor Class, but they wield powerful arcane spells that can affect multiple enemies at once.

world, the: The "normal" plane of existence; the "real world" for D&D characters, as opposed to other planes like the Feywild, the Nine Hells, or the Elemental Chaos (see *plane*). Sometimes referred to as "the mortal world" or "the world of mortals."

Index

• A •

aberrant, defined, 397
abilities
  of clerics, 140
  defined, 397
  of fighters, 131
  of rogues, 135
  of wizards, 137
ability adjustments
  of dwarves, 146
  of elves, 147
  of halflings, 148
  of humans, 144
ability checks, 19, 72–73, 397
ability modifier, 397
ability scores
  adjustments, 227–228
  armor choices, 216–217
  by class, 127, 157–158
  customization, 156
  generating, 155–157
  how they work, 151–155
  increasing, 226
  min-maxing, 294
  modifiers, 153
  of monsters, 320
  overview, 24–25, 117
  skill base, 123
  training compared to, 201
ability scores of characters
  Beryn, 54
  Calia, 38
  Chenna, 66
  Dreggu, 56
  Eberk, 68
  Jax, 44
  Lidda, 48
  Regdar, 34, 104, 106
  Shadow, 46
  Telsa, 58
  Thomm, 64
  Tordek, 36

AC (Armor Class)
  alternatives to, 79
  damage reduction, 216
  defined, 398
  overview, 120
  powers against, 81
  superior, 248–249
  target numbers, setting, 73
accuracy, 122, 192
acid arrow, 175
Acrobatics, 201, 203–207
action-denial powers, 232–233
action points, 86–87, 121, 397
Action Surge, 189, 195
actions
  defined, 397
  minor, 77–78, 94, 397
  move, 77–78, 94, 397
  standard, 77–78, 81, 94, 397
actors, 345–347
ad (astral diamond), 210, 398
AD&D (Advanced DUNGEONS & DRAGONS), 10
adjudicating results, 307–308
adjustments for race, 23
adult red dragon (level 15 solo soldier), 387
Advanced DUNGEONS & DRAGONS (AD&D), 10
adventure
  character roles in, 29, 280–281
  characteristics of, 346–347
  choices, 308–309
  components, 13–17
  creating, 323–328
  defined, 13, 14
  encounter types, 71–72
  enjoyment of, 351–354
  game rules, 17–19
  joining in, 19–20
  narration, 348–351
  objectives, 12
  overview, 9–11
  preparing, 304
  sample scenario, 330–342

adventurer's kit, 219
Adventurer's Vault, 292
aid another, 245, 249, 282, 397
Alertness, 197
alignment of characters
  chaotic evil alignment, 116, 276–277, 399
  choices of, 116
  defined, 398
  evil character alignment, 116, 276–277, 402
  good character alignment, 115, 276, 403
  lawful good character alignment,
    115, 276, 404
ally movement options, 86
ancient blue dragon (level 28 solo
    artillery), 391
anvil of doom, 167, 357–358
Arcana (training), 206, 207
arcane, 398
arcane characters, 27
arcane gate, 177, 233
arcane implement, 137, 218, 273
Arcane Reach, 194, 195
arcane spells, 83
area attack, 84, 398
arm slot items, 259
armor. *See also* magic
  Beryn, 55
  Calia, 39
  Chenna, 67
  choices, 217
  Dreggu, 57
  Eberk, 69
  fighter, 266
  Jax, 45
  Lidda, 49
  magic, 259
  overview, 215–217
  Regdar, 35, 105, 109
  Shadow, 47
  Telsa, 59
  Thomm, 65
  Tordek, 37
armor check penalty, 123, 201, 204
Armor Class (AC)
  alternatives to, 79
  damage reduction, 216
  defined, 398
  overview, 120
  powers against, 81
  superior, 248–249
  target numbers, setting, 73
Armor Proficiency, 191, 194, 196, 197

Arneson, Dave (game developer), 10
artillery, 239, 240
assets of D&D, 11
assumptions, reassessing, 241
astral diamond (ad), 210, 398
Astral Fire, 194, 196, 197
at-will powers, 27, 81, 124, 162, 398
Atari game publication, 18
Athletics, 204, 205, 207
attack rolls, 19, 72–73, 81, 119, 194, 398
attacks
  bonus, 121–122
  close, 83–84, 163, 170, 176–177, 181, 399
  covering, 167
  daily, 296
  damage, 25, 80, 87–88
  direct, 252
  melee, 133, 163
  of monsters, 319–320
  opportunity attacks, 85, 133, 134,
    243–246, 406
  passing, 165
  powers, 27, 160, 186, 235, 255
  ranged, 163
  as standard action, 94
  types of, 83–84
  with weapons, 79
attacks, basic
  Beryn, 54
  Calia, 38
  Chenna, 66
  defined, 398
  Dreggu, 56
  Eberk, 68
  Jax, 44
  Lidda, 48
  magic missile, 138–139
  options, 121–122
  Regdar, 34, 104, 106
  Shadow, 46
  Telsa, 58
  Thomm, 64
  Tordek, 36
  using, 122
avenging flame, 179
awe strike, 374

● *B* ●

backdrop for D&D, 9
Backstabber, 192

bag of holding, 219
bait and switch, 172, 366
Baker, Richard (author)
  Swordmage, 395
base damage, 122
basic attacks. *See also* attacks
  Beryn, 54
  Calia, 38
  Chenna, 66
  defined, 398
  Dreggu, 56
  Eberk, 68
  Jax, 44
  Lidda, 48
  magic missile, 138–139
  options, 121–122
  Regdar, 34, 104, 106
  Shadow, 46
  Telsa, 58
  Thomm, 64
  Tordek, 36
  using, 122
bastard sword, 196, 213, 215
bastion of health, 181
Battle Cleric
  ability scores, 158
  as caster/noncaster, 253
  as character choice, 139–140
  feats of, 195, 196
  overview, 62
  powers, 177–179
  skill package, 207
battle grid, 91–94, 329
battle order, 78
battle strategy, 237–241
Battle Wizard, 158
battleaxe, 213
battlefield control, 248
beacon of hope, 181
beast, 398
beginning players, 3
beholder eye of flame (level 13 elite
    artillery), 384
believability, 307
benign transposition, 182
Beryn (wizard), 43, 54–55
Bigby's grasping hands, 177
Bigby's icy grasp, 253
Blackiron armor, 266
Blade Opportunist, 190, 246
blazing skeleton (level 5 artillery), 380

bless, 249
blinded characters, 89
blinding barrage, 365–366
bloodied characters/creatures, 87, 318, 398
bloodied number, 118
bloodied value, 26
bloodthread armor, 273
bloody path, 172
bluff
  checks, 118–119, 172, 233
  of rogues, 171, 203, 205
blur, 175
bonus
  for ability scores, 153
  armor, 221
  attack, 120–121, 249
  charging, 242
  defenses, 81
  enhancement, 264, 269, 273
  feats, 123, 138, 141, 187
  flanking, 241
  by race, 156
  skill, 201
  weapons/weapon proficiency, 212, 221
bookstores, 20
Booster Packs, 18
boundless endurance, 166
bow, 214
boxing, 247
Brawny Rogue
  ability scores, 158
  build, 168
  as character choice, 134
  feats of, 191
  powers, 169–170
  Shadow as, 43
  skills for, 205
Broot (bugbear), 332, 333
Brutal Scoundrel, 169
brute strike, 165
brutes, 239
buffing powers, 282–283, 398
bugbears, 332, 333
builds
  character, 131
  cleric, 62, 139–140
  fighter, 32, 131, 163–164
  number of, 159
  rogue, 42, 134, 168
  wizard, 52–53, 137
bull rush, 398

Burning Blizzard, 194, 195
burning hands, 174
buying magic items, 261–262

• *C* •

Calia (fighter), 33, 38–39
campaign settings, 10, 305
cantrips (wizards), 138
carpet of flying, 262
cartoons, 10
cast a spell, 398
casters, 251, 253, 399
chainmail, 221
Chainmail miniatures rules, 10
challenge encounters, 72, 325
change history (1970s), 10
Channel Divinity, 140, 141, 196, 197
chaotic evil alignment, 116, 276–277, 399
character, PCs (player characters)
  balancing class choices, 128
  defining, 21–27
  monsters compared to, 95–97
  playing, 27–29
  role of, 13, 14, 29, 99
  selecting, 30
character ability scores
  Beryn, 54
  Calia, 38
  Chenna, 66
  Dreggu, 56
  Eberk, 68
  Jax, 44
  Lidda, 48
  Regdar, 34, 104, 106
  Shadow, 46
  Telsa, 58
  Thomm, 64
  Tordek, 36
character alignment
  chaotic evil alignment, 116, 276–277, 399
  choices of, 116
  defined, 398
  evil character alignment, 116, 276–277, 402
  good character alignment, 115, 276, 403
  lawful good character alignment, 115, 276, 404
character building
  creature reference source, 15
  epic destiny, 296–297
  min-maxing, 291–294
  multiclassing, 297–300
  overview, 3–4
  paragon path choices, 294–296
character defenses
  Beryn, 54
  Calia, 38
  Chenna, 66
  Dreggu, 56
  Eberk, 68
  Jax, 44
  Lidda, 48
  Regdar, 34, 104, 106
  Shadow, 46
  Telsa, 58
  Thomm, 64
  Tordek, 36
character equipment
  armor, 215–217
  gear, 218–219
  overview, 209
  shopping, 210–211
  upgrading, 220–221
  weapons, 212–215
character feats
  Beryn, 54
  Calia, 38
  Chenna, 67
  Dreggu, 56
  Eberk, 69
  Jax, 44
  Lidda, 48
  Regdar, 34, 104, 106
  Shadow, 46
  Telsa, 58
  Thomm, 64
  Tordek, 36
  wizards, 193
character powers
  Beryn, 54–55
  Calia, 39
  Chenna, 67
  clerics, 141, 177–182, 373–376
  Dreggu, 56–57
  Eberk, 69
  fighters, 133–134, 163–168, 357–362
  Jax, 45
  Lidda, 49
  monsters, 319–320
  Regdar, 35, 105, 107–108
  rogues, 136, 168–172, 363–367
  Shadow, 47

Telsa, 59
Thomm, 65
Tordek, 37
  wizards, 138–139, 172–177, 369–372
character sheets
  key statistics on, 25
  overview, 22–27, 111–112
  sample, 112
  sections of, 112–125
  sources of, 16–17
  supplies of, 15
character skills
  Beryn, 54
  Calia, 39
  Chenna, 67
  Dreggu, 56
  Eberk, 69
  Jax, 44
  Lidda, 48–49
  Regdar, 34–35, 104–105, 107
  Shadow, 46
  Telsa, 58
  Thomm, 65
  Tordek, 36–37
character types, race of
  clerics, 140
  dwarves, 145–146
  elves, 147–148
  fighters, 131
  halflings, 148–150
  humans, 143–145
  other types, 150
  rogues, 134–135
  wizards, 137
character weapons
  Beryn, 55
  Calia, 39
  Chenna, 67
  Dreggu, 57
  Eberk, 69
  Jax, 45
  Lidda, 49
  Regdar, 35, 105, 109
  Shadow, 47
  Telsa, 59
  Thomm, 65
  Tordek, 37
character(s). *See also* fighter
  actions of, 19, 74–75, 77–78
  battle grid placement, 93–94
  class of, 113, 123, 128–130, 160, 399

description, 117, 399
DM tasks, 308
downed, 284–285
effects on, 77, 88
episodic, 11, 12
equipment levels, 221
experience points, 223–225
feats of, 186, 187, 188
level of, 103–108, 225–228, 263
markers, 329
maximizing, 249
min-maxing, 294
players compared with, 28
roles of, 128–142, 299
victories, 12
charging, 242–243
Charisma (Cha)
  ability scores, 152, 155
  of clerics, 196, 197
  of rogues, 192
  of wizards, 194
cheating, 353
checklist, adventure-building, 327
Chenna (cleric), 63, 66–67
City of Brass, 262
class
  ability scores by, 157–158
  armor choices, 217
  buffing powers, 283
  of characters, 113, 123, 128–130, 160, 399
  cleric, 140–141
  description, 130–142
  dwarf, 146
  elf, 148
  feats, 187
  fighter, 133
  halfling, 150
  hit point determination, 117–118
  human, 145
  overview, 23–24, 127–128
  powers, 161
  weapons, 213
  wizard, 137–138
class features
  Beryn, 54
  Calia, 38
  Chenna, 66
  Dreggu, 56
  Eberk, 68
  Jax, 44
  Lidda, 48

class features *(continued)*
  Regdar, 34, 104, 106
  Shadow, 46
  Telsa, 58
  Thomm, 64
  Tordek, 36
  updating, 228
class skill, 399
cleave, 165
cleric
  ability scores, 158
  armor, 216
  bonus feats, 187
  defined, 399
  description, 61, 62
  divine prayers, 81
  feats of, 185, 195–198
  gear, 211, 218
  how to play the role, 62–63
  as leader, 29, 129
  magic items, 268–271
  overview, 24, 30, 139–141
  powers of, 27, 177–182, 373–376
  rituals of, 256
  role of, 63
  selecting, 63–70
  skill package, 207
  weapons, 214–215
  who should play the role, 61–62
climactic encounter, 327
Close attacks, 83–84, 163, 170, 176–177,
    181, 399
close powers, 254
cloud of daggers, 176, 372
cloud of steel, 170, 172, 365
color pages, 4
color spray, 176–177
combat
  basics, 75–78
  challenge/superiority, 133
  choices, 231–234
  conditions, 88–90
  cooperation, 281–282
  DM tasks, 314–317
  encounters, 72, 325
  engaging in, 78–81
  foes, adapting to, 247–249
  initiative roll during, 28
  magic in, 254
  mapping, 17
  movement in, 84–86

  powers/resources, 81–84, 235–237
  practice, 93–97
  strategy, 237–241
  tactics, 241–246, 321
combat advantage, 399
Combat Anticipation, 193, 198
Combat Reflexes, 246
come and get it, 167, 361
comeback strike, 167, 361
command, 179, 232, 233
competitive players, 12, 346–347
components, 13–17
computer games, 18
concealment, 400
condition, 400
consecrated ground, 179
console games, 18
Constitution (Con), 152, 154, 194, 196, 197
Constitution score, 117–118
construct, 400
Consult Mystic Sages, 261
Consult Oracle, 261
Control Wizard
  ability scores, 158
  feats, 193, 194–195
  overview, 52–53, 137, 175–177
  powers, 173, 176
  skill package, 206
controller
  defined, 400
  monsters as, 239, 240
  overview, 128–129
  ranged, 247
  role of, 29
  wizard as, 53, 136
conversation of DM, 313–314
cooperation among players, 12, 281–282
copper piece (cp), 210, 400
core mechanic, 17–19, 72, 153
cost of rituals, 257
counterproductive playing, 280
coup de grace, 400
cover (in combat), 245, 400
covering attack, 167
cp (copper piece), 210, 400
crack the shell, 167
crash course, 3
creatures, 400. *See also* character(s)
crimson edge, 364
crit, 400
critical hits, 80, 400

crossbow, 215
crushing blow, 134, 165, 253
cure disease, 257, 258
cure light wounds, 160, 180, 373
cure serious wounds, 180, 181, 374
currency, 210
customization, 16, 156–157, 185
cut-scenes, 350–351
cyclops impaler (level 14 artillery), 383

• *D* •

d20 dice
  in attacks, 94
  battle order determination, 78
  practice session, 94
  success likelihood, 16, 18, 19, 72
dagger, 215
daily attack, 296
daily exploits, 164
daily powers
  defined, 400
  with magic items, 266
  overview, 81, 124, 236–237
  replacing, 163
  selecting, 162
  types of, 165
damage
  from attacks, 80, 87–88
  concentrating, 248
  defined, 400
  determining, 121–122
  effects of, 94
  of fighters, 165
  hit points, 118
  ongoing, 77
  rating, 212
  reduction of, 166, 216
  spells, 175
dance of steel, 167
Danger Sense, 193
DARK SUN, 10
darkleaf armor, 268
darkvision, 400
daunting light, 181, 375
dazed characters, 89
DC (Difficulty Class)
  action success, 73
  for attacks, 79
  defined, 401

determining, 19
practice session, 97–98
rulebook samples, 75
of skills, 202
D&D Dungeon Tiles, 15
D&D (DUNGEONS & DRAGONS). *See*
    DUNGEONS & DRAGONS (D&D)
D&D Insider (Web site), 10, 15, 17, 18, 111,
    117, 150, 304
D&D Miniatures, 15, 17
D&D Miniatures Starter Set, 18
D&D Player's Handbook
  as background, 3
  for beginning players, 1, 5, 20
  classes in, 23
  combat movement, 85
  names in, 22, 113
  as reference, 15, 16
  RPG experience in, 18
D&D Roleplaying Game Starter Set, 17, 102
D&D Tiles, 17, 92
deadly positioning, 170
deafened characters, 89
death, 87, 118
death knight (level 25 elite soldier), 390
death saving throw, 87
deathjump spider (level 4 skirmisher), 378
decision points, 278
deep cut power, 170
defender
  beginning players' choice, 128
  defined, 401
  fighter as, 29, 32–33. *See also* fighter
  overview, 129
  paladin as, 141. *See also* paladin
defenses
  alternatives, 79
  attacker advantages, 80
  bonus points, 81
  of characters, 25
  of monsters, 318
  overview, 119–121
  pairing, 154
  types of, 244–245
defenses of characters
  Beryn, 54
  Calia, 38
  Chenna, 66
  Dreggu, 56
  Eberk, 68

defenses of characters *(continued)*
 Jax, 44
 Lidda, 48
 Regdar, 34, 104, 106
 Shadow, 46
 Telsa, 58
 Thomm, 64
 Tordek, 36
Defensive Advantage, 192
deities, 62, 116
delay tactic, 242, 254, 282
destinations, specific, 85
destiny of characters, 114, 297
Detect Magic skill, 206
Devastating Critical, 194, 196
Devoted Cleric
 ability scores, 158
 as caster, 253
 feats of, 195, 196–198
 overview, 62, 139–140
 powers, 177, 180–182
 skill package, 207
Dexterity check, 119
Dexterity (Dex)
 ability scores, 152, 154
 Acrobatics, 201
 armor choices, 216
 as feat, 190
 of rogues, 191, 192
 of wizards, 194, 195
dice
 attack rolls, 19, 72–73, 81, 119, 194, 398
 fudging results, 353
 rolling, 18, 19, 72–73, 75, 248–249
 types of, 16
differences from other games, 11
difficulty class (DC)
 action success, 73
 for attacks, 79
 defined, 401
 determining, 19
 practice session, 97–98
 rulebook samples, 75
 of skills, 202
dimension door, 175
Diplomacy (encounter), 203, 206, 207, 233
dire rat (level 1 brute), 379
dire straits, 278
disguise self, 253
dispel magic, 370
disruptive strike, 182

distance in combat (movement), 85
divine aid, 181
divine characters, 27
divine fortune, 140, 141
divine power, 179, 401
divine prayers, 81
dizzying blow, 165, 360–361
DM (Dungeon Master). *See* Dungeon
 Master (DM)
dominated characters, 89
downed characters, 284–285
dragon, 401
Dragon Magazine, 18
dragonborn, 150, 401
DRAGONLANCE, 10
Dragonlance Chronicles (Weis and Hickman),
 393
Dragonlance Legends (Weis and Hickman), 393
dragon's fangs, 165
Dreggu (wizard), 43, 56–57
dungeon building. *See* adventure; dungeon
 sample
dungeon exploration, 73–75
Dungeon Magazine, 18
Dungeon Master 4th Edition For Dummies, 304
Dungeon Master (DM)
 adventure choices, 308–309
 alignment choices, 116
 applicable chapters, 3
 battle grid determinations, 78
 character creation, 103, 113
 defined, 401
 deity choices, 116
 dice rolls, 75
 difficulty class, 73
 Dungeon Magazine, 18
 entitlements, treasure/magic, 264
 finding, 102
 magic items decisions, 261
 membership choices, 101
 monster optimization, 318–321
 overview, 4, 303–304
 passive perception score, 119
 role of, 13, 14, 95, 99, 304–308
 rulings, 29
 skill checks, 202, 234
 tasks of, 309–317
 team needs, 130
 veto options, 117
 weight limits, 219
 XP determinations, 224–225

Dungeon Master's Guide
  battle grid, 92
  beginning players, 5
  as reference, 3, 15
  RPG experience in, 18
  as starting point, 20
dungeon sample
  adventure, 330–342
  setup, 328–330
  wrapup, 342–344
DUNGEONS & DRAGONS Basic Set, 10
DUNGEONS & DRAGONS (D&D).
  components, 13–17
  game rules, 17–19
  history of, 1, 10
  joining in, 19–20
  objectives, 12
  overview, 10–11, 13
  plastic miniatures, 18
*DUNGEONS & DRAGONS Roleplaying Game
    Starter Set,* 15, 20
dwarf
  armor, 217, 266
  defined, 401
  Dreggu (wizard), 56–57
  Eberk (cleric), 68–69
  overview, 23
  race, 145–146
  Tordek (fighter), 36–37
  weapon choices, 213
dwarven greaves, 258
dying, 87–88, 89, 118

• *E* •

easy target, 170
Eberk (cleric), 63, 68–69, 97
EBERRON Campaign Setting, 305
EBERRON settings, 18
eladrin, 150, 401
elder purple worm (level 24 solo soldier), 390
elemental, 401
elf
  accuracy, 192
  Calia (fighter), 38–39
  cloak, 258
  defined, 401
  overview, 23
  race, 147–148

Telsa (wizard), 58–59
  weapon choices, 213
Enchant Magic Item ritual, 262
enchanting items, 262
encounter attack, 296
encounters
  combat, 78–79, 324
  defined, 401
  key to, 329–330
  powers, 81, 124, 162, 235–236, 401
  types of, 325–326
ending of adventure, 327
Endurance, 204
endure elements, 255
enemy movement options, 86
enhancement bonuses/value,
    258, 264, 269, 273
entitlements, treasure/magic, 264
epic destiny, 114, 161, 228, 266, 296–297, 402
equipment. *See also* magic; outfitting
    characters
  of characters, 12, 125, 221, 263
  of Jax, 45
  min-maxing, 294
  of monsters, 320
  overview, 26
  of Regdar, 35
escape, 402
Evasion, 190, 192, 193, 194, 196
even-handed treatment, 354
event-based adventure, 326
evil character alignment, 116, 276–277, 402
exalted armor, 270
excitement, 306
Expanded Spellbook, 194–195
experience points (XP)
  achievement level, 24
  defined, 402
  dungeon sample, 333, 336, 338–341
  gaining, 223–225
  for level advancements, 227
  of monsters, 318
experienced players, 2, 3
exploit power, 402
exploits
  of fighters, 30, 133–134, 164–167
  of martial characters, 27
  of rogues, 30, 136, 168, 169, 171
exploration, 73–75, 312–313
extended rest, 402

• F •

failure chances, 72
falchion (weapon), 213
fantasy world changes (campaign settings), 10
favored tactics, 279
feats
    acquiring, 187
    armor choices, 217
    bonus, 138, 141
    choices, 187–198, 228
    defined, 402
    description, 186
    gaining, 227
    min-maxing, 294
    multiclassing, 297–298
    overview, 26, 123, 185
    weapons, 213
feats of characters
    Beryn, 54
    Calia, 38
    Chenna, 67
    Dreggu, 56
    Eberk, 69
    Jax, 44
    Lidda, 48
    Regdar, 34, 104, 106
    Shadow, 46
    Telsa, 58
    Thomm, 64
    Tordek, 36
    wizards, 193
feet slot items, 260
fey, 402
fiery bolts, 258
fighter
    ability scores, 158
    armor, 215, 216
    as defender, 29
    defined, 402
    description, 31, 32
    feats of, 185, 188–190
    gear packages, 211
    how to play the role, 32–33
    magic items, 264–266
    martial exploits, 83
    as new player role, 103–108
    as noncaster, 253
    in opportunity attacks, 246
    overview, 24, 30, 131–134
    powers of, 27, 163–168, 357–362
    selecting, 33–40
    skill package, 204
    weapons, 213–214
    who should play the role, 31–32
fireball, 175, 177, 251, 371
fireball spells, 192
First Strike, 135, 192
flame strike, 181, 232, 374
flameburst battleaxe, 251
flanking, 80, 241, 242, 249, 281, 402
flesh golem (level 12 elite brute), 383
flexibility (character), 252
fly spell, 160
foes, 238, 248, 249.
Forbiddance ritual, 257
forced movement, 85
FORGOTTEN REALMS, 10, 18
FORGOTTEN REALMS, Campaign Guide, 305
FORGOTTEN REALMS Player's Guide, 150, 292
Fortitude defense (Fort), 79, 81, 119, 120, 402
free action, 77–78
free time, 317
frost, 266

• G •

game balance, 353–354
game optimization, 4
game rules, 17–19
game sessions, typical, 99–100
gamestation.net, 15
gaming store, 305
gauntlets of ogre power, 262
gear. *See also* equipment; outfitting
        characters
    Beryn, 55
    Calia, 39
    Chenna, 67
    Dreggu, 57
    Eberk, 69
    Jax, 45
    Lidda, 49
    overview, 26, 218–219
    Regdar, 35, 105, 109
    Shadow, 47
    Telsa, 59
    Thomm, 65
    Tordek, 37
gender equality, 117, 144

Gentle Repose, 271
gestures, 279
get over here power, 168
ghoul (level 5 soldier), 379
giant spider, 342
giant's wake, 165
giantslayer warhammer, 253
gish, 402
goggles of night, 268
gold piece (gp), 210, 403
Golden Rule of equipping, 264
good character alignment, 115, 276, 403
good-unaligned-evil scale, 276
gp (gold piece), 210, 403
grab, 403
graph paper, 17
Great Weapon Fighter
    ability scores, 158
    armor, 216
    characters, 33
    feats of, 189–190
    gear packages, 211
    overview, 131, 164–166
    powers, 164–165
    skill package, 204
    weapons, 32, 133, 163
greataxe, 213
greatsword, 213
Greenwood, Ed (author)
    Sword Never Sleeps, The, 396
Guardian Fighter
    ability scores, 158
    armor, 216
    characters, 33
    feats of, 189, 190
    gear packages, 211
    overview, 131, 166–168
    powers, 166–167
    skill package, 204
    weapons, 32, 133, 163
Gygax, Gary (game developer), 10

• H •

habitual sayings, 279
hack-and-slashers, 346–348
half-elf, 150, 403
"1/2 LVL" (level modifier), 113
Halfling Agility, 192
halflings, 22–23, 48–49, 64–65, 148–150, 403

Hall of the Spider God. See dungeon sample
hammer and anvil, 182
hammer (weapon), 213
hand slot items, 260
handaxe, 214
handy haversack, 219
head slot items, 260
Healer's Lore, 140
healing, 87–88, 129, 204, 207, 403
healing prayers, 178
healing strike, 181, 375
healing surge
    of clerics, 141
    with comeback strike, 167
    defined, 403
    of fighters, 133
    hit point restoration, 118
    as ritual cost, 257
    of rogues, 135
    using, 81
    value, 26, 118
    of wizards, 138
healing word, 141, 161, 178, 235
Heavy Blade Opportunity, 246
hell hound (level 7 brute), 378
helm of battle, 258
helpless characters, 89
Hickman, Tracy (author)
    Dragonlance Chronicles, 393
    Dragonlance Legends, 393
hit points (hp)
    of characters, 26
    of clerics, 141
    critical, 80
    defined, 403
    determining, 117–118
    of fighters, 133
    gaining, 228
    of monsters, 318
    playing the game, 87–88
    reducing, 232
    regaining, 81
    of rogues, 135
    of wizards, 138
hobby stores, 20, 101, 102
holy spark, 179
holy symbol, 218, 270, 403
honesty, 353
hp (hit points). See hit points (hp)
Human Perseverance, 195

humanoids, 403
humans
  Beryn (wizard), 54–55
  bonuses, 120–121, 123, 187
  defined, 403
  Jax (rogue), 44–45
  overview, 22–23
  race, 143–145
  Regdar (fighter), 34–35, 104–108
  Shadow (rogue), 46–47
  skills of, 123, 202
  Thomm (cleric), 64–65
hunger of Hadar, 182

ice storm, 175, 177, 370
Icewind Dale Trilogy (Salvatore), 394
icon usage, 4–5
icy terrain, 176
ignoble escape, 170
illustrations, 4
imagination as limit, 29
immediate action, 78
immobilized characters, 89
immortality path, 114
immortals, 403
immunities, 318
implements, 259, 403
improved initiative, 186, 192, 194–195
influences on D&D, 9
informed choices, 125
initiative
  defined, 404
  dungeon sample, 332, 335, 339, 340, 341
  modifier/check/log, 25, 76, 94, 404
  of monsters, 318
  order, 241–242
  overview, 119
  rolls, 28
Insight, 118–119, 206, 207
inspiring strike, 179
insubstantial, 404
Intelligence (Int)
  ability scores, 152, 154
  armor choices, 216
  of clerics, 196, 197
  of wizards, 194
Internet connection, 15

Internet resources
  D&D Insider, 10, 15, 17, 18, 111, 117, 150, 304
  for meeting players, 101
Intimidate skill, 204, 233
into the fray power, 166
invisibility, 251, 253, 255
iron vanguard, 165
Iron Will, 198

javelin, 214
Jax (rogue), 43, 44–45
joining in
  finding someone to play with, 100–102
  high-level characters, 103–108
  overview, 19–20
  typical game session, 99–100
jump, 252

• *K* •

Kathra (wizard), 25
keen weapons, 268, 292
key ability, 201
key statistics, 16, 25–26
keyword, 404
knock, 255, 258
knockout, 172
kobold
  dragonshield, 341
  dungeon sample, 332, 334
  skirmisher, 94, 96–97, 98

• *L* •

lamp oil, 219
lance of faith, 181, 249, 374
languages of monsters, 320
lanterns, 219
lawful good character alignment,
    115, 276, 404
leader, 29, 63, 129, 139, 142, 404
leaping dodge, 365
level
  buffing powers, 283
  defined, 404
  gaining, 224–228

high-level sample, 103–108
hit point determination, 117–118
magic items, 265, 267, 269–273
modifiers, 226, 228, 404
overview, 113
of powers, 24, 160
ritual choices, 256
training compared to, 201
level of characters
  clerics, 178–181, 195
  fighters, 164–167
  monsters, 225, 318
  rogues, 169, 171, 191
  wizards, 174, 176, 193
levitate power, 177, 233, 252
Lidda (rogue), 43, 48–49, 122
Light Blades, 191
Light Shield Proficiency, 216
light source, 218–219
light spell, 218
lightning bolt, 371
line of sight blocking, 247
Linked Portal, 258
list making, 219
longbow, 213, 214
longsword, 213, 262
Lord of the Rings, The, (Tolkien), 1, 9, 352
low-light vision, 404
lurkers, 239, 240

• *M* •

mace, 214–215
magic
  baseline, 262–273
  in combat, 254
  defined, 404
  as light source, 219
  overview, 251
  rituals, 255–257
  spells, 252–253
MAGIC: THE GATHERING, 10
magic items
  of characters, 124
  cleric, 269–270
  defined, 404
  fighter, 265
  finding, 261
  gear, 219, 221
  min-maxing, 294

overview, 257–262
powers of, 162
rogue, 267
selling, 261–262
wizard, 271–273
magic missile, 138–139, 160, 174, 215, 232, 369
magic throwing weapon, 214
magical armor, 221
magical beast, 405
make-believe, 2, 9
management strategy, 237
maneuvering, 233, 244, 252
mannerisms, 278–279
mantle of glory, 181, 375
mapping action, 17
mark, 405
marked characters, 89, 133
markers
  in combat, 92
  dungeon sample, 332, 335, 339, 340
  using, 329
martial characters, 27
martial exploits, 83, 168
Martial Power, 292
martial powers, 163, 405
mass cure light wounds, 180, 181, 375
master of deceit, 172
masterwork armor, 220–221, 266, 405
medium size characters, 114
melee attacks, 79, 83, 133, 163, 405
menacing behavior (opportunity attack),
    246, 247
message boards, 292
Mettle, 190, 196
milestone powers, 271, 405
min-max, 291–294, 405
mind flayer mastermind (level 18 elite
    controller), 385
minions, 239, 240
minor action, 77–78, 94, 397
mirror image, 370–371
modifiers
  ability, 153
  determining, 19, 119
  key statistics, 25
  level, 113
module, 324
money, 210
monster knowledge, 206
Monster Manual, 3, 5, 15, 18, 20

monster origin, 405
monsters. *See also* character(s)
  actions of, 71, 320–321
  DM speaking for, 306
  high-level, 389–392
  level of, 225
  low-level, 377–381
  markers, 329
  mid-level, 383–392
  player characters compared to, 95–97
  stats, 318–320
motivation, 324–325
move action, 77–78, 94, 397
movement, battle grid, 84–86, 92
multiclass, 297–300, 405
multiclass feats, 198
mummy lord (level 13 elite controller), 385
mythological world, 9

name of characters, 22, 112–113
narration, 348–351
neck slot items, 259
negotiation, 233–234
new players sample, 103–108
night vision, 268
Nimble Blade, 191, 192
noncasters, 253
noncombat encounters, 72
nonplayer characters (NPCs),
      13, 305, 320–321, 405
note paper, 15, 17
novels, 10, 18, 393–396
NPCs (nonplayer characters),
      13, 305, 320–321, 405
number of players (worldwide), 10

• O •

objectives, 12
obstacles in combat, 86
occupied squares, 85–86
ogre skirmisher (level 8 skirmisher), 380
one/two-handed weapons, 212
Online resources
  D&D Insider, 10, 15, 17, 18, 111, 117, 150, 304
  for meeting players, 101
opportunity action, 78
opportunity attacks, 85, 133, 134, 243–246, 406.
      See also attacks

orb, 218, 406
orc, 94–95, 97, 98, 343–344
Orc King, The, (Salvatore), 395
orc raider (level 3 skirmisher), 380–381
orcus (level 33 solo brute), 392
organizing games, 102
origin type and keyword, 318
outfitting characters
  armor, 215–217
  gear, 218–219
  overview, 209
  shopping, 210–211
  upgrading equipment, 220–221
  weapons, 212–215
outnumbering, 239

paladin
  armor, 217
  as class choice, 141
  defined, 406
  feats of, 185, 197
  as noncaster, 253
  spells, 182, 253
paragon path
  Arcane Reach, 194, 195
  choices, 228, 294–296, 299
  of clerics, 198
  defined, 406
  Dexterity, 190, 191
  Evasion, 192
  magic items, 266
  Mettle, 190, 196
  overview, 114
  Spell Focus, 195
  utility powers, 296
passing attack, 165
passive perception score, 119
path of characters, 114
PCs (player characters)
  action points, 86
  balancing class choices, 128
  defining, 21–27, 406
  monsters compared to, 95–97
  nonplayer characters (NPCs), 13, 305,
      320–321, 405
  playing, 27–29
  role of, 13, 14, 29, 99
  selecting, 30
penalty, 153, 216–217

pencils, 15, 17
Perception, 118–119, 203, 204, 205, 206
perception checks, 97, 331
persona building, 277–278
personality of characters, 116
petrified characters, 89
piercing strike, 170, 367
pit fiend (level 26 elite soldier), 390–391
pit fighter, 165
plane, 406
PLANESCAPE, 10
platinum piece (pp), 210, 406
play, continuity of, 11, 12
player characters (PCs)
  action points, 86
  balancing class choices, 128
  defining, 21–27, 406
  monsters compared to, 95–97
  nonplayer characters (NPCs), 13, 305,
    320–321, 405
  playing, 27–29
  role of, 13, 14, 29, 99
  selecting, 30
players, 28, 76, 345–348
Player's Handbook
  as background, 3
  for beginning players, 1, 5, 20
  classes in, 23
  combat movement, 85
  names in, 22, 113
  as reference, 15, 16
  RPG experience in, 18
"players seeking players" posts, 101
playing the game
  action points, 86–87
  combat, 75–81, 84–86, 88–90
  dice, 72–73
  dungeon exploration, 73–75
  hit points, healing, dying, 87–88
  power use, 81–84
  rest and recovery, 88
  skill challenges, 87
  understanding D&D, 71–72
positioning strike, 172
Potent Opportunity, 246
potion, 260, 406
power
  at-will, 27, 81, 124, 162, 398
  attack types, 83–84
  buffing, 283
  of characters, 12, 27, 124

  in combat, 81, 84
  defined, 406
  expendable, 235–237
  gaining, 226, 228
  min-maxing, 294
  movement in combat, 244
  navigating through, 160–163
  overview, 159
  reading, 82–83
  relative, 24
  types of, 271
power attack, 186, 190
power source, 406
powers of character types
  clerics, 141, 177–182, 373–376
  fighters, 133–134, 163–168, 357–362
  monsters, 319–320
  rogues, 136, 168–172, 363–367
  wizards, 138–139, 172–177, 369–372
powers of specific characters
  Beryn, 54–55
  Calia, 39
  Chenna, 67
  Dreggu, 56–57
  Eberk, 69
  Jax, 45
  Lidda, 49
  Regdar, 35, 105, 107–108
  Shadow, 47
  Telsa, 59
  Thomm, 65
  Tordek, 37
pp (platinum piece), 210, 406
PRACTICAL GUIDE series, 18
Practical Guide to Dragons (Trumbauer), 394
practice session
  battle grid/markers, 90–93
  practice combat, 93–97
  story elements, 97–98
prayer
  cleric powers as, 141
  of clerics, 27, 30, 177, 178–181
  defined, 406
precise strike, 358
pregenerated characters, 3
premise, 324–325, 328–329
preparation, 349
prerequisite, 406
Press the Advantage, 192
priest's shield, 179
prismatic beams, 175

prismatic burst, 175, 177
prisoners, 332
profession (class), 127
prone characters, 89
props, 351–352
protection, 253
publications, adventure, 305, 309
pull, 85, 406
push, 85, 406
puzzle-solvers, 346–347

• Q •

quarterstaff, 215
quest, 324

• R •

R.A. Salvatore's War of the Spider Queen, 394
race
  ability adjustments, 156
  of characters, 114, 123
  class choices, 127
  defined, 407
  feats, 187, 189
  overview, 22–23, 143
  powers, 161
race of character types
  clerics, 140
  dwarves, 145–146
  elves, 147–148
  fighters, 131
  halflings, 148–150
  humans, 143–145
  other types, 150
  rogues, 134–135
  wizards, 137
racial traits
  Calia, 38
  Chenna, 67
  Dreggu, 56
  Eberk, 68–69
  Lidda, 48
  Telsa, 58
  Tordek, 36
Raging Storm, 194
Raise Dead, 256–257, 258
range, 407
range penalty, 122
ranged attacks, 79, 83, 163, 407

ranged weapon, 122. *See also specific weapons*
ranger
  armor, 217
  as class choice, 141
  defined, 407
  feats of, 197
  as noncaster, 253
  spells, 182
  as striker, 130
RAVENLOFT, 10
reach, 407
reaping strike, 96, 165, 358
reckless strike, 165
reconnaissance, 253
Reflex defense (Ref), 73, 79, 81, 119, 120, 407
Regdar (fighter)
  attack bonus, 122
  characteristics of, 34–35
  defenses, 120–121
  overview, 33
  practice session, 96
  sample for new players, 103–108
Reliable exploits, 164
Religion, 207
Remove Affliction, 258
reputation of characters, 12
resistance, 253, 282, 318, 407
resounding weapon, 270
resources, expendable, 235–237
rest, short, 408
rest/recovery, 88
restrained characters, 89
retreating, 234
reward and risk, 353
righteous brand, 179, 242
righteous smite, 182
rings, 260
riposte strike, 170
risk and reward, 353
ritual casting, 138, 141, 255
rituals, 207, 218, 255–257, 271
rogue
  ability scores, 158
  defined, 407
  description, 41, 42
  feats of, 190–193
  gear, 211, 218
  how to play the role, 42–43
  magic items, 267–268
  martial exploits, 83
  as noncaster, 253

overview, 24, 30, 134–136
powers of, 27, 168–172, 363–367
selecting, 43–50
skill package, 204–205
as striker, 29, 130
tactics, 135
who should play the role, 41–42
role, defined, 407
roleplaying
overview, 28
with style, 275–280
table manners, 285–289
working together, 280–285
roleplaying game (RPG), 1, 9, 18
Roleplaying Gamers Association, 101
rope, 218, 219
round, 407
RPG (roleplaying game), 1, 9, 18
run, 407

• S •

sacred flame, 181, 376
Salvatore, R.A. (author)
Icewind Dale Trilogy, 394
Orc King, The, 395
sample starting gear, 211
saving throw (save), 408
scenario, sample, 73–74, 95–97, 330–342
scorching burst, 174
scroll, 408
seal of warding, 181
searing light, 181, 255
second chance, 192
second implement, 195
second wind, 81, 88, 244, 408
sending (ritual), 258
senses, 318
sequence, combat, 78–79
serpent dance strike, 359
setting (scenery), 349–351
shadow, 408
Shadow (rogue), 43, 46–47, 95
shadow stride, 170, 172
shield, 175, 177, 190, 216, 372
shield of faith, 181
shift battlefield action, 84, 167, 241, 244,
        254, 408
shock sphere, 174
shopping (outfitting characters), 210–211

short rest, 408
shortbow, 213
silver piece (sp), 210, 408
site-based adventure, 326
situation, evaluating, 237–238
size of characters/monsters, 114, 318
skeleton, 336
skill checks
armor choices, 216–217
computing, 201
definition of, 19
perception, 97
success likelihood, 72–73
of wizards, 206
skills
challenges, 87, 315
clerics, 141
difficulty class, 202
fighters, 133
monsters, 320
overview, 26, 122–123, 199–203
packages of, 203–207
rogues, 136
wizards, 138
skills of specific characters
Beryn, 54
Calia, 39
Chenna, 67
Dreggu, 56
Eberk, 69
Jax, 44
Lidda, 48–49
Regdar, 34–35, 104–105, 107
Shadow, 46
Telsa, 58
Thomm, 65
Tordek, 36–37
skirmishers, 239, 240
slaying strike, 170, 367
sleep, 177, 252, 371
slide movement, 85, 408
sling, 214, 215
slippery mind, 172
slot items, 259–260
slowed characters, 89
sly flourish, 171, 364
small size characters, 114
sneak attack, 135, 168
social interactions, 71–72, 102, 278, 325–326
soldiers, 239
soundtrack, 352

sp (silver piece), 210, 408
space validity, 85
special abilities, 25
special traits
  dwarves, 146
  elves, 147–148
  halflings, 149
  humans, 144
spectral ram, 174, 175
speech pattern, 279
speed, 25, 84, 121, 319
spell
  casting, 398
  defined, 408
  selecting, 252–253
  of wizards, 27, 30, 172, 174–176
Spell Focus, 194, 195
spellbook, 138, 218
Spellstorm Mage, 177
spider, 342
spiked chain, 213
spinning sweep, 165
spiritual weapon, 181, 249, 281
splitting up (in defense), 247
squares, movement in, 85–86
stack, 408
staff, 218, 273, 408
staff of the war mage, 273
stalwart guard, 168
standard action, 77–78, 81, 94, 397
standard array, 155–156
starting point, 20
statistics, 16, 25–26, 122
Stealth, 203, 204, 205, 233
stinking cloud, 247
stirge (level 1 lurker), 377
Storm Dragon (Wyatt), 394
storm giant (level 24 elite controller), 391
storm of blows, 167
story elements, 97–98
storytelling, 12
strategy, combat, 237–241
Streetwise skill, 204
Strength (Str)
  ability scores, 152, 154
  of clerics, 196, 197
  of fighters, 189
  maximizing, 293
strengthen the faithful, 179
striker
  beginning players' choice, 128
  defined, 408
  overview, 130

ranger as, 141
rogues as, 43, 134
role of, 29
warlock as, 141
structure during play, 72, 73
stunned characters, 90
Sun Tzu, 231
sunrod, 219
supplies, 15
sure strike, 92, 93, 167
surprise attack, 182
surprise knockdown, 186
surprised characters, 90
suspense, 307
sustain, 409
sweeping blow, 360
sword
  bastard sword, 196, 213, 215
  greatsword, 213
  longsword, 213,262
Sword Never Sleeps, The, (Greenwood), 396
Swordmage (Baker), 395

• T •

table manners, 285–289
tactics, 239–240, 321
"take 10," 409
taking turns, 27–28, 76
target numbers and difficulty class (DC)
  action success, 73
  for attacks, 79
  defined, 401
  determining, 19
  practice session, 97–98
  rulebook samples, 75
  of skills, 202
tarrasque (level 30 solo brute), 391
team needs/resources, 128, 130, 236, 258, 280–285
teleport power, 254
television programs, 10
Telsa (wizard), 43, 58–59, 95–96
Temple of Elemental Evil, 326
terrain, difficult, 85, 86
territorial control, 246
thicket of blades, 165
thievery, 205
thieves' tools, 218
Thomm (cleric), 63, 64–65
threat, non-existent, 239, 240
throwing hammer, 213, 214

thunder wave, 176
thunderlance, 372
tide of iron, 167, 362
tiefling, 150, 409
Tolkien, J.R.R. (author)
　Lord of the Rings, The, 1, 9, 352
Tomb of Horrors, 326
topple over, 170
torches, 219
Tordek (fighter), 33, 36–37
tornado strike, 172, 363–364
torturous strike, 170
Total Defense, 244
Toughness, 193, 194, 195, 196, 197
training, 123, 203
trick strike, 172
Trickster Rogue
　ability scores, 158
　build, 134, 168
　characters, 43
　feats of, 191
　powers, 170–172
　skills for, 205
Tripping Chain, 246
Trumbauer, Lisa Trutkoff (author)
　Practical Guide to Dragons, 394
TSR, Inc., 10
tumble exploit, 160, 170, 367
turn, 78, 94–95. *See also* taking turns
turn undead, 140, 141
two-handed weapon, 409

• U •

umber hulk (level 12 elite soldier), 384
unaligned characters, 115, 277, 409
unarmed strike, 409
unbalancing attack power, 170
unbreakable power, 166, 168, 360
unconscious characters, 90
undead, 409
unyielding avalanche, 167
upgrading character equipment, 220–221
utility powers
　4th edition changes, 255
　attack powers compared with, 160–161
　of clerics, 181
　damage mitigation, 166
　in dangerous situations, 168
　epic destiny choices, 297
　overview, 124
　paragon path, 296

utility spells, 175, 177, 253

• V •

versatility, increasing, 293
victory conditions, 12, 17
video games, 18
villains. *See specific characters; specific*
　monsters
vocation (class), 127
voice pattern, 279
voidsoul specter (level 23 lurker), 390
vrock demon (level 13 skirmisher), 385

• W •

wailing ghost (level 12 controller), 384
waist slot items, 260
walk in combat, 84, 92
walking wounded, 172
wall of fire, 247, 253
wall of fog, 247
wand, 218, 409
Wand of Accuracy, 194
war devil (level 22 brute), 389
war troll (level 14 soldier), 386
War Wizard
　builds, 137
　feats of, 193–194
　gear packages, 211
　powers, 173–175
　skill package, 206
wargames as inspiration, 10
warhammer, 213, 215, 253
warlock
　armor, 217
　as caster, 253
　as class choice, 141
　defined, 409
　feats of, 197
　line of sight blocking, 247
　spells, 182
　as striker, 130
warlord
　armor, 217
　as class choice, 142
　defined, 409
　feats of, 197
　as leader, 129
　as noncaster, 253
　spells, 182

warplate armor, 221
weakened characters, 90
weakness, character, 293
Weapon Focus
  clerics, 196, 198
  fighters, 189
  paladins, 197
  rangers, 197
  rogues, 191
  warlords, 197
weapon group, 409
Weapon Proficiency, 122, 213, 215
weapons. *See also* magic
  cleric, 139, 196
  fighter, 134, 163, 164, 166, 189, 266
  magical, 221
  melee, 121–122, 213
  one/two-handed, 133
  overview, 212–215
  ranged, 122
  rogue, 134, 135, 168, 191
  for small/medium characters, 114
  wizard choice, 136
weapons of specific characters
  Beryn, 55
  Calia, 39
  Chenna, 67
  Dreggu, 57
  Eberk, 69
  Jax, 45
  Lidda, 49
  Regdar, 35, 105, 109
  Shadow, 47
  Telsa, 59
  Thomm, 65
  Tordek, 37
web, 232, 252
Web sites
  D&D Insider, 10, 15, 17, 18, 111, 117, 150, 304
  for meeting players, 101
weight of armor/gear, 216–217, 219
Weis, Margaret (author)
  Dragonlance Chronicles, 393
  Dragonlance Legends, 393
werewolf (level 8 brute), 379
White Box version, 1
Will defense (Will), 79, 81, 120, 409
winged boots, 258
winning criteria, 11–12
winter's wrath, 177
Wisdom (Wis), 152, 155, 190, 194, 207
wizard. *See also* magic items
  ability scores, 158
  arcane spells, 83

  armor, 215
  bonus feats, 187
  as caster, 253
  as controller, 29, 128–129
  defined, 410
  description, 51, 52
  feats of, 185, 193–195
  gear, 211, 218
  how to play the role, 52–53
  line of sight blocking, 247
  magic items, 271–273
  overview, 24, 30, 136–139
  powers of, 27, 172–177, 369–372
  rituals of, 256
  role of, 53
  selecting, 53–60
  skills, 123, 205–206
  weapons, 215
  who should play the role, 51–52
Wizards of the Coast, Inc.
  4th edition, 1
  message boards, 292
  publications, 18, 305, 393–396
  supplies from, 17
  TSR purchase, 10
wondrous items, 260
working together, 280–285
the world, 410
world building, 304–305
wrathful thunder, 179
Wyatt, James (author)
  Storm Dragon, 394

XP (experience points)
  achievement level, 24
  defined, 402
  dungeon sample, 333, 336, 338–341
  gaining, 223–225
  for level advancements, 227
  of monsters, 318

young white dragon (level 3 solo brute), 378
yuan-ti anathema (level 21 elite
    skirmisher), 389

zombie, 337

Make Your Party Even Better with the Help of Another PC

THESE GUYS SPENT THE LAST THREE YEARS GETTING READY FOR THEIR NEXT FIGHT.

In the name of making 4th Edition, we've offered up countless of our own characters for use as punching bags and chew toys. Now it's your turn.

So, be ready to throw down when you pick up all three Core Rulebooks.

You know where to get 'em.

AVAILABLE JUNE 6TH

CREATE AN ACCOUNT AT:
DNDINSIDER.COM

All trademarks are property of Wizards of the Coast, Inc. ©2008 Wizards.